India Mirror of Truth

Steve Briggs

D1293905

1st WORLD PUBLISHING

India Mirror of Truth

Steve Briggs

© 2005 Steve Briggs

Published by 1stWorld Publishing
1100 North 4th St. Suite 131, Fairfield, Iowa 52556
tel: 641-209-5000 • fax: 641-209-3001
web: www.1stworldpublishing.com

First Edition

LCCN: 2005908466

SoftCover ISBN: 1595409653

HardCover ISBN: 1595409661

eBook ISBN: 159540967X

All rights reserved. No part of this book may be reproduced or utilized in any form or by any means, electronic or mechanical, including photocopying or recording, or by any information storage and retrieval system, without permission in writing from the author.

This material has been written and published solely for educational purposes. The author and the publisher shall have neither liability or responsibility to any person or entity with respect to any loss, damage or injury caused or alleged to be caused directly or indirectly by the information contained in this book.

The characters and events described in this text are intended to be enjoyed and to teach rather than present an exact factual history of real people or events.

Bharat Mata (Mother India) was painted by Mu Ramalingkam.

Book interior and cover design by Liz Howard. liz@1stWorldPublishing.com

DEDICATION

This book is humbly dedicated to
Sri Guru Dev, my guiding light.

Maharishi, whose smile has never faded,

My compassionate Mother, the Universal Devi,

The Himalayan Master who said, "Finish your book,"

My writing teacher, AA Gabriel,

The monks I journeyed with for 20 years,

My devoted Bhumi and Devala of the Kumar Club,

And Mother India and her children.

Jai Guru Dev

Table Of Contents

ACKNOWLEDGEMENTS

I want to express my thanks to those who supported the writing of this book. First there was Devala, who reviewed and edited the original manuscript, and Bhumi, who patiently read and reread the story. Later, Tony Ellis stepped forward, offering invaluable editorial feedback and professional guidance.

Of course, there were many in India who shared the journey with me. My friend and colleague, Lane Wagger, who steered our project while I went along for the ride. Will Fox, who, like a brother went everywhere with me and was as dedicated to looking after our corporate clients as he was to the pilgrim's trail. The administration and staff at Maharishi Nagar who fed and sheltered us for five years. The families and friends who opened their hearts and homes, and tutored me in the ways of Indian culture: The Rajus, Pateriyas, Soma Sundarams, Anant, Ratna, Gauri, and Jai Dehadrai, Sashi Ullal, General Kulwant Singh, General Sahney, Pundit Dinesh Sati of The Himalayan Jyotish Research Institute, Chari Vaidya, the Janis, Colonel and Mrs. Yogi Sud, Ramprasad, Ashutosh, Kankana Das, Himangi Tewari, my travel agent Mr. Saluja, our faithful driver Anil, and our cooks Maharaj and Jaya.

INTRODUCTION

My story is that of an American monk sent to India by his guru to teach meditation, a seven-year odyssey that took me from the coastal waters of Kerala to the high Tibetan plateau. Along the way, I encountered saints and shamans, politicians and pundits, astrologers and ascetics, entrepreneurs and artisans. I visited ancient holy sites, encountered swamis living at the source of the Ganges, participated in arcane purificatory rituals, experienced the excitement of thirty million pilgrims at the Kumbha Mela as guest of a maharaja, initiated India's elite into meditation, and shared the company of lamas at Tibetan monasteries in Ladakh in a journey that was as culturally rich as it was spiritually stirring. Deep in the Himalaya, my search for spiritual India reunited me with an ageless Himalayan Master who was expecting me. My dream of pursuing Enlightenment in an isolated Himalayan ashram was realized when I renounced my work to meditate night and day as my search for spiritual liberation intensified.

In late summer 1994, I was sitting with my venerated guru in a former monastery at the heart of a Dutch forest. "Go and teach business leaders," Maharishi had said. "They are the ones who will lead India out of ignorance." Having been to India many times, I had taught Transcendental Meditation to hundreds of school children and college students, but this new assignment came unexpected.

Arriving in India was a homecoming of sorts for me. I hadn't been in India in almost a decade, but the richness of sight, sound, and smell outside Delhi's international airport greeted me like an old friend. India, whose population at the time was about to reach one billion, had struggled since its independence in 1947, but the Indian soul is a gem that needs only a little polish before it shines. The prospect of introducing meditation to India's elite intrigued me, but at the same time, I wondered if it wasn't presumptuous for westerners to teach Indians what was their own. It seems Indians had begun doubting their own spiritual tradition and needed to be reassured about their extraordinary heritage.

As we traveled, our hosts told us stories of the saints and gurus their parents and grandparents had invited into their homes or visited in Himalayan retreats. These priceless spiritual heirlooms were a source of great pride for India's captains of industry. I immediately understood why Maharishi wanted India's leaders to meditate, for they had the power and vision to affect the lives of thousands. One prominent leader alone organized for 45,000 people to learn meditation.

In our work, we traveled to the remote corners of the subcontinent, where humble folk treated us as honored guests. At each stop, we taught meditation while sampling village life, often meditating in a stone shrine where a yogi had attained moksha or a miracle had occurred somewhere in the distant past. As our travels broadened, our eyes widened and we participated in the colorful festivals of the Hindu faith that are as plentiful as days on the calendar.

Although an experienced teacher of meditation, I never thought of myself as a guru. Out of respect, our students often applied that lofty title to us, but we were quick to remind them that we too were seekers of Enlightenment, eager to unearth the treasures of spiritual India. After all, that was what brought me back to India time after time.

As we traveled to exotic outposts at the edge of India and attended the religious festivals that attracted multitudes, I recorded my experiences, often sending travel logs to friends back in the States. These letters formed the nucleus of *India: Mirror of Truth*, a title I chose, having heard Maharishi describe India as a dusty mirror that, when wiped clean, would once again reflect the timeless wisdom of Enlightenment rooted in the heart. The title also reflects India's uncanny capacity to present one with exactly what one merits at every moment, be it the fructification of *punya* (merit from previous lives) or *pap* (bad karma).

No account of spiritual India can be conveyed without admiration for her people and adoration for her gods. Both are abundant and varied. India's cultural mosaic is more diverse than other countries, and I came to adore India's devas as family members, friends and teachers that took an active interest in my life. This is how the Indian household views the many forms of divinity that guide and protect them, and, as time passed, this is how I came to appreciate them also. Embracing this subtle sphere of nature at the nexus of India lies at the very heart of the spiritual journey.

Events and personalities that I encountered during my life changing seven-year pilgrimage may stretch one's imagination; they often challenged my own assumptions about what is possible, but those who have been to India know that the miraculous lies just around the corner. The scriptures teach that consciousness is a field of all possibilities and India lived up to that description again and again.

India defies description, and yet writers feel compelled to try, for the ancient land of rishis leaves a spiritual residue in one's soul that yearns to be expressed. Much of the insight I gained over the years I owe to my Indian friends who were my cultural gurus, and I their willing student. I bow down to the friends and families who treated their videshi (foreign) guest as God, and hope this account in some measure communicates the warmth and kindness that I found wherever I journeyed in the land that I call home.

ONE

Ominous Predictions

These are strange portents indeed.

—*Shakespeare's Julius Caesar*

I remember it well. Jet lag clouded my mind and my body wanted to know why I was lying in bed when it was hungry for breakfast. It was 3:00 am, but my internal clock ran five hours ahead as I lay there listening to a stampede of rodents running through the ductwork outside my room. I assumed they were mice, but whatever they were, they were a noisy bunch. After an hour of tossing about on the hard mattress and clammy sheets, I got out of bed and opened an unread newspaper. The headlines read like the title to a suspense thriller, 'Plague Invades Delhi.'

The headline story compared India's 1994 plague to the Black Death that wiped out a quarter of Europe's population in the 14th century. The highly contagious disease that had caused the Bubonic Plague 700 years ago was back and it killed 100% of its victims when not treated. According to the newspaper, the plague was transmitted through the air. As with another plague that had claimed ten million Indians early in the 20th century, rats were the principle carriers and humans infected one another by coughing. The outbreak caused a stir worldwide and 40,000 tourist bookings were canceled overnight. Many European countries stopped all flights into India. The country braced itself for the worst. 'How come no one told us about it?' I wondered as I slipped back into bed. I would find out in the morning.

I had seen the pedestrians on street corners wearing white surgical masks strapped across their faces and handkerchiefs held to their mouths, but I assumed these were just precautions against the choking pollution that afflicted the city. Although I needed to sleep, I lay there listening to the rodents, wondering where they were going in such a hurry. The thumping of feet sounded more like the home stretch of the Kentucky Derby than a few mice heading out for a midnight snack. I was suspicious. Could mice make such a racket? I would find that out in the morning too.

After breakfast I rang up our Indian host, a plump fellow with a law degree. "Namaste! Giripati, have you read about the plague that is about to reach Delhi?" I asked. Health officials believed an earthquake in western India was the cause.

"Yeees, Steveji (Indians use 'ji' as a term of friendly respect). I've been reading about it in the newspaper," he replied calmly. Giripati was always serene, totally unperturbed by project deadlines and disasters alike.

"What do you think? Is it wise to go to Delhi?"

"Continue your work, but avoid the public," he replied without emotion.

"Why hasn't anyone told us about the plague?" I asked, feeling a bit put off by the dearth of information.

"It's nothing to worry about. India has a lot of health problems. Don't give it a second thought." Somehow the fact that every state department in the western world had issued travel advisories and cancelled flights into India left me feeling less than satisfied with the answer. I was about to hang up the phone when I remembered my other question. "Uh, Giripati, we seem to have a rodent problem in the guesthouse. Those are just mice, aren't they?" I asked, hoping for the right answer.

"Housing will look into it," he said, and hung up. I was reluctant to bother my host with our domestic problems. After all, he had 200 schools to look after and dozens of other projects vying for his attention.

'Avoid the public,' I mused. 'That's easier said than done in a city of twelve million.' I wasn't satisfied with the answers, but my friend Eberhard, the German press director, who had been in India for a long time had warned me that information wasn't always easy to get. I had already been to housing, but the door was padlocked. I would find out for myself who was racing above my bed at night.

The cooks were locking up for the night when I slipped into the kitchen to get a glass of warm milk; jet lag was still bothering my sleep. It was then that I noticed a shadowy creature stealing across the pantry floor. Hoping to catch the intruder red-handed I crept into the storeroom and switched on the light. I was searching among the jute bags and storage bins when I spotted the miscreant behind a bag of chapati flour. He saw me too but was not the least bit afraid. Just as I suspected, it was a rat, and not your average rat. He was better fed than most house pets, and almost as large. Avoiding confrontation, I shut off the light leaving the fat rat to his meal.

In the coming weeks my project partner, Lane Wagger, and I ignored health officials' warnings and went about our business making corporate presentations. After all, if rats carried the plague, it seemed pointless hiding out at the guesthouse where they had the run of the place. By now the media were taking an interest in our activities. An article in a popular daily read 'Americans Teach Corporate Meditation.' The snare of rush hour traffic, which slowed our commutes to a crawl, was all that disrupted life during the day, but the nightly running of the rodents continued to disrupt my rest, and I didn't sleep any better knowing who my nemesis was.

Author (right) With Lane And A Swami

Lane had formidable business instincts and was already making inroads into India's corporate world. We would travel to a Haryana sugar factory to teach meditation to our first management group in a few days. Lane was a skilled negotiator and no one loves to bargain more than Indians. I was sure they preferred it to almost anything. I had no doubt his instincts would make our project a success. In fact, I was counting on it. Lane, a New York native, also had street smarts. Every merchant in the bazaar vied for the chance to haggle with Lane, and watching him get his bananas at a discount was every bit as entertaining as witnessing his savvy in a corporate office. Back and forth Lane volleyed with vendors, trading shots like players in a tennis match.

Delhi was just getting back to normal after an antibiotics campaign in Gujarat brought the plague under control when Giripati received a call from the Delhi police commissioner wanting to know if any foreigners were staying at the ashram. Indian intelligence had discovered a terrorist plot to kidnap westerners in the capital city. To avert the latest threat we were advised to avoid Muslim areas, alleyways, and all activities after dark.

"Giripati, our options are dwindling," I said as we sat together in his office. He paused to consider the situation. His neatly trimmed black hair and beard and pressed silk tunic suggested a meticulous personality.

"Be careful about terrorists! Muslim radicals are a bigger problem than the plague. Don't go to places like Chandi Chowk in old Delhi," he cautioned. Great, I thought to myself, at this rate we'd be quarantined to our rooms in a matter of time. I could see Giripati was too busy to think about plagues and terrorists. But I wasn't!

It was comforting to know that since all the other westerners had canceled their visits to India, Lane and I were virtually the only foreigners in the city. Naturally we assumed the terrorists would overlook that fact and leave us alone. My Scandinavian appearance read like an advertisement. I might as well have had a sign plastered on my back saying, "Available For Kidnapping." Lane, on the other hand, had dark hair and was shorter and blended in better with the locals. While Giripati and I talked, a stream of assistants entered the room soliciting advice from their rotund boss, but I was the only one quizzing him about kidnappers.

As Lane and I headed for Delhi, we joked about our predicament. "Lane, we've been advised to avoid public places, old Delhi, alleys, nighttime activities, and Muslim districts. We've got plague and terrorist threats. Have we missed anything?" I mused.

"So far the hotels aren't off limits," he replied, grinning like a Cheshire cat. "Where shall we go for lunch?"

"No kidnapper can get past those huge Sikh doormen at the Oberoi. Let's eat there," I said. My mood brightened at the thought of a plate of pasta primavera. Our favorite escape was sitting down to an Italian meal at one of the better hotels in town. As the massive Sikh doorman opened the front door for us, I was tempted to tip him off about the terrorists, but decided the crescent dagger stuffed in his belt was deterrent enough. It was peak tourist season, but we were the only westerners in the finest hotel in Delhi. Maybe I'd look into getting a dagger myself until the terrorists were caught.

"Do you hear them at night?" I asked Lane as I dove into a plate of pasta smothered in saffron cream sauce.

"Hear who, the terrorists?"

"No, the rats! It's like the running of the bulls in Pamplona. They never stop."

"I haven't heard any rats, but there's a shrew that's after my almonds. You know, those blind mice with long snouts." I knew all about shrews from a previous trip.

One evening we got home late from Delhi, and by the time I got to the dining room everyone had eaten and gone, but the food was still out. As I searched for a clean plate, I noticed a tail hanging over the edge of the rice bowl. With its hind legs balanced on the rim of the bowl, someone was sampling my dinner. I banged two metal plates together to scare the inter-loper off, but it ignored me. I went over to have a closer look and to my chagrin, a good-sized rat turned and gave me a look like, 'don't bother me, can't you see I'm eating?' I was glad someone had an appetite because I had just lost mine. I was beginning to wonder how many of these audacious rodents we had around the guesthouse. That night I dubbed our residence 'Villa de Rodentia,' a name that was more apt than I knew at the time. But despite the multiple threats to our health and safety, there was nowhere in the world I would rather have been than India, and teaching meditation was what I loved doing most.

As we headed for Kurukshetra to teach our first meditation course, I felt relieved to be out of the city. Kurukshetra, the ancient battleground of the Mahabharata War, was now an endless field of ruler straight sugar cane that reminded me of Iowa corn in August. The management at the sugar refinery was eager to interact with us, for they had almost no cultural exchange with foreigners. My group gathered for their first meditation in a small office that shared a wall with the processing plant. I always tried to make the room as quiet as possible during personal instruction, but just as I instructed my students to close their eyes, the machines started up on the other side of the wall and I found myself shouting instructions that should have been whispered. The noise was deafening. The relentless pounding of plant equipment was so loud that it was laughable and I found myself yelling at my students, hoping to be heard. I was certain my students wouldn't do well. But an hour later when I asked how they liked their med-itation, everyone in the group was satisfied. Some of the students even described profound experiences, which surprised me, since meditating in the office that day was like meditating on the wing of a jumbo jet as it revved its engines. We would soon learn that silence was easier to find deep within than on the surface of Indian life.

A Date With Fate

After returning from Haryana, I was having dinner with some European colleagues when a medium built man in traditional attire, white kurta and dhoti, entered the dining room. Judging by his aspect and attire, I guessed him to be South Indian. Although our guesthouse dining room was reserved for international faculty, ashram residents routinely dropped by to socialize. Rarely did Indians stay for a meal though, as our food was prepared without chilies or onions, rendering it tasteless to the Indian palate. The stranger approached our table and selected me from the group of westerners. In a rather grave tone, he asked, "Are you Steve Briggs?"

"Yes, I am," I replied, having never seen the man before.

Our eyes met for an awkward moment as he placed his business card in front of me and said, "Then we should exchange horoscopes."

I scanned the card for clues to the unexpected intrusion on my dinner. 'Dr. S.K. Reddy, Ayur Veda Physician,' the card read. In the next line 'astrological consultations' was printed in italics followed by a Hyderabad address. A group of Ayur Vedic physicians had recently arrived at the ashram and were about to be dispatched on tours around the world. Probably Dr. Reddy was a member of the group, but that didn't explain how he knew my name or that I was a student of Indian astrology.

"Where is your room, Dr. Reddy? After dinner I'll come by." As the man walked out of the guesthouse, I felt strangely uneasy and was not looking forward to our meeting after dinner. After four visits to India, I had become accustomed to many of the nuances of the culture, but I still had a lot to learn. The idiosyncrasies of the culture are endless. Every region of the country observes its own social protocols and most of the time I felt like a fish still learning to swim.

Standing in an unlit hallway, I knocked on Dr. Reddy's door, horoscope in one hand and flashlight in the other. He offered me a seat on a cushion less chair and began scrutinizing my horoscope with stern purposefulness. He stared and stared, and from the arch in his furrowed brow he appeared to have discovered something important, something I needed to know. But he said nothing as he continued to study my planets while I sat there defenseless, as if waiting for a verdict for a crime I hadn't committed.

Finally he looked up from the printed sheet and broke his silence. I could feel it coming before he spoke. In a solemn tone he announced the sentence, "Mr. Briggs, you are going to have a heart attack and die." If that decree wasn't sufficient, he added for good measure, "And it will be soon."

My ears heard the words, but my mind tried to block out the meaning. Now I understood why my stomach had tightened when he approached the table in the dining room. It had been a lifelong tendency for my solar plexus to intuit misfortune. I wanted to dispute the sentence, but I sat passively on the low back chair as if waiting for Bhairav, the Hindu god of death, and his black dogs to drag me off to some shadowy netherworld.

I might have reacted differently had it not been for an astrological prediction made a decade earlier. An old blind pundit living outside Delhi had made a similar prediction about my heart, although he had predicted it would fail at a more reasonable time in life. I knew from my own astrological training that a minor health affliction was present in my horoscope, but it was nothing to be overly concerned about. At least that was how I interpreted it. Knowing that astrologers are not perfect forecasters of fate, I was never much bothered by their prophecies, unless, of course, two pundits happened to arrive at the same conclusion.

"But Dr. Reddy," I protested, "why do you feel it will be fatal?"

His answer came cold and matter of fact, "Because of Sun and Mars, the planet of war. You will not survive this karma. It is destined to happen and it will be soon."

"Can you tell me the cause?" I asked.

"Government!" he stated emphatically. "Avoid government!" Easy enough, I thought. I had no plans to enter politics, but why did he have to be so adamant about it?

By the time I dismissed myself from the session, his other forecasts had blurred beyond recognition. Only the ominous prediction of the heart attack remained in my mind. After all, one's imminent demise tends to render irrelevant issues like travel and finance. Even though I had been a student of Indian astrologer for many years, my efforts to make sense of his horoscope were, at best, feeble. As I glanced at his kundali (chart), futilely attempting to predict anything, I detected something that suggested a man of severe disposition. The presence of Saturn, the planet of austerity, figured prominently in Dr. Reddy's horoscope. That insight helped explain why the man possessed the charm of an unemployed undertaker.

The lighthearted breeze in the courtyard had little affect on my disheartened mood as I passed through the guesthouse garden on the way to my room. Hoping some fresh air would revive me, I circled the gazebo a few times, inhaling the heady scent of jasmine, but it would take a far stronger intoxicant than the smell of flowers to erase the evening's forecast. Delicate jasmine blossoms carpeted the stone walk, wilting at the very peak of their brief existence. Was my predicted fate so much worse than their imminent demise?

I recalled the instruction of my octogenarian astrology teacher, the renowned Professor Gaur, who counseled, "One should never predict the death of a person as it might greatly upset the individual. But in case death is seen in the horoscope, the astrologer should recommend a gemstone to help avert the calamity." I appreciated my professor's sage advice more than ever as I tossed about the lumpy mattress. My bed felt uncomfortable, the way I imagined one would feel in a jail cell. Of course, the hardness of the mattress had little to do with my restlessness. During the course of the long night, a plan emerged. I would pay a visit to my friend Pundit Sati in the morning.

A peacock's shrill meow awakened me as the sun's early rays lit the courtyard outside my room. I lay there in bed wondering how I had offended the Sun and why he and Mars were conspiring against me. Surely this grim reaper from Hyderabad was mistaken. After all, his business card stated physician and not astrologer as his profession. I needed an antidote for this disturbing news and so I got on the blue Hero bicycle I had just purchased and rode out to see my friend, Pundit Sati, who had recently returned from a tour of North America.

Dinesh Sati was among the brightest of the six thousand ashram residents. He had toured the globe making astrological forecasts based on wisdom deeply rooted in his family tradition. Punditji, as I liked to call him, was raised in a large family; the youngest of nine children. Seven generations of his forefathers were accomplished astrologers. Punditji once proudly informed me that his father had performed yagya ceremonies for the Shankaracharya (Hinduism equivalent of the Pope) himself high in the Himalaya. I was eager to hear his opinion in this important matter of the heart.

It was still early, but Punditji opened the door and greeted me with an easy smile. Genuinely pleased to see me, he asked, "Steveji, how are you? How are meditation programs?" Pointing to a chair opposite his desk, he invited me to sit.

"I'm fine, Punditji!" I replied without conviction. "Meditation classes are going well. Many companies are signing up now." I paused before revealing the purpose of the visit. "Punditji, I have a question about my horoscope. Is this a good time?"

"Yes, yes, Steveji. What is your question?" Pundit Sati's cheerful disposition animated a handsome round face, highlighted by compassionate eyes.

"Last evening a man looked at my horoscope and made some predictions. He said I would soon die of a heart attack. Punditji, would you have a look to see if there is any truth in this prediction?" Had I not been a serious student of astrology the news might not have hit so hard. Unfortunately, I knew there was an element of truth to the prediction.

Punditji's smile vanished when he heard the prediction. Without hesitating, he took my horoscope in hand, focusing intently on the obscure geometric lines and arcane symbols on the page. After several minutes his clear brown eyes rose from the page and looked deeply into mine.

With his right index finger pointing to the ceiling, he pronounced emphatically, "Steveji, you will not die! That man should not have made this prediction. He is incorrect!" I felt immediate relief from the words, as if I had been granted a reprieve from an impending execution.

"But," Punditji continued, "in case there is some small truth to his statement, you should offer sweets to Hanuman on a Tuesday. It would also be a good idea to wear a gemstone. You are entering a period when a blue sapphire will improve the disposition of Saturn."

Punditji was relaxed and smiling again, totally at ease with himself. His calm demeanor soothed my brooding mind. The disturbance dispelled, he inquired about mutual friends in America and told me about his recent tours to Europe, Moscow, and Japan. For five years he had traveled the world counseling thousands along the way.

I knew exactly which Hanuman temple I would visit, but first I would stop at a jewelry shop to see about a gemstone.

A Stranger Saves Purari

The Vedic aphorism 'as is the macrocosm, so is the microcosm' is another way of saying 'as above, so below.' Nowhere are the similarities of the macro— and microscopic worlds better illustrated than in the behavior of planets and the activities within the human body. Molecules and atoms in the body, when viewed through a microscope, appear virtually identical to the celestial activities seen through a telescope. One could argue that an atom is a miniature solar system and a solar system nothing more than a condensed version of a galaxy. In Indian astrology, the seven planets are correlated to the seven chakras, or wheels, found in the subtle body of a person. Each planet is said to correspond to the color and vibration of a particular chakra, and exerts a powerful influence on the person.

Indian astrology, often referred to as Jyotish, is more than a method of prediction based on planetary positions at the time of birth. It combines mathematical precision with subtle intuition in its predictive process, but a unique feature of jyotish is its remedial measures. One of the more popular prescriptions is the use of gemstones. It's not uncommon in India to see a person wearing one or more precious gems for the purpose of improving health or averting unwanted events. After the unhappy encounter with Dr. Reddy, I paid a visit to a gem shop near the ashram.

Inside a small jewelry shop in Atta Market, a slender woman sat behind a glass showcase, showing gold bangles on a velvet platter to a mother and daughter seated opposite her. To their left, a handsome man in tailored western clothes scrutinized a stack of receipts. At the counter's far end, a teenage boy tapped lightly on a silver bracelet at a floor level workstation. Local power was out, and a deafening red generator chugged away outside the shop's entrance. A pleasant smile greeted me as I entered. The stylish fellow in charge of the shop introduced himself as the son of the owner of Balaram Jewelers. When I asked to see some blue sapphires, Purari invited me to sit on a stool opposite him.

"Blue sapphires are generally not worn in India as jewelry," Purari advised. "I have some nice emeralds. Would you like to see them?"

"Actually, I am interested in a blue sapphire for a specific purpose," I answered vaguely, unwilling to reveal the purpose of my visit.

"Then you probably want the sapphire for astrological reasons," intuited Purari, an obviously well-educated fellow who spoke perfect English.

"Yes, I'm looking for a clean 3-4 carat blue sapphire. Do you have any?"

Purari, having zeroed in on my needs, relaxed with an elbow on the counter. "I didn't know westerners were interested in Jyotish. Indians are fond of wearing gems recommended by astrologers, but I personally don't believe in it." The twenty-something shopkeeper's candor impressed me since, in effect, he was talking me out of a purchase.

"It's surprising that you're in the gem business, yet you don't believe in gems for astrology. Many people must come to your store for that reason," I replied. Both of us picked up on the subtle irony of the situation. The westerner readily accepted the idea of gems for astrology while the Indian was commercially motivated. I suppose it was a role reversal of sorts, but I liked this charming young shopkeeper whose brown eyes flashed gold when the light caught them.

"Tell me, how is it that you don't believe in Jyotish when it's been part of your culture for so long?" I asked.

Purari reflected for a moment, and then answered diplomatically, "There are two sides to my belief. In general, I don't believe in the ways of my ancestors. I prefer the modern way, the western way."

"What about your parents? Do they share your beliefs?"

"My parents follow the old traditions, but are not opposed to the new ones, but I've grown up with western cinema and media." Purari's frankness, if not his wisdom, impressed me.

"You said there are two sides to your belief. What is the other side?"

Purari was smiling again. "You see, I had a strange experience with a gem once. I don't tell the story often, but for some reason I think you will appreciate hearing it. Two years ago I was at a social gathering in Delhi with my friend, Rajiv. We were talking when a peculiar man joined us. The man seemed totally out of place at the party. Rajiv knew him, but I didn't. Rajiv introduced the stranger to me and the man listened silently as we continued our conversation. The whole time I was feeling somewhat uneasy as if someone was looking into my mind. Finally, the fellow spoke.

"His speech was calm and measured. 'Purari,' the man said, 'I have something very serious to tell you. A misfortune is on your horizon. You will die in an accident if you are not wearing a blue sapphire on the middle finger of your right hand by next Saturday night. I'm very sorry to bring you this news, but this is the truth. There is no doubt about it.'

"I protested," said Purari, whose eyes were now trained intently on mine. "My friend, Rajiv, who had introduced me to the mysterious man, was even more disturbed by the news. He said, 'Purari, this man is very wise. People say he's a seer, that his predictions come true. You must do as he says!'" Purari was not as relaxed now as he was when I first entered his store.

"But I didn't believe in this sort of thing, especially the idea of wearing a gem for protection. That was my attitude, and I was not going to let Rajiv persuade me otherwise." A willful nature surfaced in the young man as he told the story.

"Anyway, we left the party and I didn't hear from Rajiv for a few days. Then he stopped by my shop one afternoon. This time Rajiv was adamant. He said, 'Purari, you must take this thing seriously. Even if you don't believe the man, you are, after all, a gem dealer, so what is the harm if you wear a gem from your own shop for a few days. Please, I feel your life depends on it.'

"By now I had a strange feeling that there might be something to this, so I agreed to have one of our sapphires set in a ring and sent my boy off to Chandi Chowk—you know, the old Delhi market—to have the gem set by our silversmith." Every imaginable commodity was available at Chandi

Chowk market, which was famous for cheap electronics, handicrafts, and occasional Muslim riots.

"Few shops in Chandi Chowk have telephones so I couldn't call to check on the progress," Purari continued. "When Saturday came and the ring hadn't shown up, I decided to go and get it myself. I was now committed to wearing it, even though I really wasn't convinced something terrible was going to happen. When I arrived, the chandi walla (silversmith) hadn't finished setting the stone. He complained about power failure so I scolded him; it was just an excuse. These men take time off whenever they don't feel like working.

"Fortunately, I arrived at the shop in the late afternoon, so the silversmith still had time to set the gem before evening. When the ring was finished, I returned home." Purari was now reliving the story. He grew animated as he talked.

"I was on my motorcycle riding south on Outer Ring Road, heading for the Yamuna Bridge. It was Saturday night, so traffic was light. I was wearing the ring as instructed. I was going along when I noticed a truck overtaking me to my right. It was speeding faster than other vehicles as it came along side me, when, for no apparent reason, it veered into my lane. There was no traffic anywhere near us." By now, Purari was flashing back to the incident. His face was pale, his voice tense. His posture stiffened. "I realized he was about to run into me so I moved over to avoid him. But he kept coming closer and closer until there was no more space to my left. At that point I realized I was about to die. My heart was pounding out of control and my mind panicked. There was no way to avoid being run over. I would either collide with the truck or ram into the barrier. For some reason, the driver of the truck never saw me.

"The lorry's front wheel was so close I could hear it humming against the pavement. He was inches away. A second later I felt metal strike my right hand. It was the side of the truck rubbing on my knuckles. I had almost lost control of my bike when the truck suddenly veered away from me, careening out of control.

"I could only see its bright red tail lights as the truck sped diagonally across two lanes before going off the road where it crashed into a parked lorry. A huge explosion occurred and both vehicles caught fire. I pulled off the side of the road. I was trembling, almost in shock as I sat on the pavement, staring in disbelief at the fire that engulfed both trucks. I was sure the driver was dead.

"I was trying to light a cigarette when I noticed the ring. It looked different, so I took it off to examine it more closely. What I saw amazed me.

The sapphire was shattered inside. A web of fractures that had not been there disfigured the blue stone. The sapphire was a good one, but now it was clouded. Its surface was smooth, but the center of the stone had been shattered.

"At that moment chills ran up and down my spine. I realized what had happened. The man's extraordinary prophecy had been averted by his own sage advice. I was alive because of a gem I had worn for two hours. Would you like to see the ring? I keep it as a memento. It's in the safe."

"Yes, of course," I replied. "That is one of the more bizarre stories I've ever heard. But I don't understand one thing."

"What's that?" Purari gave me a puzzled look as he opened the shop safe. "Have a look at this!" he said as he handed me the ring. "See the center of the gem?"

"Remarkable. It's shattered inside. This wasn't there before the truck touched you?" I asked in astonishment.

"Not at all. The sapphire was clean. None of that was there before Saturday night. The amazing thing is the truck didn't bump me enough to knock me off my bike…just enough to make contact with the back of my hand." Purari subconsciously rubbed his finger as he recounted the episode. "What is it you don't understand?"

"Purari, with this unbelievable testimony…how is it you remain skeptical about the power of gemstones?"

"Steveji, I believe that the man at the party foresaw my death. But I have never been able to understand how the sapphire saved me. It's too unbelievable." Purari had obviously arrived at this conclusion after considerable soul searching.

"But surely the gem played a role, or it wouldn't have been shattered by the accident," I argued. "My guru once told me the reason one wears a gem is to keep the planet's negative energies from entering the body." It seemed ironic that I was the one convinced of the miracle and not Purari.

"I've sold lots of gems to customers at the advice of pundits. Possibly I'm skeptical because I make my living selling gems." Purari's honesty impressed me.

"But you're alive to tell an incredible story. Have you seen the man who made the prediction since the accident?"

"No. But as you may know, there are many in India with these 'gifts.' In the west you use the term 'psychics.' In India, we call them 'seers.' Our forefathers understood the stories of the ancients from Vedic times. There are many legends of rishis and saints who could look into the past or future."

"My friend," I protested, "aren't you turning your back on a profound tradition?"

"Steveji, Indians have struggled for a long time. My generation doesn't really reject the old ways, but we feel our country has to keep up with the world. We need to adopt the ways of the west. We need technology most of all."

I thought of the thousands of times power had gone out while I was in India. One of the more amusing times was in a theater where we were watching the Hitchcock thriller, *North by Northwest*. Cary Grant and his girl were hanging from Mount Rushmore in the climactic scene when, sure enough, the power went out. We waited, but it never came back on. It was amazing to see how the Indians in the theater reacted; they walked out calmly as if nothing had happened, not minding the short-circuited ending.

As I got up to leave, I thanked Purari for sharing his remarkable story with me and planned to return to buy one of the handsome sapphires he had in his inventory. He seemed somehow relieved to have confided in me. The rough chugging of generators accosted me as I left the shop and began my search for driver and car. The entire shopping district had been without electricity all afternoon and the acrid smell of diesel filled the air. Purari was right. India could benefit from better technology, but not at the expense of its ancestral legacy.

Hanuman To The Rescue

At the edge of Connaught Place stands one of the city's oldest Hindu temples. Hundreds of Delhi wallas stream in and out of the marbled temple day and night, except on Tuesday, when the numbers swell tenfold. I browsed among the row of shops outside before selecting my offering of sweets. Ladhus are believed to be a favorite of the gods, and I wanted to find the best in the market. Made from roasted chickpea flour, cane sugar, and clarified butter, and flavored with cardamom, the ingredients are rolled into golf ball-sized circles. "One dozen ladhus for Hanumanji," I instructed the jowly sweet maker sitting behind his oversized frying pan.

I crossed the threshold of the temple's entrance at the top of the stairs. Inside, shoeless worshippers moved noiselessly about carrying fruit, flowers, and sweets on stainless steel plates. Hanuman, one of the heroes of India's favorite epic, the Ramayana, was at the center of a dense cloud of commotion and incense. Flanked by priests interceding to make offerings on behalf of the throng of devotees, India's popular god was represented by a brilliant orange oval stone with a silver eye painted on it. The solitary eye symbolized all-seeing awareness achieved when one's spiritual eye is awakened.

A young pujari (priest) waved my platter of sweets in front of Hanuman before returning it to me. Because I was a foreigner, he pulled a garland off the altar and tossed it over my head. Before leaving, I paused to ask the powerful god for his protection. I put all but two of the offered ladhus in the outstretched hands of beggars, and the hungry wasted no time devouring them. A wave of relief enveloped me. Pundit Sati's prescribed mission was accomplished.

I was resting soundly in the night when a strange vision appeared before my inner eye. A form took shape. At first I couldn't make out what or who it was, but it slowly came into focus against an indigo backdrop. I recognized him; it was Hanuman, and he was smiling. His large, limpid eyes gazed benevolently at me and I felt thrills of bliss inside. The vision then faded and I drifted off to sleep, knowing that my offerings had been accepted. The following day I took prasada (offered food) to pundit Sati, who was happy to hear about Hanuman's visitation in the night. "Steveji, you are fortunate. Hanumanji is a great protector. Surely, your health will be 100% from now on," Punditji reassured me.

More Disturbances

Life in inscrutable India didn't stand for complacency. Not long after the kidnapping alert, a terrorist bomb exploded inside Nirula's where we had stopped for ice cream the previous day. Then a few months later, India's flagging tourist economy received another severe blow when a group of westerners was taken hostage by Muslim extremists. One of the hostages escaped, but the others were less fortunate. The body of a Norwegian man was found decapitated in a Kashmiri forest and the other three hostages were never heard from again. A militant group called Al Faran was blamed for the brutality that shook everyone's confidence and sent the few foreigners left in the country into a state of high alert.

Although the circumstances that surrounded us were disquieting at times, my expectations remained high. It was an anxious time in Delhi, but despite the danger and confusion, our project was gathering momentum. The meditation we offered was a needed antidote to the stress epidemic that had invaded the country. It was an exciting and perhaps tenuous time to be in India, but I wouldn't have wanted to be anywhere else. I believed a transformation of great personal significance lay ahead and sensed that there was someone I needed to meet who was expecting me. Where that person was I had no idea, but I knew that our meeting would be a reunion of sorts. Destiny had brought me to this ancient land and I willingly surrendered to it.

TWO

Darshan In A Dutch Forest

*Sages act without expectation, succeed without taking credit,
and have no desire to display their excellence.*

I had received the invitation to come to India just five weeks before our arrival in Delhi. I had known it was coming, but I hadn't known when. A blind astrologer, Sitaram, who lived on the outskirts of Delhi had predicted my return to India along with a dozen other events that had come true since our meeting a decade earlier. The wise old pundit had declared that I would one day embrace India as my home, having come to the conclusion that I was a stranger in the land of my birth. In India, he had said, I would meet my spiritual family, and I was looking forward to that day. Why I was drawn to India like a lodestone to a magnet, I can't say except that the planets ordained it. In a word, I had karma with the ancient land. India had not always been easy for me, but each visit had been life transforming. When the call had come, images of spiritual India flooded my awareness, and to have my guru extend the invitation confirmed that the time had arrived to renew the spiritual journey that I believed only India could offer.

Maharishi Mahesh Yogi, the blissful Indian teacher who had tirelessly traveled the globe for four decades, was the first fully enlightened person I had ever met, and it was his encouragement that caused me to join his corps of monks that traveled the world at a moment's notice. Maharishi's smile had leapt off the poster outside my Shakespeare class at the University of Arizona in the fall of 1972, and from the first moment I met him high in the Swiss Alps a year later, I had found his presence irresistible. I was eager for the plane to land so I could see my teacher again. A master's darshan (sight of a saint) has a way of changing one's outlook permanently, lifting one into higher states of awareness.

Upon arriving at Maharishi's headquarters in Holland on my stopover from the States to India, I had been struck by the seemingly impenetrable fortress of a former Franciscan monastery hidden deep in a Dutch national forest. For the next five weeks, along with three other Americans, we met with Maharishi to discuss plans for two proposed projects for India: establishing management institutes and teaching Transcendental Meditation to corporations. It had been almost ten years since I had seen Maharishi, and although he had aged, he still had superhuman reserves of energy and stamina. Maharishi was almost eighty, forty years my senior, but I found it impossible to keep up with him. Meetings routinely went late into the night, but he never seemed to slow down. When he finally sent us off to rest a few hours before sunrise, a secretary ushered in yet another group for their meeting. Maharishi's stamina was legendary, his focus unrelenting.

Meetings with Maharishi were unpredictable, entertaining, and always a lesson in world geography. A conference call from Latvia came in on one of the many phones manned by the secretaries. Later, with precision and patience, Maharishi answered questions on a project to build a school in South Africa and reviewed a proposal to buy laser technology for an operating theater in a Delhi hospital. Line by line he reviewed an announcement for the Washington Post and then listened to a report from his college in Cambodia. Then a delegation from Thailand was escorted into the hall followed by a Bombay industrialist and his family who offered bouquets of red and yellow tulips to Maharishi before catching a flight back to India. Maharishi then briefed a German general about implementing meditation in the armed forces. Guests and dignitaries from all over the globe came and went as Maharishi's attention moved from continent to continent with the agility of an acrobat in his relentless search for solutions to problems that even governments refused to tackle. The backlit globe on his table spun like a top as his index finger came to rest on country after country. Raise the collective consciousness of the people and you will solve the nation's problems was his rallying cry.

One late night, after the guests had gone and our work was finished, we relaxed with Maharishi in his spacious and silky suite inside the old monastery. I relished every minute with my guru, but those rare moments when the planning for the world stopped, were my favorites. An attendant served fresh juice while Maharishi enquired about our stay. Maharishi's long-time personal secretary, Nandkishore, was the only other person in the room with us. Nandkishore owned an infectious laugh even more contagious than Maharishi's and I imagined the two of them shaking with laughter for hours on end. But that night, the dynamics were different. Whenever Nandkishore spoke, Maharishi disagreed with his loyal assistant, a drama that went on for the better part of an hour.

Of course, Maharishi was the master, but I couldn't help thinking Nandkishore's ideas were sound and that Maharishi was being unfair, that he should listen to his humble secretary. But it didn't seem to matter; Maharishi dismissed everything his secretary said, sometimes brusquely. But the bearded secretary kept his cool, even laughing now and then as his proposals were shot down one after the other like clay pigeons fired from a trap.

As I witnessed what I thought was undue treatment of the long time secretary, I had the urge to tell Maharishi that he was being unfair, that Nandkishore was right on most of the issues. Finally I had heard enough, and the thought I had been suppressing pushed its way into my head. 'Nandkishore is right' flashed like a neon sign inside my brain. At that very instant, as if he had read my mind, Maharishi looked at me, raised his eyebrows, and said. "Hmm? Nandkishore is right?" Then he and his sidekick burst out laughing like two mischievous boys that had just pulled off a clever prank. I had swallowed the bait and was now dangling from the end of the master's fishing pole. It had been a test, and I had failed miserably.

The time with Maharishi was very precious. The numbers of people from faraway places coming to see him was increasing more than ever, but still he managed to find time for everyone. The amount of attention we received during our stay made it obvious that big things were expected from the projects we were taking to India. At the same time, projects were never the primary focus around Maharishi. One night I was reminded of that fact. Again, our group of four Americans was meeting with Maharishi late into the night. We were discussing India and the country's need for professional management when, for no apparent reason, Maharishi began staring above my head as he talked. This went on for a few minutes and then he looked away. I didn't pay much attention to it; after all, he often looked at people in the room. The only difference was the amount of time he had spent peering over my head.

As usual, the meeting went late. When we finally adjourned, I was asleep moments after my head hit the pillow. As I slept, a faint thread of awareness sustained itself. Then in the half-light of inner wakefulness, Maharishi appeared in front of me. He smiled, but said nothing, looking at me exactly as he had in the meeting. Without a word, he went into action. Before I had drawn another breath, he made a connection inside me, like a plumber connecting two pipes. The link made, he vanished as suddenly as he had come, and I was left wondering, 'was I dreaming or was the apparition of my Master real?'

For the rest of the night a brilliant gold and white light illumined my mind. The light was so intense that I was sure it was coming from outside; I looked around the room to find the source of the light, but the room was black. Heavy velvet curtains blocked out everything. A sublime feeling flowed through my veins that outshone even the brilliant radiance. Sweet nectar circulated from head to toe, and I felt weightless, transparent, and unable to move. The golden liquid spread throughout my body before spilling out the top of my head. Then it reversed its direction, cascading like a waterfall into every cell in my body. Hours passed in this euphoric state. I was wondering what could possibly be better than this when a feminine voice rang like a porcelain bell inside my head. It was more than a voice for a personality was present. She was Indian, and she whispered, "I am Aramati. I am with you when you wish. Now I will be instructing you." Waves of love welled up inside in response to this benevolent being, and somehow I was certain that what was happening was the result of Maharishi's visit in the night.

In the coming days, Aramati's crystalline voice came at unexpected moments; at the dinner table, on walks in the forest, during meditation, and even during sleep. A transformation seemed to be taking place. The voice advised me to 'allow it to happen.' When I saw Maharishi the next night, I waited for him to look my way so I could acknowledge his beautiful gift by sending him a wave of appreciation. He nodded ever so slightly and continued talking. After all, it was all in a day's work for a master. Having spoken to others, I knew the blessing that he had given me had been given to others as well.

Walks among the fragrant conifers provided a welcomed haven from the flurry of people and projects that came and went on the jumbo jets that touched down around the clock in Amsterdam. I needed some time to myself to digest the changes going on inside me. The needled paths formed a maze of shaded passages that never failed to deposit me at the gates of the old monastery. The Dutch loved their national forest and came on weekends to hike and pedal collapsible bikes among the benevolent pines, stopping to admire the former abbey that now hosted guests who rarely stayed long enough to adjust to the local time kept in its impassive clock tower. Strafe marks from the Luftwaffe dented the impenetrable citadel. The old chapel, with its stained glass rising to a vaulted ceiling, was our gathering place for meditation, and the monks' quarters in the attic now housed pundits and Vedic astrologers. Monastic life had been out of vogue in Central Europe for fifty years.

When it was time to leave for India, we were reluctant to go. After all,

Maharishi's presence was the essence of India, and we had him sitting right there in front of us. In our final meeting, Maharishi gave us a heartfelt sendoff. "You will be very busy," he said, "but your meditation time is always the priority. Have your cook pack lunches for you and drink fresh juice each day. This will keep you healthy." His tone was that of a doting mother sending her son off for his first day of school. Lane and I each handed the Master a bouquet of flowers, and he tapped us on the head with a rose in return. As we were about to go, Maharishi held us in his gaze, and with a broad smile, said, "Go and build a bridge between east and west. Make a beautiful rainbow between India and America." Then we were whisked away to the airport. We were on our way to the other side of the rainbow.

THREE

A Village Ashram

*The flow of life in the village is not swift, but neither is it
entirely inactive or inert. Work and leisure keep the same pace,
as if walking together hand in hand.*

—*Rabrindanath Tagore*

Autumn arrived at the ashram, bringing welcome relief from the skin-soaking humidity of the summer monsoon. A sun softened by its lower position in the sky warmed the days, but not too much. The clamminess had dissipated and the cool nights begged me to throw open the window. I drifted off each night inhaling jasmine and gardenia, and awoke at sunrise to a cock crowing. Our village ashram was beginning to feel like home.

One morning I climbed onto the flat roof of our two-story guesthouse to do my Surya Namaskars (sun salutations). The ashram and surrounding villages were just waking up. Roosters roused late sleepers, but the peacock's piercing meow from the garden was the dominant call to action in our neighborhood. It was the enchanting hour after daybreak before the sun had burned off the haze that melded crop, village, and tree together like an artist's canvas. But beyond the haze a timelessness and origination of life pervaded the landscape. Nothing appeared distinct as I surveyed the waking countryside. The transition from dawn to day is a measured process in rural India, with subtleties different from those of other lands. As I stretched and twisted on my grass mat, I thought of rooftop nights spent under the stars on previous stays in India. I had slept on a charpoy (string cot) on moonlit nights in the south, listening to the calm, believing the moon was well within my reach.

A band of red-faced monkeys watched from a mulberry tree as I performed my yoga stretches. I had never mastered the ancient system of

Hatha Yoga; the countless tennis balls I had scooped up since age six had predisposed me against serious bending. As a result, I had developed the habit of using my feet to pick up items off the floor, and took more pride in the skill than the plow and peacock poses I practiced daily.

Mother and baby monkey were peaceful creatures, but the oversized alpha male and his upstart understudies were the ones to keep an eye on. I had no doubt they were plotting mischief. Their red bottoms flashed as they bounded across the roof, but they had only come for water. The monkeys were in the habit of shaking the pipes that ran the length of the concrete roof, hoping to cause a leak. Sometimes they succeeded. Before a lid was fastened over the storage tank, the rogues were found bathing in our water supply, a situation we remedied right away. On this sunny morning, they seemed content to observe, as if they were critiquing my abridged efforts to perform the pretzel postures.

It was rush hour on the dusty bullock path that bisected the ashram. Slow moving carts that tilted from front to rear were pulled along by ungainly water buffalo, their drivers' lean legs dangling over the front of the carts as they went. Matchbox stalls selling paan (digestives) and bidis (hand rolled cigarettes) were just opening for business; a barber prepared his man for a shave and another man sat on his heels shining shoes. The chai walla deftly poured tea from one glass to another, a skillful juggler of brown liquid.

Further away, villagers waited by the road for busses as uniformed children piled onto a bicycle rickshaw and a cyclist buried under a mound of cloth pedaled along the road on his way to wash laundry in a pond. Fields extended beyond the ashram walls as far as the eye could see; the thinning haze allowed only the faintest impression of the horizon. The sight of man and animal going about their business side by side reminded me that village life relied on the interdependence of species, a relationship more intimate than in the west. The seamless panorama captured much of what I loved about this ancient culture.

Even the congested Delhi streets accommodated something of rural life. The odd gangling camel from Rajasthan towered over subcompacts packed full of urban commuters while dreamy-eyed cows lounged on raised medians ignoring the bustle of the city. The occasional sight of an elephant, forehead painted red or white, lumbering past the Tibetan market with its turbaned mahout on board thrilled the child in me. "Hati! Hati!" I called, pointing out the car window. Little by little, I was finding my rhythm in India. Like the royal gait of the elephant, I slowed myself to the tempo of the ancient land, which moved at an imperial pace, indifferent to digital time and deadlines.

Before long, our project started to catch fire. Our schedule of meetings, juggled with long hours of meditation and the daily commute to the office, demanded efficiency. But efficiency, which was second nature to Americans, could not be taken for granted in India. Our likeable driver Anil was a skilled chauffeur and ever obedient, but our arrival at meetings rested squarely on his shoulders, and he had the annoying habit of showing up late for work. Behind his sleepy brown eyes and forehead of black hair was a practical mind that knew precisely the best route to any part of Delhi depending on the time of day. Anil's tardiness was less a matter of negligence than it was the result of having grown up in a village culture where time wasn't measured by the minute hand of a clock, or even the hour hand for that matter. It never occurred to our driver and friend that arriving a half hour late for work compromised our day, and so we stopped by Khan Market one afternoon to buy Anil a watch. Indians love watches, but for reasons other than getting places on time. Anil wore the watch for a few days and it seemed to help, but one day he showed up for work without it. "Where's your watch, Anil?" asked Lane.

"Sir, I gave it to my friend,"

"But why?"

"Because he wanted it." The logic was sound, but didn't help his punctuality.

"Anil, I'll buy you another watch, but you can't give this one away," Lane pleaded. I could see that Lane was feeling frustrated, and for good reason. But not too long after Anil got used to his watch I had stopped wearing mine. Indian standard time wasn't measured in minutes, and the day I realized that was the day I took a giant step toward understanding the culture.

My Roommate's A Thief

As the days passed, I began to notice something peculiar about my room. Various items were disappearing one at a time. This puzzled me, because I always kept the room padlocked. First a toothbrush, and then a stainless steel Swiss army knife vanished. A plastic lighter followed. None of these items were sorely missed, and would hardly have been selected by a thief in favor of the stack of rupees on my desk. I was at a loss as to their disappearance, especially since the items vanished while I slept.

One night I arrived at the guesthouse late. As I was falling asleep, I heard scratching sounds and clatter in the room. Listening more carefully, I detected the source of the noise, which was coming from beneath the tall wooden almiera (dresser) against the wall. My curiosity roused, I decided to investigate.

After turning on the light, I shifted the heavy closet an inch at a time. As I moved it away from the wall, I discovered a nest made of cotton balls pulled from a comforter. It was a cozy habitat, one whose owner had escaped to safety in another part of the room. As I nudged the closet another six inches, a stash of stolen items was exposed. All my missing belongings and more were neatly arranged in a pile. Too tired to pursue the thief, I retrieved my things and drifted off to sleep; yet another rodent was interfering with my night's rest.

I rose early the next morning. The hours before sunrise were especially peaceful in the ashram. Upon waking each morning I was keen to meditate. Floating in the transcendent without interruption for hours at a time, one could inhale the soul of India deep into one's being. The early morning air brought a special prana (vital air) that enervated the body during the hour Hindus call Navaswan. As I sank deeper and deeper, a stream of bliss bathed me in serene stillness. Mundane currents of thought and emotion dissolved into a timeless sea. When the morning meditation reached its peak, the presence that had visited me in Holland appeared with the reliability of a Swiss clock. It was this daily encounter that moved me to meditate in the hours before dawn.

As the sun rose, the muffled sounds of chanting wafted about the ashram. Nearby, three thousand pundits were beginning their morning ritual. Their powerful, rhythmic recitation continued for hours without interruption, and washed over the fields and villages beyond the ashram walls. The pundits' measured song repeated itself over and over, each hymn building on the previous one. It was simply a matter of synchronizing with the group in order to become one with their subtle litany of sound and the deity they invoked.

When a group of pundits chant harmoniously together, they summon the devas (divine impulses), who respond as willingly as a mother to her child. Invoking the gods not only blesses those who chant the holy verses, but also generates a radiance that sweeps the earth, bringing peace and washing away negativity. When divinity is brought into physical manifestation through the recitation of age-old Sanskrit formulae, the world enjoys fresh waves of light and energy that expand in all directions like concentric circles spreading across a lake from the spot where a pebble has been tossed in. Although the effect is strongest at the point of origin, the vibration circles the earth, extending far beyond the reach of those chanting. India is the source of Vedic recitation in the world, and our village ashram was set apart by the presence of thousands of pundits that had gathered from villages all over India to create peace.

Pundit Boys

A sudden pounding on my door roused me from my morning reverie. I knew the knock well for it had startled me in the past. Two thumps followed by a pause, and then two thunderous thumps in case the occupant of the room was asleep. Monday morning was laundry day, and Om Prakash, our Bihari dhobi (washer man), was at the door. I was impressed by his focus, if not the quality of his work. Rarely did he lose an item or miss a scheduled pickup despite the fact that he serviced a dozen rooms in the guesthouse. Broken buttons and half-pressed collars were a bother, but I never minded the less-than-perfect condition of my clothes as much as I did the poorly timed intrusions. Sometimes my meditative state prevented me from answering the door altogether; my body simply refused to move off the bed.

Om Prakash's rounds were completed as the ashram came to life. As he rode off on his Hero bicycle with a bulbous bundle of cloth balanced on the handlebars, the kitchen crew arrived on their cycles. The old gardener sat on his heals cropping grass in the garden with a rusty sickle while a neighbor's radio played bhajans and the creaky hand pump below my window filled steel buckets for morning baths. I knew every sound and their sequence by heart. The village ashram we called Maharishi Nagar was waking up and the best hours for meditation were now past.

As I was about to lie down on the bed, I sensed that someone was watching me, and I looked around the room. To my surprise, on top of the tall dresser a tiny pair of eyes was trained on me. I remained sitting so I could observe the creature that was fastidiously observing me. I stared at him and he stared at me. I sat motionless, but he twisted his neck from left to right as if trying to figure out who I was and why I had interfered with his night. Mysteriously, the creature's presence had eluded me for the three weeks I had lived in the room, but now it was time to get acquainted. I had a packrat for a roommate!

Feeling playful, I engaged the thief in conversation. "My friend, why are you stealing my belongings? Do you really need a toothbrush? You're not one of those fat rats I saw in the kitchen." As I spoke he listened, showing no sign of fear. His just turned of his head from side to side.

The little fellow seemed quite intelligent, and although I was not happy with the fact that he had walked off with my things, I felt friendly toward him and decided to let him stay in my room under the condition that he stop stealing. Unfortunately, as the days passed, it was obvious that his habit was chronic. More items disappeared and were found under the dresser. Finally, for lack of a better idea, I vacuumed up his nest one morning while he was off burglarizing a neighbor. But the following afternoon he appeared again on his closet perch where he observed me for the better part of an hour.

Afternoon meditations, after commuting to and from Delhi, were never as satisfying as the morning and I spent the better part of one session contemplating the fate of my friend, who I had named Packs. Packs was smaller and less annoying than the fat rats in the pantry, although he was a superior thief. He had the profile of a mouse, except he was larger. Finally, I arrived at a decision. "Packs," I said, "one of us has to go. Since you were here first, I will let you stay, but you must promise not to steal from me in the future." Packs never nodded in agreement, he just turned his head back and forth like a pendulum.

Krishna Television

By the weekend I had shifted rooms and was getting things put away when two boys appeared outside my open door. "Have you seen Eberhard Uncle?" asked the taller of the two. "Tonight is Krishna television. Please tell him to come." Eberhard, the jovial Bavarian who lived next door, loved children, and a steady stream of boys and girls poured in and out of his suite.

"What is Krishna television?" I asked the boys.

"You come, Uncle. You will like. Eberhard Uncle bring you." It was Saturday and a bit of socializing seemed like a good idea. The ashram was divided down the middle by the bullock path, which was a public access road. Both halves of the ashram were walled off from the public. The foreigner's guesthouse where we lived was on one side of the ashram, and the house with Krishna television was on the other. Our side of the ashram had tall eucalyptus and flowering bushes, pruned gardens, terra cotta roads, and freshly painted buildings. Senior administrators and international guests lived on our side. The other side housed pundits and staff. Thousands of Indian villagers lived on the other side, including our dhobi, Om Prakash. A children's school was also on the far side. Beyond the walls of the 300-acre composite ashram were another 300 acres of farmland also owned by the ashram, where farmers cultivated mustard, marigolds, and paddy. Eberhard and I arrived at the far corner of the ashram after navigating cavernous potholes that tossed our vehicle left and right.

As we climbed out of Eberhard's car, one of the boys I had met earlier greeted us with a toothy smile. His three teenage sisters stood shyly behind their younger brother. The children led us into a single story house with a small-attached porch. A colorful geometric mandala (auspicious symbol) had been drawn on the ground at the entrance. After removing our shoes, we followed the children into a room full of villagers; a row of small kids sat on the floor in front of a television. The head of the household beamed as Eberhard entered the room.

"Hari Ram," intoned the round-faced fellow who wore nothing but a cotton dhoti (traditional attire for Indian men) that covered him from waist to ankles.

"Hari Bhagavan," Eberhard replied as he sat down next to the friendly fellow. As if on cue, the sound of a wood flute filled the room and the title 'Krishna' appeared on the screen. The room fell silent; all eyes were glued to the television. Although the popular serial about the life of the cowherd Krishna was in Hindi, I was able to follow the story, having read most of it in the Srimad Bhagavatam, the account of Lord Krishna's life. The lively episode brought great peels of laughter from the children who sat spellbound on the floor.

The plot was archetypal. The evil King Kansa, having learned that a divine child had been born who it was prophesied would slay him, set out to kill the baby Krishna and his brother Balaram. He hired a corrupt priest skilled in the art of sorcery and together they devised a plan whereby the priest would appear at the infants' home disguised as a mendicant beggar. The strategy succeeded and the assassin was admitted into Krishna's house. While Krishna's mother was busy in the kitchen, the evil-minded man tried to slay the infant. Using his divine powers, the baby Krishna countered the assassin while lying passively in his cradle. His efforts foiled, the priest became more and more befuddled by Krishna's powers, and by the end of the episode, he was reduced to a convulsing madman after Krishna levitated a pot of kheer across the room and dumped the pudding on the evil man's head. As the milky sweet dripped from the demented man's brow, the children roared their approval.

By the episode's end the children's eyes were wide with wonder. As in villages all over India, they gathered each Saturday night for the popular serial, a tradition that continued until the series ended. The Krishna Show was a wild success. Its producer and director, Ram Sagar, had also created another mega hit, The Ramayana, which was so popular that when one village was unable to view the show due to a power failure, its irate residents set fire to the local power station.

The neighbors departed after the show, leaving Eberhard and me behind. The women in the house swung into action preparing dinner. One daughter rolled wheat dough while another deep-fried the flatbread. Eberhard introduced me to the members of the family as they came and went. Abishek, a mild mannered ten year-old with the sleepy brown eyes of a calf, was the youngest in the family. His round face resembled his father's. Pateriya, the family patriarch, was a gregarious fellow whose infectious laughter left permanent creases around his eyes. His gray and white beard gave him a look of wisdom. Pateriya's cheerful face was as round as the melons that grew along the sandy banks of the Yamuna River and his stomach was conspicuously rotund. Bulbous bellies are a point of pride among Brahmin pundits, and Pateriya stroked and scratched his as if it were the family pet. Pateriya's three teenage daughters were named Kusum, Richa, and Neetu. Kusum was tall, confident, and in high school; the other two were shy and growing fast.

The attractive trio brought platefuls of alloo (potato) curry, moong dal, and puris (fried bread), and kept the supply coming long after I was full. The women went about serving their guests graciously. The men in the family stayed out of the kitchen. Pateriya prepared his plate like a child fashioning mud pies. He stirred the curries with his fingers before slurping the subji (vegetables) down, making loud, contented noises as he ate. When the rice and curd (yoghurt) arrived, he kneaded them with the fingers of his right hand until they were mixed to his liking. It was soon obvious that I couldn't keep up with Pateriya and Eberhard, who were larger around the middle. But the food kept coming in spite of my protests, and I was forced to cover my plate with my hands to suspend the flow. Pateriya continued with his meal, and when he was finished, more than one satisfied burp bubbled up, a sure sign that he was pleased with his meal. Mama Pateriya looked at him approvingly from the kitchen doorway. Only the men ate with such relish, and I was told the use of the fingers infused life energy into the food, which aided digestion. Judging from the sounds that came from my host, his digestion was working quite well.

Pateriya Family

After dinner, we relaxed under the stars. The autumn air was cool. The family conversed in broken English so that I could participate. Tethered near Pateriya's charpoy lay Poonam, the family cow. Poonam lowed sweetly now and then, bringing playful responses from Pateriya who clearly adored the animal.

According to Pateriya, Poonam produced twice the amount of milk as the cows in the ashram dairy. She was an exceptionally large cow and her pregnancy added to her girth. Pateriya's cow was the only one in the ashram not confined to the pasture behind his house. In fact, there was a policy prohibiting cows outside the dairy walls, but Pateriya, who was in charge of Vedic agriculture in the ashram, was given special privileges. Vedic agriculture is a unique method of cultivating crops based on age-old planting techniques prescribed in the scriptures. This explained the prolific vegetable gardens surrounding his home, and possibly Poonam's presence as well. In the course of conversation, I learned that Pateriya had traveled to Africa, Europe, and Southeast Asia, unheard of adventures for an Indian villager. It was not uncommon for him to be away for six months at a time.

Despite his globe trotting, Pateriya remained a simple villager. His happy mood was infectious, and we shook with laughter under the starry sky. Later, after the moon had risen, Richa brought an electric keyboard and Pateriya sang. Although no career awaited him, Pateriya poured his heart into each bhajan (spiritual song). I imagined this to be the way life was in rural India: A family entertaining itself under the stars, their cow joining in occasionally. The evening had flowed with the warmth and love of each member of the family, but that's how it is in a land where the guest is God. As we drove off, Eberhard stopped the car and rolled down the window. The children ran to the car and Eberhard Uncle promised to take them for ice cream the following day.

The Pateriyas came from a village in central India where their fore fathers had been farmers who shared in the priestly duties at the local temple. At the time of their marriage, Pateriya was twenty-one and his wife just fourteen. Having resisted living in ashram staff blocks that housed thousands, Pateriya built his own place on the remotest tract inside the ashram walls. Besides his expertise in agriculture, he was a trained Vedic pundit. His youngest children attended the ashram school, and his eldest daughter would graduate from public high school in the spring. Whenever he traveled abroad, Mama Pateriya fasted on rice and dal until he returned.

Bullying Tim Jones

With six kids stacked to the ceiling in the back of Eberhard's subcompact, we were on our way to Nirula's Ice Cream parlor for a Sunday treat. I was no stranger to Delhi's popular shop, but this was my first visit with a carload of children. Nirula's was more than an ice cream outlet. Its owners were Columbia University business school graduates that had cornered the

Delhi fast food market, serving 25,000 meals a day at their dozen outlets. The store had as many flavors of ice cream as Baskin Robbins, but the children knew exactly what they liked. In contrast to American kids who craved anything chocolate, the Pateriya gang wanted mango swirl and kesa pista (pistachio saffron). The kids sampled my double fudge chocolate, but it overpowered them, much the way chilies overwhelmed me.

By the time we arrived back at the ashram, the ice cream I had packed for Pateriya was a puddle of flavored cream. But it didn't matter. Pateriya waved it away, saying "too cold to put on tongue." Frozen foods were modern ideas that depended on electricity and cold storage; Pateriya preferred the old ways. The salubrious autumn day called for a game of badminton and Pateriya, being the child that he was, joined in. When my Montana friend Tim Jones showed up, Pateriya took us on a tour of the ashram goshala. The dairy maintained a herd of over a hundred cows, providing dairy for the pundits, because milk is believed to strengthen the vocal cords. Considering the boys chanted for hours at a time, it made good sense.

Pateriya was a purist in many ways. He insisted that a cow's diet should include pasture grazing. Pateriya mated Poonam with the ashram bull, but putting her in with the herd was out of the question for she was his pride and joy, and was considered a member of the family. As we returned to the house, Pateriya, Tim, and I were halfway down a narrow alleyway when the dairy's massive gray bull entered the lane from the opposite direction. He was an impressive specimen; chest and shoulder muscles rippling as he walked, his head held high. Had we stood eyeball to eyeball, the bull would have been at least my height. Tim was the first to notice that the bull showed signs of agitation. Not wanting to get too close to the burly beast, we reversed our direction, but the bull gave chase. It was every man for himself. Pateriya and I raced to safety in an open field, but the bull pursued Tim as they raced the length of the alley. The bull was closing in on Tim fast and I feared he would be gored. Without a second to spare, just as the fuming animal lowered his horns, Tim hoisted himself safely onto a concrete wall and the frustrated bull was left snorting and glaring at Tim's bottom, but his target was out of reach. The testy beast continued on his unobstructed way, looking back to see if his quarry was still out of range. Pateriya was giddy from the close encounter and Tim never quite knew how narrowly he had escaped being the bull's-eye.

Bulls were not as common on Delhi streets as their docile mates, but we spotted them occasionally. After the hostile encounter with the ashram bull, I allowed them their space and noticed that Indians went out of their way to avoid confrontation. The testosterone charged brutes were usually alone, standing in the middle of the street or grazing by the roadside, their chests swollen with pride, the skin on their necks hanging loose and rubbery. One imposing specimen near Nehru Place dwarfed all the cows in the neighborhood. I couldn't imagine any species where the two sexes were endowed with such opposite tendencies, for Indian cows were as affectionate as their counterparts were aggressive.

Vedic Agriculture

Pateriya's vegetable garden was producing nicely. His garden was organic, which distinguished it from most plots in India. It was also Vedic, which set it apart from virtually every other garden in the world. Pateriya explained that Vedic agriculture involved planting and harvesting according to the lunar cycle. It also meant planting in a prescribed manner, which included sewing the seeds by hand while certain mantras were recited. According to Pateriya, each plant has a jiva, or soul, and by following the Vedic injunctions, the farmer nurtures the plant holistically. I remembered *The Secret Life of Plants* making a point about consciousness in the plant kingdom. It made sense that the human handling of seeds added something that was lost when machines performed every function. Agro businesses in the western world were not only guilty of poisoning crops with fertilizers and pesticides; one wondered if genetically manufactured seed had a soul at all.

Poonam lay contented on a bed of straw outside the house while Abishek and his friend, Manish, piloted diamond-shaped kites that soared and dipped above the tree line. The ten year-olds skillfully controlled the flight of their craft. The white and yellow kites darted and spun around the sun like moths circling a street lamp. As we watched, Pateriya's younger daughters, Richa and Neetu, brought tea and cookies. There seemed to be no end to the sipping of tea. I was uncomfortable being the reason no one was speaking Hindi, but the girls' older sister, Kusum, who spoke English, soon joined us. Although Pateriya was as carefree as anyone I had ever met, I knew he was not be looking forward to his daughters' marriages. Despite the legal ban on dowries, the custom still flourished in rural India, and the Pateriyas were traditional villagers. Even one daughter's marriage could send a village father deep into debt, and Pateriya had three. Having grown up in a close-knit family, the company of this warm-hearted family with its outgoing patriarch taught me things about the Indian family that I might never have known otherwise.

One after another Sitaram's predictions were coming true. I tried to contact the astrologer to tell him so, but the old man had passed away. How had he known India would be my home and that I would meet my spiritual family in the process? I had known the Pateriyas for just a few weeks, but already the children were fond of coming to my door to invite me for dinner, and when I wasn't traveling, I spent laughter-filled weekends with them. The rural landscape that had looked so baked and washed out when I first arrived, I now viewed as my playground, its inhabitants, my neighbors.

I had wanted to talk to Pundit Sitaram because the crystalline voice inside told me the planets were aligning now, not for my demise as the Hyderabad astrologer predicted, but for rapid spiritual awakening. But perhaps the two went hand in hand, destruction being the father of creation. India's intuitive sciences fascinated me; they baffled my intellect but confirmed my sixth sense. But no matter what was predicted, I was intent on staying in the present. That was the great lesson I had learned as a competitive athlete. Stay in the present and the future will turn out for the best.

Packs Is Banned For Life

Although I had been in India for six weeks, it seemed like there was no end to room renovations. Electricians installed a portable water heater and rewired faulty electricals in the bathroom, while plumbers labored to get the shower running and the toilet to stop leaking. The carpenter placed plywood over air ducts and under the door in case Packs got lonely and decided to move in with me. I knew Packs was happy where he was; I was more concerned that he be barred entry for security reasons.

Villa de Rodentia, we were discovering, had the full range of rodents. In addition to Packs, rats, field mice, and shrews were on the take. While my Caribbean friend, Tony, was staying in my old room, he complained one afternoon that a large amount of rupees had disappeared from his room. It baffled him because he always kept his room locked. "I think I know the thief," I joked. "He's a chronic offender." Together we moved the wooden dresser, and as I suspected, Packs had built another homey nest, and an even larger stash of stolen goods was neatly piled, including a stack of stapled rupees. Packs' life of crime continued unabated.

FOUR

The Cowherd Krishna

The human body is like a boat, the first and foremost use of which is to carry us across the ocean of life and death to the shore of immortality. The guru is the skilled helmsman; Divine Grace is the favorable wind. If, with such means as these, man does not strive to cross the ocean of life and death, he is indeed spiritually dead.

—*Lord Krishna*

Marwari Magic

By the time our overnight train from Delhi pulled into the industrial town of Kota in the southeast corner of Rajasthan, I was ready to climb down. Legendary for its courageous warriors, sprawling hilltop fortresses, pastel-hued medieval towns, and haunting desert landscapes, Rajasthan provides ample opportunity for exploration, but first we would conduct a five-day course at the largest fertilizer plant in Southeast Asia. Our vehicle quickly escaped Kota's noisy confines and sliced its way along a narrow strip of asphalt past irrigated fields and rustic villages, overtaking farm implements as we went. Turbaned men with oiled mustaches driving red tractors were oblivious to the warnings of our speeding vehicle.

We were headed to Chambal Fertilizer, a company owned by the Birla Group. In a district of Rajasthan called Shekawati, a community of merchants once traded along the fabled spice route that connected Tibet with the Arabian Sea. These merchants were called Marwaris, and with industrialization, their community became the dominant businessmen of India. Today, half of India's industrialist families are Marwaris, and the Birla family is the most successful among them.

Shortly, we arrived at a gated community on the banks of the Chambal River. Inside the walls, a groomed, green community with paved streets, landscaped bungalows, eucalyptus groves, flowering gardens, and a modern school stood on land that was once a desolate tract. Chambal Fertilizer had selected the remote spot for its factory to satisfy its need for a plentiful water supply. In order to attract skilled managers, the company had created the eye-catching development, converting unwanted land into an extensive walled complex that is home to the plant.

The vehicle pulled up to a spacious Mediterranean styled guesthouse surrounded by rose gardens and watered lawns. The front door opened to a small solarium and an airy living room, a welcome contrast to the cramped sleeper Lane and I had shared with a pair of physicians on the overnight journey from Delhi. The plant's general manager was expecting us at the school auditorium, where our meetings would be held until the new community center opened. Following the meeting, we were taken on a tour of the recently expanded plant that stood partially hidden at the far end of the property. We were handed hardhats and taken to the control room where a wall of computer screens monitored the fully automated plant. The plant's Australian equipment produced 5,000 tons of fertilizer a day.

As I stood on the roof surveying the sprawling infrastructure, I wondered if it wasn't time for the Indian farmer to return to sustainable agriculture. Chemical fertilizers had been introduced in India on a broad scale during the green revolution that began in 1964. Fertilizers and pesticides soon became a way of life for the Indian farmer as in most other parts of the world. Initially output increased. Unfortunately, it has taken decades to fully appreciate the long-term effects of agrochemicals. Sadly organic agriculture, a hallmark of Indian farming for centuries, was abandoned in favor of methods that have now been proven damaging to both soil and environment. With a billion mouths to feed, India can ill afford to render its farmland barren in the future.

Adventures With Raj And His Bull

It was my first visit to Rajasthan and I had saved a few days to explore the enchanted land after Lane returned to Delhi. A dilapidated black and yellow 'tour car' waited outside the stylish guest bungalow while I finished breakfast. My first impression as I climbed onto the fur-lined seat was not a favorable one, but Kota isn't Delhi, and one couldn't expect a remote industrial town to offer luxurious tour vehicles catering to the exaggerated standards of foreigners. A scratchy, three-inch thick shaggy seat cover would be my throne for the trip. By mid-afternoon my bottom was pained by the broken springs pushing through the imitation black bear rug. The black and white dice dangling from the rear view mirror hinted at the gamble of crossing India's hottest state in a rattletrap that was likely to collapse anytime. Kiln-like air whipped through open windows as we lumbered along roads in need of repair. My prayers for a safe journey rested at the feet of the adorable cowherd Krishna, who stood on the dashboard, his ankles casually crossed as he played intoxicating melodies on his bamboo flute. I found his confident mood reassuring.

I enjoyed seeing new ancient sights. Our first stop was medieval Bundi, a hilltop fortress and bazaar that had no immediate plans to enter the twentieth century, in spite of the knockoff Nike and Reebok labels for sale in the market. Soon we entered a littered village named Menal. 'Sweepers must be on strike,' I thought, seeing the plastic bags and loose papers cluttering the road through town. Normally, village sweepers would have been out with their brooms in the early hours of the morning. As the car slowed to a stop, my driver Raj pointed to some ruins behind a crumbling wall. He needed lunch and this was his way of informing me. We both needed a break from the jostle of the road, heat of the engine and outside air. Relieved to be free of the coarse synthetic shag, I wandered off to have a look at Menal's ancestral heritage. It seemed legacy lurked behind every Rajasthani wall. Inside the compound, a rock precipice and dramatic gorge separated two sets of buildings of similar antiquity. On the near side was a cluster of weather stained shrines. Carved fragments and collapsed lintels lay scattered around the perimeter of the small complex, but the main structures were intact.

I entered one of the abandoned shrines, descending to a sunken sanctuary where I felt cool air for the first time since stepping out of the guesthouse that morning. A solitary flower lay on top of a rounded stone, the sacred symbol of Lord Siva. The marigold atop the hard gray stone is said to be Siva's favorite. I paused to connect with the silence. The shrine was cramped, a clue that it had once been a private place of worship. The sanctuary felt deserted; only bats and mosquitoes on their nocturnal flights paid homage to the idols that were once attended by priests and their patrons.

I crossed the dry riverbed that had formerly emptied over the precipice, creating a waterfall that plunged two hundred feet to a pool below. A small palace faced the horseshoe falls. It was the twelfth century retreat of King Prithivi Raj on the Menal River. Low doorways led to dusty bedchambers and sitting rooms, and I imagined silk-clad and jeweled Rajput royalty and their minions reclining on sequined cushions, pulling on hookah pipes and plotting their defense against Muslim invaders from the north. Rodents now ruled the retreat, and one shy mouse scampered across a threshold hoping to avoid being seen. I seemed to be running into the little fellows everywhere. The building made good shelter from the searing heat, but I felt uneasy, as if I had entered someone's home without permission.

Outside, a stand of trees had rooted in a ravine upstream from the falls. I sought shade, and leaned against the base of a tree. Heat-induced daydreaming overcame me, and it was some time before I returned to my senses and stumbled over the rocks heading toward the car. Stepping along the riverbed, eyes to the ground, I nearly fell headlong into a string hammock hung between two trees. I had thought I was alone among the ruins, but when I peered into the meshed cord, I found a young woman asleep. 'This can't be real,' I mused. Either the Rajasthani heat had completely overcome me, or I had lapsed again into dream.

From her appearance I knew she was European. The tag on her day-pack said Air France. I stared for a moment in disbelief. Her milky complexion, strawberry hair, and slender form were as lovely as Lady Guinevere's, but I was no Sir Lancelot. To wake her would have invited suspicion, and so I made a careful detour to avoid disturbing her slumber. If she was traveling with friends, they were not among the ruins. Probably they had wondered off while she napped. I marveled at the free-spirited way Europeans traveled the subcontinent, and, at the same time, worried for her safety. Was the fabled Rajput chivalry already entering my psyche, or was it just the sun?

From Menal we headed for Chittorgarh, capital of the former Mewar state, and one of Rajasthan's most eulogized fortresses. Doubt crept into my mind as our beleaguered vehicle chugged and sputtered up one side of the Aravali hills and coasted down the other. It remained to be seen whether we would arrive at our destination before the old chariot died. The coasting tactic was an effort to conserve fuel on the part of the driver. Raj, like many professional drivers, favored second and third gear, avoiding first at all costs. Consequently, the vehicle stalled a lot, squandering precious drops of petrol with each start of the engine.

The drive took us over barren hillocks and through vast parched stretches hostile to all but the most resilient life forms. Little protection was available from the sun, but under a lean tree here and there a docile cow and its master huddled in the shade. But primary shelter came from the attire of the nomadic herders. Brilliant red turbans wrapped low over the foreheads of the men measured thirty feet when stretched out to dry. Loose cotton gowns covered everyone. Even with proper attire, the sun could debilitate one in minutes, an eventuality that I would face should our vehicle expire, for service stations were non-existent in these parts. Raj carefully planned his stops. We were passing through a region of obvious scarcity, a land where hardship had forced many to the streets of Jaipur and Delhi.

It was approaching evening when we pulled into the dusty lot of The Padmini, one of Chittorgarh's better hotels. Our decrepit Ambassador's endurance had won my confidence. It survived on determination alone. I would not have lasted much longer on the road, but neither, it seemed, would our vehicle. When Raj shut off the engine, the vehicle convulsed as if to shake off the dust it had collected, and then stood motionless after a final spasm. To the east, the sun reflected off the awesome russet walls of the old fort. The rocky hillock wore a contoured crown of stone extending seven kilometers. Aglow against the setting sun, the fort lured me onto the balcony of my room. Again chivalrous thoughts bounced about my head, and I imagined a distressed princess imprisoned within the fortress' walls. I was drawn to the hill; if this was the magic of Rajasthan, I felt its enchantment already.

Rajput Royals

The road to the fort led through one massive gate after another, seven in all, as we chugged up the hill. After a lengthy ascent, we entered the seven hundred-acre fortress containing the remnants of a former Rajput capital. At its zenith, 75,000 people inhabited the now vacant fort city. Palace ruins from the reigns of kings spanning a thousand years were in various stages of decay. Scattered about the dusty landscape were pavilions, water tanks, elephant and horse stables, and over a hundred temples and shrines, one of which was an intricately sculpted nine story monument called 'The Tower of Victory.' Whenever I explored these places with their low passages, I came out with a lump on my head. The tanks, secluded for the private baths of queens, had been dug alongside their palaces. The pavilion of one particular palace played an intriguing role in the fort's extraordinary history.

At the peak of the Mewar dynasty, a queen of legendary beauty lived within the thick walls of Chittorgarh. Her name was Padmini. Stories of

Rani Padmini's beguiling looks reached the powerful Muslim Sultan, Ala-ud-din, who desired an audience with the queen. One day Padmini's husband, King Ratansen, received word that Ala-ud-din wished to meet his wife. The king naively instructed Padmini to receive the Sultan, but the queen was suspicious, and refused. King Ratansen insisted that his wife receive the Sultan, and so Padmini consented to the meeting on the condition that Ala-ud-din 'view' her only through a mirror. Having had a glimpse of the queen, the desire-struck sultan wanted Padmini for the crown jewel in his harem.

To obtain her, the Muslim emperor kidnapped King Ratansen, and then demanded that Padmini be given in exchange for the king's freedom. But the Chittorgarh generals devised a plan, and the following morning, a hundred-fifty palanquins from the fort arrived at the Sultan's camp, supposedly carrying the queen and her coterie of handmaids and attendants. The Muslim army was caught off guard when armed Rajput soldiers leapt out of the palanquins, freeing their king, and escaping on horses taken from the Sultan's stable. Ala-ud-din was furious, and ordered his army to attack Chittorgarh. But the fort was not so easy to overwhelm. Having seen the impenetrably thick walls encircling the community, it seemed inconceivable that any invader could seize the fortress no matter what their strength. Unable to sack the fort, Ala-ud-din cut off supply lines and waited for provisions to run out. After six months, King Ratansen had no choice but to order his soldiers to attack the huge Muslim army. Badly outnumbered, the Rajputs rode to their certain death.

Meanwhile, inside the fort, Rani Padmini and the women of Chittorgarh faced an equally desperate situation. They could follow their men in death or face dishonor and debasement at the hands of the ruthless Sultan and his troops. The decision required little thought. In a Rajput tradition called johar, a huge pyre was lit, and the women and children rushed into the fire rather than be taken captive. When Ala-ud-din's elephants smashed through the massive gate, the Sultan found only the charred remains of his wanton mischief. Rajasthani folksongs honor the brave ones who perished at the hands of the licentious Sultan.

The Rajput warrior lived an ideal similar to his knighted counterparts in Europe. Chivalry, valor, and codes of honor brought the Rajput kings into conflict not only with Muslim invaders, but kept them at odds with each other. Unwilling to unite forces against the common Muslim enemy, the Rajput kingdoms eroded over time. The desire for sovereignty undid one alliance after another between the warring clans. But in spite of their contrary ways, the Rajput kingdoms survived for a thousand years,

Two hundred-fifty years after Ala-ud-din's brazen efforts to capture the breathtaking Padmini, yet another drama unfolded between a Muslim conqueror and a Chittorgarh royal. An Indian by birth, the young Emperor Akbar delved passionately into the study of yogis and their mystical powers. The practices of Hindus, Jains, and Sikhs fed his eclectic appetite, and Akbar even invited Portuguese padres from Goa to his court so he could learn about Christianity. His religious broadmindedness, a departure from Mogul rulers past, gave his citizens the freedom to practice their faiths openly and without fear of reprisal. Akbar had thirty-three wives in his harem, but his favorite was the Hindu daughter of a Rajput king.

As a young ruler, Akbar's spiritual search led him to Chittorgarh. Fascinated by the legend of a Rajput princess who composed and sang ecstatic lyrics to her beloved Lord Krishna, the youthful Akbar wanted to meet the pious princess. Knowing the Rajputs hated the Moguls, Akbar slipped into Chittorgarh disguised as a Hindu monk accompanied by his court musician, Tansen. The ochre-robed men went straight to the temple where the guileless Krishna devotee prayed and sang to her lord day and night.

The princess' name was Mira, the daughter of a Rajput king. When Mira was a young girl, a wedding procession passed by the palace window, causing Mira to ask her mother, "Where is my bridegroom?" Her religious-minded mother took Mira by the hand and introduced her to Lord Krishna, saying, "Here is your husband. Love him and serve him as a good wife would love her husband." The innocent child took her mother seriously and abandoned her childhood play.

When it was time for Mira to marry, her parents arranged a match with a young prince known for his valor. Mira selflessly looked after her husband and his parents, but despite her devotion to her in-laws, they objected to her worship of Krishna, insisting that she adopt their family deity, the goddess Durga. But over time, having witnessed the intensity of his wife's spiritual bhava (mood), her husband Bhojraj built a temple where Mira could worship Lord Krishna. When they arrived, Akbar and Tansen found the breathtaking princess singing in her temple. Whenever Mira sang, devotees came to hear her soul stirring voice. Akbar and Tansen were deeply moved by her piety, and before leaving, they touched Mira's feet and offered gifts to Krishna.

Word spread that the great Mogul emperor had secretly come to Chittorgarh disguised as a monk and that he had touched the feet of the young princess. Bhojraj was outraged by the news and demanded an explanation from his wife, but Mira remained silent. The furious prince ordered his wife to drown herself in a nearby river. Mira did not protest, and left the fort carrying her beloved Krishna in her arms. As she was about to leap into the river a blue form appeared before her, causing her to fall unconscious. When Mira woke up, her beloved Krishna instructed her to go to Vrindavan, the storied city of the cowherd's childhood. Without informing anyone, Mira made the long journey to Vrindavan on foot in an ecstatic state. A short time after Mira arrived in the holy city, devotees began gathering to hear her captivating songs.

In time, Bhojraj heard about the Vrindavan saint who was called Mirabai. Suspicious that it was his wife, he disguised himself as a mendicant and went to the city to find out whether Mira was, in fact, still alive. When he found that it was Mira, he begged her to return to Chittorgarh, promising that she would be allowed to worship her beloved Krishna. She agreed to return. Then ten years later, Bhojraj died. Again Mirabai's cruel in-laws harassed her, insisting that she immolate herself on her husband's funeral pyre. But Mirabai refused, saying she listened to none but her beloved Krishna. Incensed by Mirabai's insolence, her father-in-law mixed a bowl of poison and sent it to her. Mirabai drank the poison with a smile on her face but nothing happened. Mirabai was no longer welcome and soon left Chittorgarh, wandering like a sadhu from place to place before ending up in Dwarka, the town where Krishna's kingdom once stood on the shores of the Arabian Sea.

By now Akbar had established himself as one of the world's most powerful monarchs. He ruled over a territory three times more populous then Western Europe, but the pious ruler allowed everyone to worship however they wished. Akbar's love of art and music led him to sponsor schools where artisans trained, and his friend and court musician, Tansen, became one of the great musical masters of India.

The Rajput capital of Chittorgarh provided an improbable backdrop for the meeting of two all-powerful Muslim rulers and the enchanting Rajput royals that entranced them. The fortress was attacked by Muslim invaders again and again, and was laid waste three times. The worst of the sieges resulted in the death of 30,000 Rajput soldiers. Again, those left behind in the fort chose johar. Accounts of the outnumbered Rajput warriors riding to their death reminded me of Tolkien's Rohan and his three hundred horsemen who challenged Saruman's army of 10,000; the notable difference being the fact that the Rajput tales are true.

As I sat on the enormous wall of the fortress, watching shadows grow and the subtle shades of light play on the desert, I imagined the sentry's gloom when his watchful eye caught sight of a wall of men and horses stirring clouds of dust and intimidation in the distance. Like the ominous anvil of an impending storm, it moved with force and fury. The sentry knew the outcome could be delayed, but not averted. Even the bravest hearts would have withered at the sight of a sea of men marching toward the hilltop capital. As I walked about the deserted property, past edifices eulogizing the men and women whose romantic notions caused them to make the ultimate sacrifice, I marveled at the madness of men. One of Mirabai's poems is titled 'I am Mad,' but the truth is, her life was an isle of sanity surrounded by a sea of madness. The singular legacy of the heroic Rajputs lives on in ballads sung by villagers across Rajasthan to this day; many of them composed by Mirabai.

After repeated attacks, Chittorgarh's king Udai Singh fled the fortress during its final siege in 1567. Having escaped capture, he sought a new location for his kingdom. One morning, while hunting near the shores of Lake Pichola, Udai Singh came upon a meditating sage. He described the siege of Chittorgarh to the sage and asked him where he should build his new kingdom. The sage replied, "Right here where your destiny has brought you." And so the city of Udaipur sprung up, flourishing in the protective sanctuary of the Aravali Hills. Today, Udaipur ranks among India's most popular destinations, renowned for its Lake Palace and white washed monuments tranquilly reflected off the glassy waters of Lake Pichola.

Srinathji

From Chittorgarh we headed for Nathdwara, the site of one of India's most revered Krishna temples. The drive curled around and between rock outcroppings and colossal boulders as we crept through the Aravali Hills. Our battered Ambassador had performed far better than I had envisioned; it still stalled when in a sullen mood and strained on steep inclines, but Raj knew just how to finesse the old bull to our destinations without unduly paining its arthritic joints. The wobbly machine screamed when the fan belt slipped, but thus far we had not been stranded in the desert sun. I attributed our good luck to Krishna's presence beneath the rear view mirror.

Raj had this peculiar habit of listing as he steered the car, his head cocked so far to the right that it nearly stuck out the window. I worried that he might fall asleep at the wheel, and never complained when he pulled off the road for a cup of coffee. The cool breezes that whistled through the hills swept through the back seat. A town came into view in the distance. At the crest of a hill stood Nathdwara, a cluster of white-washed buildings. On similar hills throughout Rajasthan, abandoned forts battled the elements.

Everywhere one traveled in Rajasthan, one encountered the legendary Rajputs and their Mogul adversaries. Nathdwara was no exception. Four centuries ago, a coal black statue of Lord Krishna called Srinathji was in danger of destruction at the hands of the Moguls. The idol that is believed to be 5,000 years old had been originally installed by Krishna's grandson in a temple near Vrindavan. During Aurangzeb's fanatical rule, every Hindu temple in India was in danger of being razed to the ground and their idols crushed into gravel to make footpaths leading into mosques.

Aurangzeb, who was well known for his merciless disposition, had executed two of his brothers and imprisoned his emperor father in order to usurp the throne. His unfair taxation of Hindus, wars of expansion, and ruthless means of quelling uprisings made him a feared and hated man. News came that Aurangzeb's army was approaching Vrindavan and that it would be unsafe for the ancient Krishna statue to remain there. Consequently, Srinathji was secreted away to a succession of hideaways around northern Rajasthan. Wherever Srinathji was taken, his devotees were reluctant to let him go. As a result, it took three years to complete his journey to Nathdwara. According to legend, the wheels of Srinathji's chariot got stuck on the road to Udaipur, and the cart couldn't be moved. The idol's escorts interpreted this to mean that Srinathji wished to remain where he was, and so a temple was constructed on the spot and a town sprang up around it. Nathdwara has since become an immensely popular pilgrimage center and community of artists.

Although history adds to the popularity of pilgrimage sites, subtler influences conspire to attract Hindus to sacred shrines. This was the case with the Nathdwara temple. I entered the temple compound in the afternoon, joined by hundreds of enthusiastic Rajasthani villagers. The temple, with its open courtyard, looked more like a haveli (ranch-style house) than a place of worship.

A large crowd stood outside the sanctuary so I sat in the corner of the courtyard to wait. Drowsy from the heat and travel, I was soon fast asleep, my chin resting on my chest. During my nap, daylight waned. Vaguely conscious, I was roused by clamor from inside the temple. Free of my fatigue, I settled into a long, deep meditation. Impervious to the fever-pitch noise coming from the temple, I remained in my transcendental state. A powerful energy began coursing through me, and soon I was no longer leaning against the courtyard wall, but sat bolt upright in response to the surging energy.

Light now filled my meditation and vaporous bliss flowed up and out the crown of my head. A thread of golden light no wider than a hair passed through wheels that spun along my spine. The ascending light caused each sphere to open like pastel flowers in soft sunlight. A peach colored blossom opened in my chest. Then, one by one the chakras rose above me where they spun and danced playfully. Golden prana poured down into my body, and I breathed in and out, long loops circulating from the base of my spine to the top of my head, and then returning again. The slow inward and outward breath brought immense bliss, and a golden liquid filled me.

The sublime experience slowly dissolved and I opened my eyes. But what I now saw was a different courtyard. I squeezed my eyes shut more than once, but the scene in the courtyard looked totally different than it had an hour earlier. The people and objects now appeared like extensions of my own being. Objects appeared illusory like images without substance, and my best thoughts were no more than withered flowers compared to the state of no thought I was immersed in. I could do little more than sit and observe, and had no desire to move at all. It was enough to be; the question of doing anything didn't even arise.

By now, the crowd inside the temple had reached a frenzied state. With great effort I got up and took my place in line, waiting for the next group to enter the sanctuary. As the congregation exited the main sanctum, our group jockeyed for position to fill the empty space. Like a limp rag doll, the crowd carried me into the temple. Once inside, devotees cried out and made supplications, their outstretched hands shaking like poplar leaves in an autumn breeze. A few spun in circles where they stood. Moist eyes and tender expressions appeared on faces that had been severe moments earlier. I was still reeling from the courtyard meditation and stood there silently.

A collective devotion cloaked the group as if the fine silk worn by Shrinathji enveloped everyone in a gossamer field of pious energy. Involuntarily stitched together, we swayed back and forth, hearts pulsing in devotional song. I had been ushered to the front of the sanctuary, an unexpected kindness in a temple open to Hindus only. Srinathji Krishna stood just a few feet away. His soft body stood passively, his left arm raised above his head, symbolic of one of the many miracles attributed to his childhood.

According to the Srimad Bhagavatam, the king of the gods, Indra, was unhappy with the cowherd community of Vraj. He was jealous of the love the villagers showered on the child Krishna. At Krishna's instruction, his kin had stopped their annual offerings to Indra in favor of honoring their cows. In a fitful rage, Indra sent torrents of rain and terrifying lightning that flooded and shook the countryside. The frightened people, fearing for their lives, ran to Krishna for protection. To calm his people, the ever-playful Krishna casually hoisted Govardhan Mountain above his head on the little finger of his left hand, shielding them from the deluge. Indra was humbled by Krishna's miraculous feat, and felt remorse for failing to recognize the divine child.

Lord Krishna

Srinathji's eyes are hypnotic. His affectionate gaze is both personal and aware of the great expanse beyond. A sparkling diamond, said to have been the gift of Akbar, decorates his handsome face. Garlands drape about his neck and silk garments are changed before each worship session. His devotees dote over him like a child, giving him toys to play with and fresh milk from a temple cow. Milk sweets are his favorites, and he is fed large quantities. The temple doors close early so the youngster can have his rest, but Krishna doesn't rest much at night, for that is when he enjoys nocturnal sport with his adoring milkmaids.

Merging

Shrinathji is the same Krishna that Mirabai adored, and, in all likelihood, she composed songs for him in Vrindavan before he was taken to Nathdwara. Mirabai's tender lyrics express devotion to God devoid of pretense or formality. She never relied on scriptural authority to guide her, but was content to immerse herself in His prema, divine love, which served both as her boat and boatman as she crossed the ocean of ignorance. She writes,

> Guide this little boat over the waters,
> What can I give you for the fare?
> Our mutable world holds nothing but grief,
> Bear me away from it.
> Eight bonds of karma have gripped me,
> The whole of creation
> Swirls through eight million wombs,
> Through eight million birth-forms we flicker.
> Mira cries. Dark One
> Take this little boat to the far shore,
> Put an end to coming and going.

Could such tender lyrics possibly be ignored by the loving Krishna? The popular belief that Krishna's relationship with his milkmaids was adulterous sadly misses the point. Krishna, as Supreme Absolute, permeates every grain of creation. Therefore, when his lovers, be they trees, cows, or milkmaids unite with him in his universal heart, both He and His creation thrill in rapturous union. However, sensuous metaphors are both justified and justifiably misunderstood. Their use is appropriate because conjugal union offers a fine sampling of ecstatic bliss. It is one of the great primal inclinations, but the difference between physical union and divine union is significant both in intensity and duration. The Upanishads claim that the bliss of one who has attained eternal truth, Liberation, is a thousand times greater than the enjoyment of a king who has every pleasure in his kingdom available to him. Divine union is said to be many times more satisfying than anything experienced while waking, dreaming, or sleeping.

As significant as the intensity of bliss is its duration. Divine Love has the potential to permeate one's reality without end for it underlies and flavors every aspect of day-to-day experience. For many, the experience of bliss is fleeting at best. For the less fortunate, even life's peaks are flattened by monotony. The Romantic poet Keats exalted over love's eternal beauty in one stanza, lamenting its loss in the next, wishing the moment could be frozen for all eternity. Poets immortalize love's transitory nature. But Divine union, since it isn't confined to time and space, has infinite capacity. It's simply a matter of learning to access prema and the human heart is designed to do just that.

The secret lives of yogis are inscrutable to the average person. How, we wonder, can one enjoy life as a lonely hermit? But yogis are far from alone, and the secret of their contentment lies in their ability to enliven the subtle currents of prana-light and shakti (divine energy) that remain dormant for most. With the disciplined practice of age-old techniques, the yogi and yogini become surcharged with bliss until he or she is permanently immersed in the divine union of God Consciousness. This was Mirabhai's mystical state.

If an electrical cable capable of transmitting 1,000 watts of electricity were suddenly charged with 30,000 watts, fuses would be blown and a short-circuit would result. For this reason, yogis meticulously prepare their bodies over time to accommodate higher and higher energy frequencies through meditation and the use of herbs. The increased capacity allows bliss to flow unimpeded through the nerve fibers of the body where it is experienced as inexpressible love. To draw on 30,000 watts of Divine Love, one simply needs to prepare the nervous system properly. The potential already exists; it's simply a matter of opening the floodgates and allowing prema to flow through us. Mirabai, through her devotion, opened the gates, achieving what all yogis aspire after. She courted the Supreme, expressing her love for the Divine openly and honestly.

Unbreakable

Unbreakable, O Lord,
Is the love
That binds me to You:
Like a diamond,
It breaks the hammer that strikes it.

My heart goes into You
As the polish goes into the gold.
As the lotus lives in its water,
I live in You.

Like the bird
That gazes all night
At the passing moon,
I have lost myself dwelling in You.

Meditation is as at once a fine art sculpting the heart's tender feelings and a scientific technique for raising consciousness. After establishing the habit of settling deep into meditation, *para bhakti* (transcendent devotion) begins to awaken the lotus petals of the heart, lifting one into the states of ecstatic absorption described by saints and yogis, and recorded in the scriptures of every religion. Intense inner bliss takes place as one merges with divine presence. Merging occurs when one unites with another being. Traditionally, it is thought of as a conjugal experience, but the highest spiritual merging occurs between the seeker and his/her beloved Lord. The value of merging lies in bringing a being of lower vibration into unity with one of higher vibration. This process is extremely beneficial because it elevates the aspirant's awareness.

Over time the disparity between the two levels of vibration is reduced until there is little difference at all, at least while merged. Duality dissolves into the unity of Divine Oneness the way water reaches a common level on both sides of a dam when the gates are opened. The seeker has found her way into the protective harbor of her Beloved. In Mirabai's verse, the 'little boat' guided by Krishna has arrived safely at the shore, the state of spiritual absorption. In its beginning stages, merging occurs for short periods, but done regularly and with purity of intent, spiritual strength grows from it and the awareness expands, allowing the heart to swell in tidal waves of universal love.

Bliss lubricates the nervous system the way oil lubricates an automobile engine. The potential is limitless. There is no nectar in creation so sweet as Divine Love, no balm so healing. Divine bliss melts the hard rocks of ignorance and mends the deepest wounds. The practice of merging is highly evolutionary for it heals mind, body, and soul. Merging allows Heaven to be experienced within the heart as it was intended.

The Divine Melody

The image of the cowherd Krishna playing his wood flute is familiar the world over. According to legend, the youthful Krishna was walking along the banks of the Yamuna River at sunset when he came upon a bansuri (bamboo flute) master. The music teacher, who was fond of Krishna, handed him a flute and offered to teach him, but to the astonishment of the teacher, Krishna placed the instrument to his lips and played a sublime melody. He then walked away serenading river and sky, immersed in bliss.

Among the Vedic gods, Devi Saraswati plays a stringed instrument called the veena, and Lord Siva is fond of the drum. During Krishna's carefree youth as a cowherd, lilting melodies filled the forests and meadows around Vrindavan. His enchanting melodies overwhelmed the young milkmaids, causing intense longing in the hearts of those who knew him. The gopis sang and danced after their work was done, meeting Krishna in the forest on moonlit nights while their families slept.

Krishna's flute is named Murli and subtle significance is given to the hypnotic instrument. It is Krishna's soft breath flowing through the hollow of the reed creating sublime melodies that bewitched the milkmaids. In a similar way, in the quiet of meditation, the subtle nervous system is enervated by prana (vital air). This refined breath moves along a passageway in the spine called Sushumna, said to be the size of a fiber in a lotus stalk. The awakened energy flows up the spine moving successively through seven energy centers known as chakras, or wheels. Like the seven chakras, Krishna's flute has seven finger holes through which his gentle breath passes as he plays. Both Krishna's breath and the prana flowing along the spine are capable of generating indescribable bliss.

Every spiritual aspirant, like the lovesick gopis, desires union with the Supreme Absolute. It's an innate tendency. The passage of pranic energy thrilling the nervous system awakens one in the same way Krishna's flute aroused the milkmaids to unite with Him. They are the same phenomenon. Krishna's music enlivens the same subtle energy that is awakened during deep meditation. They're simply different paths to the same goal. Bhakti Yoga is for the devotee of Krishna what Raj Yoga is for those inclined to practice meditation. The two paths are complimentary. In fact, they merge at the goal where all streams of consciousness become One.

Mirabai's lyrical ballads tell the story of a life spent merging with Krishna. Her simple poems have inspired people toward higher spiritual awareness for centuries. In the last months of her life, Mirabai fed the poor outside a temple in Dwarka. On the final night of her life, she entered the inner sanctum of the Krishna temple in an ecstatic state. The sanctum doors are said to have swung shut behind her and remained closed all night. When the temple doors were opened the following morning, Mirabai had vanished. Only her sari was found wrapped around her beloved Krishna.

FIVE

Cape Comorin And The Malabar Coast

A good traveler has no fixed plans and is not intent on arriving.

—*Lao Tzu*

After attending some meetings at our Madras management institute, I departed by train for Kanya Kumari at the southernmost tip of the sub-continent. But track repairs derailed the second leg of my journey. In order to proceed south from the town of Trichy where I had been enjoying the vast Ram temple, I boarded a local bus crowded with villagers. The inconvenience was best endured with a sense of humor, patience, and plenty of water. Seated on the laps of some of the passengers were sacks of vegetables and even a live chicken or two. I was sandwiched on a two-seat bench between two villagers, with my knees pressed against the metal seat in front of me. Within moments of getting underway, both men had drifted off to sleep despite the incessant jarring caused by worn shocks and wild swerving as we careened down the road, horn blaring to warn one and all that our vehicle was basically out of control. We leaned left, then right, and even veered off the road to avert calamity twice, leaving great clouds of dust in our wake. To take this unsafe situation seriously would result in anxiety, something of little benefit to anyone. Certainly my bench mates weren't uptight about it. During the three-hour thrill ride the men slept soundly, their heads resting on my shoulders most of the way. Although I desperately needed to stretch my legs, I was being used as a pillow and couldn't move. And so I sat there like a nut in a straight jacket. Despite the reckless antics of our madcap driver, I found the green fields and red boulders outside soothing to look at.

Chartreuse paddy stretched in every direction, and villagers were bent from the waist, coaxing the young plants along with their hands. Hitching their loose garments at the knees, they slogged about the waterlogged fields tending to the tender sprouts that produced the staple that fed Southeast Asia. While in the south, I subsisted on a dozen rice dishes: uttapam, idli, lemon rice, and masala dosa appeared on every menu.

Our zigzagging box on wheels and most of its occupants arrived miraculously intact at our destination, the temple city of Madurai. A handful of passengers had climbed down along the way, either having arrived at their destinations or come to the conclusion that walking in the midday sun was less hazardous than continuing on the bus. I considered climbing down myself, but after seeing a flock of vultures picking at a carcass by the road, I stayed put. Sandwiched between my snoring travel companions, I amused myself with wild fancies while being fanned by the gusts of hot air pouring through the open windows.

The Madurai bus station looked vaguely familiar as we pulled in. I had departed on a trip to the island pilgrimage center of Rameshwaram from the depot fifteen years earlier. As the ten-rupee thrill ride came to a welcomed conclusion, a long forgotten image surfaced in my travel weary awareness. On a torrid afternoon, while waiting for my bus, a sadhu garbed in brown hemp had wandered among the busses, soliciting rupees from reluctant passengers peering down from open bus windows. As if his coarse garment was not sufficient austerity on that blistering South Indian afternoon, when I glanced at the mendicant's face I needed a double take to fully comprehend what I saw. To my chagrin, the long blade of a knife protruded out of the man's cheeks. When the mendicant noticed me, he came over so that I could have a closer look. The blade had been there for a long time; its entry points passed through thick, calloused skin. I handed the man the rupees he wanted, understanding that the blade was a symbol of his silence, a common penance among sadhus.

Madurai, the city of Dravidian dynasties mentioned in Greek records dating back 2,500 years had extended its boundaries since my eight-week stay fifteen years earlier. Despite its growth, the population's pulse was still centered in the old city. At the heart of a series of narrow concentric streets that fanned out in rectangles, resided the ancient city's favorite deity. Within fortress-like walls, fierce yalis (gargoyles) perched on ledges above towered entryways. A massive quadrangular enclosure housed Meenakshi, the fish-eyed consort of Lord Siva. Strict rules forbade foreigners from entering the multi-towered temple when I visited Madurai in 1981, and I had passed by the goddess's abode daily without entering. On my return, however, wearing a fresh cotton dhoti, I moved confidently past the guards flanking the main entrance. Temple policy had eased and I entered without incident, passing the spot where a 'Hindus Only' sign had been posted fifteen years earlier.

The myriad forms and symbols inside the Meenakshi temple were not easy to decipher. The colossal complex is reputed to have thirty-three million figures, but I didn't count. As I walked among the forms, both painted and sculpted, I was overwhelmed by opportunity for contemplation. The aloof scrutiny of beings staring down from the tops of ornate pillars followed my steps; the convoluted corridors with their multicolored mandalas sketched on ceilings mystified the intellect. The sacred geometry defied analysis, and it was only after I approached them with alert intuition that I made any progress. But maybe that was the point. Surrendering the intellect allowed the flow of holistic consciousness to take over.

The carefully crafted archetypes appeared as portals to magical realms and vast realities, extending far beyond the compound walls and my limited comprehension. Only an adept could competently decode the messages embedded in the mandalas. As my perception mingled with the forms, I surrendered to the elusive spirit of the place, finding myself engulfed in an architecture whose creators had simulated a layered cosmos, one that had as many points of entry as a lotus has petals. Still the entry points were not easily unlocked. I searched for a key, seeking familiar reference points, but neither sun nor pole star was there to guide my way.

I was crossing a spacious assembly hall near the Siva shrine when a family seated on colorful cloth coverings signaled to me. They must have noticed my isolation as I moved among the unsociable inhabitants of the labyrinthine place. A welcoming woman filling platters with food invited me to join them for their meal. I hesitated, reluctant to intrude on the family function, but the woman's husband reinforced the offer and a space was made for me. A dozen hands passed potato curry and lemon rice, and I felt happy to be part of the celebration.

The boy's father explained that the occasion was a special day for his son Murghan. Grandparents, aunts, uncles, and children had gathered to witness the sacred thread ceremony, a Vedic ritual performed for Brahmin boys between ages eight and twelve. The initiation ceremony, like Christian confirmation or Hebrew Bar mitzvah, bestows a spiritual blessing on the youngster and carries with it the responsibility of living according to prescribed principles of the faith. Hindus believe that contact with the world from birth causes the loss of a portion of one's purity and the ceremony restores that purity through the investiture of a sacred thread worn over the left shoulder. The thread represents the second birth of a boy and the awakening of his soul into the realm of spirituality. The length of the thread is equal to the boy's height and has three interwoven cords to remind the wearer of the three debts owed in life: the debt to one's spiritual teacher, one's ancestors, and the gods. During the ceremony, the teacher asks the gods to bestow strength, long-life, and enlightenment on the boy while he gazes at the sun, the giver of life.

The newly placed cotton thread hung diagonally across the boy's bare chest as he spooned in yellow rice and yoghurt with his right hand. The picnic celebration had followed the morning ritual. The invitation to lunch reminded me of something Maharishi had said to a group of westerners departing Europe for South India. "You will find the Tamil people warm and friendly," Maharishi said, "but don't eat the chilies, they are too hot for you." The beads of perspiration on my temples confirmed his assertion, but I didn't mind. I was happy to be on the receiving end of such kindness in this aloof monument to the gods.

In former times, parrots chanted Meenakshi's name continuously inside the temple. Brilliant idea, I thought. What higher purpose for a bird than repeating one of God's names? Nor for a human for that matter! The sacred bird, often seen in the left hand of a Hindu goddess, is a symbol of peace. Near the inner sanctum, pilgrims dipped their feet in the rectangular lotus tank before making offerings to the goddess. I found a place in the men's darshan line, watching to observe how South Indians honored their gods. When my turn came, I placed a garland at the feet of the goddess who was wrapped in a fuchsia sari. A still moment at her feet ended much too soon and another man took my place.

I had not been allowed into the temple on my previous visit to Madurai, but I understood. At that time I knew nothing about temple worship, but now I better appreciated their subtle implications. A granite idol that has been worshipped daily for centuries is more than a stone image of a Hindu god. First the statue is carved from quarried stone by craftsmen who follow a design scheme from Sthapatya Veda (sacred Vedic architecture). When it's time to install the statue, a consecrating ceremony called Prana Pratistha is performed to breathe life into the stone. The ceremony is said to transfer the vital force of divinity, which then resides in the murthi (idol) forever. But the real Prana Pratistha takes place in the heart of the devotee. The murthi is there to remind the worshipper of what resides within.

I wandered about the enigmatic complex, lost among endless pillars and recessed shrines housing gods faintly illumined by flickering oil lamps, some familiar, some not. Walking the length of the thousand-pillared corridor was a journey through time itself, the concepts of past and present blurring as I went. The long history of the temple endured. Mogul warriors had plundered Meenakshi's riches, stealing gems and precious art and damaging her abode time and again. Each time, Madurai's religious minded kings dutifully reconstructed the halls where their forefathers once worshipped. The current temple has stood for four centuries, but the goddess Meenakshi has been there for over two millennia.

Monkey Business

Madurai's devout kings built temples everywhere, and an old Vishnu shrine stood at the base of a forested hillock fifteen miles outside the city. Local busses to the temple were unpredictable, but I crowded onto one as it pulled away. Some of the passengers sat on the roof while others, including myself, dangled from the entrance platform, hoping the vehicles we overtook kept a good distance from us. Getting sandwiched between busses was a real possibility. Road adventures are normal in India, but I was relieved when the bus stopped at the edge of a forest where a trail led to a temple in the distance. The simplicity of the white tower against the emerald hillside drew me closer. I kicked off my sandals and entered a dark chamber. The quiet of the glade and absence of light in the temple sanctum lured me into meditation.

Outside I followed a shaded path deeper into the forest until I came to a large rock where I sat down to have some fruit. As I lunched on a sugar sweet banana, I thought how much the gods must appreciate forested solitude. From time to time, passing pilgrims greeted me with friendly smiles, inviting me to mug for a snapshot. As I was about to push a second banana into my mouth, an elderly man startled me. He came rushing at me waving a walking stick, screaming something I couldn't understand. Thinking he intended to use the stick on me, I braced myself for a blow, but he ran right past me yelping and screaming like a madman. I assumed the poor man was crazy, but when I turned to see where he was headed, I saw the motive behind his tirade. A band of rhesus monkeys had shrewdly snuck up from behind, planning to rob me of my fruit. The old man's timing couldn't have been better; the monkeys were almost upon me when he chased them off, his stick flailing in the air. I thanked the Good Samaritan and offered him some of my snack, but he just shook his head, muttering "naughty monkeys."

Although life in Madurai centered on its famous temple, South India's oldest city once traded with ancient Greece and Rome. The shops lining the narrow lanes of the old city were filled with sculpted mounds of red, gold, and russet spices and intricately woven textiles sought by the Mediterranean cultures. The stores of dried red chilies seemed unreasonably large, a perception exaggerated by my disdain for the burning peppers. Hand woven silk and cotton fabrics were dyed in traditional ways in small textile houses. Jasmine grew easily and profitably around Madurai. In some neighborhoods, its delicate scent drifted into homes. Madurai's literary tradition has produced the finest Tamil classics. South India was so much more India than the north, which was how I had remembered it fifteen years earlier. Its traditions remained intact, the pace of life grounded, in rhythm with nature and inner spirit.

The Little Girl Goddess

After the Madurai reunion, I traveled by train to Cape Comorin at the tip of the subcontinent. As I journeyed south, memories of an earlier trip through Tamil Nadu surfaced. The humble Indian train had a way of ushering fond memories into my head. Twelve years earlier, we had been traveling by car through Tamil Nadu on our way to Ramnad District, a region infamous for its lawless bands of dacoits (robbers). Every time we mentioned our destination to anyone, they were horrified and tried to convince us not to go, but we had been assigned to teach in Ramnad District, and we were determined to do it. CECRI, the government research institute in the district, treated us like kings and three liberal arts colleges enrolled their entire student bodies in our program. My students drove me back to the hotel on the back of their scooters each night in the moonlight. I was in bottomless bliss. Upon departing, we had to purchase suitcases just to carry the gifts that were lavished on us. Our efforts to visit the remote district had been amply rewarded.

It was Thanksgiving in America the day we journeyed to Ramnad District, but of course, no one knew about the holiday in south India. Our driver passed a Catholic school. Impulsively we instructed him to stop. A group of Belgian nuns that had been teaching at the school for forty years were running the school. The nuns welcomed our team of four westerners who had come to teach meditation to schools and colleges. When we told them it was Thanksgiving, the senior nun invited us to stay for dinner. Miraculously, the nuns prepared a banquet that included many of the same dishes my Swedish grandmother served when I was growing up, including a delicious apple pie. It was hard to say who was happier, the nuns for their opportunity to serve, or our group for the banquet we feasted on.

The nuns had taken vows not to return to their native Belgium. They could write to family, but not visit. Some of the nuns were just teenagers when they arrived on the shores of south India by steamer from Europe. They were a dedicated team who lived together as family.

That night I remember sleeping exceptionally well. Maybe it was the second helping of mashed potatoes, or the fresh baked bread. Probably it was the love that went into the meal. During the night I dreamt I met a man under a towering banyan tree. The young man was handsome in appearance; his long black hair and beard gave him a religious look. He wore a white fryer's frock, but he was Indian. Around his neck hung a heavy wooden cross. The priest and I stood there talking under the tree for a long time and then the dream faded.

I had forgotten about the dream when ten days later we stopped for water in a Tamil village on our return journey from Ramnad District. I was stretching my legs when I saw a man standing under a sprawling banyan tree on the opposite side of the road. As I crossed the pavement, I was attracted by his pious appearance. He had shining black hair and beard, and wore a white frock with a broad belt around his waist. As I came closer I saw the hand-carved cross around his neck. Then I recognized him as the man in my dream. Immediately, his great compassionate eyes drew me into his peaceful world, and we exchanged greetings in English and Tamil as if we were old friends. As we stood there talking in the shade of the tree, I felt like I had been reunited with a part of my distant past. He asked about my work and I quizzed him about his. He knew about meditation and I knew about prayer, each man recognizing the subtle irony of our role reversal. The silence surrounding our words was filled with déjà vu; an understanding that bridged great expanses of time and culture was shared in that moment of communion. Then my car pulled up and I was whisked away, never to see the man again. As if our lives had been intertwined in some parallel universe, dream and waking states had collided like Himalayan streams for the briefest moment, only to be wrenched apart again. As we drove away, I looked back at the priest beneath the yawning tree, an image that is as clear today as it was the day it happened. The brief overlap of lives left me unsatisfied; the way one feels when interrupted at a critical point of a good book.

It was late by the time the slow moving train pulled into Kanya Kumari's deserted station. As I walked out of the station, a commotion followed me. A railway worker was running as fast as he could to catch up with me, his thongs making a loud 'clap clap' sound on the concrete. "Sir, ticket! Sir, sir, ticket!" he shouted. No one had checked tickets on the journey and the man wanted to be sure I had one. Satisfied that I was all right, he left me to find my way to a hotel where I took a room overlooking the ocean. The soothing rhythm of rolling waves dissolved the impressions of road and rail, and I fell fast asleep.

The sun ascended behind Vivekananda rock, enveloping the island shrine in shades of crimson as I bathed in the sea behind the Kanya Kumari temple. The waters around the small island where Vivekananda meditated in preparation for his famous journey to America are infested with sharks, but that didn't dissuade the great swami from swimming to the holy spot where legend says Devi Kumari stood on one foot for a thousand years. A small footprint is embedded in a stone marking the spot. I took the ferry to the shrine rather than try my luck against wave and fish.

A barrier of rocks buffered the tide creating a calm pool to bathe in. Already, the beach was busy with pilgrims wandering about, vendors close behind. As I finished dressing, a small girl approached, selling one of the popular beach mementos. She looked up expectantly, holding out a packet filled with several colors of sand. Three bodies of water converge at the cape: the Indian Ocean, Bay of Bengal, and Arabian Sea, each washing ashore a distinct color of sand. The little girl's packet contained white, red, and black sand. The colors represent the three aspects of time. Black symbolizes past, the present is red, and the future white. A fourth color, gold, was also in the packet. The timeless omnipresent!

The endless procession of waves that deposited the sands on the shore reminded me of the analogy India's spiritual teachers use comparing the conscious mind to an ocean. The silent depth of the mind, where thought originates, is calm and settled, while the surface mind is often turbulent and agitated. The flood of thoughts running through a restless mind is like the incessant activity on the surface of the ocean. The guru teaches that the active mind never rests, seeking satisfaction in impressions from the past and hopes for the future, but the mind never finds satisfaction in past or future, and so it returns to present, only to wander off again. The cycle repeats itself endlessly, life after life, until one day the mind finds its quiescent source within, the ocean of infinite bliss consciousness. Only then does it find lasting fulfillment, only then does the prodigal son return home.

I felt refreshed and ready to enter the temple as I knotted the white dhoti cloth around my waist without putting on a kurta. The sign at the temple's entrance read *No upper garments for gents*. The red and white candy-striped temple opened to the north and stood so near the water that

I imagined high tide washing right over the feet of the goddess. Three priests placed my offerings in front of the blue stone image of a young girl with a garland draped over her shoulders. The pujaris allowed me to sit in front of the goddess while pilgrims came and went. The rustling of saris and dhotis was the only sound the worshippers made as they passed in front of Devi Kumari. The inner sanctum was charged with her sweet and clear presence, like a celestial bell ringing in the heavens. One could easily get lost in the bliss of Kanya Kumari. After sitting for some time, I felt a pull toward the deity and watched as a lotus flower floated out of my chest in the direction of the deity. Amazingly, the same thing happened with the goddess. A beautiful golden lotus came out of her heart and met mine in the air where they formed a ball of swirling light, multicolored and lovely to look at. Then the ball of light rose into the sky above the coastal waters. Cascades of bliss descended as sparks of light, showering all below. From Kanya Kumari, Devi's light reached every corner of India and beyond.

Upon stepping out of the temple, I wandered up and down the beach, admiring endless sea that merged with endless sky at the horizon. Objects that normally appeared distinct now ran together like pastel watercolors. With the merging of hearts in the temple, everything I gazed at turned transparent like the ocean that washed over my feet. It was all I could do to stay upright in the frothing surf that rushed across the sands and wetted the end of my dhoti.

A coconut vendor approached, breaking my trance by lopping off the tip of a golden ball filled with sweet, clear water. I sipped the king coconut's cool liquid. According to the rishis, the coconut contains the totality of Vedic wisdom. The surface of life is seen in the coarse husk, the light-energy of creation is found in the kernel or fleshy meat, its milk symbolizes the sweet essence of creation, and the uncreated universe exists in the empty space within. But despite the fruit's rich symbolism, I had purchased it as refreshment, and not as an aide to self-discovery.

The Puranic legend of Kanya Kumari is a familiar one, but with a unique twist. The goddess manifested at Cape Comorin at the request of the gods who called for help to kill an evil demon. Lord Siva, who resided in nearby Suchindram, fell in love with the goddess and arrangements were made for their marriage. However, it had been decreed by Brahma that only a virgin could destroy the awful demon, and so the gods had to put a stop to the marriage that was to take place at exactly midnight. As Siva made his way to the seaside village for the ceremony, he heard a cock crowing. Thinking he had missed the auspicious hour he returned to his abode, but the cock was a god in disguise. Because Siva never came, Kanya

Kumari never married. After slaying the demon she took up residence at the seaside shrine.

After visiting the temple, I followed the beach along the Bay of Bengal. The sun was now high overhead. Even locals don't take the South Indian sun lightly, so I took shelter in a seaside church. The sanctuary, with its tall ceiling and wooden pews was flooded with sunlight and saline air. Outside, waves broke in cadence and palm trees clicked responsively to the wispy sea breeze. The light, balmy atmosphere in the church was a welcome asylum. As I sat in a pew looking at the venerable symbols of the church, I wondered if Christian favorites like 'How Great Thou Art' were sung on Sunday mornings.

Late in the day, after the sun had softened, I explored the village where children played among weathered dugouts and salt worn nets. Although the image of Christ suffering on the cross seemed out of place in this simple fishing village, one could easily envision Jesus healing villagers on these tranquil beaches the way he had on the shores of the Sea of Galilee. There is ample evidence that St. Thomas brought Christianity to south India soon after the crucifixion. In fact, the Christian faith was practiced in India 1,400 years before it reached the shores of America. Whether Christian or Hindu, the languid coastal lifestyle had changed little over time.

Maya Amma And Her Canines

Fifteen years earlier I had met a saint on this same Cape Comorin beach. After visiting the temple we had been taken to the entrance of a grass hut some fifty meters from the Kanya Kumari temple. The simple dwelling appeared to be inhabited by a pack of stray dogs that lounged in the entryway. Our guide approached the hut, bending to peer inside. Tamil words were exchanged, and then he returned, saying, "Brothers, you are in luck, Maya Amma is here today."

Pilgrims and holy men alike from all over south India came for Maya Amma's blessings. We were told the saint was nearly ninety years old, although no one knew her exact age. Her peculiar lifestyle prevented that sort of information. Maya Amma was a yogini who rarely spoke and had so completely renounced the world that even basics such as food and material needs had long since been abandoned. We were told she very often disappeared for weeks at a time while roaming about the forests.

Her favorite pastime was riding driftwood at sea. When the tides receded, she could be seen clinging to a piece of driftwood that soon vanished, as if swallowed up by the sea or one of its creatures. For days she floated about the ocean without food or water until the tides deposited her on a beach somewhere. Fishermen who had witnessed the bizarre ritual far out at sea documented this extraordinary fact, describing her lying on a piece of driftwood like a surfer on his board.

A tiny figure wrapped in a cotton cloth slowly emerged from the hut. As she came close her weathered skin gave me the impression of an ancient mariner recently returned from years at sea. As she stepped into the sunlight she seemed unaware of her physical environment, like someone who had come out of a dark room but had not yet adjusted to the light. Two young chelas (disciples) emerged from the hut behind Maya Amma and led her by the hand over to our little group where she sat in the sand facing us. We had come with bunches of delicious red skinned bananas. She motioned for us to sit near her and we instinctively obeyed. The motley dogs joined us.

We offered bunches of bananas to Maya Amma, but a disciple returned them, instructing us to offer them one at a time. I peeled a banana and handed it to her, and she broke off bite size chunks, placing them into our mouths one by one. The motherly gesture was touching, but no one was expecting the shabby dogs to receive pieces of banana as well. The peculiar process alternated human mouths and canine mouths. Each of us was fed a bite and then we waited for the others to have their turn before the process started all over again. The feeding sequence repeated itself until all the delicious morsels were gone.

While Maya Amma fed me, I looked into her brilliantly abstracted eyes. Although her skin was thick and wrinkled like the elderly Tibetan women I had seen, her eyes radiated total freedom, an independence of boundary, whether time or space. She was so deeply absorbed within that I doubt she made any conscious distinction between my mouth and the scruffy creature at my side. But the dogs were docile and well mannered, as if they knew proper etiquette in the presence of a saint. They never stole my bite and I never went for theirs. The saying 'we are all one in the eyes of God' surely applied here. No words were exchanged after the fruits were distributed, but each of us touched Maya Amma's tiny feet. Her smile was all motherly love as we departed. Once again, India had shattered my assumptions about life and how it should be lived.

Humanity lives predictable lives. But at the tip of civilization at Cape

Comorin, Maya Amma broke all the conventions of society and was venerated for it. She was a God-Realized saint who followed her inner convictions, or possibly the convictions prescribed for her by Nature itself. No one could fathom her purpose; most would consider her mad until they looked into her eyes and experienced her loving glance and unqualified acceptance. Even then, many would doubt, but I couldn't. But it was not just Maya Amma's peculiar lifestyle that shattered my assumptions about life; India was a gem of a million facets and as many tests, always knowing what lesson needed to be learned next. It had taken roughly two years to align myself with the culture, to reach a point where I knew India was the place I wanted to spend the rest of my life. I had joined the family, and my relations numbered over a billion.

A cool evening breeze moved the air as I returned to the spot among the rocks where I had bathed the previous morning. The local temple priests had told me a story, which ran through my mind as soft waves splashed against the rock I sat on, and then withdrew. Maharishi had arrived at Kanya Kumari unexpectedly one day. After sitting in the presence of the goddess for many days, he gathered the priests together and explained to them that the goddess was unhappy with the way she was being worshipped. According to one of the priests, Maharishi had said, "Devi Kumari is a young girl and should not be treated like a grown woman." After reviewing their practices, he showed them how to propitiate the young goddess properly. The priests claimed the instructions had brought them increased happiness and better fortune to their families. Having observed the priests in action, one wondered if the goddess wouldn't be happier being worshipped by young girls or young boys. After all, wouldn't a little girl feel shy in the presence of grown men?

The sublime setting at Kanya Kumari inspired the poet-sage Shankara to compose a poem dedicated to the divine goddess. He wrote,

> *Thy right eye, being of the form of the Sun,*
> *Begets the day, while thy left,*
> *Of the form of the moon, begets the night.*
> *The third eye, resembling a slightly blossomed golden lotus,*
> *Brings forth twilight, which intervenes day and night.*

The sunsets at Cape Comorin are extravagant displays in both sea and sky. Brilliant hues of bronze and gold glistened and danced as the fading light silhouetted small sailing vessels on the light-flecked Arabian Sea. Taut sails stretching from angular masts appeared like the fins of giant aquatic creatures gliding along the surface. As the sun retired in the west a translucent moon ascended in the east, and three seas deposited sands at the steps of her temple. At the heart of it all, Devi Kumari presided over the confluence of earth, sea, and sky.

The Land Of Green Magic

I found it difficult to leave Kanya Kumari. Even as I boarded the wood-benched coach I considered climbing down. Having immersed myself in the tender spirit of Cape Comorin, I headed up the coast on the Trivandrum Express, but my heart was still in Kanya Kumari. Express hardly described the velocity of the train that crept along at speeds allowing me to greet villagers by the track. The daily passenger trains provide an informal means of sharing news with communities up and down the coast. The sixty-kilometer journey to Trivandrum took almost three hours, but the lush paddy interspersed with coconut groves soothed the senses and kept the mind cool. A high-speed train racing through the region would have been out of character in these unhurried environs.

Kerala was my destination. The coastal state has been dubbed the 'California of India,' because of its dramatic coastal geography, golden beaches, and temperate climate. But Kerala is unique in the world for as many reasons as America's gold coast. Its dense tropical vegetation includes thousands of potent Ayur Vedic plants nourished by countless rivers and waterways. The state is also an odd mix of communism, Catholicism, and perhaps the purest Brahmin tradition on the subcontinent. I planned to tour the state as much as possible on primitive canoe-like boats taking in the culture in its timeless simplicity.

My first stop was Trivandrum, an unhurried, shaded city. Greenery hadn't been cemented over in the state capital the way it had in other Indian cities. The telltale signs of the spring festival honoring the goddess were present everywhere as our bus lumbered in the direction of Kovalam Beach, one of the state's geographical gems where land and sea meet in a delightful dance. It had been fifteen years since my first visit, and I wanted to see the fishermen and their communal rituals again.

A brash, new tradition heralded the arrival of spring and the nine-day festival of Mother Divine. At regular intervals along the road, giant stereo speakers had been erected for the celebrations. The stacked speaker boxes reached as high as the windows of the bus, bombarding us with earsplitting music. It seemed our bus was running an auditory gauntlet that forced its passengers to cover their ears, but blaring music was no stranger to me. I had been awakened many mornings by the sound of crackling speakers outside temples. We reached the ocean after a journey that should have been serenaded by tropical birds, a more soothing herald of spring.

In 1982, Kovalam's crescent beaches were deserted, and we had enjoyed the surf before wandering up the beach to a fishing village. The mending of nets and lifting of heavy dugouts beyond the reach of high tide was part of the daily duty of the men and boys who lived in a cluster of thatched habitats that depended on the day's catch. We had watched as the men organized the tools of their trade: nylon nets, crude oars, and rough-cast rigs. The launching of the boats was a coordinated effort; each boat was responsible for a portion of the netting. One fisherman, probably the village's best swimmer, rode the waves while clutching the main body of the net that needed to be properly spread to ensure a good catch. The boats didn't venture far out to sea. Despite timing the launch to take advantage of the receding tide, it would have been difficult to venture too far from shore given the wind and choppy waters.

The boats buoyed several hundred meters offshore before returning. As the team of men pulled the net in they broke into a chant-like song, one man pounded out a rhythm on a crude drum. The singing galvanized the group; each individual's effort becoming part of a whole that was more than its parts. With heels dug into the sand, their bodies tensed at sharp angles. Pulling the netting onto the beach strained the men's faces. As each few meters of net was retrieved, the crew rotated positions. A new lead man replaced the old, who took a position at the rear. This procedure distrib-uted the work evenly as the 'tug of war' with the sea inched their catch homeward. After half an hour of exertion, the tangled net lay in a pile on the sand. As if it were the first time they had performed the task, all eyes were riveted on the net as the senior member of the group untangled it. From the discouraged look on the men's faces it must have been an unsat-isfactory catch. As the dozen fish were distributed among the men, a small dispute arose, presumably over who got what. A pound more or less might mean having enough leftover to sell at the market or exchange for needed foodstuffs.

European Spice Trade

It was time to move further up the coast. The journey on the Kerala Mail was an agreeable adventure past languorous backwaters and thick tropical vegetation. Known for its balanced climate, well-distributed rain-fall, and rich, loamy soil, Kerala grows many of the plants used in Ayur Veda, India's indigenous system of natural medicine. I arrived in the scenic port city of Cochin, found a suitable room, and took a walk through one of the city's water front parks. Easy going ice cream vendors pushed white iceboxes on creaky wheels along sidewalks lined with flowering bushes, stopping to peddle their frozen bars and cones. Balmy, saline breezes wrinkled the cobalt harbor where titanic iron freighters from distant corners of the globe were anchored. The nationality of the ships painted on their massive bows told of ports in Europe, South America, and the Middle East. Blessed with a protected natural harbor, Cochin, sometimes called the 'Queen of the Arabian Sea,' has attracted a variety of European traders, settlers, explorers, and missionaries over the centuries. A Portuguese navigator had landed in Cochin a few years after his countryman Christopher Columbus discovered the continent he thought was India. The Portuguese established an island settlement in Cochin harbor where the explorer Vasco de Gama is buried.

Curiosity took me on a ferry tour of the harbor to see some of these historic settlements. One of the older communities was Jewtown on Mattancherry peninsula where Jewish settlers have traded locally grown spices for eight hundred years. Their shops warehoused large open bags brimming with colorful spice powders that discharged an array of aromas, sweet and pungent. Black pepper, cardamom, clove, cinnamon, ginger, nutmeg, turmeric, curry leaf, vanilla; the heady smells were reminders that Arab, Chinese, and European ships had crossed the Indian Ocean in search of riches in the form of spice trade.

Foreign governments and their surrogate trading companies had vied for centuries for control of the lucrative industry, which led to colonization up and down the Malabar Coast. Spices made foods taste better and last longer. In particular, Europeans coveted Kerala pepper, an effective preservative that helped prevent food spoilage. Maritime battles were waged to gain control of the waters off the Kerala coast. The Portuguese were the first to control the Indian Ocean, although Arab vessels pirated merchant ships and profited handsomely in the process. Today's annual global spice trade is 500,000 tons, half of which comes from India. Spices like turmeric and ginger are in demand today not only as taste enhancers, but because they possess potent medicinal properties. The rush by western companies to patent indigenous plants would seem ludicrous if not for the potential profits at stake.

Although the five hundred year old Franciscan Church looked innocent enough with its fresh coat of yellow paint, its walls had witnessed more than its share of cutthroat European colonization along the coast. Built by Portuguese Friars in 1502, the church fell into the hands of protestant Dutch little more than a century later. The British in turn, pushed out the Dutch. The game of dominos ended when Kerala Christians inherited the modest church after the Anglicans were sent packing. The checkered history of St. Francis Church seems to contradict the spirit of the guileless saint the church is named after. The legacies of colonialism and spice trade on the Malabar Coast are as complex as the network of waterways in the nearby Kerala jungles.

Real Backwater Towns

The harbor tour with its white ferryboats was picturesque, but my greater mission lay along the serene waterways that form transportation arteries throughout rural Kerala. I signed up for a guided tour with a group that advertised for those 'having an interest in the ecology and knowledge of Ayur Veda.' Kerala's plant life is a sacred life, and our tour began with a visit to a cluster of thatched huts where farmers were cultivating medicinal herbs. The process of planting, harvesting, and drying these plants involves techniques passed on from generation to generation. Ayur Veda preparations often involve twenty or more different herbs that are formulated through numerous painstaking steps of refinement that may take months before a preparation is ready for use.

Our guide pointed to creepers, bushes, and trees, while describing some of their medicinal uses. As we moved along the canopied trail, we inhaled vigor from the vibrant life around us. The path led to a simple dock where two roughhewn, grayish dugouts were tethered among the reeds. Four oarsmen prepared the boats for launch while a group of westerners scrambled to untangle their cameras and hi-tech packs in anticipation of the daylong adventure into the unknown. We had escaped into another of the many timeless treasures of ancient India.

Not a ripple disturbed the glassy surface as a pair of sinewy boatmen clad in lungis (cotton waist wraps) propelled our boat upstream. Beautifully painted birds serenaded us as we glided easily in and out of the dappled shade of overhanging trees. Soon we came across a coir (coconut fiber) processing house where coconut husks were being stripped, soaked, and cured for use in bed mattresses. Fishing families and their thatched homes dotted the shoreline. An auburn colored mother cow tenderly nursed her young one. Children played as mothers gathered fodder for their cows. Men pulled buckets of sand from the river bottom presumably for construction purposes. A small barge transported a load of lime colored coconuts to a distant dock. Everyone engaged himself in one form of activity or another.

I could hear chanting deep in the jade jungle. Puja was in progress. The spring festival to the goddess of fertility was being observed with greater civility in the jungle than along the speaker-lined road to Kovalam Beach. It was springtime, and the villagers desired a successful planting. The priest's voice, sweetened by sincerity, echoed off the water. His shrine was close by, and his prayer was as much a part of the festive atmosphere as the bluebird's song overhead. I wanted to go ashore to pay homage to the local deity, but our oarsmen continued on in unbroken cadence. A riotous flock of parrots shot past and disappeared into the jungle.

Just as suddenly as the streaking green flyers veered off, our craft made a right turn into a narrow canal. The hand dug waterways transported locals between larger communities because there are no roads in these jungles. There was just space enough for an approaching dugout to pass. We could easily reach out and grab hold of the other boat's oar as it slipped past. We passed a simple village without plumbing or electricity. The absence of garden plots implied reliance on river and jungle for foodstuff, except for a few grazing cows.

At the halfway point in our journey, we stopped. Our boatman pulled a curved machete from the hull and scrambled barefoot up the side of an overhanging coco-palm, where a cluster of green balls hung beneath a crown of serrated leaves. He hacked away, sending large green spheres crashing to the ground near our feet. A second machete carved away the tops of the coconuts; creating a natural bowl from which we sipped the clear, cool juice. As we refreshed, curious village children peered timidly from behind trees, giggling at the site of such large and pink humans.

As our boat moved further along the narrow canal, two boys tossed an old tennis ball back and forth while engaging me in simple conversation. I held out my hand to receive the ball, but the boys guarded it jealously, smiling all the while. With some encouragement they tossed it to me and I tossed it back. The game of catch went on until we arrived at a second waterway, which took us to our jeeps.

Giving Up The Farm For The Street

My journey through the south was coming to an easy end. The gentle sway of the sleeper car brought me in and out of awareness as the train made its way to Madras. I had not set foot inside a temple in over a week. On the other hand, I had not stepped outside nature's sanctuary either. Peering out the sleeper car's window, I gazed absentmindedly at villages about to rise from their collective slumber. The peaceful cadence of village life was about to resume as it had for thousands of years. The train rolled into the Victorian station as Madras awoke to the sounds of street vendors, chai wallas, and the growing din of a motorized city—six million people pressed together, many having migrated from villages on trains like the one I rode. It's hard to fathom the urban migration that devours villagers all across the subcontinent. Rural south India has always been a traditional life of farming and fishing, a way of life that demanded perseverance and even hardship, but life in the city has resulted in much less for so many. India's massive reassignment from rural to urban life is, without doubt, the single largest demographics shift occurring in the world today, and is reshaping the lives of tens of millions of people.

Many Indian cities will double their populations in the coming decade. The migration to Bombay alone reached such dizzying proportions a few years ago that municipal leaders imposed a ban on people moving to the city; the strained infrastructure simply couldn't handle the influx of a thousand newcomers a day. Housing has become so scarce in Bombay that middle class families have little choice but to live in slums or face many hours of commuting each day.

One day, from a Bombay penthouse overlooking a white capped Arabian Sea to the west and an endless sea of tenement roofs to the inland side, I left the plush digs of our corporate guesthouse in search of the Bombay I had glimpsed from the window of our car on the ride from the airport. I walked wide-eyed all afternoon through the narrow lanes separating haphazard dwellings assembled adhoc from assorted discarded materials. A twisted strip of corrugated steel, a sheet of torn plastic, some bamboo poles, a straw mat, a piece of broken plywood, a few stones and mud cooperated to keep the deluge of the monsoon at bay while sheltering a family of four or more. The shocking condition of the ramshackle huts hadn't surprised me, but the people did. Ignoring the overwhelming smells that hung invisibly in the air, the journey through the ghetto was a walk through a playground of laughing children, mothers frying foods in strong spices, and plywood shops vending paan (a kind of chewing tobacco) and bidis to men who relaxed before heading off to work in the concrete city. TV antennas fixed to the roofs of the slapdash hovels confirmed what my friends had told me: that there were plenty of middle class families living in the Bombay slums. As I passed the inhabitants of the hodgepodge community within the megacity, I was greeted by curious looks and shy smiles, and I scarcely noticed that my feet and sandals were caked with mud and effluent until I stepped into the sparkling elevator that returned me to my privileged roost at the top of the lift. Standing once again on the balcony, clean saline breezes washed over me, the same air that had been scented with incense, spice, and sewage when it confounded my nostrils in the hutment below.

The Indian villager, like the rest of the world, wants to be part of the global culture. To that end, he has swapped folk songs for rap music, bhajans for MTV, starry nights for smoky skies, and tilling the land for whatever way he can support his family in the concrete megacities. But Indians are no strangers to migration, for they have successfully adapted and thrived on every continent. Their triumphs, east and west, are a tribute to the culture itself, and to the Indian family, which preserves its core values wherever it goes, ideals that have never been challenged more severely than they are today.

The Bhagavad Gita is India's treatise on dharma, a discussion about one's allotted duty in life. For centuries, the sons of farmers have tilled the same soil their ancestors did and fishermen have cast their nets in the same waters as their forefathers, but these ageless traditions are now endangered. In a single generation, the sacred dharma of Hindus is at risk. What will be the outcome? I wondered, having witnessed the swelling numbers on Delhi's street corners, and the sweeping epidemic of children begging on Bombay streets.

Will the dharma of the Indian farmer be lost among the tangle of alleyways in cities like Bombay and Delhi? In his Gita discourse, Lord Krishna said the loss of dharma ultimately brings the destruction of society. But the mass migration of rural India is as much about hope as it is about joining the global culture. The coming decade will sorely test India's resilience as villagers continue to arrive in cities like Madras on trains like the one that delivered me.

SIX

The Black Goddess

It is unanimous where I come from,
Everyone agrees,
It is no fun when God is not near.

—*Hafiz*

East Meets West Over Dinner

A sign with the names 'Lane and Steev' painted on it greeted us as I pushed a squeaky luggage trolley out the exit at Dum Dum airport. The crowd of taxi drivers and hotel hawkers vied for our attention, but we easily spotted the company man who had come for us. Mr. Choudhry was tall and stood out in the crowd. Insisting that we call him Mr. C, the gregarious Bengali was our host for our stopover in Calcutta. A cement company who employed Mr. C had flown us in to make a presentation at its factory in Orissa. The proposal under consideration included eight hundred employees, a commitment that needed the support of plant management.

Mr. C, an affable liaison officer who looked after the company's Calcutta guesthouse, would take us to dinner and then on to the train station where we would catch an overnight train to Bhubaneswar. We had no idea what we were sitting down to with our outgoing host for the evening, but the events of the night still bring a smile to my face.

"Friends, what kind of beer you would like?" Mr. C asked as we pulled up to the table at a popular Chinese eatery.

"Bottled water is fine," I replied, opening a menu.

"Yes, yes, we order bottled water, but you have beer. It's imported beer, not Indian beer." Without even waiting for my response, Mr. C instructed the waiter to bring three beers. Mr. C had apparently decided we wanted beer, just not *Indian* beer.

"Mr. C, we don't drink," Lane said politely.

"No drinking? No drinking at all? Hmm," puzzled our host. "Yes. Yes. You have beer with me. I order Black Label. Best beer. Waiter!" For some unknown reason, Mr. C seemed determined to get us a beer. I could only assume that he thought every American drank it. I glanced at Lane and he raised his eyebrows slightly.

"Mr. C, Lane and I don't drink! For thirty years, no alcohol!"

"Thirty years, no alcohol." Mr. C was in mild shock.

"But tonight you have some with me." Somewhere there was a gap in our communication.

"Mr. C, it goes against our spiritual practice," I protested. "We are meditation teachers. We don't drink!" That was the best I could do, and I hoped it was enough, because Lane was about to jump in.

"I see, I see," said Mr. C. "Alcohol no good for meditation. But only little alcohol in beer." He wasn't getting it.

It was Lane's turn now. "Mr. C, I'll order beer for you, but Steve and I will have lime sodas."

"Very good," Mr. C said. Lane had a definitive way about him, which Indians almost always accepted. Mr. C seemed satisfied. "Waiter, one beer and two lime sodas." Lane had figured it out. Mr. C obviously wanted a beer, but social convention prevented him unless we joined in. Since Lane had suggested he have a beer, it made it all right.

When the beer (a 32 ounce bottle) and sodas came, Mr. C made yet another attempt to get us to share his beer with him. "See, this special import. Best beer! Try some of mine," he said as he started to pour Lane a glass. By now we were feeling a bit impatient with our host. It was time to order our meal.

"I order for you, ok?" Mr. C offered. "This restaurant has best chicken in Calcutta. I recommend sweet and sour chicken. Fish curry excellent too. Very tasty! Waiter, bring us…" Lane rolled his eyes at me as if to say, 'here we go again.'

"Wait, Mr. C," I jumped in. "You see, Lane and I are vegetarians. We don't eat meat. And we avoid onions and chilies too." I was not about to let our host order meat for us. Now we were defending our choice not to eat meat and the routine with the beer repeated itself, only this time over chicken. I could see that our host was having a hard time with the idea that his American guests didn't eat meat. I just hoped his beer would pacify him enough so we could enjoy our dinner. The scene bordered on the ridiculous. The beer-drinking meat-eating American stereotype was evaporating fast. Mr. C was just trying to be a proper host and it was his duty to take care of us, but we were more than he had bargained for.

Then, as if a light suddenly switched on in his head, Mr. C exclaimed, "I get it. No beer, no fish, no chicken, no chilies. You are yooogis! You want yooogi food!" Unfortunately, he didn't get it. All we wanted was a tasty vegetarian Chinese meal and we were having the time of our lives getting it.

When the meal finally came, we settled down to a better than average dish of stir fried vegetables. Despite the confusion, Mr. C entertained us with his favorite stories of Calcutta, and we found him to be a very likeable guy. As we walked out of the restaurant, the irony of the dinner dialogue brought a smile to my face. Here were two Americans from a flesh-eating culture fending off offers for meat and alcohol by a guy from a traditionally vegetarian, tee-totaling culture. East meets west over Chinese food had proved entertaining, but I wouldn't want to do it every day. As we drove to the train station, Lane advised Mr. C to call ahead to alert our hosts in Orissa about our dietary preferences. After rattling off a list of items we liked, Lane added, "And have them stock the freezer with plenty of ice cream …and chocolate sauce." Lane's boldness would be our saving grace in the years to come.

Sleepless In The Sleeping Car

To get to the train station, we crossed the Hooghly River, an artery of the Ganges that empties into the nearby Bay of Bengal. The arched cantilever bridge is an engineering triumph connecting Calcutta and Howrah district. From the bridge, Calcutta's skyline was partially obscured by brown gauze that gave the city an eerie, desperate look, as if its life force were failing. Traffic came to a standstill again and again as men, clad in soiled lungis, pushed wagons or carried back breaking loads across the span, their taut muscles strained by pain and exertion. The men transported everything from steel to bricks to coal, their almond skin glistening from their Herculean efforts. I had seen men spent from athletic exertion, but these were more than feats performed in a gymnasium. Nearly broken by the weight of their loads, the men stepped gingerly trying to reduce the backbreaking concussion. Pedestrians, cyclists, and motor rickshaws jockeyed for position. Everyone who had a whistle, bell, or horn used it, making it impossible to make sense out of the warnings coming from all directions. According to Mr. C, who was helping our driver navigate the confusion, the scene went on day and night. After nearly an hour, we reached Howrah Station, bewildered by what we had seen on Howrah Bridge.

Howrah Station is a colossal Victorian terminus with dozens of interstate departure platforms housed under a massive vaulted roof. The incessant 'attention please' announcement scarcely dented our awareness as we dodged left and right to avoid passengers making their way to trains headed for places like Madras, Bombay, Patna, and Varanasi. Inside the station, a bevy of faded, red-coated coolies competed for the opportunity to porter a foreigner's bag. Our carriage, at the far end of the train, tested our slender coolie, who strained under the weight of the load he had stacked on his head. To the dismay of the weary man who had cleverly outmaneuvered his comrades in the expectation of a handsome bonus, Mr. C insisted on taking care of the tip. We should have intervened, but as Mr. C's guests, it would have just added to the complications that had plagued our evening. I was almost sorry to be leaving Mr. C behind. The twelve-hour train ride would seem dull without him.

By the time we boarded the sleeping car on the Howrah-Puri Express, I was ready for some rest. Mr. C promised to meet us on our return, and then got off the train as it was about to pull out. We sized up our rolling accommodation, which slept six. A young family of four occupied three births, and an elderly man was already asleep on a fourth, which meant the two ground level benches were ours. Two pair of innocent eyes peered from beneath blankets on the middle tier opposite us; our strange appearance aroused the curiosity of the young boy and his sister. The three tiers of bunks on either side were separated by a space in the middle that was already stacked high with luggage. Our compartment was segregated from the rest of the car by a curtained glass door that could be shut and bolted. It was a snug fit, but we would all be asleep in minutes.

Sitting by the window, I watched the chaotic scene inside the cavernous terminus. Howrah station, built by the British at the turn of the twentieth century, is the busiest train station in the world serving a million passengers a day. Five hundred trains departed daily from the drab concrete platforms reachable by a narrow walkover.

The endless stream of Bengali and English announcements provided a suitable soundtrack for the drama that played around the clock. Howrah station is a self-contained city employing thousands, functioning as a staging area for rural refugees who have staked their futures on a better life in Calcutta. All shared a common goal: to secure a trickle of rupees in a city where the unemployed exceeded the employed. In addition to the hoards of passengers, a legion of uniformed Indian railway workers, 1,500 baggage coolies, and hundreds of vendors selling magazines, books, fruits, tea, bottled water, snacks, and umbrellas eked out a living inside Howrah station.

The conductor entered and punched our tickets before moving on to the next compartment. I was about to lie down when a group of men pushed their way into our cabin. Two of the men sat down beside me while their companions placed their bags on the floor, made obsequious gestures to the seated men, and climbed down from the train. Moments later, as the train pulled away from the station, the conductor entered again and spoke to the new arrivals in Bengali, a language I didn't understand. Neither man was a ticketed passenger, however, the man with a paunch sitting next to me spoke assertively as he presented some papers to the conductor. The conversation ended with a gesture of satisfaction from the conductor.

Lane was already resting, and I was not in a mood to converse with the new arrivals, having had my quota for one evening with Mr. C. On the other hand, I couldn't lie down because the new arrivals were occupying my berth. It was an awkward situation. The fellow with the substantial girth, spotty complexion, and bushy black hair was in charge. He muttered a guttural greeting from a throat used for barking commands and I said "Hello" in return. The headman's cohort was slightly built and seemed ill at ease; his feet fidgeted nervously on the vinyl under the bench. I switched off the light, a not-so-subtle gesture on my part designed to inform them that my intention was sleep. But the intruders ignored my hint.

After an hour I decided to say something and mentioned that I wanted to lie down, to which the heavyset fellow replied, "Yes, yes, we will be getting down at the next stop. Panch (five) minute only." He seemed sincere enough. I was relieved to know they would be getting off the train soon. But when many more stops came and went, I began to wonder if the men really intended to get down before Bhubaneswar. It was now past 2:00am, and it had been a long day. Surely the conductor would have a solution, so I went in search of him.

"Sir," the conductor replied with a pained look, "I am very sorry. There is nothing I can do. These men are local politicians. Unfortunately, I cannot ask them to move." And so I returned to my seat, understanding why they had produced official looking documents for the conductor when they first arrived.

Despite the insincerity of the politicians, the fluid motion of the train soothed me, and I settled in, resigned to a night of discomfort. Swaying from side to side, the train moved majestically, massaging my tired limbs. The amusing dinner with Mr. C replayed itself as I stared at another six hours in the cramped compartment with the graceless politicians. It was not the first time I had been entertained in a foreign city by a well-meaning host who badly misinterpreted my desires.

Not many years after graduating from college, I visited West Germany where the Klipper Club, a century-old tennis club had offered me a position training their talented crop of junior players. After dinner at a rooftop restaurant overlooking Hamburg's deep-water harbor, my host had taken me on a walking tour of the city by the River Elbe. A pulsating nightlife flashed audaciously near the port. Herr Wenzel, whose gracious Bavarian wife and teenage daughter had taken tennis lessons from me earlier in the day, guided me through the Reeperbahn, Hamburg's legalized red-light district, where ruby-cheeked women were on bold display behind plate glass windows, looking like scantily clad mannequins in a Berlin department store. I was young and found it all quite amazing. The frauleins, wearing cherry lipstick and eye-catching corsets, enticed passing sailors with a seductive toss of the head or pucker of lips. Barrel-chested Germans and slender seamen from the Mediterranean and Middle East prowled the streets, their passions fueled by robust steins of German beer. I had never seen men shop with such purpose.

Suddenly our walking tour diverted into a dark tunnel that emptied into a badly lit hall. The breathy flirtations of a saxophone filled the cavernous chamber where a craving as thick and sticky as peanut butter clutched every man that entered the concrete garden. Hundreds of lithe young women milled about, like ripe summer fruits waiting to be plucked from tree or vine. The hot stream of men ahead of us eyed the orchard of pretty women, lissome limbs grafted from Asia, Africa, and the Mediterranean.

I was wearing a fashionable Italian tennis sweater, and one after another of the women approached to touch and coo over the creamy pullover. I found the scene quite amusing until Herr Wenzel suggested I choose a girl, or two if I liked, his eyes swimming in murky pools of imagined pleasures. Apparently, the prospect of walking out with a girl in each arm had erased wife and daughter from my host's restive mind. Whether the strong German lager had gotten the best of him or not, Herr Wenzel had misjudged his guest. As we exited the surreal body bazaar I was saddened by the thought of so many young women sentenced to unhappy lives. But I could not censure my German host any more than I could complain about Mr. C's off-key performance, for Herr Wenzel had spent the dinner hour recounting the horrors he had survived as a Russian prisoner of war where all but a few of his comrades had starved or frozen to death.

Wounds of that nature heal slowly, and it was not my role to judge the therapy he chose.

The brakeman pulled his lever, producing a high-pitched screech as the train slowed to a stop and my mental journey to Hamburg came to an end. "Sir," I asked the man next to me, "tell me, are you going all the way to Bhubaneswar?"

"I am legislative member," he bristled, "and can take any seat I wish on this train. If you want sleep then find another berth." His rudeness was beginning to wear on me.

As I was about to respond, the conductor opened the cabin door and spoke to me. "Sir, a berth is now vacant. Please come."

"But don't you think since this is my assigned berth, it would be only fair if they shifted?" I protested. The conductor was in a difficult position. He knew the answer to my question, but couldn't contradict the politicians, who enjoyed a higher position in society than his.

"Please sir, come," he pleaded. Wanting sleep more than justice, I gathered my belongings and followed him out.

"Don't you think those men should have shifted?" I asked the conductor, wanting to understand the situation.

"Sir, Indian politician not good people." His response was sufficient. As he left, I handed him a small tip for his effort. Finally, some rest.

A soft predawn light seeped through the curtained window as the fluid movement of the train prevented me from fully waking. As the trustworthy iron steed slowed to a standstill, I opened the curtain to have a glimpse of Bhubaneswar, the state capital of Orissa. In contrast to Calcutta where concrete buried the landscape, stretches of vibrant green were interspersed among residential and commercial buildings. Before the final rotation of the train's wheels was completed, a troop of coolies filed onboard in search of employment. Like a colony of worker ants, they scooped up everything in their path, hoisting bags onto their heads with assembly line efficiency. As I stepped onto the platform, I saw the politicians and two new fawning sycophants scurrying after them like sand crabs on a beach.

Cementing The Proposal

A handsome company representative named Mahapatra greeted us at the station. Mahapatra was as affable and sincere as the politicians had been disingenuous. A square bottom cream-colored handspun shirt worn outside his trousers and braided sandals captured his relaxed manner. I soaked up the morning calm and Mahapatra's warm smile as we conversed on the platform, happy to be standing on ground that wasn't moving. The sun shown brightly in the clear sky, the languid scene soothed the senses. Indian mornings radiate a spiritual vitality like few other places. By the time our uniformed driver had loaded our bags into the dickey of the car, the previous night's disruption was already a faded memory.

Outside Bhubaneswar, the verdant scenery never looked so good. Delhi had its stately trees, Mogul gardens, and weathered monuments, but scenery was not a feature of most Indian cities, especially Calcutta. Calcutta accosted the senses, burning the nose and stinging the eyes, and pinching the heart with its procession of humanity resigned to lives as beasts of burden. The emerald landscape of rural Orissa soothed the sting and pinch; its waterways were alive, succoring the fields. We had entered timeless India on our way to the cement meeting. As we continued, we crossed a narrow viaduct above a stream where a small herd of water buffalo bathed. Submerged up to their flared nostrils, the cool water pacified the unorthodox beasts while stick-legged egret debugged their black scalps. Two bare-legged boys in white T-shirts, looking a bit like oversized egrets, busied themselves skipping rocks off the water while keeping an eye on the herd. Fields of paddy and legumes stretched to the horizon, tended by irrigation ditches and farmers who cultivated with wooden plows hitched to the reliable creatures in the water. Life in the Indian countryside moved at the pace of the slow moving buffalo, and the fields waited while the deliberate creatures had their bath and head massage.

The meeting with Orissa Cement was in an industrialized district. A fine coating of grayish powder covered everything within a hundred yards of the faceless factory. Every tree and blade of grass, every scooter and automobile in the parking lot needed a good scrubbing. Senior management liked our proposal and agreed to our program for its eight hundred workers. The details would be worked out at the head office when we returned to Delhi. As we were leaving, the plant manager suggested a visit to nearby Nandankanan, where some Bengal tigers lived.

Tiger Tales

We were pleasantly surprised at the habitats provided for the majestic and mysterious cats at the animal park. The Bengal tiger, the main attraction at zoos and circuses the world over, is an awesome creature. Mature males measure nine feet from nose to tail and weigh over four hundred pounds. In the wild, they hunt at night, consuming up to sixty pounds of meat in a single meal. Their strength is legendary. When necessary, they can drag a five hundred pound water buffalo a quarter mile. They also sleep sixteen hours a day.

Bengal tigers have two distinct color schemes. The more common is the reddish orange coat, accented by thick black semicircles that give the beast a fashion conscious look. Its sibling, the spectacular white tiger, with its blue eyes, pink nose, and cream-colored fur, is also a Bengal tiger. All white tigers are, in fact, descendents of a cub captured in India. Whether white or orange, the pattern of a tiger's stripes is as unique as the fingerprints of a human. No two tigers carry the same set. Blessed with extraordinary vision, their gaze can be mesmerizing, their roar paralyzing. Looking into the eyes of the Bengali tiger, even with a fence between us, was a haunting experience as their fiery yellow-orange eyes project pure predatory passion. In the Hindu tradition, the tiger symbolizes Shakti, or divine power. In West Bengal, the goddess Durga rides on a tiger named Amba.

Housed in a shaded acreage surrounded by high fences, the tiger compound at Nandankanan is well-fortified. Although male tigers typically live alone and mate with tigresses in their territory, one tiger in the zoo had a loyal mate who lived in the wild. Distressed by the loss of her companion, the female was often heard crying in the nearby forests. Then one day, an astonished zookeeper discovered an extra tiger inside the compound. The tigress had been so lonely for her partner that she scaled the restraining fence and swam across a moat to be reunited with her mate. The tigress, given the name Kanan, gave up her freedom to live for eleven years in captivity.

Approximately sixty percent of the tigers in the wild are found in India. In the Indian subcontinent, the Bengal tiger's habitat is being rapidly destroyed by human encroachment, and those fortunate enough to remain in their native environs are threatened with extinction by ruthless poachers who export the skin, teeth, and bones to Arab countries, China, and Japan where parts of the tiger are believed to aid male potency and possess medicinal qualities. The Indian government, with the support of organizations like WWF (World Wildlife Federation), has established preserves to protect the tiger, but the task of protecting creatures that roam over large distances isn't easy. It is estimated that three hundred and fifty tigers alone live in a region east of Calcutta.

A Road Through Hell

The overnight return to Calcutta passed without incident; no obnoxious politicians crashed our compartment and no one pushed alcohol on us. Mr. C waited dutifully on the platform to greet us as our train pulled in. Standing next to him was a bright little girl, who Mr. C introduced as his niece, Laxmi. To our delight, her uncle had assigned Laxmi the task of taking us sightseeing. I suspected Mr. C had had enough of tee-totaling foreigners and figured his young niece would make an appropriate tour guide for anyone who disdained such basics as beer and chicken. Our destination was the renowned Dakshineshwar Temple on the outskirts of Calcutta. Mr. C's driver, Mr. Roy, would make sure we arrived at our destination safely. Laxmi, who was twelve years old, but looked ten, was perhaps more mature than her uncle. Dressed in a pretty cotton frock, she was not at all intimidated by the foreigners she would chaperone to the abode of Kali, the Black Goddess of Calcutta.

Sitting in the front seat next to Mr. Roy, little Laxmi was barely able to see above the dashboard. With poise, she answered questions from the back seat about her family, school, and city of birth. Her little brother, Ravi, was eight years old, and her English medium school was closed for a government holiday. Yes, she liked Calcutta.

Laxmi's deep brown eyes took in everything, but she was undaunted by the tangled snare of traffic that Mr. Roy labored impatiently to free us from. Every intersection required a Herculean effort by the graying driver, who skillfully maneuvered his car within inches of rickshaws, pedestrians, and bicycles as the human hordes made their varied way through Calcutta's narrow arteries. The arduous ordeal was due, in part, to the lack of a public transportation system. No busses were on the streets; the only gesture of mass transit was a handful of antiquated red streetcars running down the center of major streets.

Upon extracting the vehicle from one impossible snare, another would leap out to entangle us like a tentacled monster. With a sudden spin of the wheel and long blast of the horn, we were moving again. Smaller conveyances yielded to us, but the unwritten rule of the Indian road was that the bigger vehicle had the right of way. During one testy jam, a man pulling two plump women in his bicycle rikshaw bumped our fender. Instantly, Mr. Roy leapt out of the car and launched into a rancorous diatribe while the timid rikshaw walla cowered. Tempers frayed easily on Calcutta's gridlocked streets. Mr. Roy appeared to be fifty, but the war he waged each day was killing him.

Soon we found ourselves on Barrackpore Trunk Road, which took us through the heart of a heavily industrialized district along the east bank of the Hooghly River. The British built and operated jute mills a century ago along the river, taking advantage of waterpower and transportation. Jute is a coarse fiber from the bark of a tree used in sacking and rope, and is a major export in the region. Its factories employ thousands of unskilled workers. However, the transportation infrastructure in the industrial district is negligible. If Calcutta's congested downtown streets seemed impossible, we had now entered a zone where an envoy of commercial vehicles monopolized the road, and most of their drivers were in a sullen mood.

The bright orange lorries, built for Indian roads by TATA, have a narrow wheelbase and high walls enclosing their cargo. Seated in the cabs next to the 'professional' drivers were young apprentices whose job it was to navigate. The lorries were decorated with colorful peacocks and parrots. Some had menacing faces painted above the windshield, presumably to ward off evil spirits in the form of oncoming traffic.

As we inched along the narrow asphalt, sandwiched between lorries front and back, opaque plumes of indigo and gray belched from the exhaust pipes of oncoming traffic. Closing the windows was not an option because of the heat; we had no choice but to breathe the noxious fumes. Surrounded on every side without an escape route, we did our best to pacify Mr. Roy, who honked continuously in a futile effort to free us from the smoky confusion. The deeply etched lines on our driver's face became rivulets of perspiration as he tried in vain to move us forward a few feet. Even a driver with the calmest disposition would be severely tested by the daily turmoil of Calcutta's roads that moved countless rickshaws, pedestrians, bullock carts, pack animals, assorted bicycles, scooters, and pull carts about the metropolis. Mr. Roy's profession had exacted a heavy toll on him over the years, and a volatile pot of frustration and anger boiled over at the slightest provocation. Despite our gentle admonitions, our driver's road responses were aggressive and exaggerated. Unfortunately, the 'Biggest Rules the Road' policy placed our sedan at a distinct disadvantage among the trucks.

Ours was a civilian vehicle caught in the crossfire of a military maneuver. We had unwittingly entered a war zone where combatants were armed with ear piercing horns and raging engines. Every road warrior seemed compelled to respond to the painted sign on the vehicle in front of him, which read: 'Horn Please.' Most vehicles in the envoy had exclusive spellings: 'Horn Pleez,' 'Horn Pleas,' 'Horn Pleese.' The poor spelling seemed to sanction the disregard for any and all forms of courtesy. The scene was a disturbing contrast to Orissa's tranquil countryside.

Drivers muttered curses through open windows at the least provocation. By now, Mr. Roy was badly wounded, his psyche so agitated that his blood pressure throbbed in a vein on his temple. Casualties were strewn along the oil-stained sidelines where grease-covered mechanics peered under raised hoods and into exposed underbellies of lorries propped up by hydraulic lifts. Drivers of the broken vehicles sat for a meal, chai, or hand rolled bidi before reentering the fray. The scene on either side of the road was uniformly drab. Endless rows of gloomy gray repair shops, chai stalls, and dabhas (open air restaurants) lined the road, each eatery an imitation of the previous place with its row of aluminum pots manned by a cook in a turmeric-stained undershirt. Boys younger than Laxmi ladled soupy dishes onto metal plates while hungry dogs looked on, keeping a safe distance. The distinguishing feature of a dabha was the choice of cola stenciled on its wall. The cola wars were being fought along the Hooghly too.

After an hour we had traveled just a few miles on the bumper-to-bumper inferno called Barrackpore Trunk Road. Our destination was not yet in sight. If there was a road to hell, we were on it. Engines roared and horns blared in frustration as drivers inhaled their own vehicles' poisonous fumes. Contorted expressions were etched on every face. In places, the narrow road doubled its width as drivers improvised like a flash flooding river in search of an opening that would inch them forward, even if it meant driving through the yard of a repair shop. Amidst the confusion, little Laxmi stoically observed the insanity. It must have seemed surreal to her innocent mind, although I'm sure she had seen far more in her young life than either of the grownups in her care. As another interminable wait ended, our hostess grew pale, and I was afraid she would be sick; the noxious atmosphere was getting to all of us. Mr. Roy, who was due for another meltdown, exhaled in frustration.

After a second torturous hour, our seven-mile journey came to a welcome conclusion as the car pulled into a grassy lot adjacent the Dakshineshwar temple complex. Our senses had been thoroughly accosted by the journey. Eyes burned, eardrums ached, the caustic taste of petrol lingered, and diesel residue filled our nostrils. We felt thoroughly defeated as we climbed down from Mr. Roy's steaming chariot. After checking our flight time to Delhi, we knew that if there were even a short delay on our return, we would miss our flight. We would pray to Mother Kali that our return would be less painful.

Ramakrishna's Playground

Rising majestically into the clear sky stood the multi-domed Dakshineshwar Temple, the abode of the black goddess of Calcutta. The spacious courtyard between the shrine and the Hooghly River was filled with worshippers as we approached. We had arrived not a moment too soon at the spiritual oasis. Standing on an elevated landing, a line of devotees wrapped itself like a skirt around the temple. Before joining the queue, we removed our shoes, washed industrial Calcutta from our faces, hands, and feet, and purchased biscuits and juice for Laxmi, who looked drained by the trip. Hibiscus blossoms and coconuts seemed to be the popular offering to the goddess. We insisted that Mr. Roy join us for darshan; his strained mind was in need of a potent balm.

At the back of the courtyard enclosure, a row Siva shrines faced the temple crowned by a two-tier curvilinear roof and nine domes. The graceful Bangla architecture was auspiciously conceived. A wealthy widow named Rani Rasmani planned a pilgrimage to the holy city of Varanasi where she would worship the Divine Mother. Elaborate preparations were made for her trip, which was to be made by boat on the Ganges. Twenty barges would carry relatives and servants, including one for her cows. On the night before the procession was to depart, Kali appeared before Rani Rasmani in a dream. The black goddess said, "There is no need to go to Banaras. Install my statue in a beautiful temple on the banks of the Ganges and arrange for my worship there. Then I shall manifest myself in the image and accept worship at that place." Rani Rasmani immediately cancelled her trip and began planning for the temple. Eight years later the Dakshineshwar temple complex was completed. To inaugurate the new temple, a wise old Brahman was selected to be the head priest. After his death a year later, his responsibilities were passed on to his younger brother, Ramakrishna, who would rise like a meteor, bringing great fame to the temple as one of India's most revered saints.

For centuries Kali has been the favorite deity of Bengali culture. Kali, which translates as 'the black one,' is the most fearsome form of the mother goddess in India. With fiercely bulging eyes, red tongue dripping blood, and hands wielding weapons, she is the primordial symbol of destruction, an appropriate symbol for Calcutta. Her enemy is ignorance in all its forms. The garland of fifty severed heads around her neck represents the destruction of the multi-faceted ego that blinds one. The dismembered limbs covering her waist is karma; her disheveled black hair, shooting out in all directions, boundless awareness. The third eye on her forehead represents inner vision and transcendence. Kali personifies invincibility;

nothing can hurt her and, it is said, nothing can hurt those whom she protects.

Our moment in front of her fierce form had arrived. The black basalt image teemed with life. Ornamented with a gold nose ring and flowered earrings, her pearl necklace contrasted her dark skin and red tongue. The scene was chaotic inside the sanctuary. Coconuts smashed against the checkerboard marble floor and hurtled through the air in the direction of the goddess, priests barked incantations, garlands came to rest around the goddesses' neck, and great clouds of incense choked the room. Crimson champak (hibiscus) blossoms blanketed her feet. Devotees received the auspicious marking of red kum kum (powder) on their forehead before departing. I felt the intense energy devouring one and all. But beneath the upheaval, a liquid bliss flowed like a cool stream through the shrine.

Kali's maya (illusion) is layered, and one must dive beneath the surface in order to taste the sublime. Like a lake covered with green algae, deeper waters are clear and refreshing even though a filmy surface obscures them. I looked beyond the physical and found the thread of peace. As I penetrated the transparent fabric permeating the sanctum, I was enveloped in a great expanse of blackness under a moonless sky. Countless stars fell through the indigo canopy, showering the earth like flower petals. The sky was an all-pervasive sea of stillness, and my mind melted into the enveloping abyss. Then I saw Her swaying form in front of me. The skulls that were Her necklace rattled menacingly as She danced, and I felt a forest of fire rush through me burning pride, doubt, and fear. She was eating the champak blossoms the priest had just offered on our behalf, and She laughed riotously as She rubbed kum kum powder on the skulls around Her neck. Her hair blew wildly about as if in a storm. Then She faded, leaving a message for my mind, 'too much of my darshan will burn you up.'

The heady vision faded and I was faced with Kali's menacing glare again, only this time it was the face of the statue. A pujari placed red dots on our foreheads and poured sips of holy water into our right hands before a uniformed guard ushered us outside. Our darshan was over. Despite her terrifying appearance, I knew Kali was a compassionate mother, and hers was a world I wanted to know better. As devotees filed out of the sanctum, some wiped a tear from their cheek, others like me shuffled out spellbound, stunned by her darshan. Most were content to savor the prasad given them by a priest, a consecrated blessing from the goddess.

Reeling from the sudden infusion of shakti, Laxmi led our little group across the courtyard to the river. The red-tiled surface of the courtyard burned the bottoms of my feet, but no more than the fire that had engulfed me inside the temple. As I stumbled along, led by Laxmi like a puppy whose feet had grown faster than its body, I was happy to see the winsome smile return to Laxmi's gentle face. Her perseverance had been amply rewarded. Laxmi was familiar with the temple garden having visited Dakshineshwar with her family many times, and I followed our young guide, hoping no one would notice my incapacitated condition. Gradually my senses gained clarity and I was better able to absorb the lovely garden setting than when we arrived. In the southwest corner, outside the garden walls, stood the music hall, a favorite nighttime haunt of Swami Ramakrishna where the magic of the shennai (reed instrument like an oboe) commingled with the intoxicating aroma of jasmine as they wafted about the river.

Since its inception in 1855, the atmosphere at Dakshineshwar has been steeped with spiritual vibration. The childlike Swami Ramakrishna, by virtue of his pure and ecstatic nature, set a high standard of worship at the garden temple. His spiritual presence at Dakshineshwar continued for thirty years until his passing in 1886. The ardent saint's sublime experiences as a young temple priest have been frequently chronicled. One of many lucid accounts was recorded in the book, *Great Swan*. "After receiving the direct vision of Mahakali, my blissful Mother with Her scintillating Black Form rising out of a golden ocean, with gigantic waves rushing at me from all sides, I remained in a constant visionary state. It was literally impossible for me to tell any difference between night and day, so brilliant was Her radiance, permeating my entire mind and senses."

As we approached the stairway to the bathing ghats, highly scented bushes flanked us. Oleander, China rose, gardenia, jasmine, and five-faced hibiscus graced the embankment. One could imagine Ramakrishna's fragile form moving about the grounds, his impulsive behavior baffling even his most intimate disciples. The spacious temple complex proved an ideal playground for the childlike Bengali saint. By no means an austere and humorless renunciate, Ramakrishna's moods were kaleidoscopic. He prayed, danced, sang, laughed, counseled, and cried without pretense in the presence of anyone who happened to be nearby. One moment he swooned ecstatically before an image of his beloved Mother, the next he presided over discussions with erudite scholars and members of Calcutta's cultural elite. Rich, poor, saints, sinners, Hindus, Muslims, and Christians alike were mesmerized by his spellbinding personality and extraordinary insight into the realities of inner life.

The Gospel of Ramakrishna provides the following description of the great sage: "Ramakrishna was a small man, thin and extremely delicate. His eyes were illumined with an inner light. Good humor gleamed in his eyes and lurked in the corners of his mouth. His Bengali speech was of a homely kind with a slight, delightful stammer. He held men enthralled by his wealth of spiritual experience, his inexhaustible store of simile and metaphor, his power of observation, his bright and subtle humor, his wonderful catholicity, his ceaseless flow of wisdom. Ramakrishna viewed as 'mere straw' the Bengali intellectuals who debated him with nothing more than bookish understanding behind their religious fervor. He often asked, 'What will a man gain by the words of the scriptures alone? Ah, the fools! They reason themselves to death over information about the path (to liberation), but never take the plunge. What a pity!'"

It was with a small group of youthful disciples that Ramakrishna lovingly shared the priceless gems hidden within the treasure trove of his heart. Among them, a boy named Narendra showed great promise. Of his days with his mentor, Narendra later wrote, "It is impossible to give others any idea of the ineffable joy we derived from the presence of the Master. It is really beyond our understanding how he could train us without our knowing it through fun and play, and thus mold our spiritual life...Besides meditation and spiritual exercises, we used to spend a good deal of time with him in sheer merrymaking. Sri Ramakrishna also joined in with us, and by taking part, enhanced our innocent pleasure."

The Master's alchemical ability to transform metal into gold, to turn teenage boys into spiritual lighthouses, occurred as naturally as the jasmine, tuberose, and gardenia bushes bloomed in his garden. Molding young minds as they matured was something Ramakrishna longed to do. He said, "I would sacrifice twenty thousand incarnations to encourage even a single Seeker of Truth." The playful activities so fondly remembered by Narendra were not without rigorous discipline at their foundation. It was Ramakrishna's firm belief that his monks should eschew a full night's sleep in favor of long periods of meditation while observing strict vows in daily life.

As Laxmi guided us about the garden, we passed the Panchavati (five sacred trees), Ramakrishna's favorite spot for meditation. In the grove, timeless wisdom was entrusted to a handful of teenage monks destined to create a spiritual renaissance both in India and abroad. Seven years after his master's passing, Narendra boarded an ocean liner headed for America. The turbaned young man's passage was registered in the ship's log under the name Swami Vivekananda. The swami's first talk, a stirring lecture at the World's Parliament of Religions at the Chicago World's Fair in 1893,

captured the imagination of the seven thousand representatives in attendance. His 'unity of all religions' theme echoed his master's lifelong cry that
all religions lead to a common goal.

Swami Vivekananda was the first Indian teacher to visit America
where his fame grew rapidly, and the press dubbed him 'India's spiritual
ambassador to the west.' His words were printed in bold letters in leading
papers, and because of his powerful aura he was described variously as
cyclonic Hindu, warrior prophet, and militant mystic. With his iron
resolve forged in the fire of renunciation, Swami Vivekananda's razor-sharp
intelligence penetrated the minds of Americans, inspiring thousands to
practice their faith with renewed commitment. At the World's Fair, he
received a rousing ovation following these closing remarks: "If the
Parliament of Religions has shown anything to the world, it is this: It has
proved to the world that holiness, purity, and charity are not the exclusive
possessions of any church in the world, and that every system has produced
men and women of the most exalted character. In the face of this evidence,
if anybody dreams of the exclusive survival of his own religion and the
destruction of the others, I pity him from the bottom of my heart."
Vivekananda's hugely successful American tour would not have surprised
his master who prophesied, "Very soon Narendra will shake the world by
his intellectual and spiritual powers." At America's bicentennial celebrations in 1976, a portrait gallery paid tribute to great persons who visited
America from other countries. Swami Vivekananda's picture was captioned
with the following statement: "The Swami charmed the audiences with his
magical oratory and left an indelible mark on America's spiritual development."

Widows' Watch

Our garden tour took us to the river's edge. A relaxed smile now
spread across Mr. Roy's face, the tension brought on by his unenviable job
had eased. We all felt content as we watched people performing ablutions
in the river. As we walked past a shaded lane we passed a row of withered
faces, faded blossoms escaping the midday sun. In front of each woman
was a small pot. I couldn't help noticing the many pairs of eyes trained on
us as we passed the beleaguered bunch. These elderly widows, dressed in
dusty black gowns, depended on the coins dropped into their pots by worshippers, and they were not a cheerful bunch.

Our visit to the famed Dakshineshwar temple was over; it was time to
depart if we were to make it to the airport in time for our flight. As we

moved past the begging women, I dropped a coin into each bowl until they ran out. But to our vexation, as the last coin clanked in the container, the entire group of women rose to their feet in unison and began pursuing us. We easily reached the car ahead of the arthritic crowd and climbed in, waiting for Mr. Roy, who had gone off to smoke a bidi. Within moments a mob of weathered faces was pressing against the car windows on every side. The cacophony of noise outside sounded like a flock of quarrelsome crows squabbling over a scrap of food. The commotion would have been amusing had it not been so heartrending. The women grew increasingly agitated, and began complaining and pounding on the glass as they vied for our attention, hoping for baksheesh (a donation).

Little Laxmi, who was alone in the front seat, sat poised as the gaunt women pressed against the windshield and tried to pry open the car doors. Lane reached into his pocket and pulled out a handful of rupee notes. Speaking to one of the women who understood English, he said, "You must divide these rupees equally." But to our chagrin, the gesture created even more dissonance. One woman replied angrily, "Don't give it to her, she'll keep it for herself." The women seemed incapable of cooperative effort. Little Laxmi, having assessed the situation, counseled, "She is right, the woman won't share. Better not give any rupees to anyone." Lane looked at me, palms turned up, as if to say, 'They expect others to share with them, but can't even share among themselves.' The situation had reached an impasse. Only the arrival of Mr. Roy resolved the stalemate. He started the engine and off we went leaving a throng of shrouded forms in our dusty wake.

Dum Dum Racing

Our prayers were being answered as we sailed smoothly in the direction of Calcutta. According to Mr. Roy, traffic had been backed up in the morning because there was only one option for crossing the river, a narrow bridge a few hundred meters beyond Dakshineshwar. After crossing the river the transport vehicles joined the Grand Trunk Road, the major east-west artery across northern India.

As we headed for the airport, a vehicle like ours sped past us and then cut sharply in front of our car, forcing Mr. Roy to slam on his brakes to avoid a collision. Although a common tactic among Indian drivers, Mr. Roy took offence to the maneuver and returned the favor, paying back the thoughtless driver with an equally foolhardy ploy. Before long we had a battle on our hands. Mr. Roy had exceeded his limit for the day and was engaged in the skirmish he had been unable to wage against the trucks he had faced earlier. Tempers flared and speedometers shot past sane levels. Soon the two Ambassadors were jockeying for position like thoroughbreds on the stretch run of the Calcutta racetrack. For three treacherous miles our vehicle veered in and out of the path of certain death. Mr. Roy and his nemesis sped along so close to one another that their bumpers appeared welded together. Finally, the drivers slowed down, their sanity seemingly restored. But as the cars came to a halt, we realized their intentions; the combatants planned to settle their score face to face on the pavement. Once again, Mr. Roy's pulse throbbed; a career's worth of suppressed road rage pounded against his temples. An explosion was imminent. As the drivers climbed from their chariots, they reddened with wrath, pit bulls poised to attack. We had no choice but to issue an ultimatum.

"Mr. Roy, NO TIP!" Lane shouted out the open window. It was the leash we hoped would restrain our man, and it worked. Mr. Roy stopped in his tracks. For a brief moment he pondered his course of action, but after exchanging angry stares with his foe, he meekly returned to the car and drove off. The aborted battle would have caused us to miss our flight. The pent up frustration of a thousand blasts of the horn begged exorcizing, but the prospect of losing a hard earned wage was deterrent enough. Tranquility restored, we arrived without further incident at Dum Dum airport. After tipping Mr. Roy and showering praise on Laxmi, we entered the terminal, an oasis of orderliness and air-conditioning.

As our Indian Air flight prepared for take-off, the events of the previous days played on the screen of my mind like a fast-forwarded video. Some of the scenes were comic, others tragic; a few were an odd mix of each. The script for our trip had been written as we went. The nightmarish sequences of Howrah Bridge and Barrackpore Trunk Road, interloper politicians and withered beggars, the surreal dance of the black goddess and cold stare of the Bengali tiger were extraordinary images patched together in dreamlike sequence, suitable material for any filmmaker. The comic Mr. C and his caricatured driver Mr. Roy, and the languid Orissan countryside rolled across my mind like scenes from a Fellini film.

Cement, our principle purpose for coming to Orissa, had been obscured by more compelling vignettes, and in the process, India penetrated still deeper into my soul. Like an eccentric grandmother whose life was from another era, India was family, and I found it easy to connect to that world as long as we met on her terms. For all its chaos and distraction, the journey to Calcutta and beyond had awakened me, and I now knew that my purpose in India lay beyond corporate meetings, crowded trains, and smoky streets. I was resolved to dive deep into the crystalline waters that bathed the feet of the mystifying Kali Ma, to drink the spiritual nectar that flowed from the soul of India itself.

SEVEN

Bhairav's Birthday Bash

Fate is nothing but the deeds committed in a prior state of existence.

—Ralph Waldo Emerson

After our trip to Calcutta and Orissa, we returned to Delhi to teach a group of executives from Oriental Bank. Will Fox, my easygoing Texan friend, had a birthday, and a couple carloads of Americans headed for the Sheraton Maurya to celebrate. After dining on dishes fit for a Mauryan king, the partygoers decided to pay a visit to the Bhairav Temple at Delhi's Old Fort. Although the Bhairav Temple is one of the city's oldest, I knew nothing about Lord Bhairav except that he was the god assigned the unpopular task of meting out punishment to those performing evil actions in life. Consequently, I was in no hurry to get to know Bhairav, and wondered if we had chosen wisely in bringing the birthday boy for a visit to the grim reaper. Something about the visit didn't bode well, but I couldn't put my finger on it as we approached the temple.

By strange coincidence, on the Hindu calendar, it was also Bhairav's birthday, and a huge crowd had turned out to celebrate. Hearing that it was Bhairav's birthday, I relaxed a bit, thinking that my intuition had been dulled by the second piece of chocolate cake I had eaten at the party. After all, no one metes out punishment on his birthday.

To get to the temple, which was built against one of the outer walls of the old stone fortress, we passed through a crowd of thousands who had come to honor their god. Most were poor folks seated on the ground. Before entering the temple, we left our shoes with an attendant, who placed them inside a small shed. Once inside, the crush of people made it impossible to move and almost as difficult to breathe. Bodies were wedged against one another like matches in a matchbox. As we stood adhered to one another, a zealous man started pushing his way forward, forcing everyone to move with him, or be further compressed together. The scene was claustrophobic; the fellow's intense desire to reach the altar jostled everyone. The crowd inched its way toward the deity as one massive organism, but many heads prevented me from having a look at Bhairav. When we finally reached the altar, I stood face to face with Lord Bhairav. To say he looked intimidating was an understatement. Bhairav held a severed skull in one hand and a sword in the other, and wore a necklace of snakes. He was not a particularly friendly looking fellow.

Bhairav is said to ride on a black dog, live in a cremation ground, and punish people for their misdeeds. I pleaded for a light sentence in case he was displeased with my behavior in this life. After my brief supplication, I moved toward the exit. Being the first one outside, I went to get the birthday boy's shoes. The scene outside was almost as congested as the one inside. Many eyes followed me to the shed where I turned my back on the throng to collect the shoes. Something was in the air, but I couldn't put my finger on it. As the attendant handed me Will's size fourteen shoes, I felt an odd sensation on my leg, like someone had put a mouse in my pocket. Then it hit me. A theft was in progress and I was the victim.

In a flash I turned to nab the pickpocket, but to my astonishment, the sea of humanity behind me sat perfectly still, exactly as it been when I turned away. No one fled the scene. No one pointed a finger at the guilty party. No one revealed anything at all. The group sat as if anesthetized. Hundreds must have witnessed the theft, but all stared back at me as I scanned the crowd. I scrutinized the men at my feet, casting accusing glances at one or two characters, but it was too late! My valuables were gone including my passport, which I had brought along for a visit to the bank.

By now Will and the others were outside. Half the group found the temple atmosphere intoxicating; the suffocating crowd had bothered the other half. I was preoccupied with my stolen passport. One of my friends joked that I had received the blessings of Lord Bhairav, the patron saint of thieves. Had I known the gathering outside the temple included some of Delhi's better pickpockets, I would have been more cautious.

The US Embassy processed my passport without delay, and within a week I had a new one. The Indian women at the embassy were courteous and helpful every step of the way. When I told one of them how I had lost the passport, she admonished me, "You shouldn't carry your passport to a place like that." It seemed everyone knew the reputation of the place but me.

The next stop was the Indian Home Ministry for a visa replacement. I wasn't looking forward to this stop; my prior dealings there had severely tested my patience. When an indifferent bureaucrat asked how I lost my passport, I replied, "It was stolen at the Bhairav temple."

"Be more careful," he warned, instructing me to fill out some forms and return the following day. I returned the next day and sat for three hours, but when my turn came the same official said, "Come back tomorrow."

I repeated the patience testing vigil for the next four days. Each day, after a long wait, I was told, "Come back tomorrow." I asked the bureaucrats questions, but got no answers. Frustrated, I decided to speak with the officer in charge. During the weeklong ordeal, a mysterious man sitting idly at a desk in the main hall had befriended me. His task appeared limited to directing visa applicants to the photocopier down the hall, but after we got acquainted, he confided, "I am really an intelligence officer assigned to observe the Afghan immigrants pouring into Delhi. Five hundred a month," he said, pointing to a family dressed like nomads.

"Sir, maybe you can help me. I need to speak with the officer in charge. As you know, I've been coming every day for a week. Still no visa."

The undercover officer motioned to an assistant, who led me into a spacious office where the man in charge sat behind an oversized desk. I had barely sat down when two cups of tea arrived. If only the bureaucrats could process files as efficiently as they prepared tea, I thought. From behind his desk, the babu in charge signed documents placed in front of him by an assistant as he listened to my story. When my empty teacup hit the saucer, the senior man dismissed me, saying, "Come back tomorrow." I had heard the instruction one too many times and was determined not to leave without my visa, so I remained in my seat, causing the officer to peer coldly at me over his glasses. I had felt his disdain from the moment I entered the room.

"Sir," I said respectfully, "I've already spent a week here. I'm not leaving without my visa." His indifference was starting to wear on me.

The officer was caught off guard by my demand, and instructed his assistant to check its status. He then replied in his seasoned bureaucratic way, "We are having some difficulty finding your file. Please be patient." His tone was insincere, but there was still hope.

To my relief, within twenty minutes I had a fresh visa stamp in my new passport. No doubt it could have been issued the first day, but it seemed everyone had to suffer the whims of the government babus. I was certain the delay was a ploy to extort money, but I wasn't about to have my pocket picked twice. Self-serving bureaucrats who made life difficult for the people had bothered Mahatma Gandhi too. In his autobiography, he wrote, "It has always been a mystery to me how men can feel themselves honored by the humiliation of their fellow beings."

The following morning a police officer showed up at my door. "Sir, your lost passport has been found." It was too obvious; the timing couldn't have been a coincidence. After wasting a week at the Home Ministry my passport showed up the very next day. What a strange sense of humor Lord Bhairav had! I thanked the officer, but told him I had already gotten a new one. He looked saddened by the news, and I could only assume that he too had hoped to be compensated for his efforts.

Karma And Conduct

Hindus embrace the belief in karma, a concept familiar to almost everyone these days. Christ stated it best when he said, "As ye sew, so shall ye reap," and physicists have known for decades that there is an equal reaction to every action in the universe. But somehow people are reluctant to apply physical laws to personal behavior. Hindus define karma much the way physicists do. It is simply the law of action and reaction governing the physical world. As such, karma is inherently neither good nor bad, but people are fond of saying "It's my karma" when misfortune befalls them, but are less likely to invoke the phrase when something good happens in their life. Australian Aborigines invented the boomerang, a remarkable weapon that cuts a circular path through the air before returning into the hands of the person who throws it. Karma is like a boomerang— it's programmed to return to its owner with the reliability of gravity.

The loss of my valuables at the Bhairav temple was a reminder that karma lurks in the shadows at the unseen edges of life. It waits patiently until time and circumstance are ripe, and then the mail gets delivered when we least expect it. Consequently, we're often blindsided by our karma, whether it's an accident, serious illness, or loss of something we value. In rare instances we may have premonitions about future events that prepare us for tragedy or heartbreak.

In 1982, I spent six months with a group of monks at a former Benedictine monastery in a German hamlet called Boppard. Nestled against the banks of the Rhein River, the cobblestone village has a favorable climate for vineyards and fruit orchards. It was an idyllic setting, one that took me back in time to Medieval Europe.

Maharishi had given our group strict instructions not to leave the

13th century Christian citadel, and the men who had gathered from around the world for the most part followed his instruction. We had not come for a holiday; our purpose was to create a meditative influence to help heal the division between the two Germanys. During a visit to the monastery, Maharishi had surprised everyone by saying that East and West Germany would be united again one day, and even instructed some artists to create a large map of a unified Germany, which was displayed in the chapel where we met each evening.

One day an American named David slipped off to Bonn, an outing that was not approved. The commute to Bonn was a short, scenic ride along the Rhein past impregnable castles overlooking the river. David and his friend planned to take the morning train to Bonn and be back at the monastery by lunch. By the time they reached the departure platform the train was already pulling out of the station so they chased after it. Catching up with the train, they lept onto one of the cars. The first fellow made it safely, but David fell beneath the train and his leg was crushed.

When Maharishi heard about the accident he admonished us for not taking his instruction more seriously. The next day, security guards were posted to insure that outsiders did not enter nor inmates exit. Maharishi warned us that karma lurked outside the monastery walls.

A week after the accident I was walking with the fellow who had gone with David that fateful day. He narrated a story that sent chills up my spine. David had had an ominous dream the night before the accident. In the dream, a being appeared to him, and said, "Choose either your leg or your private parts" to which David replied, "my leg." When he awoke in the morning, he had no memory of the dream. Then the accident occurred. Days later, while lying in a hospital bed, he recalled the strange premonition. He had been given a choice as to how his karma would be repaid, and his subconscious mind had chosen his leg. The Masters say karma is like an arrow heading for a target. When people have presentiments or 'gut feelings' about events looming on the horizon, it often involves an important karmic lesson.

The actions we perform in life never fail to boomerang back to us. The mailman who delivers our karmic packages is simply an instrument of nature assigned to help balance the karmic debts we have incurred. A person prone to angry outbursts is sure to receive a heated response when they least expect it. The deliverer of our karma is also working out his own karma in the process. Most karma is not as traumatic as David's, but accidents, business failure, heartbreak, or serious illness can be life-altering events necessary to balance the ledger of our actions. The Hindu scriptures say there is a Karma Board that evaluates each action before assigning the method of repayment. I imagined they kept long hours. Like a checking account, karma needs to be balanced periodically.

Of course, good actions return to the doer as well. When a fireman rescues a family from a burning home, his meritorious action does not go unrewarded. Nor does a smile shared with a stranger. No action great or small, goes unnoticed. Premeditated actions that are of malicious intent warrant the strongest payback. They may be the ones Bhairav is called upon to repay. Each act is carefully recorded in the individual's cosmic record, which is encoded in the etheric field that surrounds a person. Everyone has mountains of personal karma, but we only carry a small suitcase of it with us each lifetime. The suitcase contains samples of the karmas we have accumulated over many lifetimes. Meditation and meritorious action help reduce one's karmic load. Karma can also be reduced by the grace of the guru or God. The scriptures say, "No act is wholly meritorious nor wholly wicked. In all acts, something of both is seen."

I remember playing a round of golf with my dad while back in the States. It was a perfect day, and we were enjoying a competitive game. Halfway through the round, I was preparing to hit a shot when for some inexplicable reason I raised my head instead of swinging, something I never do. As I lifted my head, I heard a whizzing sound and felt a rush of wind on my throat. Then I heard a man shout "Fore," the warning golfers use to inform you that you are about to be knocked unconscious by their errant shot. The man's drive, traveling at high speed, missed my larynx by a fraction of an inch. Had I been struck in such a vulnerable place, there is little doubt I would have been killed. The close call left me out of sync for a hole or two and I had trouble concentrating. Had a karmic arrow somehow been averted? Or was the near fatal miss just one of the hazards of public golf? My intuition told me that an arrow of karma had missed the mark, but I would never know for sure.

The sages say that arrows of karma can be diverted before they strike the target. Although the principle of karma is as inexorable as a law of physics, grace provides us with the opportunity to rise above the consequences of mistakes made in the past. Nothing is etched in stone regarding the law of action and reaction. As one dives deeper into the Universal Self through meditation, misguided actions are absolved. Grace is a state where one has risen above the wheel of karma that has been spinning round and round for thousands of years and hundreds of lifetimes. When a state of Grace is attained, one is no longer subject to karmic law. It is Grace that carries the saint through life, manifesting what he or she needs as they need it. Grace is fueled by gratitude, a feeling rooted deeply in the heart.

A Good Walk Spoiled

I was enjoying a holiday in Nepal one autumn while my business visa was being renewed at the Indian consulate in Katmandu, a process that takes about a week. It was a crisp fall day and the valley had a golden glow about it. A game of golf seemed like fun. I started slowly, hitting crooked shots and trying not to mind the rented clubs. Despite my poor shot making, I felt as free as the raptors I had seen soaring among the pristine peaks. My Nepalese caddy and I were exchanging stories when I heard someone shout my name in the distance. "Briggs, Briggs. Are you Briggs?" The sharp voice pierced my bubble momentarily, but I went on playing. As I walked up the fairway, a man approached out of breath. He introduced himself as Baxter, and asked if he could join me.

I was playing alone, so I said, "Why not?" and off we went. The American expatriate was from New Jersey. Apparently, the manager of the club had suggested we team up, which explained how I could be in a country where no one but the hotel manager and Indian consulate knew my name and still have an American track me down on a golf course. What were the odds of two Americans teaming up for a game of golf in the Himalayan Kingdom of Nepal? It had the potential for a match made in Karmic Heaven.

"Briggs, want to bet on the game?" Baxter suggested. I was experienced at identifying competitive fire and knew my playing partner had some to spare. I was also no stranger to golf wagers, having played with my dad and his buddies since high school, and knew that betting changed the game a little, sometimes a lot.

"If you like," I replied indifferently, ignoring an inner voice of protest. Having spent the past five years in India I had come to appreciate the less competitive personalities of Asians.

"Damn!" exploded Baxter as his putt missed from short range. I looked at my placid caddy, who raised his eyebrows. We had barely begun and my opponent was already complaining about the condition of the greens and the fact that he wasn't playing well. He was unhappy about everything, but his histrionics seemed out of place. This was, after all, not the U.S. Open.

Baxter's antics reminded me of some of the coaches I had trained under as a teenager. His competitiveness made him short-fused and impatient, not the kind of guy you'd want along on a trek around Annapurna, but maybe the cool Himalayan air would bring out a more agreeable side. Like my high school basketball coach, Baxter's mood fluctuated with his play. If we were winning, my coach was pleasant, but whenever our team fell behind, he stood on the sideline with his hands on his hips, making it clear to one and all that he was upset.

When I found my ball wedged against a rock, Baxter shouted across the fairway, "Briggs, don't forget to take a penalty." Baxter was the type of playing partner I avoided. My bubble of Himalayan bliss was rapidly deflating, but I was not about to let this guy get under my skin.

I had been away from America for a long time, and felt like a civilian in the custody of a marine sergeant. Before I knew it I was competing with the intensity of my former incarnation as a teenage athlete. As we reached the final hole Baxter took a look at the scorecard and announced, "Briggs, I'm one stroke up on you." Maybe Bhairav would teach this guy a karmic lesson or two, unless of course I was the one who needed the lesson. Win or lose, we had just one more hole to play. I summoned what remained of my badly eroded golf skills and placed my drive well beyond my opponent's, but both of us reached the green on our next shot.

As my putt missed the mark, Baxter let out a distinctly American "YEAH!" It was not a gracious gesture, but I wasn't expecting one. As we shook hands Baxter's euphoria was beyond his control, but I couldn't begrudge the victor his moment of exaltation. I had never understood the American humorist Mark Twain's comment, 'Golf is a good walk spoiled' until my game with Baxter. If there was any consolation in my poor play, it was the fact that I would soon be sitting down to gourmet pizza at Fire and Ice, a café owned by an Italian friend. Marie's Napoli pizza and fresh strawberry ice cream were the best in Katmandu.

But Baxter wasn't finished with me. "Briggs, want to do it again tomorrow?" he asked. No doubt Twain would have found the victor amusing, and probably the vanquished too, but I didn't take the bait for I had already decided that my last day in heaven would be spent in the mountains outside Katmandu.

After pancakes at Mike's, everyone's favorite American in Katmandu, I rented a motorcycle and rode into the foothills to a ridge where the spellbinding views of Langtang left me longing to trek again. The wall of magnificent peaks that divided Nepal and Tibet was awesome, and I could easily make out Ganesh Himal among them; the elephant god's large ears and curved trunk were clearly etched into the side of the mountain. As I inhaled the breathtaking panorama, I thought about the folly of the previous day's encounter. To come to Nepal and not spend every waking moment among these peerless pinnacles was a mistake I wouldn't make again.

I was hiking along the ridge, feeling close to the peaks in the distance when I came upon a monument. The commemorative inscription described a tragic airplane crash. A decade ago, a Japanese airliner had slammed into the Langtang range as it flew out of Katmandu. Karma, I reflected, becomes even more unfathomable when disaster claims hundreds of lives.

The Binding Influence

The south Indian saint Amma often reminds her students, "Children, we need to respond, not react to our environment." Reacting is the equivalent of the old teaching 'an eye for an eye,' which keeps the wheel of karma revolving. Christ revised that idea when he taught his students to "turn the other cheek" in response to what we perceive as unfair treatment. Forgiveness breaks the vicious cycle of action and reaction. I was making progress with my karmic mailmen, those patience testing bureaucrats and aggressive golf partners, by looking inside myself to see what lessons I needed to learn.

When my passport was stolen, I mused, 'Why did this happen?' I could have easily blamed it on my friends who talked me into going to the Bhairav temple in the first place, or the Delhi police who allowed pickpockets on the streets. I could have even blamed it on Bhairav, but the mind's response to karma is unreliable. It often distorts and reshapes reality to satisfy the ego, the backstage puppeteer that manipulates the strings of our psychology and emotions. All too often, the connection between cause and effect is missed, which is essential if we are to learn our lessons.

Karma is the great teacher, humanity its students, and the world a classroom. The Chi Gong master knows how to respond to any form of attack; he simply steps out of the way of a forceful blow, rendering it ineffective. A master may even reverse the flow of energy, returning it to its source like the aborigine's boomerang. The sages were so attuned to nature that they remained in their caves when the stars were inauspicious. It is said that a Master knows the time of his passing six months ahead of time and may choose to elude death if he wishes to extend his life.

In a state of God Realization, the soul has separated itself from its mountain of karma. Maharishi once said the action of an enlightened person is like 'drawing a line on air,' it leaves no impression on the mind at all. Consequently, no seeds of future karma are sewn; the mind is at peace. A farmer knows seeds won't grow in saline earth. The saint's mind is like salty soil. Existing in a childlike, unconditioned state, karma cannot touch him.

Not long after my fateful visit to the Bhairav Temple, Lane and I were walking to our Bombay hotel near Nariman Point. The street was poorly lit, and as we passed a dark alleyway I had the feeling that danger lurked. Instinctively, I placed my hand over my back pocket at the exact moment a thief was reaching for my wallet. As he was about to snatch it, our hands touched and the pickpocket sprinted off empty-handed into the night. I was learning to respond to internal messages in a timely manner.

A few months after our visit to Bhairav, we returned again. I had some misgivings after my first experience at the temple, but didn't want to prevent my friends from going. My lesson learned, I left my valuables in the car and suggested that everyone do the same.

"Remember what happened last time," I warned.

"C'mmon, Coach. It's safe! Nothing will happen," my friend Tim said optimistically.

"I'm leaving my stuff in the car, and I suggest you guys do the same," I replied as we headed for the entrance. I had the feeling that we needed to be careful, but I couldn't be sure my feelings weren't due to the earlier pickpocketing.

The temple was chaotic if not as crowded as before, and we made our way to Bhairav more quickly this time. When it was Tim's turn to stand in front of Bhairav, he offered a small prayer. But as he turned for the exit his face suddenly paled. He grabbed for his wallet, but it was too late. Bhairav had already blessed him.

EIGHT

Silence

The holy time is quiet as a nun,
Breathless with adoration.

—*William Wordsworth*

Ringing In The New Year

The Christmas season had arrived in Delhi, and the markets were clad in gold and silver. Although I didn't see Santa, Christmas trees and snowflakes decorated store windows, which amused me since most Indians had never seen either. As expected, government offices were closed for the holiday. The twenty million Christians in India, whose ancestors were some of the first to adopt the faith, attended church services and celebrated quietly in their homes. One of the wise men present at the nativity is believed to have made the long journey from India. My last minute shopping was not motivated by the holiday season, but was preparation for a self-imposed internment to begin New Year's Eve. It was our tradition to observe a week of silence to give an auspicious start to the New Year.

Of greater interest than the bags of fruit and nuts squirreled away in my dresser was the condition of my room heater and bathroom geyser. January was cold and damp, and needed air and water heaters. The hot water heater had already broken twice, and I was determined to have it repaired before beginning my silence. But this was risky business at the ashram; repaired electronics often came back in even worse shape. The competence of our staff was dubious at best, but I had no option if there was to be any hope of hot water. When the water heater sputtered and died on the second day of silence I shrugged my shoulder, knowing that cold showers were my only option. The wiring had sizzled during morning meditation and by the time I could get to the bathroom, a cloud of smoke hung in the air. 'There goes my hot water,' I rued. The outlet was charred and the caustic smell of burnt wires called for strong incense. I only hoped the room heater wasn't next.

As with ships at sea, the mind requires a wide arc when reversing its course from worldly duties to deep silence. By the third morning, my navigational settings had been revised and the new coordinates propelled me into a tranquil port. Having cast overboard the jetsam of my mind, I sailed home on a light breeze. Anchored in the silent depths of my favorite harbor, I was blissfully ensconced in my routine. Except for meals and picking up a decoction prepared by our Ayur Vedic physician, there was no need to leave the room. The medicinal supplement, which we called the 'Green Rasayana,' was unlike anything I had ever taken; it tasted a bit like kelp mixed with olive oil, and its creator, Dr. Raju, had left instructions to take it before meditation.

Snowbound In The Borscht Belt

My first extended silence had begun one snowy January in the Catskills Mountains in up-state New York with the cryptic instruction to just 'Be' for the week. Free to roam about the inner landscapes I rarely ventured outside the farmhouse where I lived. My bedroom window framed an expanse of white that swirled about like waves in a stormy sea, and I was content to watch the snowy matinee each afternoon. The whistling winds sweeping across our mountain heightened the stillness rather than diminishing it. The drifting snowstorm served as a fine conduit for silence, and the white blanket connected me to the deeper realms of nature where I was free to navigate the ocean of Being. On afternoon walks my mind observed the azure, forest green, and white landscape as if for the first time. Half filled tracks, some human, some deer, and some rabbit, were the only signs of life among the conifers and on the glossy sheet of ice called Lake Shandelee. My mind roamed about freely, and the days were differentiated only by sunrise and sunset.

Nights outshone days in the silent landscape. Inner wakefulness was like a steady lamp illumining sleep and dream. One late night, as incandescent light filled the inner chamber of my mind, a form precipitated in front of me. Entranced, I watched the oval of light slowly take shape. At the center of the pearled radiance, the sublime image of a goddess appeared. Her benevolent eyes held me in loving embrace for an eternity and then her right hand slowly extended toward me. As her index and middle fingers touched my chest, my heart swelled in waves of devotion and I lay there transfixed, unable to move for a long, long time. Then the vision faded and I drifted into the kind of blissful slumber usually reserved for children.

Upon waking, snowflakes danced again outside my window, but they appeared different that morning. As if the bedroom window had been wiped clean, I was seeing more clearly. The intricate crystal pattern of each flake possessed a beauty and definition that had previously eluded my vision. I felt acutely alive inside, born anew, as if the energies in my body had been recalibrated. But her unexpected visit brought more than an impartial increase in voltage for the flow of energy had a disposition of compassion and joy, and I felt a greater connection to all things, animate and inanimate. Who the beautiful lady was, I may never know, but her blessing opened a door in my heart that I would enter often from that day on.

Maharishi Nagar couldn't match the snowbound Catskills for beauty or depth of silence, but it had an appeal all its own. The haunting meow of the peacock, the cawing of crows, and the sounds of children playing in the courtyard outside my room floated around the periphery of my silent bubble without bursting it. Only the thump-thump at the door one morning ruffled the calm. Om Prakash hadn't read the Hindi sign on my door because he couldn't read. The washer man's banging along with the chilling bucket baths were small distractions in an otherwise unbroken quietude.

The thought kept coming during silence: 'What's in this green rasayana?' Dr. Raju was often evasive when asked questions about his medicines, but no one minded because they were so effective. This time, however, I would not let the winsome doctor off the hook. The drink, bolstered by the morning chants of three thousand pundits, put me in a euphoria that I hoped would never end. Losing track of time is an extravagance reserved for cloistered monks and renunciate yogis, but sampling that world made me want more. Silence, although at the very core of our existence, is easily obscured by thought and emotion, and responsibility. The nonstop mental activity the mind engages is like a poorly tuned radio. It distorts the sublime symphony within. During my week of silence, the static dissolved and the music of the heavens flowed unimpeded.

Seven apples had been stored on the shelf, one Kashmiri gold for each day. Only one remained. As I fell asleep, a voice penetrated the night. It was Pateriya singing in the moonlight. Even from the opposite side of the ashram I could feel his devotion as he sang beneath the stars. I would pay him a visit when my silent vigil was completed. The week had unfolded like a continuous meditation. All thoughts ceased when they merged at a point between the eyebrows where mental calm was as receptive as the serene surface of a lake. More than ever, I appreciated the sage who said, "To the mind that is still the whole Universe surrenders."

Mama Pateriya's Pudding

Silence ended and the Pateriya household bubbled with excitement over its newest member. Poonam had given birth to a calf named Radha. Pateriya himself had assisted in the late night delivery of the healthy girl with big brown eyes, rubbery ears, and knobby legs that angled at the knees. It was my first time around a newborn calf, and I felt as awkward as Radha looked. The calf was still getting acquainted with her body, and stayed near her mother who rested comfortably under a jute blanket.

No matter the time of day, tasty treats simmered on Mama Pateriya's propane range, and Pateriya's round belly was ample proof. In honor of Radha, the preparation of a special kheer (pudding) was in progress. The slow process of reducing milk resulted in a thick creamy dessert made delicious by jaggery (unrefined sugar), rose water, and ground cardamom. Tonight's kheer, Pateriya claimed, was special, and I was privileged to share it. I liked milk puddings flavored with butterscotch or chocolate, and quickly acquired a taste for kheer. Mama Pateriya herself brought two small bowls of dessert into the room, one for Pateriya, and the other for me. I noticed the pudding's strangeness immediately. It was thick from condensed dairy, but there were these mysterious lumps in the concoction. A transparent glob slid off my spoon when I raised it to my mouth. On the next effort the glob slid down my throat in a slimy sort of way. As I swallowed, my taste buds searched, but were unable to identify the elastic mass. Pateriya meanwhile was relishing his serving with audible sighs and so I pretended to enjoy mine. After forcing down yet another bite, I asked Pateriya about the peculiar dish.

"Pateriya, what's different about this kheer?"

Before her father could answer, Richa jumped in, "Uncle, don't say 'kheer,' say 'kheeeer!'" Richa found my Hindi amusing and wanted me to exhale slowly as I pronounced the word.

"Kheeeer!" I said, causing Richa to spasm with joy. "Pateriya, what's in this kheeeer?"

Pateriya chuckled at my pitiable Hindi. "Steveji, this kheer is good nutrition. Special taste. Best food for you!"

I sensed that from the earlier conversation. "What's so special about this kheer?"

"This kheer only possible when baby born," Pateriya replied. Now I was suspicious. "Calf gets special nutrition from mother to make strong. If human eats, he become strong too." I had never been one to mix health food with my dessert. That was strictly reserved for salads.

"Pateriya, did this…come out of Poonam's womb?" I asked pointing at the transparent blob in my bowl. By now I suspected the worst.

There was a distinct possibility that key information was about to be lost in translation so I called Kusum into the room. Kusum understood what I wanted to know immediately. "Uncle, this special kheer is made with, how you say…"

"Placenta?" I asked horrified.

"Yes, placenta!" Pateriya wiggled his oval noggin in agreement and called into the kitchen in Hindi. Another bowl of the slippery stuff promptly appeared in front of me.

"Steveji, you eat special kheer and swastik problem nahin (no health problem)," my smiling friend explained with conviction. I didn't have the presence of mind to explain my philosophy about sweets, but was resolved not to eat another bite of it. Radha needed the nourishment, not me.

"Pateriya, please, one bowl is enough. Others should enjoy. The children are growing. I'm already healthy," I protested. By now the entire family was hovering over me. Mama Pateriya, a delicate woman with a slender face and a few streaks of gray in her oiled back hair, had come from the kitchen to see how her guest liked the pudding she had specially prepared.

"Aacha kheeeer (tasty pudding)!" I said in my best Hindi, trying to imitate Richa's pronunciation. I didn't want to disappoint Mama Pateriya.

"Steveji, aacha (good) Hindi!" Mama Pateriya cried with delight, her voice huskier than her physique.

Avoiding eye contact with the second bowl of kheer, I turned to her daughter, "Richa, you teach me Hindi, Teech hain (ok)? Then I can talk to Mama better."

Henna On My Hands

By now Pateriya was eating the extra bowl of kheer and the children were teaching me Hindi. My poor pronunciation brought peals of laughter from the girls who no longer felt shy around me. As they taught me Hindi, Neetu, the youngest daughter, drew designs on her sister's arms with a liquid that she squeezed from a plastic tube. I had never seen this before, and marveled how artistically she applied the reddish brown fluid, creating flowers and geometric shapes. The Hindi lesson soon lost its momentum, and one of the girls took my hands. Neetu applied the russet liquid, drawing hieroglyphs all over my hands and arms. According to Richa, the liquid was made from dried leaves that were crushed and mixed with mustard oil. The technique was an ancient ceremonial art called mehindi, and was popular among village girls. It was the custom of an Indian bride to have the henna designs drawn all over her hands and arms the night before her wedding. If the designs were still there in the morning it boded well for the marriage.

Before long the girls had painted tattoos that were far more conspicuous on my pink skin than on their almond complexion. The henna looked good on the girls, but looked weird on me. The evening had been filled with the usual Pateriya household merriment, but it was getting late and I had a presentation to make the following day. Before departing, I went to the hand pump to wash off the henna designs. I scrubbed and scrubbed, but the brown stain didn't come off.

"Pateriya" I asked, "How do I get this off?"

Pateriya's eyes rolled with laughter. "Steveji, henna no come off." The girls giggled and I frowned, wondering how I would hide their handiwork at the lecture. If I awoke in the morning with henna on my hands, I would not consider myself nearly so fortunate as a young bride.

The next day, standing in front of a roomful of senior executives, my hands covered with lotus blossoms, I felt as self-conscious as the day I forgot my talk at a citywide middle school speech contest. It would have been one thing to be lecturing in a large auditorium, but the conference room was intimate. My shirtsleeves covered my arms, and I kept a marking pen in one hand and the other buried in my pocket. The executives attending our corporate seminar would not have understood the mischief we enjoyed in the village ashram.

Soma Plants

That evening I stopped by Dr. Raju's room to thank him for the green rasayana he had prepared each morning during my week of silence. Standing at the door, a short man dressed in a raw silk kurta and bordered white dhoti greeted me. A full head of silver hair disguised a smooth, youthful face that showed no signs of ageing. Large milk chocolate eyes beamed benevolently at me, peering deeply into mine. I felt as though I was being scanned from head to toe, as if an x-ray machine were compassionately viewing my brain, heart, liver, and lungs. Dr. Raju was one of those rare human beings who lived to serve others. Day and night, he looked after anyone in need.

"Steveji, how were your meditations?" Dr. Raju asked with a knowing smile.

"Never better!" I replied. "What was in that concoction? The effect was magic."

With a sparkle in his eye, Dr. Raju confided, "The green rasayana is a special formula using the soma plant."

"Soma plant!" I said in disbelief. "Are you saying the drink had soma in it? But where did you find it?" The Vedas ascribed miraculous properties to the soma plant, but I had understood the plant to be either extinct or extremely rare.

"Yes, Steveji, it was a soma drink. Soma plant grows in the Himalaya in special places. Did you like it?"

"Yes, very much, but it's difficult to separate the effect of the soma from the silence. They complimented each other."

"Exactly," enthused Dr. Raju. "That's why I waited to prepare until now." Again and again Dr. Raju amazed me. When I had cooked for him at our Catskills retreat a decade earlier, I discovered that he possessed rare skills and subtle awareness. A friend and I had prepared meals for him during his stay and he enjoyed the food, but one day he didn't touch his meal. When we asked him about it, he replied mysteriously, "Never be distracted while cooking." At first I didn't understand his comment, but then it hit me. During the meal preparation that day many friends had dropped by the kitchen, curious to see what foods Dr. Raju liked. Apparently the intruders had caused Dr. Raju to skip lunch altogether, although he couldn't possibly have known about the steady flow of inquiring visitors. Dr. Raju's comment had dumbfounded me at the time, but after getting to know him, nothing surprised me. His intuition was flawless, his knowledge of herbal formulas rivaled India's greatest sages.

As Mahatma Gandhi wrote, "Everyone who wills can hear the inner voice. It is within everyone." But for the inner voice to be heard the radio needs tuning, and extended meditation and periods of silence were the rishi's ways of tuning in to the right frequency. Dr. Raju's radio was certainly well tuned and his elixirs of life equally well prepared.

NINE

Exceptional Souls

Sages wear a coarse cloth covering with precious jade at the center.

—*Dao De Jing*

As busy as we were with our corporate programs, I couldn't help noticing an elderly Swami going to and from the ashram on a red motorcycle. He was in the habit of parking his vehicle in front of our guesthouse so I suspected he was staying in the housing block nearby. His braided gray beard, long flowing hair and white cotton ensemble seemed incompatible with his urban mode of transportation. But, at a time when the modern and traditional collided at the very heart of Indian culture, incongruities such as this were commonplace.

We had arrived in India at a time when disparate traditions were competing for the soul of India. The previous year, lawmakers had opened India's economy to the world, and with the new trade laws came a massive influx of western products and trends. By day we interfaced with this burgeoning influence in boardrooms across India, but by night we retreated to our ashram. Although only a handful of our corporate executives acknowledged spiritual development as a reason for their interest in meditation, most had been introduced as children to the idea that man's inner nature is divine.

Corporate friends quickly revised my idealized vision of the Indian family, explaining to me that the complexities of the contemporary Indian family were substantial. Traditionally, a child was expected to follow the path of his forefathers. The son of a doctor would one day become a doctor and the son of an army officer was sent off to join the military when he was old enough to fight. An Indian boy's life was mapped out for him from birth; he would fill the shoes of his father and assume the responsibility of looking after his parents in their old age. Consequently, the pressures to do well in school and excel in a career were strong. Many counted on their sons and grandsons.

Swami Narayan, the free spirit on the motorcycle, was an anomaly in the family system for he had eluded the noose of householder life, choosing instead to dedicate his life to the pursuit of God. He had chosen, as if by providence, a life of renunciation. Although as a boy he couldn't possibly have comprehended the age-old customs that would decide the future of others his age, an inner voice impelled him to live outside the conventions of society. Our ashram friend Brahmachari Ajay offered to introduce us to Swami Narayan and translate for us. One Sunday we listened to Swami's story as he sat on the cot in his room.

From a small stool near his bed I watched childlike expressions dance playfully across Swamiji's face. His twinkling eyes darted about as he narrated the account of his life. Swamiji began his story by saying, "I left home at age ten to search for God." Not a trace of pretentiousness betrayed the straightforward statement. Most parents, east or west, would have been horrified at the events that shaped this gentle man's childhood, and his stories kept us spellbound the entire morning.

"What compelled you to leave home at such a young age?" My friend Tim asked.

"It must have been an impression from my past, a samskara. I felt a strong desire to search for the divine and so I left home," he said matter of factly.

"Did you have a destination in mind? Somewhere you planned to go?" I asked.

"No. I just wandered about."

"How did you find food and shelter?" Tim asked.

"I usually had something to eat, but not always. Sometimes I went to sleep hungry. Eventually I began living in a dense forest."

"What was life like in the forest? Wasn't it difficult, living in such a lonely place?" I asked. I wondered how a ten-year-old could have chosen the isolation of a jungle with its uncertainties and potential dangers over the security of his parent's home. Certainly one of the many ashrams around India would have provided the food, shelter, and spiritual training necessary to help him realize such a lofty ambition.

"It was not so difficult. I made a shelter out of grass and sticks for protection from the monsoon. I was never lonely. My friends were the animals. A cobra came each morning to share the pot of milk the villagers brought me. I grew up with nature as my friend and teacher. I had no formal education and no interest in the world." Swamiji's eyes conveyed great warmth as he talked.

"Did you ever consider returning home?" I asked.

"No. I felt a closeness to God in the forest and never thought of home."

"Swamiji, boys ten years old don't normally do that sort of thing…you know…live alone with wild animals," Tim said.

"I felt a kinship to the plants and animals. Nature was my family. I was quite content. The deer and birds were my friends. They were not afraid and I was not afraid." Swamiji's words, however unusual, were spoken with utter sincerity.

Swamiji paused for a moment, then jumped off his cot and crossed the room to a table where a picture of the god, Hanuman, leaned against the wall. On a brass tray in front of the picture was a plateful of ladhus. Swamiji examined the sweets carefully before picking out three beige balls, and then he returned to his bed. He handed one to each guest. He seemed pleased with the spontaneous gesture; his eyes danced again with delight as we ate the offered sweets.

It is common for sanyasis to worship Hanuman who is famous for his devotion to Lord Ram. Hanuman was Swami's favorite. I reached for the mace that rested against the wall and raised it into the air, proclaiming, "Hanuman Ki Jai." Swamiji was enjoying himself, swaying side to side, shaking with laughter at the gesture.

"Swamiji, how long did you live in the jungle?"

"In years I can't say, but when I left the jungle I was fully grown. I had received my education from nature. Mine was a happy childhood, a fine education," he said.

I marveled at the statement. Swamiji had spent a decade in the lap of nature with no guarantee of food or protection. But unlike most Indians who have been exposed to the elements, his face was still youthful and soft. I guessed his age to be seventy-five, but there was no way to verify it.

"Swamiji, when you left the forest, where did you go?" Tim asked.

"I felt the urge to go to the Himalaya. It's the tradition of those seeking God in this country. I wandered for many months, possibly years in the mountains, visiting the holy shrines in India and Nepal. In Nepal, I met a holy man who lived on milk only. We called him 'Dudh (milk) Swami.' We walked from place to place with our belongings in a pouch. We were not attached to anything."

"Swamiji, I met a Dudh Swami at a Siva temple outside Katmandu," I said. "He had been living on milk for the past seventeen years. Do you think it was the same man?" Dudh Swami was a calm soul who lived in a kutti (hut) near the river at Pasupatinath, Nepal's most venerated temple.

"It must have been him. Dudh Swami was a devotee of Siva."

"So you walked about the Himalaya with only the clothes you were wearing?"

"I had a blanket and bowl. What more does one need?" replied Swamiji matter of factly. It takes a renunciate to understand a renunciate, and I found the psychology of complete detachment foreign to me.

"Swamiji, after wandering the Himalaya, what did you do?" asked Tim.

"I lived in a cave by the Ganges. I had a friend who stayed in a stone hut nearby." The first time I saw these cave dwellings I noticed most of them had been enclosed with masonry and wooden doors, allowing their owners to lock them when they were away.

"I spent my time doing japa (a type of rosary), but after some months I became restless and so I told my friend I was going in search of a guru. My friend was sympathetic, but he told me there was no need to search for a guru. He said to stay put, that my guru would find me.

"On the advice of my friend, I returned to my cave. Then one day the door to my gufa was flung open. The light from outside was blinding. Two holy men were looking in and laughing. The man in orange robes asked what I was doing. I showed him my japa bag (indicated he was doing japa). Then the white robed man spoke, saying 'you come with me.' I felt compelled to follow these men, as if they possessed a power over my mind. I didn't know who they were, but I got up and followed them. As we walked along the Ganges I learned that the man in saffron was the Shankaracharya of Joshimath and the man in white robes was Maharishi Mahesh Yogi.

"Maharishi took me to his ashram in Rishikesh, where he gave me diksha (initiation). He taught me deep meditation. He was the guru I had been restless to find. My friend had been right when he said, 'your guru will find you.' I served in the ashram under Maharishiji's divine guidance for some years before he began traveling around the world. Eventually he stopped coming back to Rishikesh altogether."

Rishikesh ashram sits on a forested bluff overlooking the Ganges with dense jungle around it. Bands of monkeys routinely raid the ashram in search of food and once we found our belongings strewn about the back seat of our car while the guilty party screeched abuse at us from overhead limbs as they munched on our cashews and bananas. That day, the ashram manager had insisted we depart well before sunset because of the danger of meeting elephants on the road. A rogue elephant could charge a vehicle and trample its occupants, and an elephant had been heard trying to break through the ashram's wall in search of food the previous night, according to the manager.

"Were you there when the westerners started coming?" I asked. Rishikesh ashram was where the Beatles and Beach Boys had come to be with Maharishi.

"Yes. Maharishi was very patient with these young people, but they lacked discipline."

"Can you tell us some stories about Maharishi?"

"During monsoon season it is quite dangerous to travel in the Himalaya because of landslides. One day, Maharishi announced that all his chelas should get into the jeeps for a trip to Jyotirmath, which is deep in the Himalaya. The brahmacharis and other swamis were afraid and refused to go. When the heavy rains come landslides are common."

"It is the duty of a master to test his chelas. Seeing the resistance, Maharishi made a small concession, saying, 'Ok, all the vehicles will go ahead of me. Mine will be the last. With this, all will be safe.'

"This brought some relief to the group and reluctantly we climbed into the vehicles. I was assigned to Maharishi's car. The caravan departed in the direction of Joshimath, an eight-hour journey. Maharishi's vehicle came last. About three hours into the journey heavy rains came. The caravan was crawling along the narrow road when we heard and felt a faint rumbling. The sound and sensation grew and before we knew it, huge rocks were tumbling down the mountain directly above us. Everyone was sure we would be buried under the rocks, but Maharishi just sat quietly next to the driver. 'Go little faster,' Maharishi instructed the driver as the rocks pelted the pavement. As we were about to be buried by the falling section of mountain, Maharishi's car passed the most treacherous spot just as the landslide buried the road behind us. We were all thinking, 'what would have happened had the caravan arrived even a few seconds later?'"

It is said that the guru's tests become increasingly more difficult as the disciple matures in wisdom and experience. I too had been exposed to some of Maharishi's tests over the years, but none quite like the one Swamiji described.

Swamiji told another story about a visitor that came to the ashram. "One day we were sitting with Maharishi in the kutiya (house) garden when a fakir entered the ashram gate. He approached respectfully. 'Guruji,' he said, 'I possess a special power. If your holiness would like to ask any question, I can answer it by means of my djinn (spirit guide).' This amused Maharishi, who innocently played along with the fakir. 'Please, ask any question you wish and I will give the answer,' repeated the man.

"We were all curious to see what Maharishi would do. He thought for a moment and then asked. 'Alright, why am I so fond of this ashram land?' After asking the question, Maharishi got up and went into his kutyia a short distance away. By now the fakir was lying on his back on the ground, eyes closed. He had entered a sort of trance, and his body twitched once or twice as he lay there.

"At the exact moment the fakir opened his eyes Maharishi came out of his kutiya and returned to the garden. 'You have my answer?' asked Maharishi, as he sat down. 'Yes' replied the fakir. 'Guruji, you love this land because two thousand years ago you also had an ashram on this very same land. Is it not so?' Maharishi nodded, but said nothing."

After telling the story, Swamiji reached above the head of his bed, and grabbed an old black and white photo from the shelf. "See, this is the picture of the fakir with Maharishiji. That's me," he said, pointing to a young monk standing next to Maharishi. The fakir was lying on the ground in the foreground of the photo.

It was clear that Swamiji adored his master. Each time he said, "Maharishiji," his voiced was filled with tenderness. It must have been difficult for him when Maharishi began traveling around the world in the early seventies. There was no knowing when or if he would return, and there were stories that more than one chela became discouraged by Maharishi's absence. In time, Swamiji resumed wandering. However, now he was equipped with deep meditation, which Maharishi likened to a jumbo jet that could bring one quickly to the goal.

"When you realized Maharishi was not going to return to Rishikesh, what did you do?" I asked.

"I started doing tapas (penance) on the banks of the Ganga. First I sat submerged in the Ganga for twenty-eight days with only my head above the water. Then I performed a more difficult austerity, called 'Panch Agni' (five fire sacrifice)." These austerities are described in the scriptures as practices that bring spiritual benefit to the person, but they demand unwavering discipline and fierce determination.

"The Panch Agni sacrifice was difficult. First you build a fire on four corners of a square and then you sit in the middle. The fifth fire is the sun, which is the hottest of the five. I performed this yagya (offering) for many days. After completing the yagya, I began wandering in the Himalaya again."

"What has brought you to Maharishi Nagar?" I asked.

Swamiji was quiet for a moment. "I have been visiting a heart specialist in Delhi who wants me to have surgery, but I am not inclined that way. I am old now. Brothers, I feel the end for this body is near, but I am at peace."

"Maharishi stays in Holland now. We will be seeing him soon. Is there a message you would like us to take to him?" I asked.

Swamiji thought for a moment before speaking. "Please tell Maharishiji that Swami Narayan loves him." Everyone's eyes in the room moistened as he spoke; Swamiji's emotions were so spontaneous, so humble.

Here was a man who had left home at an age when most children are playing with toys. And, yet, Swamiji never lost his childlike innocence. We spent another Sunday morning with Swamiji before he passed one winter night. When I heard the news I knew that the light that had guided Swamiji's life would surely lead him to his destination.

The Miracle Of Chattarpur

Tour busses, taxies, and auto rickshaws raced along a narrow strip of asphalt, shuttling tourists, foreign and domestic, to one of Delhi's most popular historical sites. The Qutbh Minar, a pencil shaped landmark at the south edge of the capital city, was built in the 13th century so the muezzin could call his brethren to prayer in a nearby mosque. The towering red sandstone World Heritage Site is visible to everyone in the vicinity and for decades has provided a livelihood to vendors lining the roadside, including a diminutive sadhu whose hut was close to the greasy strip of pavement.

Babaji was a passionate young man laboring to preserve the religious heritage of a city that has suffered countless invasions over the centuries. Miraculously, the Hindu faith survived the brutal attacks. A few kilometers from Babaji's hut lay the ruins of Tuglukabad, the seventh city of Delhi, once ruled by a merciless Sultanate named Tugluk. Now, the ruins are a sanctuary for exiled vultures, but Tuglukabad once housed an army that preyed upon the inhabitants of north India. At the peak of his cruelty, Tugluk's men marched one hundred thousand barefoot Delhi residents across the scorching Rajasthani desert for 'relocation.' Only the hardiest survived.

Babaji's life revolved around a tiny Durga shrine, a makeshift structure that accommodated one worshipper at a time. His self-assigned mission was to help poor vendors keep the faith. A coin or two from a shop owner's paltry earnings was placed at the feet of the goddess, and in return Babaji waved a camphor light in front of the deity and dotted a forehead with red powder, a blessing from the goddess.

India's roadside vendor leads an insecure life. Food and shelter for his family depends on a meager income from the sale of cigarettes, chocolates, string, camera film, paan (a slightly narcotic mix of lime betel nut); anything that will sell to a tourist can be found on his plywood shelves. It is no surprise that these beleaguered merchants stopped to pray at Babaji's shrine before bicycling home hours after the sun had set.

Late in the night as one of the world's largest cities slumbered, after the blaring bus horns and revving engines were quiet, Babaji sat in front of his beloved Durga Ma. It was his favorite time for worship. He prayed to his Mother for the world, for he had adopted humanity the way an issue-less couple adopts an orphan. Babaji's greatest desire was to build a home for the goddess and he prayed to her nightly to grant him that wish. Then one lonely night she appeared to him and whispered, "My son, your wish is fulfilled, build a temple for me."

Babaji went to work planning a beautiful white marble temple for the goddess. But as the days passed, he grew anxious, wondering how it would come about. Again, late one night he prayed. "Ma how can I build a temple for you when I am penniless? I am willing to do the work but YOU must provide the means. Please Ma! Please!"

In the coming weeks something miraculous happened. More and more people began stopping at his tiny shrine and one day a basket full of fruit was left in front of the goddess. In the bottom of the basket was a huge sum of rupees. As the months passed the miracle repeated itself again and again. Enormous sums appeared as if by magic, giving Babaji the confidence to begin construction of the temple of his dreams. As time went by a powerful momentum seized control of the Chattarpur temple complex and one after another beautiful marble structures were constructed.

When we met Babaji for the first time, the colossal temple complex was nearing completion on a groomed ten-acre plot south of Qutbh Minar. Babaji himself was small in stature and suffered from a debilitating lung condition that forced him to interrupt his work to receive oxygen from a respirator. Although his health was poor, it didn't slow him down. As we talked, he leaned against a podium that supported his frail body; a tube ran from his nose to a machine at his feet.

"Friends," he said, "have the blessings of Ma Durga and then return. My staff will prepare food for you."

As we enjoyed his kind hospitality, his assistants explained how Babaji personally oversaw every aspect of the temple complex. He walked the grounds each morning inspecting the new construction, modifying plans as necessary. According to one assistant, Babaji received the design idea, which included a dozen beautiful temples, directly from the goddess.

During Navaratri, the festival honoring Mother Divine, we attended Chattarpur's festivities as Babaji's guests. Enormous crowds gathered each day; more than one hundred thousand lined up in the roped walkways to attend the nine-day celebration. As the Chattarpur complex blossomed, donations continued to pour in. The poor left a coin at the feet of the goddess and the wealthy endowed the temple trust generously.

But with expansion came growing pains. As the crowds mushroomed, administrative responsibilities grew. In time, conflict arose as to how the resources should be used. Babaji was unaware of the discord; he was fully absorbed in serving his beloved Ma. But when the differences of opinion couldn't be resolved, Babaji was asked to intervene. In a meeting attended by Chattarpur administrators, he listened quietly while others spoke. At the close of the meeting, Babaji looked into the eyes of each person in the room, and said, "My work is finished here. I will leave tomorrow."

Those attending the meeting were troubled by the foreboding remark. The following morning all were grief stricken by the news that Babaji had passed away in the night. I heard the news when Babaji's senior assistants came to my door to invite us to the saint's memorial service, an emotional event attended by religious leaders, politicians, and industrialists. A humble man's dream, conceived in a roadside shelter in the shadow of a Delhi landmark, was miraculously realized through unshakeable faith and years of devoted service. The marbled halls, sculpted towers, and flowering gardens that Babaji envisioned will endure over time and maybe one day they too will become a heritage site, a fitting tribute to an exceptional soul.

TEN

Tennis, Anyone?

*What a polite game tennis is… admiration of each other's
play crosses the net as frequently as the ball.*

—*Sir James Matthew Barrie*

Our week of silence was followed by a flurry of courses around Delhi,
but despite a full schedule Lane and I were missing our recreation, and
decided to find a regular game of tennis. After checking out the facilities
around Delhi, we joined a weekly game of doubles at the Gymkhana Club.
Gymkhana was built by the British in the 1920's, and still retains a fair
dose of stuffiness. The extensive club occupies prime real estate near the
polo grounds and is adjoined by the prime minister's mansion on one side
and Indira Gandhi's former home on the other. The stately clubhouses'
central hall is a sunken dance floor with a row of game rooms at the side.
The billiard room is next to the bridge room, which is next to the chess
room, which adjoins the men's locker room, but we rarely went inside the
clubhouse. After all, we weren't members, and Members Only signs were
prominently displayed. However, for the winter season we managed to
finesse our way into the Thursday afternoon doubles competition.

Gymkhana boasts two rows of superb grass courts, with a backup of
red clay courts for use during monsoon season, when the grass is soggy.
The lawn tennis court is on the endangered species list the way wood rackets and canvas sneakers were twenty-five years ago, but space-age racket
technology has had little effect on the style of play at the staid club. White
flannel trousers were worn on at least a few courts, and spin preferences
were graceful slices and clever chops, rather than the roundhouse topspins
and two-fisted swats seen on today's pro tour. Sportsmanship superseded
winning, except for an aggressive pair of Americans who played to win.

Towering shade trees kept everyone cool, including the pickers (ball boys) who retrieved our errant shots. At half past four the bell rang, and contestants retired to courtside tables where tea with cream was served along with buttered bread; the crust carefully sliced away. I had never been so coddled on an athletic field. Over the course of the winter, we never heard a disagreement on the courts. Although the gracious games lacked the intensity of a good college match, we enjoyed ourselves on the perfectly manicured courts, and after a game with the director of Hewlett-Packard, we were invited to teach meditation at his office. My college teammates would have had a good laugh at the wood rackets and white pants worn by some of our opponents, not to mention my sluggish movement around the court.

Remembering The Alamo

I learned to meditate because of tennis. On a postcard Saturday in Tucson, I sat for my first meditation. When my instructor asked me how I liked it, I gushed, "Fantastic. It's just like playing tennis in the zone." Those matches when the racket worked like a magic wand and every shot landed within inches of its intended target; those were the moments of peak performance that athletes trained for. It was the elusive 'zone' that transformed mundane exertion into pure poetry of motion. How ironic, it had seemed at the time that such lucidity of experience could be found in meditation from the very first sitting, when athletes trained for years to achieve it.

Our University of Arizona team was one of the strongest in the country, and a talented batch of newcomers had joined the squad in 1971, the year I arrived. In addition to the rookies, the Wildcats had two returning All Americans, seniors with reputations for playing hard and partying harder. Each year before the conference season started, the team traveled over spring break to California or Texas. In my freshman year, we went to Texas to play some of the top teams in America. Our results were good; we hadn't lost a match by the time we reached San Antonio for our final match of the trip against Trinity, a private college that had put together one of the finest teams in collegiate history.

By the time our squad reached San Antonio we felt satisfied, having defeated a string of top teams. But we knew Trinity, a team that boasted a lineup of national junior champions (three of whom would go on to become top professionals) overmatched us. The night before the Trinity match, our senior co-captains, Bud and Butch, decided we should celebrate, and went out to get the needed party items, returning with an impressive selection of intoxicants. The party was rolling along well past midnight when Coach Snyder decided to check in on his team. Coach was a straight-laced guy from Kansas who worked his team hard, but didn't interfere much away from the courts.

Coach walked into the party with a smile on his face, but walked out wearing a frown. He didn't say a word about the bash, but before leaving, he told everyone "Be ready to go to the Alamo at eight." Very few heard the comment, and the party raged on into the early morning. Most of the guys had only been asleep a few hours when Coach came around, knocking on doors. As he had promised, we piled into the van to do some sightseeing at the Alamo. More than a few of the guys had to prop themselves up against the old garrison walls while Coach and the freshmen toured the site of the famous attack by the Mexican army that massacred Texas cavalrymen in a battle for independence.

At the Trinity courts, as our own massacre was about to commence, Bud and Butch called the guys together for a last minute team briefing. In his laid-back Santa Monica surfer's style, Bud rallied his teammates with the cry 'Remember the Alamo,' and then placed a black tablet in each of his teammates hands with instructions to take it before starting the match. Most of the guys didn't even know what they held in their hands, but had there been drug-testing thirty years ago, the entire squad would have failed it. To everyone's amazement, including Coach Snyder, we matched Trinity shot for shot for the next two hours. Not until the final tiebreakers were played did the home team prevail; it seemed the effects of the amphetamines had worn off too soon. But that was only fair. Whatever the reason, Arizona came closer to defeating the champions than any other team did all year.

Coach Snyder typically showed little emotion on the bleachers, but after hearing his players cheering each other on, he too was heard shouting, "Remember the Alamo." The following day, as our van full of weary Wildcats crossed west Texas on its way home, Bud and Butch, self-confident as ever, sipped beers in the back seat. But when the team reached Tucson, Coach called the senior co-captains into his office and suspended them for the remainder of the season. He was understandably upset about the wayward example the two seniors were providing the rookies. Without the seniors, our young squad went on to win the first of three conference championships in a major upset that came down to the final match. A week later we finished in the top eight at the NCAA tournament in Athens, Georgia, which Trinity won in the most lopsided finish ever. By the following fall, Coach Snyder had departed, taking the head-coaching job at his Texas alma mater, and five members of our young Wildcat team were meditating, a trend that was to become popular with college and professional teams all over the country.

A Bird's Eye View

While in Calcutta, I spent an evening with Jaideep Mukherjee, India's genial Davis Cup captain. Jaideep and I met to discuss our meditation program as a potential training tool for his players, one of whom had collected a medal at the Olympics. After all, five former Wimbledon champions had incorporated TM into their regimens, and at one point, twenty-five top pros prepared for their matches with meditation. Again and again, the tennis pros opened their eyes from their first meditation, and said, "I've had this experience before. It's like being in the zone." Jaideep knew all about the zone, and said playing tennis in the zone was the most effortless thing in the world. Every accomplished athlete said the same thing about it, and the tennis pros that learned meditation found it easier to achieve the zone after meditating.

Jaideep, a former top twenty player in the world, proved as agile a storyteller as he had been an athlete. When we got onto the topic of Indian weather, Jaideep conceded that even Indians couldn't cope with the blistering temperatures on the courts. Jaideep was playing in an international event at Delhi's Gymkhana Club, where lofty trees line the perimeter of many of the courts. His opponent was Ken Fletcher, an Australian Davis Cupper who, like all Aussies of his generation, was a superbly conditioned athlete. It was a typical sizzling Delhi day and the two were locked in a protracted battle that left them both exhausted by the middle of the final set. The physical demands of tennis are often underestimated by the undiscerning public, which perceives the game as more glamorous than grueling, but having played most American sports as a boy I can say that high level tennis requires the stamina of a marathon runner and the grit of an amateur boxer. More than one tennis player has been carried off the court at the end of a punishing three-hour contest, the victim of dehydration.

With the match even in the final set, an uninvited spectator joined the gallery. The uncouth observer, according to Jaideep, chose a seat on an overhanging limb above the court. The observer was a vulture and he had not come for the tennis. Peering down at the combatants, the unsightly carnivore watched intently as if trying to determine which man would succumb to the heat first. Both players saw the bird, but refused to surrender to the heat or the intimidating stare of the hungry onlooker. Fletcher, who possessed a wry wit, headed to the sideline for water where his doubles partner sat, cheering him on. When the dog-tired Aussie reached his chair, he pointed his racket at the vulture and quipped, "Mate, if I don't make it, don't let him get me." Jaideep, who was sitting next to Fletcher, doubled over in laughter. After the match, the spent gladiators retreated to the club-house, but the winged spectator was not invited inside.

ELEVEN

Gomoukh

How sweetly the Ganga smiles and glides,
Luxuriant o'er her broad autumnal bed!

—*William Jones*

I was about to plunge into the Ganges when Mataji walked up. The heavy chains wrapped around my wrists would have made me look like a prisoner on a road gang, except for the fact that I was standing knee deep in the Ganges in my underwear. We always stopped in Hardwar to bathe in the Ganges before heading into the Himalaya, and the kindly Mataji who had pressed red dots on our foreheads over the years spotted us immediately. She greeted me with her usual wag of the head and waited while I submerged three times in the swift waters before performing her quaint little ritual. The white-haired woman was as much a part of the holy town of Hardwar as the river itself, for she had been blessing us since our first visit.

It was time to escape to the Himalaya, and Hardwar signaled the beginning of another spiritual adventure. We arrived in the town dubbed the 'Gateway to the Gods' in the late afternoon, feeling dusty after a typical hair-raising ride from Delhi. After our bath and blessing from Mataji, we began our search for Modi Bhavan, the riverside bungalow of a Delhi magnate who had invited us to stay at his family's vacation home. Little did we know that the house sat right on the river and had its own private bathing ghat. For our morning bath we just stepped from the veranda into the brisk waters rushing past.

Daylight was failing as we made our way through the narrow alleyways that connected Hardwar's ghats and temples. We were headed to Hari Ki Puri, where thousands gathered at sunset each evening for the ceremony of lights (aarti) honoring Mother Ganges. A huge crowd had assembled in the amphitheater setting surrounding the ancient bathing ghat, but we found a place on the crowded clock tower island moments before the ceremony began. The pious crowd joined in heartfelt song to Mother Ganga as brass oil lamps with three-foot flames cast shimmering reflections on the river and leafy boats filled with rose petals and candles floated past. It was a superb spectacle. Ganga aarti was a favorite of mine, and the sweetness of community song erased the bumpy ride from Delhi and prepared us for our journey into the Himalaya.

Mataji At Hardwar

Ananda Mayi Ma

Hardwar is nestled against the Shivlik foothills at a point where the Ganges empties out of the Himalaya. The pilgrimage center is recorded in the oldest scriptures and was once the residence of the great Bengali saint Ananda Mayi Ma, who stayed there in the latter years of her life. Indians revered Ma as an incarnation of the Divine Mother and Prime Ministers and industrialists sought her darshan and council, but even more astonishing was the fact that India's holy men came in great numbers for her blessings. This was unheard of at a time when Indian women rarely even ventured into the public.

After meditating in the shrine containing Ma's physical remains, we met an old Frenchman named Swami Vijayananda who had been a close disciple of Ma. The octogenarian shared with us the extraordinary story that had brought him to India fifty years earlier. As a young physician, Vijayananda had booked a berth on a steamer to India where he planned to visit a well-known south Indian saint. But a week before his ship depart-ed, he learned that the saint had passed away. Discouraged by the news, he considered canceling his trip, but at the last moment he decided to go any-way. It was to be a crossroad in the young doctor's life, for when he arrived in India, the spiritual lure of the culture captured his heart and he never returned to France again.

Swami Vijayananda spent thirty years with Ma, but he told us that he had struggled to learn Hindi in his early years in India, and was frustrated because Ma typically spoke in Hindi at public gatherings. Then one day she sent him into seclusion in the Himalaya. When he returned a year later, he went to see her, and again, she was speaking in Hindi. However, to his great surprise, he could now understand every word she uttered. Even more astounding was the fact that he himself could speak fluent Hindi, for he had made no effort to learn the language at all. He attributed the miracle to Ma.

While in Hardwar, we were the guests of the Modi family, who were also devotees of Ananda Mayi Ma. One day Mr. Modi was on a business trip when his plane developed engine trouble. The pilot informed the pas-sengers they were about to crash, and that there was no hope of averting it. The passengers panicked, but Mr. Modi remembered Ma's teachings and advised everyone to think of God, saying their prayers would take them directly to Him when they crashed. Miraculously, the plane made it safely to an airport where the engine was repaired. Mr. Modi and a handful of others, however, didn't feel good about continuing on the flight, so they stayed behind. The ill-fated plane crashed immediately after takeoff and everyone on board perished. By following his inner voice, Mr. Modi believed the grace of his guru saved him.

Ananda Mayi Ma was not a guru in the traditional sense. According to close disciples, she gave diksha (initiation) to only a handful of devotees. Once, during evening satsang, Ma stood up and walked out of the hall without saying a word to anyone. She went straight to the Hardwar station and boarded a train, leaving a group of befuddled devotees in her wake. Two stops later, she climbed down and walked to the home of an old woman who had been crying to Ma for help. Ma spent the evening com-forting the ailing woman, and later told her assistants that she had known a devotee was in distress and needed her help. Ma had simply followed her kheyala (divine guidance), which led her to the home of the distraught devotee.

Ma's teachings were as practical as they were poignant. Once she told a group "Whenever you have a chance, laugh as much as you can. This will loosen all the rigid knots in your body. But to laugh superficially is not enough; your whole being must be united in laughter, both inwardly and outwardly. You simply shake the merriment from head to foot…I want you to laugh with your heart and soul, with all the breath of your life."

Ma slipped into exalted states of God Consciousness easily, and never seemed to mind whether it happened in front of a large group or in private. Once she stayed in a yogic state for five days. When she was asked how she had felt during the samadhi, she replied, "It is a state beyond all conscious and supra-conscious planes—a state of complete immobilization of all thoughts, emotions, and activities, both physical and mental—a state that transcends all the phases of life here below." Sublime yogic states had come naturally to Ma since she was an infant.

Miracles were commonplace around Ananda Mayi Ma. Swami Vijayananda wrote in his book, "The miraculous atmosphere around Mother has impressed me since the first day I met her. It is a daily experience in our relationship with the Mother. Mother can call down rain at will. When she toured in South India in 1952, there had been an acute scarcity of rain for a prolonged period. I was present when a delegation came and prayed to Mother to bring about rainfall. Subsequently, abundant rainfall was reported in the newspapers due to Ma." Once Ma was walking along a road with some of her devotees when they came upon a man whose leg had been badly broken in two places. He moaned in agony over the injury and Ma stopped to help. By simply running her hand over the injured limb, the pain ceased, and when the man was examined at the hospital there was no sign of the breaks.

During our corporate tour, we taught at the companies of many prominent businessmen. Among them was Mr. Jaipuria, who had once owned *The Pioneer*, the newspaper Rudyard Kipling worked for as a young journalist. Mr. Jaipuria told us that he enjoyed hosting saints, but that Ma would never stay inside the family's house, so a small guesthouse was built for her in the garden. During one of her visits, it was monsoon season, a time when snakes are flooded out of their habitats. One evening Ma was walking in the garden when a cobra bit her on the ankle. The Jaipurias were horrified when they learned about the accident, but to their great relief, Ma showed no sign of pain or discomfort from the bite. The snake, however, died.

According to Swami Vijayananda, Ma did not need much to sustain her. For six months, she ate only three kernels of rice a day and once went without water for almost a month. When her devotees asked her about her peculiar habits, she told them that her body didn't really sustain itself on food and water, but rather it was her meditation that provided the nourishment she needed. Through prana (vital breath) alone she could get the essence of things.

During my travels, I stayed at some of Ma's ashrams, including several on Himalayan mountaintops. In each retreat, a shrine is kept in her memory. We always meditated in those rooms, which were places where she had stayed. With remarkable consistency, each room felt as if she was still very much present.

Ananda Mayi Ma

Rough Road Ahead

After our stop in Hardwar, we headed for the source of the Yamuna River. On the narrow paved road, prehistoric looking creatures appeared now and then in the form of a grassy ball perched atop slender brown legs. These odd characters were village women bent over at the waist under the heavy load of fodder, which they gathered for their animals. We also encountered gujjar, nomadic herdsmen and their families, who pitched camp and grazed their water buffalo along the mountain roads. The herds, on their way down the mountain from high summer pasture often obstructed the way, but the Muslim gujjar were always willing to create an opening so we could pass.

The road we traveled to Yamnotri (source of the Yamuna River) follows the Ganges for a couple hours before it forks to the east. The summer monsoons had not yet ended and it rained steadily, which worried our driver. Rain in the mountains bothers drivers because it increases the chance of falling rocks. Despite our driver's concern, I was enjoying the lush vegetation as we made our way through the Yamuna valley. Blessed with mature forests that enriched the soil, crops grew easily in the region and the villagers we passed looked healthy and well fed.

We were almost to the Yamnotri road head when we came upon a small landslide that had spread a thick layer of scree and mud over the road. With considerable effort, our driver maneuvered the car across the debris. We continued on for another few miles in the drizzle until we came to a line of stalled vehicles on the road. A much larger landslide had dumped a portion of the mountain on the road, including a boulder three times the size of our car. As we sat there deciding what to do, the scene reminded me of Swami Narayan's story of Maharishi and the landslide. It would be several days before the slide was cleared and the huge rock chiseled away piece by piece. This was the hazard of traveling in the Himalaya during rainy season. Pilgrims from the tour busses were plodding past the slide to jeeps that shuttled them to the road-head, where they would begin the ten-mile hike to the river's source. Lacking rain gear, we turned back and headed for Gangotri, the source of the Ganges River. It was the second time our efforts to visit Yamnotri had been thwarted.

As we retraced our route, we crossed the smaller landslide we had negotiated earlier. A rough patch tossed the car violently, slamming it against some rocks. As our driver continued down the road it was obvious that something was wrong with the steering mechanism, not a good situation on these treacherous roads. The driver was having trouble on the switchbacks, so we stopped to have a look underneath the car. It didn't look good. A steering rod connected to the left front wheel was badly bent, and although it needed fixing, our driver felt he could keep the car on the road until we reached a repair shop in the next village. Unless one has been on a Himalayan road, its difficult to imagine the danger involved in negotiating hairpin turns and cliffhanging sections of road without sound steering. The slightest miscue would have sent us tumbling thousands of feet to our death. It was a tense situation, but we had no better options, so we crawled along until we reached the next village, which was twenty miles away.

We limped into a shop where a Sikh mechanic lay on his back under the car and repaired the twisted part. He labored hard for forty minutes, but when we asked him what we owed, he said "twenty rupees." We couldn't believe it. Fifty cents for repairing our car! Lane insisted on giving him more, but he politely refused, and so we thanked him for his good work, to which the turbaned mechanic replied, "My duty to serve, sir." By the time we arrived in the town of Uttar Kashi the clouds had cleared; in fact, we never saw rain again the remainder of the trip.

Bus Accidents

Having scrapped our plans to trek to the source of the Yamuna River, we headed for the Ganges valley and arrived in the pilgrimage town of Uttar Kashi late in the day. The rush of the Ganges that surged through the town was swift, and a local cautioned us to choose our bathing spots carefully. I left my room early in the morning for a dip in the cascading water that split the town down the middle. The footbridge spanning the river was a parade route of blue, green, and beige uniforms as hundreds of boys and girls marched to school burdened only by the weight of their school packs.

We were keen to journey on to the source of the Ganges, a pristine region known as the Valley of the Saints. Before departing for Gangotri I was having breakfast at a local restaurant when a group of men gathered in front of a television in the dining room. News of a bus accident near Gangotri was being broadcast. A pilgrim bus had lost control and plunged over a cliff into the icy waters below. These tragedies occurred from time to time so we instructed our driver to exert great care in negotiating hazardous sections of road as we climbed to our destination. Certainly we didn't need more damage to the car.

Our drive to Gangotri took us past the spot where the vehicle had veered over the escarpment. Army personal was already on the scene, pulling the wreckage from the rapids below. Apparently the bus had picked up a group of stranded pilgrims whose bus had broken down. The extra weight added to an already full bus and poor suspension caused the driver to lose control as he traversed a rough patch of road caused by an earthquake a few years earlier. No survivors were found. As we crept past the scene of the tragedy I remembered my Rishikesh friend Swami Direndra's harrowing tale.

Direndra had asked me for medication for his chronic hip, which bothered him now and then. When I asked him about it, he told me how he had been meditating in a window seat when his bus lost control and plunged over a steep cliff. Thrown from the bus, he landed headlong in the river where he was in a serious predicament because he didn't know how to swim. As he flailed about swallowing water, he grabbed hold of a tire that floated past. Moments later, a small girl who was also in the rapids was swept alongside him, so he pulled her to safety. Direndra and the girl were the sole survivors in the accident that claimed sixty lives. The following day the local headline read 'Miracle Survival of Godman.'

Swami Direndra

Gangotri's Hermits

After repairing a flat tire, which our driver blamed on an unscrupulous repair shop that had placed nails on the road, we negotiated a dramatic ascent over cliffhanging sections of road and multiple crossings over deep gorges before arriving safely at our goal. Gangotri is as picturesque as it is spiritual. As we approached, Mount Bhageerathi loomed in the distance. Superbly framed by the valley, the stream emerging from the glacier field at the base of the mountain forms the source of the holy Ganges.

Gangotri is redolent with Himalayan atmosphere. Deodar (cedar) forests cover the mountainsides and parts of the valley. Clusters of birch trees and multicolored shrubs attire lower portions of the mountains in shades of red, orange, and yellow, and the Ganges cuts a deep gorge through the region that has attracted ochre-robed mendicants to her banks for thousands of years.

On our first morning, after meditating near the river, I hiked through a deodar forest. The trail followed the precipitous gorge carved by the river. Above the trail, a hermit had used overhanging rocks and a bit of ingenuity to fashion a shelter out of timber and fallen rocks. He acknowledged my presence by raising his hand as I passed, and I returned the gesture without speaking. The solitary figure was as much a part of the landscape as his neighbors, the peaceful pine and cedar trees. Whenever I encountered one of these self-sufficient monks, I felt the aura of ahimsa (non-violence) around them. The needle-covered trail continued until it ended abruptly on a precipice. Below, the Rudra and Ganges rivers converged in a tumultuous rumble of water in the narrow canyon. The thunderous roar was deafening.

Gangotri reminded me of photos of the old mining towns that sprung up during the Colorado gold rush, except that its inhabitants panned for inner treasures. Dharamshalas (pilgrim housing) dotted the valley and small rock hutments sheltered mendicants. The slow chants of sadhus echoing off the hills told a story of renunciation. We stopped at Gaurikund Falls, where rivulets of water poured over fluted gold and white rock formations. The trail near the falls led past the hut of a baba named Maharaj, whose matted locks were stacked on top of his head, forming a cylindrical beehive. Maharaj had eyes that probed like a hawk's from beneath his mountain of hair. After scrutinizing us closely, he invited us to sit by his dhuni (fire), although our seats were outside his circle of sadhu friends, beyond the tarp awning that protected his constant companion, the sacred fire. Maharaj didn't speak English, but his chela did. The young disciple Vishwanath translated while Maharaj stirred the fire and asked about our purpose for being in India. He was familiar with westerners and their spiritual quests, and asked about our meditation project.

"Have you seen the birds diving into the falls in the early morning?" Maharaj asked.

"No."

"They are yogis coming for morning bath."

"You mean sidhas (perfected ones) who can transform themselves into birds?" I asked incredulously.

"Exactly."

The following morning I sat on a boulder hoping to see the birds diving into the falls, but I didn't see any so I visited Maharaj again. This time, I barely recognized him sitting by his fire. The holy man who wore nothing but a loincloth was covered from head to toe with ash from the previous day's fire. Maharaj sat on a tiger skin; his gray ghost-like appearance looked almost humorous, but I was sure the vibhuti (sacred ash) served a serious purpose. The powdered remains of his dhuni exaggerated Maharaj's slender features, but Vishwanath explained that it helped a yogi maintain body temperature, which I had been unable to do in the dharamshala despite a thick cotton comforter.

Maharaj wanted to know how much time I devoted to my spiritual practice each day and quizzed me about Indian philosophy. Satisfied with my answers, he nodded his approval. I could see from his shining eyes that Maharaj had good light within, so I asked him, "Maharaj, are you awake during sleep?" Many would have misunderstood the question, but Maharaj knew what I was getting at. Perpetual wakefulness is a trait of the enlightened and I wanted to find out if Maharaj had achieved such a lofty state. He reflected for a moment before answering. "During sleep I visit the planets in my astral body. Mangal (Mars), Chandra (Moon), Guru (Jupiter)," he replied, pointing to the sky indifferently as he spoke. Then he took a stick from the fire and drew circles in the dust. "Each circle is a solar system and between each solar system is a Brahmasthan (sacred space)," he said, with a knowing look. "This is Vedic wisdom."

I asked Maharaj what he thought was important for rapid spiritual progress, but without answering me, he fired a question back at me. "Have you eaten meat in this lifetime?"

"Yes," I answered apologetically. Although I had been pure vegetarian for twenty-five years, I had been raised on a typical western diet. "Then take a cave here in Gangotri to prepare for your next life," he replied matter of factly. While I appreciated his candor, the thought of being buried under fifteen feet of snow in the dead of winter with nothing but sacred ash and a faint fire to keep the freezing cold out didn't appeal much to me. I was flattered to think that my yogi friend felt I could approximate his austere lifestyle, but Maharaj lived a life few yogis could emulate, and the lifestyle he proposed would surely have finished me off in short order. If I didn't freeze to death, I would have starved in no time.

Maharaj never wandered far from his fire. Day and night we found him sitting there, staring into the red-gold flames or meditating eyes sealed shut, his spine arched like Ram's bow, palms upturned on his knees as if waiting to receive gifts from the sky. The sadhu's dhuni is his connection to the cosmos, to the subtle realms of the devas and pitris (ancestors). Sitting statue-still at flame's edge, the mantras Maharaj whispered were conveyed to their intended deity by Agni, the spirit within fire. The dhuni communicated a sadhu's prayers to his god much the way a translator interpreted a conversation.

The following day I hiked along the Ganges, beyond the blue-roofed Sivananda ashram to a spot where some caves were hidden among the rocks. Marigolds bloomed in a small plot in front of one hermit's abode and huge stores of wood were piled near another.

After wandering further upstream, I came upon a recluse sitting in front of his cave. The man appeared to be in his thirties, and wore sleeveless orange robes that exposed strong arms and broad shoulders. The mendicant looked up as I approached, but didn't speak. He motioned for me to sit, and placed his hand over his mouth, a gesture I interpreted to mean that he didn't speak. "Maun (silence)?" I whispered. He nodded, and picked up a scratch pad. He seemed willing to communicate by writing notes, and his written English was perfect. As a result, a unique dialogue evolved. I spoke, and he scribbled on his pad. The method worked quite well. I soon learned that the swami had been observing silence for eight years and that a benefactor periodically brought him food and supplies. The swami's name was Paranand Tirth. He invited me to come again, and so every day after my morning meditation we met in front of his cave. If I didn't find him outside, I knew not to disturb him.

Swami had been an honors student at Delhi University and was raised in an affluent family. His serene face lacked any signs of wear and tear that one might expect as the result of spending long winters without heat at 10,000 feet. Swami lived on a diet of powdered milk, nuts, and dried fruit. He did not cook with fire according to the vows of renunciation he had taken. His danda (wooden staff) stood beside him as he sat on the ground in front of his cave. In the days that followed, I rarely saw him without a scripture in his hand for he was a deeply philosophical man.

When I told Swami that Maharishi was my teacher, he scribbled, "Is Maharishi's university still in California?" I was surprised to find a cave dwelling Himalayan recluse who knew about the university, no matter how outdated his information. During the course of our daily dialogues I learned that while Swami was staying in a Varanasi ashram, an American had told him about Maharishi International University, which had since relocated to Iowa.

Swami and I sat outside his cave each morning. I think he looked forward to our conversations as much as I did. One day he wrote, "The guru is the embodiment of spiritual power. There is little need for communication. The preceptor has been maintaining spiritual blessings for his disciple for a long period, waiting until the time is right to bless him. He can transfer the blessing by seeing you, or touching you. You never know when the blessing will come. But it will come." Swami's cave was named Hansa Gufa (Swan's Cave) after his guru, Swami Hansa, who had lived in the cave for thirty-seven years before giving it up due to age and infirm health.

Swami invited me to meditate with him in his cave one morning, a cavernous hollow beneath a massive crag. His apartment was simple and never needed paint or roof repairs. Inside, there was an extra saffron robe, a torch, a box of matches, some powdered milk and nuts, a picture of his guru, a grass mat on which he slept, and a blanket. There was no furniture but I noticed a stack of books, pencils, notepads, and an oil lamp. Swami had composed a poem of 108 verses, called *Matrika Harem* (The Garland of Alphabet Having Divine Powers). One verse read, "Let the creeper of karma fructify incessantly bearing good, bad, and mixed fruits. We sanyasis (recluses) do not participate. So we are fearless."

After one of my visits to Swami, I met his neighbor, Arun, who lived in the cave next door. Born in Rajasthan and raised an orphan, Arun was placed in the care of a Tibetan yogi near the border of China at the tender age of eight. For twelve years he served his master, an accomplished yogi whose remote cave, at 13,000 feet, was perpetually shrouded in fog. According to Arun, much of the time it was impossible to walk outside for one could easily step off a cliff in the dense fog. When Arun was twenty, having faithfully served his master, the yogi informed him that his training was complete. The next day his master disappeared and was never seen again.

Arun had just finished a vigorous workout and invited me inside his cave. Like Swami, he also wore orange cloth, but his was tailored in the style of an exercise outfit. Unlike Swami's cave, Arun's was an unusual synthesis of ancient and modern technology, and was decorated with a touch of style. Italian tiles trimmed the floor, solar panels lighted his apartment, and a gas range cooked his food. Arun's cave was as convenient as Swami's was austere. Arun even had a plan to be connected globally from his Himalayan hideaway via a satellite hookup. It all seemed incongruous for a recluse, but Arun admitted he wasn't really a hermit. He had spent a decade in California, and at summer's end he would leave for Afghanistan where he would oversee the construction of a major oil pipeline.

The Source Of The Ganges

It was a flawless autumn morning as I set out in the direction of the Bhageerathi sisters, three soaring peaks that rose above the glacial fields that create the Ganges. Only one of the peaks could be seen from the lower portion of the valley where I walked. As the trail twisted and turned, more pristine peaks appeared, each one an inspiration to continue on the trail. After an hour, I had to decide whether to go on or turn back, and opted to play the role of sanyasi for the day, having nothing with me but a few of rupees in my pocket. A short distance outside Gangotri I met up with an Australian priest named John, who had taught at a Jesuit school in Bihar for thirty years. Together we moved at an easy pace, enjoying the peaks, shimmering leaves, and intoxicating air. Stands of silver birch and juniper grew in the valley, but they were at risk since firewood was still the fuel source used for cooking among sadhus.

I didn't expect to find a Jesuit hiking to the source of the Ganges, a spot revered by Hindus, and asked him if he had come for the trekking. When he first arrived in India, John had found the culture incomprehensible with its myriad gods and rituals, but as the years went by he began to appreciate the depth of spirituality in the culture and the goodness of the people. His three decades in India had given him a deeper appreciation for his own faith. He was surprised to find that many Hindus recognized Jesus as a divine personality.

We shared the trail for most of the morning, but the Jesuit looked puzzled whenever I stopped to pick an herb that grew abundantly on the side of the mountain. Himalayan tulsi (basil) is known to have therapeutic properties that make it easier to breathe at high altitudes. Its effect reminded me of eucalyptus, opening the sinuses and penetrating deep into the lungs. Nature seemed to be providing whatever was necessary to get me to the goal, but I hoped it would provide food for I would be hungry by the time we reached our destination.

We fell into a rhythm on the trail that looked down to the Ganges and up to snowy pinnacles as we ventured deeper into the valley. As I walked, I maintained my respiration by breathing in a deep, measured way and sniffed tulsi leaves from time to time. The yogis knew the secrets of conscious breathing. Some of their methods kept the cold away, others energized the body or helped it settle for meditation. Advanced yogis were said to nourish their bodies through breath alone, and didn't need much food. I would be invoking that technique myself before returning to Gangotri if no one offered me food. The yogic breath I practiced on the trail drew air in through the nose, creating a soft snoring sound in the cavity of my throat as I inhaled and exhaled. The technique was energizing, and felt like a fresh breeze passing through a cedar. River and peak, conifer and shrub fed my senses as we climbed toward the glacier in the distance, the fabled source of the Ganges. Like a ladder, the Ganges is said to be a passage to heaven.

We were not the only pilgrims on the trail. Halfway to our goal we overtook four Bombay businessmen. I had seen them arrive with their families the previous day. They seemed out of place on the trail with their dress shirts and dark slacks, but they too were sincere in their desire to reach the source of Mother Ganga. The men labored on the trail and were out of breath by the time they reached a tented chai stall where I sat with them. One of the men poked fun at their poor conditioning, but the wheezing quartet had not taken precautions against altitude sickness and shortness of breath. As they sipped their tea, barefoot women old enough to be their mothers passed them on the trail, moving at a steady pace. Everyone was friendly and I joked with these fellows who seemed anxious about their physical discomfort. When a guide showed up with a pair of mules, two of the men jumped at the chance to ride, leaving their friends behind. The two walkers considered turning back, but I encouraged them to continue despite sore feet and aching heads.

Deeper into the valley, the trail became treacherous for the inexperienced hiker. According to the guides that led mules up the valley, serious accidents had occurred on the trail. In places, landslides had erased the trail altogether, leaving me no option but to cross the slippery scree rapidly in order to avoid sliding down the mountain. Even sure-footed mules had tumbled to their death with their riders. A young girl riding a mule had gone over a cliff just a few days earlier.

The autumn weather reminded me of the Rockies after the aspens turned as gold as a Rajasthani bride's nose ring. It was late in the day when we arrived at Bhojbasa, a tiny settlement near Gomoukh where I spent the night in a cramped dormitory with a dozen European trekkers and climbers. The guesthouse had only a handful of rooms, and the Bombay businessmen were holed up in one of them. I looked in on them to see how they were doing. They were happy to see a familiar face, but the men were a pitiable sight lying there side by side on a mattress meant for two. Four swollen faces peered out from under a comforter that kept the chill away but couldn't hide their wounded pride. I asked them if they needed anything. As a single voice, they asked for tea. The pain on the faces of the two that had walked drew a sympathetic response. The foursome looked lost without their wives, who had stayed behind with the children; they had little option but to endure the altitude sickness. It had been a full day on the trail and I was also looking forward to crawling into bed.

Mount Sivling

I was the first to rise in the room full of Europeans, and set out before sunrise for Gomoukh. As the sun climbed over the peaks to the east, Mount Shivling, a magnificent pyramid of granite and snow, refracted the earliest rays of light above Gomoukh glacier. Glittering in the morning glow, I was irresistibly drawn to the peak and my mind was unable to focus as I scrambled over the rocks separating me from the source of India's holiest river. As I arrived at my destination, I was lifted higher and higher as I entered an ice palace sculpted by time and nature. The effect of the altitude, no doubt, contributed to my euphoria, and by the time I reached the river's source I was soaring.

Alone amidst the pinnacles and silver-blue stream that emerged from an oval opening at the glacier's base, I reveled in a transcendent mood. Seated on a boulder, I scanned the escarpments overhead. The amphitheater of rock and ice inspired reverence. If heaven and earth had a meeting point, I was sure this was it. I had reached the source of the Ganges, the wellspring of the Hindu faith, and I soaked up its sanctity. I thought about plunging into the freezing waters for the ultimate holy bath, but my rapture was short-lived when a boulder tumbled off a lofty crag and came crashing to the ground a few feet away. The thunderous concussion echoed from all sides, and my relaxed reverie was short-circuited. Startled by the displaced rock that had nearly crushed me, I moved closer to the sapphire stream to watch the chunks of ice as they floated past. I reached down to test the water and realized the foolishness of my plan for a bath. As I peered into the oval opening called Gomoukh at the base of the glacier, a massive block of ice broke off and plunged into the stream, sending a wave washing over my shoes. The pristine atmosphere was unpredictable, and my thoughts reflected that uncertainty. After christening myself with the holy water, I retreated.

Gomoukh (Cow's Mouth)

Lunch With A Yogi

As I climbed out of the glacier region, the gnawing emptiness in my stomach begged attention. I had not eaten a proper meal for thirty-six hours and was beginning to question the wisdom of approximating a mendicant's life, if only for a day. As I retraced my steps to Bhojbasa, suddenly, out of nowhere, a sadhu appeared on a rock above me wearing nothing but a loincloth. His matted hair, beard, and nakedness gave him the appearance of a madman as he stood there on the boulder waving his arms at me wildly. But when I drew close enough to see his eyes, I knew he was anything but crazy. His face was serene; his eyes clear like glacial pools. He gestured for me to join him in his hut and I followed him into his rough abode. He didn't speak, but motioned for me to sit near the fire. Silence seemed to go with the territory.

His slender hands moved efficiently as he prepared tea and leafy greens. The chill mountain air made the warm drink appealing. The fire swelled and crackled as the hermit blew into it through a flutelike tube. After chai, my host served a tasty bowl of sag subji, seasoned with a pinch of salt. I was fortunate to be the guest of the recluse, as I had only a coin or two in my pocket. After eating, we sat for a time, enjoying one another's silent company. The sadhu had wrapped himself in a coarse blanket that gave him a prehistoric look, but there was nothing primitive about his crystalline eyes. I felt an affinity with this kind soul who had shared his simple meal with me, and as I departed I bowed to him and placed the coins in my pocket on the stone altar outside before setting out for Gangotri. Years later, while browsing in a Delhi bookstore, I came upon some pictures of a Himalayan yogi in a coffee table publication by an Italian photographer. When I looked more closely I recognized the ascetic who had fed me at Gomoukh. His name was Swami Bhalawan and he was a Hatha yogi.

Doon Boys

The trek down the mountain was easy. The Ganges gurgled, rushed, and sometimes roared as it sped past boulders that had fallen into its path during landslides. Before long, I overtook a group of schoolboys. One of the boys started up a conversation as we walked. Although I had been enjoying an introverted walk, I welcomed the company. Mukesh and his classmates were from Doon School, India's most prestigious prep school where Prime Ministers and captains of industry had studied over the decades. The teenagers were on a camping trip, but the boys were unused to the cumbersome equipment strapped to their backs. They looked weary and in need of a warm bath and a good meal.

Mukesh wanted to know why I was visiting Gomoukh, and seemed as surprised to see me, as I had been to find the Jesuit, John, making a pilgrimage to the source of the Ganges. His class had come for nature study, and they had chosen an idyllic place for their assignment. After we had walked together for almost an hour, Mukesh asked me what I thought about Hinduism, but before I could respond, he asked a second question. "There are so many gods," he complained, "How do I know who to worship?"

"Worship the one closest to your heart," were the words that stumbled out of my mouth. Mukesh seemed satisfied with the answer, but I could see he was thinking as we walked. The hermit's greens had helped, but my hunger was stronger than ever. I was prepared not to eat before reaching Gangotri. After all, I had begun the trek in the spirit of renunciation. The boys stopped to have lunch on the trail and I wished them luck as I headed off. As I passed the headmaster he invited me to share their meal. I gladly accepted the offer and sat with the schoolboys on the rocks near the Ganges, enjoying cheese sandwiches and chocolate bars. Their spirits buoyed by the meal, the boys were smiling again, and I continued walking with them for the next few miles. It astonished me that thousands of wandering sadhus walked these mountain trails without any idea where their next meal would come from, or where they would rest for the night. Since running out of rupees I had been the recipient of unexpected hospitality twice. Maybe this is how those who renounce worldliness are looked after, I thought.

When I reached the last tea stall before Gangotri, I stopped to rest. The clever owner was drumming up business and tried to coax me into spending the night in his stall. He warned of bears on the trail, but I was too famished to spend another night on the trail. And I was penniless.

Sitting on a bench across from me was a British fellow who was also trekking alone. I struck up a conversation with the man who was a professional photographer, and while he ate, he told a traumatic tale. He had been on a Himalayan photo shoot and was hiking on a trail like the one leading to Gomoukh when a team of pack mules approached from the opposite direction. Somehow the mules managed to pass between him and the mountain, a mistake that nearly cost him his life.

The first mule made it past him all right but the second mule had a wider load, which knocked the Brit off balance, forcing him over the cliff. As he was falling, he flailed wildly in the air, groping for something to grab hold of. He was sure it was the end when, at the last second, his hand latched onto a rope dangling from the mule. He held on with all his might, hoping his weight wouldn't pull the animal over the cliff with him. The mule held its ground and the photographer pulled himself back onto the trail. As he told the story, his face tensed and his voice constricted, and I felt the fright in his heart jump into mine as he talked. It was a good reminder to always lean against the mountain when animals passed, unless of course, one encountered a Himalayan black bear.

The forces of nature in the Himalaya are not to be taken lightly. One spring, after our third visit to Gangotri, a huge section of ice broke away from Gomoukh glacier and made its way down the mountain before becoming wedged in a narrow part of the valley, causing the river to dam up. When the ice thawed enough to dislodge itself, a massive wall of water rushed down the valley sweeping away everything in its path, including the hermits that lived along the banks of the river above Gangotri. None of our friends were lost in the tragedy, but I often wondered how Swami and Maharaj survived the whims of winter.

The King Of Nepal Honors Maharaj

Maharaj was away when we stopped by to see him, but Vishwanath was sitting by the fire. Maharaj's chela was obviously well educated. He spoke fluent English and had plenty to say when his master was away. Vishwanath invited us to sit while we waited for Maharaj to return. In the presence of Maharaj, Vishwanath only spoke when translating, but now he seemed eager to talk. I asked him about the tiger skin that Maharaj had been sitting on the day I found him covered in vibhuti.

Vishwanath said Maharaj had not spent the previous winter in Gangotri. He had gone wandering, leaving Vishwanath behind. According to Vishwanath, Gangotri winters were extreme with 10-15 feet of snow everywhere and frigid temperatures that even the best fire couldn't counter. Only nine sadhus stayed year-round and those included Swami Paranand Tirth, Swami Bhalawan, and a handful of other ascetics we had met. Vishwanath performed all the household chores for Maharaj: cooking, cleaning, and gathering kindling. When Maharaj returned in the spring he had the tiger skin with him. It had been a gift from the King of Nepal.

I asked Vishwanath how it happened that Maharaj had received such a gift from the King of Nepal. Maharaj had gone to Orissa to attend a convention of sadhus. Tens of thousands of wandering monks had congregated in Puri along with the guest of honor, the King of Nepal, who was visiting Orissa at the time. The King, whose royal hunting reserve is home to leopard, deer, and tigers, had brought a stack of skins with him to give to the sadhus, because Indian holy men believe certain animal skins enhance their spiritual power when they sit on them. The king had walked through the throng of monks, handing out skins as he went. A tiger skin is rare and much coveted by sadhus. He had just one, and he saved it for last. After passing many sadhus, the king came to Maharaj, and placed it in his hands. From the telling of the story, it was obvious that Vishwanath was extremely proud of his master.

The Blind Baba

Maharaj didn't return that afternoon, so we went up the trail to visit the Ram temple I had passed on the way to Gomoukh. The Ram temple had a welcoming air about it. Saffron flags fluttered in the breeze atop the entryway as Lane and I entered the complex, which included simple accommodations for the staff. After silently exploring the property nestled at the edge of a precipice above the river, Lane disappeared through a wood doorframe while I leaned against a pillar in the sunlit courtyard.

A few minutes later Lane reappeared, saying, "There's an old baba inside. I went in and sat in front of him. When the baba spoke I could see that he was blind. In a loud voice, he said, 'please join me, but bring your friend who is outside in the courtyard.'" It puzzled Lane that the Baba knew he was not alone.

Lane and I entered the room together and sat in front of the baba, who was bent with age. Ram Baba, must have been eighty years old. His cataract clouded eyes stared at the wall above us as he inquired who we were and what country we came from. It pleased him that foreigners were interested in a far-off place like Gangotri, and he offered us prasad as he told us the story of how he came to live in this remote region of the Himalaya.

As a boy, Ram Baba had seen the ascetics wandering through his village and wanted to join one. One day he decided to leave home and so he walked along the Ganges until he reached Gangotri. When he reached the Ram temple, he found an old recluse living there alone. Ram Baba was fascinated by the holy man and stayed with him for a few days. He began helping out, doing simple chores like fetching water and washing the old man's cloth.

After a few weeks, Ram Baba asked the holy man if he would accept him as his disciple, but the old renunciate refused him. Ram Baba persisted and again approached the old man with the request that he be allowed to serve the man as his disciple. Again the old man refused him. By now Ram Baba was feeling desperate, and said, "Guruji, if you will not accept me as your disciple then I will throw myself from the cliff into the Ganges." Now the old man was faced with a dilemma, for he was wise and felt the intense conviction of the youngster and so he allowed the boy to stay on the condition that he agree never to leave this holy place. Without hesitation, the boy agreed.

Ram Baba honored his master's request by spending seventy years on the banks of the Ganges, enduring Himalayan storms that buried the valley in snow and summer monsoons that swelled the river beyond its banks. Even after Ram Baba lost his eyesight he continued his sadhana at the temple. When we met the kindly old man he was nearing the end of his life, but I'm sure he had no regrets about his decision never to leave the Valley of the Saints.

Goodbyes

Our days in Gangotri were as carefree as the hermits we met. We had made friends with a number of local holy men, and when not meditating or hiking, we sat with them by the fire. Before departing for Delhi, we dropped by Maharaj's hut to say goodbye. Having heard Vishwanath's stories of the hardships they endured during the long winters, we brought some supplies to help get them through the winter. We also hauled a large block of firewood to his camp. Maharaj was amused by the piece of wood that we strained to lift. Before we departed, Maharaj reminded us that we should take a cave in Gangotri, but I was quite sure I wasn't ready to sit on a tiger skin covered in ash.

After seeing Maharaj, I went to Swami's cave. Swami's sentimental response to our departure surprised me since those who take vows of renunciation are expected to be indifferent. Before parting, he scribbled a final note on his pad, "All those who meditate are connected in a subtle way. Anyone doing meditation can transfer bliss to another on that level. We are connected through the subtle currents of consciousness." I was touched by his words, and some months later I had a vision of Swami in his Gangotri hideaway, and knew that he was well.

After visiting Swami I ran into Arun who was wielding an axe outside his cave. When I told him we were leaving, he thought for a minute, and said, "You will be passing through Uttar Kashi. If you want to meet the last mahatma (great soul) in the Valley of the Saints, go to room 23 at Kailash ashram. There you'll find Hansa Swami who lived in Swami's cave for 37 years. He is 109 years old and not in good health. Bring him mangoes, its his favorite food, and tell him Arun sent you." I thanked Arun for the tip and wished him well on his project in Afghanistan, where he planned to spend the next three years.

The Last Of The Living Saints

We arrived at Kailash Ashram with enough mangoes to feed a bevy of monks, but the fruits were gifts for Hansa Swami. Infirm health had forced Hansa Swami to abandon his Gangotri cave for a modest room near the Ganges where a senior disciple looked after him. When Lane and I entered his room, we found the revered old saint sitting on his bed, giving guidance to a couple that sat at his feet. Shortly after we arrived, the couple departed, and the old swami turned his attention to us. His articulate English surprised me as he praised us for making the pilgrimage into the Himalaya. He repeated many times, "I wish you moksha (enlightenment) and all blessings of the Himalaya." The meaning of the words went deep into my heart. His method of darshan was to look deeply into one's eyes, and his awareness seemed to pass right out the back of the head of the person he looked at. I watched as he interacted with Lane, whom he obviously liked from the moment we entered the room. Lane sat on the floor at his feet, soaking up Hansa Swami's kindness. When his powerful gaze shifted to me, I found it difficult to speak, so I simply stared back. Despite his infirmity, I found his eyes penetrating, his darshan commanding.

After blessing us generously, he announced, "I take leave." We interpreted the message to mean that it was time for us to go, so we touched his feet and backed out of the room, hands pressed together. Outside, Lane and I sat side by side on a bench, watching the Ganges flutter past for a long time. We were both unable to speak. When we finally emerged from our silent reverie, we giggled like children. Swami was extremely fortunate to have had such an enlightened guru. After sitting with Hansa Swami, I better understood one of the messages Swami wrote outside his cave; "The guru is the embodiment of spiritual power. He can transfer spiritual blessings by simply seeing you." Not long after our visit, we heard the news that Hansa Swami had left his body.

Ananda Mayi Ma encouraged people to be around saints whenever possible. She said, "A saint is like a tree. He does not call anyone; neither does he send anyone away. He gives shelter to whoever cares to come, be it a man, woman, child, or an animal. If you sit under a tree it will protect you from the scorching sun as well as the pouring rain, and it will give you flowers and fruit. By sitting under a tree you will get shelter, shade, flowers, fruit, and in due course you will come to know your Self." Great gurus are givers. They expect nothing in return. Knowledge flows from a true guru like Ganges water. The guru's holy current purifies everything in its path and helps things grow to their fullest. One can always recognize a guru by their capacity to give.

The Ganges, the celestial river that is said to fall from heaven, had been our refuge for a fortnight, and I had felt its purifying authority when bathing in its waters, meditating on its banks, and sitting with those who lived near it. Yogis have always known the secrets of sacred water. The relationship between monk and river is one that has existed throughout the ages. As outrageous as it sounded at the time, maybe Maharaj was right, maybe we should take a cave by the banks of the Ganges to prepare for our enlightenment, even it wasn't to come until next lifetime.

TWELVE

Kolkata's Children

Before I built a wall I'd ask to know
What I was walling in or walling out,
And to whom I was like to give offence.
Something there is that doesn't love a wall.

—*Robert Frost*

Although Maharaj was serious about our move to Gangotri, the prospect of retiring to a Himalayan cave was sheer fantasy, at least for the time being. Calcutta was to be our home for much of the spring. A uniformed driver collected us at Dum Dum airport and whisked us off to our guesthouse in south Calcutta. Sadly, the city looked even more afflicted than I remembered. A dense gray lid hung over Calcutta, trapping its inhabitants in a container of stale, suffocating air. The effects of the noxious cloud were reflected in the drawn forms shuffling listlessly along the cluttered streets. On our way we passed a stagnant pool emitting a stench that closed windows couldn't hold out. I wondered if some sort of preternatural urban ogre hadn't devoured the refuse in the area, and, suffering the ill effects of its gluttony, belched up the appalling odor.

The unsavory sights and smells along the road were enough to dampen anyone's psychology, and so I fortified myself with a story I had heard Maharishi tell. There was a saint who had a reputation for seeing the good in everything. One day, a cynical man wanted to test the saint's cheery disposition and led him down an alleyway where they came upon a dead dog. As they passed the offensive scene, the man pointed to the animal, saying, "Mahatma, how awful that looks," to which the blissful saint replied, "But see the pearly white teeth, how beautiful and shining." As we drove through the city, I was glad I had been trained to see the pearly white teeth.

It was a powerful technique for happiness. Ananda Mayi Ma instructed her devotees to accept both good and bad with equanimity. She said, "Keep your thinking on a very high level; praise and blame, filth and sandal paste must become alike. Nothing in the world should be repulsive to you."

Turning into the tree-lined cul-de-sac off Bollygunge Circular Road we escaped Calcutta's decrepit facade. A pair of security guards eyed us suspiciously at the barricade blocking the street before allowing us into the posh residential enclave. Once inside, we were stopped at a second security checkpoint, the gated entrance to an impressive estate. As our car entered the driveway, white-jacketed staff gathered under a vine-covered portico to receive us. A uniformed attendant pulled open the car door and escorted us into what was to be our Calcutta home for many weeks.

Two Englishmen living in India founded The Williamson-Mager Group in 1869. Over time, the company prospered, weathering the vicissitudes of international markets to become a major tea producer. When the British were forced out of India, the B.M. Khaitan family purchased Williamson-Mager and continued to build on the company's tradition of producing world-class teas. The company now owns fifty-four gardens in the Himalayan foothills around Darjeeling, along the southern border of Bhutan, and in the fertile Brahmaputra valley in Assam, making the company the largest private tea producer in the world.

We had been invited to Calcutta to instruct Williamson-Mager's management in the art of meditation, and the spacious mansion where we would be staying was the former residence of the Khaitan family. The antechamber of the master bedroom alone was larger than the room I had shared with Packs at Maharishi Nagar. My balcony overlooked a spray of blossoming bushes and citrus trees bordering a manicured lawn. I had not even opened my bag when a young Assamese bearer knocked on my door with a platter of fruit and cookies. Out of habit, I tested the mattress, but such concerns were uncalled for in this palace. This was, after all, not a roadside motel. Were we really in infamous Calcutta, I wondered, or had our driver magically transported us to some idyllic Shangri-La? As Chandra adjusted the air conditioner, I thought how Delhi, which we had dubbed 'Oven on Earth,' was already heating up in anticipation of summer.

Dinner for two served at a table for sixteen required getting used to. The guesthouse staff, 'the boys' we called them, shuttled one delicious dish after another into the dining room. We quickly grew accustomed to having meals served over our shoulders and were pampered by turned bedcovers, room service, and chauffeured cars. The staff readily grasped the nuances of our lifestyle, something Mr. C never could have done. The freezer was kept full of ice cream and the cook knew exactly how Lane liked his chocolate sauce. Chandra brought fresh coconut water and mangoes to our rooms without being asked, noted our preference in newspapers, and looked after us in a dozen other ways. The guesthouse remained our private palace for the duration of our stay in Calcutta. As time went by, I began to wonder how I would fare when the time came to return to Maharishi Nagar. A friend who had grown up with domestic help once confided that it was easier adapting to servants than doing without them, having become accustomed to convenience.

Of the Indian cities we had visited, we were treated like kings in Calcutta, but our coddled lifestyle came unsolicited. We lived in perhaps the most exclusive part of the city. A neighbor across the street employed a servant to polish his mint condition Rolls Royce and sporty XKE. On Sundays, the vehicles were driven to one of Calcutta's ritzy clubs, but I couldn't imagine being chauffeured through the streets of Calcutta in such luxury. In the distance, beyond the protective walls of our home, the hum of humanity went on day and night. Even our meditation seminars were held in the living room of our residence, so we rarely went out. The tea managers talked enthusiastically about their benefits, reporting better relations at work as well as improved golf games.

On days when we ventured beyond our fortified enclave, we witnessed humanity on the edge. On the streets beyond our Eden, gaunt figures stepped around the homeless who slept on threadbare blankets or less. Decrepit buildings in need of more than paint appeared on the verge of collapse. The infusion of new energy, resources, and vision that every great city requires never arrived in Calcutta; its debilitated condition was the result of decades of municipal neglect. Layers of faded handbills defaced public walls, giving them a papier-mache look. Crumbling walls bore faded hammer and sickle logos, and smelled of decay. Partitions guarded properties everywhere, preventing squatters from moving in. The negligence that littered Calcutta was as much a symbol of failed socialist governments as were the washed out Maoist icons stenciled on the city's walls.

Golf In The Kingdom Of The Rajas

The privileged belonged to swanky private clubs scattered around South Calcutta. Spacious cricket fields, manicured lawn tennis clubs, upper-crust social clubs, and two of the oldest golf clubs outside the British Isles provided sanctuaries for Calcutta's moneyed residents. One particularly lush playground was Tollygunge Club, a golf and tennis club built by the

British, who once frolicked on the former Indigo plantation turned golf club. Tolly, as the locals call it, is a watered oasis of tree lined fairways, equestrian trails, swimming pools, tennis courts, and guest lodging; a recreational utopia capable of boosting the spirit when life outside its walls became oppressive. The two-hundred-year-old clubhouse stood elegantly among flowering magnolia trees. The property's previous owner, the exiled Muslim ruler Tippu Sultan, turned his private paradise into a royal park that included fifty species of trees imported from far off places like Australia and South America. The abundant flora, in turn, attracted exotic species of birds, adding music to Tolly's playfields and neutralizing the drone of the city outside. At the invitation of our hosts, it was not long before we were going to Tolly regularly.

As a boy, I had read a story in a golf magazine about a professional tournament held in India. The article described how an American had found his ball in the tall grass with a cobra coiled around it. When he approached it, the deadly snake flared up, ready to strike. With the help of his Indian caddy, he managed to remove the intruder without injuring reptile, caddy, or player. Tolly's layout was narrow, but not unreasonable if one had the skill to maneuver shots between the overhang of eucalyptus and magnolia trees. After a round or two the course played rather benignly, despite rented clubs, tennis sneakers, and the imagined threat of snakes lurking in the rough.

One afternoon I met a tall, handsome Bengali named Arjun, one of the pros at Tolly. I liked Arjun's easygoing manner, and suspected his golf game matched his disposition. We decided to play a round together. Arjun and my caddy Durga were waiting for me at the first tee on a languid morning when the sun blazed bright and hot above the city.

I imagined Arjun would want some incentive so I suggested we wager one hundred rupees. In reality, the bet would be his wages for the day, a trick I learned while teaching tennis in Europe. My students liked playing against the pro, and if they managed to win a game, the session was free; otherwise they paid the going rate. It made things interesting for everyone. Arjun liked the idea and offered me a handicap. I was delighted to be teeing off with a skilled partner, and I planned to give the young pro the rupees even if I managed to come out on top.

Vibrant shades of olive and emerald garnished with yellow blossoms flanked the fairways. Hidden in the lush foliage were songbirds warbling without a care in the world. From years of sporting experience, it didn't take much to put my mind into a focused flow, a meditative zone that athletes, both amateur and professional, pursue religiously. The game of golf itself is a meditation when approached with a measure of openness and reverence. Arjun played effortlessly, coasting around the front nine a stroke over par and appeared to be the one in the competitive zone. Watching my handsome playing partner stride fluidly down the fairway, I was witnessing a man at the peak of his physical prowess, a competitor who looked as much like a Greek god as he did an Olympic athlete. My play, bolstered by a couple of handicap strokes, kept me close on his heels, but still I felt more like Arjun's caddy than his playing partner.

Arjun had a classic caddy's swing, but despite the self-taught technique, his coiled and coordinated moves generated towering shots that soared above the tree line, bending gracefully to distant targets. On the back nine, with the sun scorching anything not sheltered by the stately trees, the silver spoon that I had enjoyed since arriving in Calcutta suddenly dropped out. Fate shifted slightly and the graceful game became as venomous as a coiled cobra in tall grass. The first indication of impending doom came when my approach shot splashed into a pond fronting the twelfth green. As Durga handed me a fresh ball, Arjun pointed to a shirtless fellow sitting under a tree.

"For five 'bucks' (rupees) that guy will fetch your ball," Arjun said.

"How will he do that?" I asked incredulously. My ball had found a watery grave. I had never heard of anything like that before.

"Watch!" Arjun signaled ahead to the fellow, who waded into water up to his chest in search of my ball. While we waited, Arjun and I chatted.

"Arjun, how did you get started?" I had an inkling how it happened, but wanted to hear his story.

"I started coming to Tolly with my brother when I was small. Our family lived in a nearby tenement. We began as pickers (ball collectors) on the range, and later I got a bag (became a caddy)."

"Did you learn the game by imitating good players the way caddies do?"

"More or less. The club pro let me practice on the range sometimes; the caddies were only allowed on the course when the members were finished." A kid from the ghetto, Tolly had been Arjun's finishing school. The Queen's English flowed from his lips as gracefully as his powerful swing sent shot after shot soaring above the shade trees and water hazards that harassed mine. Arjun possessed the poise and polish of a Cambridge graduate although I was certain he never finished high school.

"Do you have a family?"

"Two children."

By now the attendant had retrieved my ball. No other club in the world provided this kind of service. Scuba divers scoured the lake bottoms of American courses, reselling the balls they found. But this was India, the land where cobras claimed errant shots and special attendants waded into murky water, employing nimble footwork to find lost balls. The man promptly delivered my ball to Durga. The entire process took just a minute or two, and cost me ten cents, a fraction of the cost of a new Titleist.

The next hole had a boundary wall running along the right side. As usual, Arjun struck his ball high into the azure sky, leaving an iron to the par five green. My drive was nearly as good, my best of the day. It ended up in the fairway a few meters inside the wall. As Arjun and I walked to our balls, I vaguely noticed a figure slip onto the fairway before disappearing again into the shadows. When I reached my ball it was nowhere in sight. I had watched it arc close to the boundary before drawing safely onto the short grass. Durga and I searched in vain. Then I saw him; a ghost of a man squatting on top of the wall, golf ball in hand.

Durga and I stared accusingly at him; my caddy became angered by his conversation with the man, but I couldn't understand a word of it and Durga was unable to tell me what he found out. Meanwhile, the guy on the wall kept muttering, 'Sahib, Ball OB, Ball OB, Das (ten) Rupees Sir, Ball OB' (ball out of bounds). I understood what he was saying and protested in my best Hindi. I gestured to the ball burglar that I wanted my ball back, but he stuck to his line, "Ball OB, Das Rupees Sir." I was in no mood to be blackmailed, and refused to pay for the theft of a well-placed drive. In mock anger, I waved my club at him and the thief panicked, probably the result of having been attacked by other indignant victims. As mysteriously as he had appeared, he vanished, having dropped to the ground outside the boundary wall.

The bizarre intrusion was over as abruptly as it had begun and I was left standing, assault weapon in hand. Durga replaced the stolen ball, but I had no idea what the rulebook had to say about a stolen ball. In frustration, I swung at the helpless white sphere at my feet, sending it high into the air and onto the putting surface, only to lose yet another hole to Arjun who made an easy birdie.

The combined effects of the larceny and an afternoon sun that bore relentlessly down on me, left me depleted, so I turned to Durga who failed to produce a bottle of mineral water. Instead, he wandered off while I played my shot. I was fading fast and needed some liquid for the finishing holes. Durga soon caught up with me and handed me the water bottle. Feeling the effects of dehydration, I was about to drain the liter when a voice inside my head whispered, 'stop.' I pulled the bottle away from my mouth, and held it up to the sunlight to have a look at its contents. The water was foggy and sedimentation floated about.

"Bhaiya (brother), where did this water come from?" I asked Durga, hoping he would understand.

Durga obediently pointed to a hose that was leaking water profusely. Had I drunk a liter of Calcutta's non-potable water, I would have swallowed enough disease to put me in intensive care or worse, as even Calcutta's treated water was unsafe for a westerner. Irrigation water was drawn directly from one of the city's woefully polluted rivers. I could hardly blame my caddy for the miscue. He was only trying to help. Fortunately, Arjun came to my rescue, and handed me a sealed bottle from his bag. It was a close call and I dreaded the thought of what would have happened had I drunk the tainted contents.

Einstein himself couldn't have calculated the odds of having a golf ball stolen and the close encounter with contaminated water on consecutive holes. Clearly, the lords of karma were in a payback mood on the back nine and my mind rapidly shifted to red alert. My stroll through Tolly's luxuriant flora and fauna had become a labored march. Long shadows now extended across the fairways as sprinklers sprayed the lawn behind us. We were the only golfers on the course, but we were not the only ones playing.

I had observed the boys on other days, but today they were out in unusual numbers, chasing soccer balls up and down the vacant fairways. Fifty barefoot urchins clad in soiled shorts laughed and screamed at each other as they raced about, having the time of their young lives. I was astounded that club management allowed the boys on the course; most clubs would have run the intruders off. But the exuberant kids charged about as if the impassable barriers to privilege were no impediment to their innocent fun. The walls that protected the venerable old club, and every other private property in the city were impenetrable. Calcutta's classes were distinct, the disparity titanic, but whatever tension existed between club members and these slum kids was not evident at the moment.

"Arjun, did you sneak onto the course when you were their age?"

With a wry smile, he answered, "yes and no. I did, but once I was allowed to caddy, I stopped. I separated myself from the others."

"Do you know these kids? Are they from your neighborhood?"

"I know most of their families. They are poor kids. Their fathers are rikshaw drivers and laborers. Good people, but poor." Arjun spoke to a couple of the boys who clearly admired their 'older brother.'

The neighborhoods surrounding Tolly had many crude shelters where families lived in difficult conditions. For the moment, the boys had escaped their hand to mouth existence by scrambling over the wall for some fun. Arjun himself now lived in a middle class flat thanks to his job at the club.

I was enjoying the contest again. As Arjun and I stepped onto the tee, the boys gathered around to watch us tee off. The boys, knowing that their presence was tenuous, became as silent as spectators at the British Open. Some of them lay on the ground while others kneeled or stood in the back. Our target was small; a marshy pond lurked to the left and another boundary wall ran along the right side of the fairway. I scanned the wall, but no ball burglar waited. Arjun played first, and cracked his patented fade safely onto the fairway, drawing a pitter-patter of applause from the boys. I found the gesture charming.

Now it was my turn. I had played sports in packed stadiums, but the ragtag group assembled around the tee made me uneasy. Somehow, when a crowd is hushed, it's even quieter than when no one is present at all. Calming myself, I struck a solid shot that arrived near Arjun's ball, despite having followed a different flight pattern. As I reached down to collect my tee the applause of the peanut gallery felt especially sweet. But I wasn't prepared for the response of one smudge-faced boy kneeling on the grass. As I picked up my tee, he chirped, "Lovely shot" with the cultured accent of an urbane Oxford professor. All bets were off as I fell to the ground, doubled over in laughter. P.G. Wodehouse couldn't have timed a better response. Seeing my reaction, the others joined us in a chorus of merriment, dancing about and parroting 'lovely shot' to one another. Even Arjun and Durga burst out laughing. When I finally recovered, the Oxford urchin gave me a casual 'high five,' and again I nearly collapsed in a spasm of hilarity. Before I knew it, every last kid was lined up to take his turn sharing 'high fives' with the foreigner. It was a moment that has far outlived the friendly competition in my memory. In the twinkling of an eye, I felt a kinship with those Calcutta kids who knew nothing of class and cultural barriers. From that day, the fun loving soccer boys were as much a part of my Tolly experience as the members who paid to be there.

The match ended with Arjun the victor, but as often happens in sports, the seeds of friendship had been sewn, and not just with Arjun, for every time I passed the soccer kids in the coming weeks, they hooted and waved, and shouted 'lovely shot.'

Slum kids have few opportunities compared to other children and Arjun was fortunate to have seized his chance. But given opportunity, underprivileged children will surprise you. In an experiment conducted by NIIT, India's top computer literacy institute, the head of research placed a computer in a city slum, recessing it into a boundary wall. The executive also placed a hidden camera in a tree to observe the computer and its users. Within days, illiterate youth were surfing the Net, and soon they were creating folders, playing computer games, and downloading their favorite Hindi tunes. A digital paint site was popular with the users. The kids, who had never held a pen or used a sheet of art paper, were drawing for the first time. The average age of the children was six to twelve.

India was an ongoing odyssey into the unexpected, and that was part of the reason I loved it so much. After all, I was not wired for a nine to five job. An innocuous game contested on a manicured lawn became fraught with intrigue and peril, and fun. As with every other aspect of life in this ancient land, a round of golf in the kingdom turned an ordinary afternoon into compelling drama. In the scented evening air of our guesthouse patio, perspective coalesced. I had condemned the thief without knowing the circumstances that had provoked his desperate act. The fellow was obviously destitute, and the sale of a golf ball might feed his family for several days. The man's act may have been the noble deed, and mine a misguided response. The din outside the walls of our idyllic world reminded me that the struggle for survival went on around the clock in this inscrutable metropolis.

The incessant commotion of the city overwhelmed me sometimes. On days when more than a round of golf or game of doubles was needed, I sought refuge in the countryside. One day I visited an old Kali shrine outside Calcutta in the middle of a mango grove. After carving up as many golden mangoes at I could consume, I paused to listen to the quiet, realizing that it had been weeks since there hadn't been noise in the background. There was something about an Indian countryside anywhere on the subcontinent, which felt welcoming. I was sitting alone on the hardened earth among rows of fruit-laden trees when I became aware of the deep spiritual undercurrent that reverberates through the very ground of India like the continuous hum of a great mantra. I realized that this sound was what distinguished India's soil from other countries. All the many times I'd walked in virgin forests and remote mountain regions in other parts of the world, I had never encountered such a quality in the land itself. It came out of the earth, pulling my awareness within. Could this be why India has always had such a strong spiritual tradition and why whenever I arrived from the West, I was inclined to touch the ground and inhale its strong smells? Just being conscious of it as I sat there was like a dive into deep meditation. As I probed more deeply, I became aware that the subtle sound was not exclusive to the spot where I sat, but actually spread far in all directions, which may explain why India is often referred to as Ved Bhumi, the Land of the Veda. Spirituality resided in the land itself.

Princes And Paupers

Meditation classes convened each morning in our living room, and our Calcutta friends took their new practice seriously. The Khaitan family seemed to have a Midas touch at everything they did, from tea growing to competitive golf to philanthropic service. Meditation was their newest undertaking and before long we were conducting courses in the homes of their industrialist friends around the city. The first family of tea had not only developed the largest private tea enterprise in the world, they were also the first family of Calcutta golf. The Calcutta tea growers association held an annual competition, a tradition established when the East India Company presided over the city's trade two hundred years ago. The Khaitan team had recently won the competition and was celebrating at Royal Calcutta Golf Club.

We passed through the wrought iron gates of India's most exclusive club, congregating on the lawns of the oldest golf club outside Great Britain. Royal Calcutta's handsome Tudor clubhouse was erected in 1829, and its walls showcased sepia photos of its early members. The collection of photos was a virtual caricature of the stiff, bearded Brits wearing starched shirts and knickers, and wielding hickory-shafted clubs. The pale Europeans would have looked absurd enough on the streets of Calcutta without their peculiar golf outfits adding to their oddness. Our invitation to RCGC was not an invitation to play golf, but to celebrate it. As a rule, we avoided large social gatherings; they simply didn't fit into our lifestyle. But the Khaitans were princely hosts, and we were honored to attend the function; our primary purpose, of course, being dinner.

Sumptuous spreads overflowed tables around a pool area decorated with ice statues that slowly disappeared as the evening passed. Spectacular tropical bouquets were on display in the dining rooms. White-jacketed staff put the finishing touches on steaming dishes and dispensed ice cream from sterling buckets. We made multiple passes at the spread, picking and choosing among the elegant fare, avoiding dishes evidencing chilies and flesh. The early hours of the party included grandparents who circumspect-ly guided toddlers to and from the buffet, seemingly overwhelmed by the lavishness of the affair. The Gandhi generation did not easily embrace extravagance.

Speeches were made, toasts proposed, and trophies awarded. Following the presentations, the very old and very young toddled off to bed as a glossy Bombay band took the stage. Their hybrid beat would have raised some bushy eyebrows had the starched Scots on the club's mahogany walls come back to life. The high decibel music spun my head in circles. We had missed our cue by not slipping out with the elderly and the kids.

Indians love their music, and everyone else's too. They have a knack for fusion, artfully blending sounds and cultures, whether Punjabi masala, Jamaican reggae, or Motown soul. They also love to dance. Indian culture, as reflected in its cinema, identifies intimately with music and dance. I can't remember a Bollywood film without choreographed interludes involving scores of talented dancers whirling about while heroes and heroines enticed one another with suggestive gyrations. The RCGC crowd was starting to shake. It was time to retire.

Our vehicle moved through the iron gates and past a canvas shelter pitched within range of the party's throbbing sound system. A fire licked the bottom of a pot illumining two contracted faces focused intently on the contents of the charred vessel. Their meal in all probability would be a bowl of watery lentils with vegetable scraps and chapatis. The couple would have barely enough, if they had that. We, on the other hand, had recklessly discarded what would have been a feast for most of Calcutta. The Hindu faith considers it a great sin to waste food, and I now felt uneasy about our transgression. How many would go to sleep without a proper meal? The firelight scene awakened me from my negligence, for I was seeing clearly again. Inexplicable moments of lucidity came unpredictably when a misty veil lifted like curtains on a play. At times the windows of perception revealed life as substandard to the soul's dignity. Both sides of the wall staged surreal dramas. Was hardship any more real than opulence, I wondered? The pair of opposites, pleasure and pain, alternated endlessly like a pendulum, and I was committed to anchoring myself at the still point between them.

Kalighat

On one our infrequent outings, we instructed our driver to drop us in front of a row of stalls in the heart of the old city. Marigold and hibiscus garlands hung from the corrugated awnings that protected the delicate inventory from sun and monsoon. Beneath the strings of flowers, straw baskets full of blossoms were on display. Before entering the narrow lane leading to an old shrine, we purchased a handful of crimson hibiscus.

Tentatively, we stepped onto the path leading to Kalighat, the two hundred year old temple from which the anglicized name Calcutta is derived. Indian cities were reconnecting with their roots, and Calcutta had reclaimed its former name, Kolkata.

It was night, the perfect time to pay homage to the Mother of Kalighat. As we entered the dark alley, we passed an open door to a room crowded by a sea of cots that gave the impression of a single floating mattress. Young women in white garments moved about like guardian angels administering care and compassion to those too weak to move. The modest facility was Nirmal Hriday (Place of Pure Heart), a part of Mother Theresa's broad network of charitable services that extend assistance to Calcutta's destitute and dying. The facility came about as the result of a visit Mother Theresa made to Calcutta's town hall one day.

Mother Theresa was already in the habit of caring for the poorest of Calcutta when she came upon an unconscious woman lying by the side of the street outside one of the city's crowded hospitals. She carried the woman into the hospital and asked that the woman be looked after, but her condition was beyond treatment and the hospital refused to take her. Finding many more homeless in the throes of death on the streets, Mother Theresa appealed to the city health department to provide her space in an empty building. Nirmal Hriday became Calcutta's first hospice where 40,000 destitute individuals have been cared for since it's opening.

Mother Theresa and Kali-Ma, although icons of different faiths, served side by side at Kalighat. Kali's urban abode is confined to a cramped tract hemmed in by ageing neighborhoods and crowded markets, but the temple is a sacred heart pumping spiritual life into a metropolis in the throes of cardiac arrest. A branch of the Ganges once flowed beside the temple, but with the acute demand for water, the artery has long since dried up, except during monsoon.

Kalighat predates Calcutta. Centuries ago, the dense, marshy jungles separating the finger channels of the Ganges concealed a place of pilgrimage visited by Bengali villagers. Set amidst thick, tangled vegetation and swamplands inhabited by tigers and crocodiles, a simple shrine to the black goddess was erected after a devotee discovered a brilliant light emanating from a riverbed. A peculiar carved stone was determined to be the source of the light, and so a shrine was built around it. A narrow path through the jungle was the only trail leading to the place of worship. As the jungle was cleared and a metropolis grew up around it, the secret shrine became known as Kalighat temple and the footpath became Chitpur Road, one of Calcutta's busiest thoroughfares.

Kolkata is as much a victim of fate as the careworn people crowding its streets. History and politics have dealt the Bengali capital a difficult hand. The city which grew out of many small villages clustered at the mouth of the Ganges became a commercial and administrative center under the British Raj, an era when Kolkata's warehouses were filled with tea, jute, and cotton grown in outlying fields.

Bengal was split down the middle by partition, becoming East Pakistan and the Indian state of West Bengal, placing the two regions under the control of hostile governments. In November 1970, one of history's worst cyclones devastated the heavily populated flood planes of East Pakistan. Fatalities were officially estimated at 300,000, but some placed the death toll as high as a million. The aftermath of the storm brought drought, epidemic, and political instability. The Pakistani government responded to the situation with military force that claimed tens of thousands of lives. Hindus were the primary targets. India came to the support of her oppressed neighbors, and soon India and Pakistan were at war, forcing eight million refugees to flee to India. Kolkata absorbed more than its share.

Many of India's greatest saints have roots in Calcutta. Swami Ramakrishna, Swami Vivekenanda, Yogananda Paramahansa, and Ananda Mayi Ma are among them. Ananda Mayi Ma had thousands of devotees in East Bengal (East Pakistan). After all, Dakha was her native place and where she first became recognized as a saint. Prior to partition, before anyone had any inkling of the upheaval and violence that loomed on the horizon, Ananda Mayi Ma went to each of her families individually and instructed them to move to Varanasi. She did not tell them why, and many wept over the prospect, but all did as they were told. It was only much later, after the multiple disasters of typhoon, drought, and genocide that her devotees realized that Ma had saved them from the extreme privation almost every Hindu faced in East Pakistan after partition. Many of her families wanted to relocate to Kolkata, but Ma directed them to Varanasi, knowing that Kolkata would not be a friendly place to live when the massive influx of refugees started flooding its streets.

Kolkata humbled and often overwhelmed me, but despite the city's crowded and crumbling facade, it easily found a place in my heart. Certainly we had been treated like rajas, but it wasn't the pampered lifestyle that inspired me. Bengalis were open and fun loving, intellectually curious and passionate, very passionate. Bengal has raised India's most illustrious saints, finest musicians, and best minds, and it was that profound underpinning that attracted me to the city of joy. Both sides of Kolkata's boundary wall, privileged and poor alike wove the vibrant colors of the Bengali mosaic. India, which I considered to be the soul of the world, had Bengali culture at its heart.

THIRTEEN

Gardens in the Sky

God blooms from the shoulder of the elephant
who becomes courteous to the ant.

—*Hafiz*

A plan evolved one clammy evening on the terrace of a senior executive's home. After two months of corporate seminars, golf and tennis at the clubs, and languid evenings at the homes of Calcutta's business leaders, I was ready for an adventure outside the city. While lounging on the veranda of a spacious Lutyen (the British architect who designed New Delhi) bungalow, the conversation turned to Himalayan tea gardens. Our hosts thought I might enjoy Darjeeling and the region bordering Bhutan, an idea that appealed to me.

I boarded a plane for Bagdogra, the nearest airport to the tea estates where a Gypsy jeep waited outside the terminal while I secured the necessary stamp in my passport allowing me to enter a region where Maoist extremists had been a problem over the years. After the man had examined my passport, he looked up and said in the best English he could muster, "You are America. Fine country! You go to place where communists live. Danger! Be careful." I appreciated the compliment as well as the advice, and paid him for the stamp in my passport.

After some bumpy hours on the road, I was shaking hands with Subhir Gosh, the general manager of Williamson-Mager's tea plantations in Central Duars, and my host for the stay. Subhir was a family man with two teenage daughters, but lived alone at the plantation while his children attended school in Delhi. The manager was a big, gentle fellow who seemed totally at ease with himself and everyone around him. It was no surprise that a man who excelled at human relations would be in charge of a tea plantation. Tea operations employed as many as two thousand workers and relations between management and pickers were often contentious. Our tour of the gardens and processing plant confirmed my suspicion that Subhir was well-liked throughout the garden. His easygoing manner, ready smile, and boyish appearance could disarm even the most hostile union boss.

It was surprising to see how small the tea bushes were. The meticulously pruned plants were no more than three feet tall, making it easy for pickers to walk along the row, plucking the two or three most aromatic leaves from each plant. Rain trees were scattered around the garden, the only break in the long rows of perfectly groomed bushes. The unique taste and aroma of a cup of tea comes almost entirely from the plant itself, giving rise to the expression 'tea is made in the field.' The atmosphere around the garden was refreshingly calm and orderly after Calcutta's incessant noise and chaos.

Subhir's wood-framed bungalow was surrounded by bougainvillea. The property included a tennis court and a manicured pitch and putt golf course. Subhir was one of Williamson-Mager's champion golfers, and golf memorabilia from St. Andrews and Pebble Beach decorated the cottage built by his British predecessors. A handsome writing desk and brass bed in the guest room were original decor.

Best Cup Of Tea, Worst Cup Of Tea

I slept soundly that night; the incessant itching of cricket legs was a pleasant contrast to the drone of Calcutta's ceaseless activity. After a superb meditation, Subhir's cook served breakfast on the porch, a suitable plantation repast to go with the company's finest cup of tea. Toast with orange marmalade and porridge, both British staples, reminded me of the fare at a Stratford-Upon-Avon bed and breakfast, and I imagined there was no shortage of drama in these wilds. Somehow, a Calcutta newspaper found its way onto the porch each morning, but I had no interest in the events of the city I had recently fled.

"Subhir, how long have you been managing this garden?" I asked.

"Three years. We have three gardens in Central Duars that I look after."

"Does your family come to visit?"

"My wife comes up once a month, but she stays with my daughters in Delhi. You see there aren't proper schools up here."

"Will you spend your entire career here?"

"No. The company rotates us in and out every few years. I like it here, but most managers don't. They miss their families and want to get back to Calcutta as soon as possible."

"What's the biggest challenge running a garden?" Subhir had shown me the operation, which seemed pretty straightforward.

"Worker relations. With 2,000 employees, things can get tense if the union leaders start agitating. But our relations are good."

"Are most of the workers locals?"

"Not at all. Most of our workers are Nepalese. We also have pickers from Bangladesh. After breakfast, we'll play some golf at the airstrip. A Bhutan friend will join us." From the paraphernalia around the bungalow it was obvious that Subhir was an avid golfer. His broad shoulders and large hands would make him a powerful player.

"How far is the Bhutan border?" I asked. I had a secret desire to visit Bhutan, but knew that it wasn't so easy traveling there.

"You're looking at it. See those hills? The estate runs right up to the border." Bhutan was literally in Subhir's backyard.

After breakfast, we headed off to Subhir's private club, a nine-hole golf course he had cut around the company's airstrip. Subhir's friend, the police chief of a nearby Bhutanese town, joined us. After the friendly game, the chief invited us to his home. Subhir, despite being from an upper class Calcutta family, enjoyed the frontier life, and drove his own jeep most of the time. Wearing his aviator glasses, he headed straight for the Bhutan border, the jeep bouncing violently over a potholed trail. We were entering Bhutan through the back door.

"The riverbed is the border of Bhutan," said Subhir. "By crossing off road, we avoid the Bhutanese authorities, who would delay us since you are a westerner. Bhutan has strict laws, you know, regarding tourists, but because I know Jagman, no one will bother us once we're in Pheutselong." I had read that foreigners could only travel in Bhutan if they spent exorbitant amounts of money for the privilege.

We reached the river, which was mostly dry except for a shallow stream at the far side. The jeep lurched about and stalled as we crossed the riverbed, but when we reached the far side, it sped up the bank as if delighted to be in the Buddhist kingdom.

It seemed strange that entering a country should be easier than entering our Calcutta guesthouse. The regions on both sides of the border are called Duars, which means door or gate. There are said to be eighteen doors entering Bhutan from India, although Subhir had discovered a nine-teenth. Like a burglar slipping in through the back door, Subhir routinely entered Bhutan this way. Of course, it helped to know the right people and the police chief was definitely the right person. No physical barriers exist between the friendly nations and Bhutan serves an important defense function for India. The mountain range in Bhutan's interior forms a natural wall between the two largest populations in the world: China to the north and India to the south. Ours was a simple social call to one of Pheutselong's most influential men.

The bouncing stopped as we reached the paved road. "Subhir, why did the guy at the airport warn me about Communists?" I asked, seeing that Subhir could relax again as he drove.

"It's the Naxalites. The insurgents got their start in this area, actually near Darjeeling. I'll tell you a story. I was driving on a road like this, returning from the market late in the afternoon. My driver was sitting next to me, holding a flat of eggs when I came around a turn and spotted a barricade of tree limbs and rocks on the road. I suspected foul play, so I speeded up. As I approached, a group of men opened fire on us. Bullets ricocheted off the hood and shattered the windshield, spraying glass about. I had small cuts everywhere."

"Did you have any idea who was firing at you?"

"I suspected they were Naxalites." I had read about the Maoist insurgents in the Calcutta papers. They had a reputation for being ruthless and violent.

"I grabbed my driver by the back of the head and pushed him below the dashboard so he wouldn't be hit by a bullet, but the jeep couldn't make it over the barricade. Armed men surrounded us, pointing rifles in the window. Fortunately, we weren't injured, except for the fact that when my driver sat up, he had egg yoke all over his face. He looked so comical that I started laughing, but the situation was really not a laughing matter. They released my driver the next day. They only wanted me."

"Why did they want you?"

"They demanded a large ransom from the company. It's against the law to pay these ransoms, but if the company doesn't pay, the fate of the hostage isn't good as you might imagine."

"You must have been worried."

"I was worried, but what could I do? I thought about trying to escape, and I might have, but I decided to wait for Mr. Khaitan to respond. I believed he would do everything possible to free me." Knowing Mr.

Khaitan, I would have trusted him with my life also.

"Were these people ruthless?"

"There were about a dozen of them. Some were just teenagers. All were armed, but some of the rifles were parade guns that fired only blanks." Subhir smiled at the memory. "But most of the guns were real. The gang made strong demands, and openly threatened to kill me if the ransom wasn't paid in two weeks time."

"Do you think they were bluffing?"

"No. I think they were serious, but fortunately we never found out. We moved constantly, shifting locations at night to avoid detection. I'm told the police scoured the area, but they couldn't find us." Subhir drove aggressively as he talked. We were entering the town of Pheutselong where his golf buddy Jagman lived.

"We moved about on bicycles, and on foot. The hardest part was moving at night, because I never got much sleep. They treated me well though, and after a few days they became quite friendly." This didn't surprise me. Subhir had an endearing personality. I couldn't imagine anyone treating him badly once they got to know him.

"Mr. Khaitan secretly sent the money and I was released after ten days. I was tired by the time they released me, and was happy to have a bath and some proper food." Subhir had emerged from the tense episode unscathed, if a few pounds lighter.

"What will prevent them from doing it again?"

"They could, but I don't think they will. It's just a gut feeling." Subhir was a courageous fellow and a first rate storyteller. From the cavalier way he drove about the countryside, the kidnapping had left no scar on him.

"Can't the authorities round up these Naxalites?"

"It's not so easy. They're very clever. They hide deep in the jungles and the villagers provide protection."

It was generally believed that the Naxalites were sponsored by China, and were causing major problems in Nepal where they controlled many eastern districts. They had camps in the jungles, and engaged the authorities in violent exchanges from time to time. Local villagers kept them informed about police search parties.

We arrived at the police chief's bungalow where we sat in his sunny parlor room. Tea was served almost immediately. I had already been treated to the best cup of tea I had ever tasted at breakfast. Subhir's choice blend mixed with cream from a local dairy and wild honey was exceptional, especially when served on his porch.

Our Bhutanese refreshment was called suja, a tea made from yak butter, salt, and roasted barley that was not much in demand in the international tea market, and for good reason. Large mugs arrived. Yellow oil
floated on the surface of the liquid. I waited to see how the others drank it
before putting the heavy mug to my lips. Subhir mixed the butterfat into
the tea and sprinkled barley grounds over it, so I did the same. Then I took
a drink. I would need time to adjust to this brew, possibly lifetimes. The
drink was almost nauseating, but I didn't want to offend my hosts, so I
sipped it as we talked. What a contrast to the breakfast tea at the plantation.

Jagman, who suggested we have a look around the mountains above
the city, saved us from a second cup. Pheutselong is nestled in a crease in
the Shivaleks, which rise to become the snowcapped Himalaya soaring
above the clouds at the country's interior. The town spilled up the hillside,
and we stopped at a vantage point overlooking the hazy Indian plains, a
property owned by Bhutan's queen mother. Her vacation palace on the hill
had a colorful pagoda, which we circled, turning the prayer wheels as we
walked. The town below appeared unhurried and traditional, but not without amenities like electricity and motorized vehicles. Jagman said there was
very little crime to contend with, and judging from his golf game, he had
plenty of free time on his hands.

Subhir And Jagman

Bhutan lies within the protective aura of the Himalaya, beyond the reach of globalization that has crashed the gates in neighboring India and Nepal. Tourism has never been encouraged in Bhutan. If anything, the opposite was true, according to Jagman. Although Bhutan has plenty to offer the world, most of it is closely guarded.

Because of its towering peaks, dense forests, and rugged terrain, modernization has been slow. There are very few roads through the interior of the nation, which is about the size of Switzerland. Bhutan's two million inhabitants are poor by western standards, but their collective spirit is attuned to the harmony of nature, an intrinsic wealth few western societies can claim. Cow and yak herding is done at higher altitudes during the warm season, and crop cultivation is the principle means of support. Bhutan's land is seventy percent forested, confining small scale farming to lower altitudes. Its climate is volatile. The forceful monsoons that collide with the immovable mountains unleash torrential rains on the land for three months of the year, resulting in three inches of rainfall per day, which swells the rivers while shrouding the mountains in perpetual fog.

The serene presence of Buddhism pervades the culture with its altruistic values and adherence to spiritual practices. Prayer flags fluttered in the hills. Equally visible are the white chortens and multi-colored stupas. Mahayana Buddhism, the national religion of Bhutan, teaches reverence for the land, and respect for all beings great and small. It emphasizes the interdependence of life, a principle neglected in other parts of the world. The culture's popular fable, the tale of the four harmonious friends, captures the spirit of Bhutan beautifully.

A bird flew from a distant land, carrying a seed in its bill. It dropped the seed from the sky and a hare caught it. A monkey sowed the seed in the soil and an elephant shaded it as it grew. Over time the seed grew into a majestic tree. When its fruits were ripe, the four harmonious animals desired to enjoy the harvest. The elephant stood at the base of the tree, and his friend, the monkey, climbed on his back. The rabbit stood on the shoulders of the monkey and the bird lighted on the head of the rabbit. It collected the fruits, and shared them with its companions. The trusting animals, acknowledging each other's role, created a pyramid of interdependence in order to achieve their common goal. The tree represents the 'tree of life,' symbolic of the ripening of the fruits of wisdom based on tireless self-sacrifice for the benefit of all. The wisdom of Buddhism extols the value of performing good deeds to all sentient beings, from the lowest to the highest. This practice is rooted in the Buddhist belief in reincarnation, which places every living being, from the humblest to the supreme, in the great chain of Being. One may be a human in this life, but in previous incarnations the same soul embodied in lower forms on its journey to discovery and mastery. From this perspective, it's understandable why Buddhists view compassion as a great virtue.

It is no surprise that Bhutan has the highest tree cover of any nation in the world. The absence of deforestation underscores the country's desire to protect the environment. Law and religion forbid hunting. The intentional slaying of a crane, a bird sacred to Bhutan's monks, brings life imprisonment. The mature Buddhist, especially the monk, sees the impermanence of all beings. Change is the rule in creation, and encourages the Buddhist to focus on that which is imperishable, the eternal Bodhisattva. It also compels him to work for the advancement of humanity, so all can attain the state of inner transcendence.

Perhaps Bhutan's greatest gift to the world is its flowers. Over 6,000 varieties flourish in the kingdom. The profuse number of indigenous plants fascinated European botanists, who returned to their native lands with many exotic and beautiful species. Rhododendron, lilies, poppies, orchids, and clematis all have ancestral roots in Bhutanese soil. Fifty-four variety of rhododendron in shades of lavender, pink, yellow, and white blossom each spring. From the mountainsides of the Himalaya, many prized flowers have found their way into gardens the world over. Seeds are an appropriate endowment to the world, for the seed is the central symbol in Bhutan's favorite allegory. Bhutan's fertile soil grows the most beautiful flowers in the world—humanity's favorite expression of the heart.

I was reluctant to leave Subhir's kingdom of tea. My host had the grace of a benevolent monarch, and a golf game to match. Our friendly competitions among the bougainvillea and rose bushes each evening were great fun, and the bungalow itself had the calm of a monastery. The absence of television and computer turned one to a good book or evening walk. Life on the tea estate, I imagined, had not changed much since the days of the British, except for the occasional thrill ride over Maoist barricades and rocky riverbeds.

Having heard the kidnapping saga, I felt a greater kinship with Subhir's reserved driver as we headed for Darjeeling. After crossing the northern plains, we began a steep ascent through a rain forest. Fir and teak trees towered over cascading rivulets that tumbled down the mountain. Pinks and purples and crimsons adorned the hills. On the opposite mountain, ribbons of water fell great distances from rock outcroppings. The road up the mountain ran parallel to the narrow gauge tracks that had transported Mark Twain to Darjeeling in 1896. Twisting switchbacks tested my drivers' strength and skill as we maneuvered past slower vehicles, averting their smoky trails.

The 'Toy Train,' as it was christened, crept along the ridge ahead of us, issuing plumes of smoke from its stove-piped locomotive as it chugged up the mountain, its shrill whistle alerting those at the station ahead. The infant train moved along tracks two feet wide, zigzagging and looping about the mountain, negotiating curves aptly named Sensation Corner and Agony Point on the world's most spectacular amusement ride. The dare-devil curves on the exposed ridges left passengers suspended above steep precipices. There were no tunnels obscuring the breathtaking views. Groups of school children hiking along the road, cheeks burned red from UV exposure, screamed and waved at the baby blue novelty that crept along like a brightly painted centipede. Daring boys leapt aboard the train from time to time, more for the thrill than the transportation. We pulled into Darjeeling just ahead of the Toy Train and I watched the Bengali tourists climb down.

Again, I was the guest of Williamson-Mager. The Darjeeling gardens grew on the side of a steep mountain; nearly everything did in this vertical land. At over 7,000 feet, Darjeeling's pure air and wet climate produced some of the world's finest tea. Dubbed 'the champagne of teas' due to their unique red wine flavor, tea bushes flourished under the watchful eye of experienced managers and the benevolent presence of Kanchenjunga, the 28,000 feet leviathan that dominated the horizon to the north. We were just a trek away from the Nepal border and the base of the world's third tallest peak. Kanchenjunga appeared almost extra-terrestrial, its mid-section girdled by clouds, its top hovering in endless blue. Upon viewing the unrivaled vistas, Twain hailed Darjeeling 'Queen of the Himalalyas,' writing,

The one land that all men desire to see,
And having seen that once by even a glimpse,
Would not give that glimpse
For the views of the rest of the world combined.

Having learned about tea and its production from Subhir, I spent my days exploring the colonial hill station and monasteries that were a short drive around the mountain from the tea estate. When two British officers discovered the region, it was in the hands of Gurkhas from eastern Nepal. After battling the tenacious Nepalese, the British seized control of the idyllic ridge and proceeded to raze forests, build bungalows, plant tea, and construct a railroad. I would have gladly taken up arms with the Gurkhas to save the virgin forests and mountains, but the fate of so much of India lay in the hands of the industrious Brits at the time.

For centuries, a peaceful Tibetan monastery named Dorje Ling had stood on a narrow ridge overlooking the broad basin to the east, but the ambitious foreigners had other plans for the emerald Shangri-La. The British anglicized the monastery's name, christening their frontier town Darjeeling. Although Dorje Ling is no more, wine-robed monks still go quietly about their contemplative lives at gompas in the meditative presence of Kanchenjunga.

Clouds enveloped Yogachoeling Gompa the day I visited the monastery outside Darjeeling, and I needed an umbrella in the steady drizzle. The friendly lamas invited me to step out of the silver fog and into the main shrine where a towering statue of Maitreya stood. The stunning Buddha was impassive, an invincible symbol of dharma.

In the library, rare handwritten manuscripts were preserved. No doubt, the ancient texts would have been tossed into the fire had the Chinese found them before they were secreted away from Tibet. The monks invited me to meditate on the cushions they used for their own meditations. Immediately, I felt the settling effects of the misty shroud outside and serene atmosphere within the hall, and sank into transcendence. The serenity of the Himalayan gompa induced both clarity and depth as I sat there like a novice eager to know the secrets of the faith.

It wasn't long before I arrived at a place of inner light. In this peaceful realm, robed beings appeared before me holding a large book. The book had beautiful gold script, which I was unable to decipher. When I asked the angelic keepers of the tome to translate the text, I was instructed to touch my head to the cover of the book in order to gain the wisdom contained within it. I did so, sensing that it contained ancient records of the genesis of man and the Earth's role in the greater scheme of things.

The ancient text indicated that the earth and its inhabitants were at a crossroads. The road ahead appeared as topsy-turvy as the tracks the Toy Train traversed, and Agony Point and Sensation Corner seemed appropriate names for the collective ride humanity was about to embark upon. The long predicted upheaval seemed imminent, but the storm would pass, and when it did, humanity would rise out of its shrouded ignorance to find a higher destiny. Wherever Tibetans lived, the ancient records were preserved, and I felt blessed to be in the presence of such spiritually attuned souls. These simple lamas, after centuries of safeguarding their ancient wisdom, were now sharing it with the world at a decisive time.

The vision at the gompa conspired with the awe-inspiring environs, and I left the gompa with my head in the clouds, my feet barely touching the ground. I returned to Darjeeling and continued my absentminded walk, stumbling over the cobblestone paths around the idyllic town. The fog had lifted, and Kanchenjunga rose majestically to the heavens in the distance. A necklace of clouds adorned it. The day had turned to magic, and my wanderings up and down Darjeeling's steep lanes took me past quaint wood and stone hotels and forest green bungalows. Neatly pruned rose gardens seemed scarcely real in the awesome Himalayan setting, but the Brits had committed a grand folly in their compulsiveness to civilize the world. It had taken a monumental effort to create the verdant hill station with its toy train and tea gardens, but compared to the unparalleled splendor of the mountains themselves, I questioned the need for proper English gardens and guesthouses with ginger bread trim. No doubt the ancestors of Subhir's Nepalese laborers had been ordered to fell the forests that altered the landscape.

Just above the town resided a small group of indignant natives. As much as the sight of animals living outside their native environment saddens one, there are few opportunities to view the enigmatic snow leopard, one of the habitat's prized residents. Even the author of the book bearing the shy cat's name failed to spot the elusive creature on his extended Tibetan expedition. The retiring beige and cream-colored creature with its exaggerated tail kept to itself, unwilling to socialize, which I fully appreciated. But its neighbor, the Himalayan black bear was feeling feisty, and spent most of the morning on his hind legs staring down tourists. Like the snow leopard, this furred fellow was yet another diminutive version of larger relatives found in other parts of the world. While on treks, villagers had warned us about the testy bear that prowled the night. Had a fence not separated us, he would have lived up to his spirited reputation, for he had already entertained his quota of tourists for the day. Another group of indignant residents in nearby Naxalbari had created the first Maoist revolt in 1967.

Having sampled life on two tea gardens, one on the plains and the other on terrain better suited for goral and snow leopards, my journey was complete. The process of turning leaves into the world's favorite drink is a ritual observed all over the globe. The Chinese have their version of a good cup of tea, as do the Japanese, the Indians, and the British. Even America has gone for fruit-flavored teas in favor of the cola brands. Bhutan's salty tea posed little threat to the popular drinks of the world.

The Land of the Thunder Dragon has kept global trends outside its gates, holding fast to its time-honored traditions. Bhutan's Himalayan fortress safeguards the Buddhist ideals, its monasteries preserve the myths of Shangri-la, and its soil nurtures the seed. I understood its motives for keeping the rest of the world outside its gates. Despite Bhutan's reticence to enter the global community, it has richly endowed the gardens of the world, and in doing so, has spread its message of peace.

FOURTEEN

Crossing Over in Varanasi

*There is the land of the living and
the land of the dead and the bridge is love.*

—*Thornton Wilder*

"Banaras (Varanasi) is older than history, older than tradition, older even than legend, and looks twice as old as all of them put together!" proclaimed a wide-eyed Mark Twain after visiting the fabled city. I had to agree with the perceptive humorist. Varanasi is believed to be the most ancient city in the world, and archaeological evidence suggests the city is 3,000 years old; however, Vedic literature claims that it's much older. The holiest city in India, Varanasi sits on a hill on the western bank of the River Ganges at a point where the river takes an uncharacteristic turn to the north. The river that is exhausted by the time it reaches Kolkata runs broad and full as it skirts Varanasi. In the early morning, the sun strikes the city's weathered buildings, casting a golden aura over the community referred to as the City of Light. Like many, I arrived in the ancient city to deposit the ashes of a recently departed soul into the holy river. It's a strange sensation carrying someone's physical remains around, and I was anxious to email my friend, saying 'mission accomplished.' It was this duty that caused me to set aside a few days to visit Varanasi, for I had the ashes of a friend's mother with me.

Numinous light reflected off the river in brilliant shades of amber and gold. It was early and the sun was just above the horizon. A fresh water dolphin surfaced near our boat, rippling the placid water before disappearing into its watery playground. Countless temples, shrines, and bathing ghats lined the three-mile stretch of river, and massive stone steps descended to river's edge where pilgrims stood waist deep in the gentle current, offering flower petals, grains of rice, and lighted wicks in tiny clay bowls to Mother Ganga, the sacred river of heaven. For a city where people come to die, the city was very much alive. The bright-colored saris of women ornamented the drab stone landings at water's edge as pilgrims went about their rituals while we glided silently past. Everywhere I looked, someone was summoning the gods.

Many of the pyramid spires rising above the Ganges are dedicated to Lord Siva. Interspersed among the shrines are dharamshalas sheltering thousands of elderly and infirm who come to Varanasi to spend their final days. The famed cremation grounds play a vital role in the riverside community, as Varanasi is considered the most auspicious spot in India from which to pass on to the realms of the pitris. In fact, Varanasi is reputed to be a Tirtha, or crossing over point from this world to the next. In many ways, Varanasi is not of this world.

We settled into the heart of the old city at a hotel near the river. Outside my room, humanity flowed endlessly to and from the ghats. The clanging of bells and litany of vendors added to the clamor on the street that continued into the night. It was wedding season, and apprehensive grooms on white steeds led processions up the street to the sound of brassy horns and thumping drums; merry dancers following in their wake.

Away from the river, Varanasi is like other Indian cities. But as we came close to the Ganges, the city compressed into crowded lanes that were further reduced to footpaths clogged with foraging cows and vendors' carts. Pilgrims bargained for everything: garlands, crimson powders, fruit, brassware, but the seasoned merchants always seemed to have the upper hand. The stalls added congestion and color to the cracking stone walkways, as did the bands of mischievous monkeys who sat on ledges waiting to pounce on unwary piligrims carrying nuts or fruit. The city has an aged appearance, but not a tired one. Its energy throbs like the pulse of a rikshaw walla pulling a carriage full of children. The moment I entered the ghat district, I felt the pulsation, a spiritual adrenaline that flows through the constricted lanes connecting temples, residential enclaves, and bathing ghats. The emphasis in the city is on the spirit for the material has withered like the bodies of Varanasi's infirm that wait patiently for their time to depart this earth.

Hindus believe Varanasi to be the city of Lord Siva, in existence since the beginning of creation. In important ways, Varanasi captures the essence of the Hindu faith. Bathing in sacred waters, making holy pilgrimage, and worshipping the Divine in His or Her many aspects form the basis of daily life in the city. But these ancient rituals, visible wherever the eye falls, are imbued with an urgency and purpose not found in other places. The scent of rose petals and sandalwood, and the ringing of bells and chanting of prayers are reminders that this city's central purpose is ministering to the thousands of souls who have come to be ushered safely from this life to the next.

As we negotiated the labyrinth of narrow alleys, becoming more disoriented at each turn, we arrived at the courtyard leading to the temple of my old friend Bhairav who is known as the 'Black Terror' around Varanasi. Being the god of death, Bhairav plays a pivotal role in Varanasi. I had no reason to dispute the ominous moniker after my unfortunate encounter with him in Delhi. But to come to Varanasi without paying a courtesy visit to Bhairav would be foolhardy, since he is said to know everyone's purpose and metes out punishment as he sees fit. Lying on the ground outside his temple were four black dogs; black dogs are said to be Bhairav's assistants. When the pack saw us coming they were on their feet instantly, checking us out. Although they didn't attack, none of them seemed particularly pleased to see me, nor was I enamored to see them. Not wanting to take any chances, I entered the temple, wallet in hand. We didn't stay long and I didn't have the courage to complain about my stolen passport.

Night was upon us as we boarded a rough-hewn boat at Raj Ghat for a nocturnal glimpse of the city from the water. A light breeze cooled us as our boatman plied his way upstream against a mild current. Only the swish of the oar stirred the water. Monks in an ashram situated on a bluff above the river chanted sonorously; cymbals clashed and a conch sounded, evoking otherworldly feelings while invoking beings unseen to the physical eye. Although it was night, our craft passed through the shadows of anonymous buildings that had congregated on the bluff to witness the surreal dramas unfolding on the waterfront. The eerie scene reminded me of the ancient Greeks' journeys to the world of the departed beyond the River Styx. But unlike the Greek myth, no demons haunted this tranquil river, at least none that I could see.

Just ahead, the reflection of a solitary flame shimmered on the water as a priest circled a brass lamp above the river. He paid tribute to the river goddess, a nightly ritual for many. Everyone, it seemed, was involved in some sort of supplication or another. Further upstream, smoke rose into the darkness from a half dozen fires. We had arrived at Manikarnika Ghat, Varanasi's principle cremation ground. As I climbed out of the vessel, the boatman pointed to the fires, saying laconically, "Burning is learning." It was not an attempt at humor on his part; perhaps it was all the English he knew, but priests and guides around the ghats parroted the cliché. By the time we departed Varanasi, I had indeed learned a great deal about life and death.

At the ghat, we didn't linger among the smoke and ritual, but climbed to a platform a respectful distance from the pyres that burned around the clock. Huge stores of wood surrounded our vantage point above the burning grounds where we silently watched the solemn ceremonies in various stages of completion below. Silver clouds hung about the temple towers, as families watched the blazes reduce to ash the vestiges of lives in transition.

Purificatory Rites

Every religion utilizes nature's elements in their rituals. Water is used in Christian baptism, Hindu puja, and Buddhist ritual. Fire is also used for worship. Candles and oil lamps are found on the altars of cathedrals and stupas, and the same is true for incense, which the Catholics, Tibetans, and Hindus use to purify the atmosphere. Each ingredient used for worship is symbolic of a particular element. Candles represent fire, incense the air element, and water itself.

Hindus employ fire as a purificatory element in their worship. Fire, perhaps the most sacred of the elements, transforms matter more effectively than the other elements. For this reason, cremation is preferred in the Hindu tradition. The cremation ritual is believed to release the soul in the most expedient way from its earthly bondage, the result of a lifetime of attachment to physical form. Rather than allowing the slow process of decay, cremation hastens the process, insuring that the departed soul doesn't linger in the vicinity of the physical body, thus preventing the soul from becoming earthbound.

We watched as a shrouded body on a bamboo bier was carried three times around the pyre before it was placed on a bed of wood. Then the eldest son lit the pyre with a twig of burning grass handed him by the dom, one of the priests that oversees the cremation process. After lighting the fire, the chief mourner circled the pyre three times counter clockwise. With the fire ablaze, the body was offered to Agni, the god of fire. After the fire had died away, the ashes were collected and sprinkled in the Ganges where they slowly dispersed with the current as the mourners walked away without looking back.

The ritual was complete, but the bereaved family would gather in their home for an eleven-day ritual called shraddha, to ensure the safe journey of the departed soul to worlds determined by one's actions in this life. Many Indian families refrain from temple worship and attending religious festivals for up to a year after a family member has passed away. However, it's considered inauspicious to grieve excessively; Hindus believe the departed soul is attuned to the emotions of loved ones and the family is careful not to disturb the departed one. Hindus are taught that death is a time of celebration and birth a time of reflection, because in death the soul is liberated, while birth brings renewed bondage to the wheel of karma.

In the ghat below, as soon as one cremation was completed, another body wrapped in cloth, white for men and red for women, was carried in. The ritual continued day and night. To a realized saint, all levels of reality are accessible. The Bengali saint, Swami Ramakrishna, while visiting Varanasi, observed the rites being performed at Manikarnika Ghat from a boat. After closing his eyes for a long while, he described to his disciples what he had seen with his spiritual eye. Ramakrishna described seeing Lord Siva impart the Taraka (sacred) mantra to the departing soul while Siva's consort, Parvati, held the soul in her arms. Then the soul began its spiritual journey. Scriptures assert that those who die in Varanasi are never reborn. This is the legacy that draws Hindus to the City of Light. To gain the benefit of Varanasi's spiritual gift, one simply needs to go there. The Puranas say, "The city of Siva requires nothing of people but their presence. The rest is a gift of grace." The city's awesome spiritual current was palpable from the moment we first arrived.

View Of Varanasi Ghats

Our visitation completed, we climbed down to the stone landing where earlier in the day a plump priest sitting under a sun umbrella had assisted me in dispensing my duties for my friend's mother. He had read slokas (verses) from a dog-eared scripture while I scattered the ashes I had brought from the States into the river. The ashes had drifted off, dissolving as they went.

The color and commotion that vied for one's attention on the ghats during the day was gone. Varanasi slept and the river rested. Only the ghat's great, gray foundation stones remained as I dangled my feet above the water, my mind immersed in images reflected on the river's indigo surface. As I digested what I had seen from the balcony above the burning grounds, the soothing presence of the river aided the process. In the smashan (cremation ground), roles are reversed; the material becomes insubstantial and the invisible becomes real. That is why the yogis seek out smashans, for the ghats are places of transition, neither a part of this world nor the next.

The Psychology Of Dying

Above the ghats stands Kedarnath Mandir, Varanasi's oldest temple. As we entered the otherworldly abode, evening oblations were in progress. Kedarnath, which means 'field of liberation,' is at the heart of Varanasi's crossing over point, and the temple was filled with devout figures absorbed in prayer. The shrine resounded with the resonant tones of brass bells meant to invoke the gods. Thick plumes of smoke wafted about the heavy stone columns like dense fog, as worshippers moved noiselessly from altar to altar. Everyone in the temple shared a common purpose; all were preparing to depart this world.

It is unfortunate that death is often viewed with uncertainty, confusion, and fear. After all, death is as much a part of life as birth. While medical science has done much to promote longer, healthier lives in the West, it has also taken the dignity out of dying. I became aware of this sad fact as I watched my dad's health fail in a nursing home. He was being kept alive by an endless battery of drugs, implanted tubes, and surgical procedures. Finally, after a torturous year, his compassionate Greek physician gathered the family together, and counseled, "I think we should let him go. There will be no quality of life from here on. Life support will be necessary." In support of dad's wish not to be kept alive through life support, we consented and he passed a short time later; but the family was left with the emotional residue of having abetted the termination of his life.

At times during my dad's ordeal, I wanted to snatch him off to Varanasi. The Indian way, I believed, was more humane than what I observed in my dad's nursing home where 150 elderly Americans were in as bad or worse condition than my dad, many being kept alive by medical technology alone. Fortunately, hospice care is now playing a growing role in helping us pass with dignity. The naturalness with which Indians deal with death and grieving is impressive. Intuitively, people know how to die. It's really not so different than falling asleep or going into a deep meditation. At the same time, the period leading up to it provides an opportunity for the individual to prepare for the soul's journey. Indians, when they know their time is near, try to balance the ledger of their life, which frees the individual to give his of her undivided attention to matters of the spirit.

Hindus believe that the final phase of life should be one of renunciation where the individual withdraws from his responsibilities in favor of time spent in meditation and worship. While staying with friends in Allahabad, I noticed that Grandma spent many hours meditating, chanting, and performing puja. The peace and composure she radiated as a result of her spiritual practice made a profound impression on me for she was preparing for the journey.

The most auspicious way to live the final months of one's life, according to Vedic scriptures, is to distribute one's wealth and possessions, and then go to Varanasi to live peacefully until the time arrives. In contrast, as I passed through the halls of my dad's care center, I observed residents listlessly watching television day after meaningless day. I remember one room in particular where the man had been in a comatose condition for thirty years as a result of a motorcycle accident. It was unsettling to see the fellow laying on his bed day after day, the television permanently tuned to a cartoon channel.

The Last Thought

Hindus believe that the thought one entertains at the time of death determines the direction the soul takes on its journey into the realms beyond. There are scriptural stories of people who reincarnated as a deer or a cow because they were thinking of those animals when they died. Indian parents like to name their son or daughter after a god or human virtue because they will have their child's name in their heart when they pass. This tradition inspired Varanasi's elderly to immerse themselves in temple worship in their final weeks. The resolute intent of worshippers who repeated

Lord Siva's name over and over at the close of their lives charged Kedarnath's inner sanctum with a potent atmosphere. A powerful impulse to cross over hung in the air as we made offerings to Siva. The pull to turn inward was undeniable and I welcomed it.

From Kedar Ghat I entered an alley leading to a poorly lit hall. Inside the small chamber a fire blazed from a sunken pit in the center of the stone floor. Sitting in the firelight, a father and his two young children made offerings into the fire while a priest recited from a tattered book. After each mantra, the father tossed a few kernels of rice into the blaze. His young son and daughter made the same offering as the grains crackled and sputtered. I stopped in the doorway, realizing that the fire sacrifice was a solemn ritual being performed for the children's mother who had passed away. Bright orange flames flashed across their faces as the family bravely participated in the religious rite to invoke blessings for their departed loved one. I felt their hurt for I too had performed a similar ritual. Having witnessed the cremation ghats, worshippers at Kedarnath temple, and the fire sacrifice in the shrine, I was reminded that Hindus had been crossing over in this holy city for thousand of years. This was the pulse one felt upon entering Varanasi.

Rebirth

Hindus embrace the philosophy of reincarnation, a belief that eases some of the anxiety surrounding death. A Harris Poll indicates that over one-fourth of all Americans believe in reincarnation, and even one in five Christians now accept the concept. The debate continues whether reincarnation was originally a part of Christian theology, taken out by a council of church fathers in the fourth century. Whatever one believes, evidence in favor of reincarnation is mounting as the memories of past lives have become commonplace. Church leaders can do little to discredit personal experience, although there was a time when those whose inner experiences didn't conform to church dogma were burned as heretics. I hope dogma will one day be buried for the ball and chain it has become.

One of the founders of the TM movement in the 1950's was a pragmatic businessman named Charlie Lutes. Charlie was an executive with a California cement company. He had studied eastern philosophy and esoteric traditions, and was acquainted with the idea of reincarnation long before he met Maharishi. While testifying in a court case to determine whether TM was a religious practice, the lawyer asked him, "Mr. Lutes, do you believe in reincarnation?" Without missing a beat, Charlie fired back, "Yes, and you will too five minutes after you die." Charlie was not afraid to swim against the current.

When death claims someone close, it challenges our deepest assumptions about life no matter what our personal beliefs. When my dad passed away, a friend sent me a poignant elegy.

Life Is Eternal

I am standing upon the seashore. A ship at my side spreads her white sails to the morning breeze and starts for the blue ocean. She is an object of beauty and strength and I stand and watch her until at length she hangs like a speck of white cloud just where the sea and sky come down to mingle with each other. Then someone at my side says: "There! She's gone."

Gone where? Gone from my sight - that is all. She is just as large in mast and hull and spar as she was when she left my side, and just as able to bear her load of living freight to the other place of destination. Her diminished size is in me, not in her; and just at the moment when someone at my side says, "There! She' gone", there are other eyes watching her coming and other voices ready to take up the glad shout, "There she comes!"

—Author Unknown

Maharishi's master, Swami Brahmananda Saraswati, urged his students to prepare. He said "One who has come has to go. Nobody can stay here. Every moment keep your luggage packed. Nobody knows when death will call. One cannot think of appealing against it… Think of when your father, grandfather and great-grandfather had to leave, then how will we be able to stay? Since going is certain, keep ready from the beginning so that the travel will be comfortable. If you are not ready then you will face difficulties. Whatever a man does while living, be it good or bad, it comes to be remembered at the moment of death. Therefore, one should always be cautious such that no sin happens so that one has no regrets at the time of death."

The Buddha Of Compassion

Along the Grand Trunk Road, India's longest highway, we traveled from Varanasi to Bodh Gaya where Lord Buddha gained nirvana while sitting under a Bodhi Tree. Sandwiched on the road among countless transport trucks, we were entertained by an unusual and somewhat comical scene. We were flanked by hundreds of young camels being herded by Rajasthani nomads to West Bengal, a journey of a thousand miles. The docile, almost effeminate creatures moved awkwardly by the roadside, stopping to munch tree greens and shrubs along the way. We were charmed by the herd and jumped out of the car for a closer look. The gentle creatures are said to be unsociable, but they seemed quite happy with their afternoon snack. The creator of these odd beasts clearly had a sense of humor for their crumpled noses, bony legs, and long eyelashes conspired to make a rather homely look. After some friendly banter with the camel herders we returned to our taxi. Much to our bemusement, as we were about to drive off, one of the men thrust a hand through my open window and shouted "baksheesh" (money). I couldn't imagine why we needed to pay him for climbing out of the car so I instructed our driver to move along, leaving the mustached gypsy standing empty-handed by the road.

It was proving difficult to reach Bodh Gaya. When our taxi arrived at the Bihar border, we weren't allowed to pass until we paid an exorbitant road tax. Some of these tollbooths were phony, but this one had a metal barrier blocking the road. After paying the excessive toll, we spent the next six hours bumping and bouncing over some of the worst roads in India. It was obvious that the revenues had been diverted; into the pockets of politicians, we guessed.

We arrived at the tranquil oasis in central Bihar where Buddha gained nirvana 2,500 years ago. We had also achieved a nirvana of sorts having arrived at our destination intact. Bodh Gaya is a mecca for Buddhists, and Southeast Asian countries have constructed beautiful shrines and monasteries in honor of their divine personality. We had arrived just a few days after the Dalai Lama's departure. He had come to bless those on pilgrimage from all over the globe. Although we missed the revered Buddhist leader, we were left with sweet encounters with Tibetan, Korean, Thai, Japanese, and Burmese monks who went about their lives with focus, simplicity, and purity of intent.

We visited the monasteries to observe the routines of the lamas, and watched trained fingers pass over beads and turn prayer wheels in a never-ending process of mantra japa. The aids kept the mind from wandering, something anyone who meditates appreciates. We sipped tea with a group of genial Tibetan lamas as they paused between rituals. They happily engaged us in conversation, but had little to say of their own accord. Their path was more an emptying of the mind than the filling of it, a favorite past time of inquisitive westerners. It seemed the lamas had successfully cultured the habit of never having the same thought twice. Later we visited the exquisitely ornate Thai Stupa, a magical place with layered roofs and upturned eaves that reminded me of a Viking ship run aground. Inside the powder blue pagoda, at the center of a rose garden, was a magnificent bronze Buddha with an ornate crown of flames that rose to a point above his head.

In the evening, as the sun set, the ancient Buddha shrine and nearby Bodhi Tree provided a captivating setting for worship. Set in a sunken ter-raced garden with as many yellow chortens (votive monuments) as pruned bushes, innumerable butter lamps glowed like fireflies on a mid-west sum-mer night. Pilgrims slowly circumambulated the tall stupa on the Cankamana (Cloister Walk), prostrating before images of the Buddha, and touching their heads to the trunk of the Bodhi Tree, all the while whisper-ing prayers recited since childhood. One elderly Tibetan woman prostrat-ed every few steps while circling the main stupa, a ritual that took over an hour. A young monk in wine-red and yellow cloth prostrated again and again on a wooden board, wearing padding to protect his hands. For some, the body was being strengthened as much as the spirit. We flowed like a circular stream around the shrine, a human mandala united in purpose. Some trained their attention on rosaries while others pressed palms togeth-er above their heads as they walked. Many placed a flower, candle, or stick of incense at the feet of one of the granite images of the Bodhisattva. Few gatherings involve people from so many cultures; everyone moving as a family. No one conversed; all energies were turned within.

Inside the Maha Bodhi Temple, Buddha sat in perfect equipoise against a royal blue backdrop. His serene golden form, wrapped in stun-ning saffron, was among the most sublime figures I had ever seen. His eyes were open, but not fully. Like a lamp in a doorway that lights a room both inside and out, the wisdom of inner and outer worlds was reflected in his serene eyes. His face inspired calm. Of all the divine personalities, Buddha is the one most associated with meditation. Having lit lamps burning at his gilded feet, we went within and remained there for a long time.

Later, I sat under the Bodhi Tree, a descendent of the sacred tree that Siddhartha, the young prince who became the Buddha, had meditated under the day he gained nirvana; the reason why Bodh Gaya exists today. The trunk was wrapped in orange cloth, and I found myself inhaling the sanctity of the ancient tree and the scent of joss sticks along with it. Sitting alone at the shrine, I thought about the life of Siddartha who began his spiritual journey so austerely that those who had known him failed to rec-ognize his emaciated form. He had made a different kind of crossing than then the one made in Varanasi when he attained nirvana under the Bodhi Tree, for he had overcome death itself.

It was only fitting that I pay homage to the Great One. My first exposure to eastern philosophy had come as a high school English assignment; Hermann Hesse's Siddhartha was among the choices our class had been given, and not knowing a thing about either the author or his work, I chose the story for my term paper. The account of the prince's single-minded pursuit of liberation had opened a door, giving me a glimpse of the spiritual journey at an age when I was not yet ready to embark on it. Having read about and reported on the very tree I was now sitting under, a seed had been planted that would sprout later. Although I was not a part of his tradition, Buddha was the first to illumine the path for me.

Road Warriors

It was time to make the three-hour journey to Patna. The drive to the Bihar capital kept us slightly on edge. I had read about a foreign journalist who had been robbed not once, but twice on the same road we traveled. Tollbooths were not the only form of larceny in a state that had the reputation for being among India's most corrupt. Armed gangs battled one another over land and politics. The national media reported that dozens of politically motivated homicides were committed in Bihar each year. It was a state teetering on the brink of anarchy, and it showed.

Traveling to the state capital, no bandits assailed us, but rutted roads harassed us most of the way. As is often the case when traveling in India, time evaporated and we found ourselves in a race to get to the airport in time for our flight. Half way to Patna, a pothole flattened a threadbare tire. Every minute counted now, but by the time we reached Patna our luck had run out. Our driver missed the airport road, a miscue that trapped us in the gridlock of transport trucks spewing diesel fumes.

Precious minutes passed as we idled among hundreds of other vehicles, slowly asphyxiating ourselves. Surely we would miss our flight. Then, as if possessed, I climbed out of the car and stopped the crawl of oncoming traffic long enough for us to reverse our direction. However unlikely it would be for us to make our flight, at least we were once again headed in the right direction. Greasy repair shops lined the industrial road where daylight was all but extinguished by dense clouds of exhaust and the sun was obscured by a hideous yellow-brown sky.

Patna, once the home of India's most prestigious university, appeared to be under siege. Swarms of people overran its crumbling structures like ants dismantling a piece of leftover cake. I was sure the same politicians that pocketed road tolls were the cause of the anarchy. Amidst the chaos and smoke that enveloped us, I saw something that distressed me still more than the deplorable condition of the city. At the edge of the pavement, a light brown puppy had been run over moments earlier. It was alive, but its hindquarter was crushed. I watched as the desperate pup dragged itself along the road just inches from the convoy of trucks. When our car came alongside the hapless creature, I looked into its innocent eyes, but they showed no pain. No puppy comes equipped to face the steel and asphalt jungle he landed in, and the scene wrenched at my heart.

Moments later, traffic was flowing again and we were on our way to the airport. Our only hope was that our flight had been delayed. The departure time was already past. When we arrived, our flight was indeed delayed, but we needed every extra minute to settle with our driver who now demanded a substantially higher amount than had agreed upon at the outset of the trip. When I disputed his price he refused to unlock the trunk, holding our bags hostage until we met his unreasonable demand. After phoning his boss in Varanasi, we got the mess straightened out. From the sublime visage of Buddha to the confusion around Patna, it was all in a day of sightseeing.

As our plane rose above the smoke and chaos, I lacked the contentment found on other pilgrimages. I was not bothered by our driver's efforts to extort money or the deplorable condition of Patna. Nor did the face of death in Varanasi unsettle me. Rather, I was preoccupied with the story of the Buddha of Compassion. The Buddha was about to enter nirvana when he looked back to earth and saw an animal in distress. He was so moved by the pain of the creature that he decided not to enter nirvana. He couldn't bear his own liberation while another continued to suffer, so he begged his father's permission to return to Earth to help the animal. His father agreed, saying, "My son, there are so many in torment that in order to see them all I will give you a thousand eyes and to help you save them, I will give you a thousand hands." Somehow I hoped the Buddha of Compassion had seen the helpless puppy by the road and had freed him from his suffering.

FIFTEEN

Immortality

The mystical techniques for achieving immortality are revealed only to those who have dissolved all ties to the gross worldly realm of duality, conflict, and dogma.

—Lao Tzu

Godmen

I had waited too long. Devraha Baba, one of India's greatest yogi saints, was gone. While attending the 2001 Kumbha Mela, the world's largest religious festival, we heard stories of a yogi who lived an extraordinarily long life. His name was Devraha Baba and he had roamed the banks of the Ganges for centuries. According to his close disciples, the Ageless Yogi had left his body in 1989 at about age 250. Devraha Baba liked to sit on a wooden platform on a sandbar at the confluence of the rivers Yamuna and Ganges and toss fruit to devotees who came for his darshan. The yogi, who reportedly ate nothing and drank only Ganges water, was a favorite at the festival, which draws tens of millions of devout Hindus.

The first president of India, Dr. Rajendra Prasad described meeting Devraha Baba when Prasad was just a young boy, somewhere around the turn of the century. The sparsely clad saint was already an old man according to Dr. Prasad, whose father had also come as a child to receive the elderly Devraha Baba's blessings. The saint's extraordinary longevity fascinated the Indian public, and parents and grandparents like to tell about his legendary feats. Prime Ministers and members of parliament, rich and poor, saints and sinners; everyone who attended the Kumbha Mela visited the enigmatic personality referred to as Premaswarupa (The Incarnation of Love).

India's yogis have bewildered foreigners for centuries. The British arrived in India armed with rational minds and linear thinking, and a game plan to impose order on a complex culture, only to have their world turned upside down by phenomenon they could neither understand nor dismiss. Trailanga Swami is one of the enigmas that left the British scratching their heads with their cricket bats. You see, Trailanga Swami was no ordinary yogi who avoided the public at all cost. Born in 1601, the outsized swami weighed 300 pounds and was widely known to a dozen generations of Indians who marveled at his extraordinary feats. Among his miracles, Trailanga was observed drinking poison on many occasions with no ill effects, and he enjoyed floating on the surface of the Ganges near Varanasi's cremation ghats. He sat on top of the water as if it were solid ground. His 'divine powers' were made all the more spectacular by his enormous size and the fact that he went about stark naked. Trailanga tried to teach the people that the human body need not depend on normal conditions. Being a master of secret yogic techniques, he displayed abilities known only to the adepts, most of whom never appeared in public.

Varanasi's British constables wanted to remove Trailanga from the public eye because he refused to cover himself. Out of frustration, they locked him up one night in the local jail, but when they returned the next morning, a smiling Trailanga was found sitting naked on the jailhouse roof, his cell still locked. One can only imagine how, over afternoon tea, the befuddled Brits explained Trailanga's enigmatic behavior. According to records, Trailanga lived to be nearly 300. What is so endearing about 'god-men' (a title Hindus give those with mystical powers) like Devraha Baba and Swami Trailanga, is their childlike innocence. In their super conscious states, humanity amused them as much as their preternatural acts bewildered the public.

Accomplished yogis are part of India's unsurpassed spiritual legacy. Devraha Baba and Swami Trailanga were sidhas, perfected souls whose inner journey was complete. Due to their mastery over mind, ego, and senses, they displayed superhuman skills in daily life that most of humanity could never understand. But none of their mind-boggling feats were performed by magic; all the powers they possessed were the byproducts of fully developed consciousness.

The Death Of Dying

Scientists have observed yogis stop their heartbeat and suspend their breathing, giving the empirically minded a clue as to how one might add decades or even centuries to life while slowing the aging process. But, like it or not, death is a fact of life. Like gravity and oxygen, the human race has to live with it. Today's average lifespan of 70-80 years (less in places where nutrition and health care are substandard) is a foregone conclusion, but there have been exceptions to the norm. Anomalies like Devraha Baba and Swami Trailanga defied what was believed possible and their examples offer a ray of hope that man's life on earth need not be quite so tenuous as we think.

Mankind has always been fascinated by the idea of immortality. In Vedic lore, gods and demons alike coveted a drink called amrit, the nectar of immortality. European explorers also pursued the elusive elixirs of life. Ponce de Leon discovered Florida while searching for the fountain of youth and myths about the Holy Grail have captured the imagination of thoughtful writers and philosophers since medieval times. Sir Lancelot rode his steed across Europe in search of the Holy Grail, Christianity's symbol of immortality. Immortality, however, remains a fanciful flight of the imagination that scientists hope one day to turn into reality and a profitable business. In an age when biogenetics can reconstruct a human body from strands of DNA, eccentrics obsessed with longevity entertain the idea of freezing their genes until scientists can find the answers to ageing and mortality. Imagine waking up in the future and being told by a geneticist that you are now immortal, imperfections and all.

But freezing the human body is a flawed concept for it implies that humans have only one lifetime, and therefore, no matter what the cost, they should try to preserve something of that life for a future when the riddle of life has been solved. If one understands the simple truth that we have unlimited opportunities to experience and enjoy life, then it takes the pressure off preserving a genetic artifact. Fear of death remains only as long as one is ignorant of the incredible journey the soul makes in its evolution up the spiral staircase. Once Maharishi was asked by one of our management students whether reincarnation was real or not. In a fatherly tone, he replied, "Yes, its real. Sometimes its necessary to move into a new house." The body inevitably grows old so one gets a new and hopefully better one, according to his or her karma. Reincarnation is a wonderful gift for the advancement of the soul, eliminating the need for indulgences like body freezing or cloning.

Lotus Cups

According to Biblical lore, Jesus drank from the Chalice of the Eucharist at the Last Supper. Since then, the chalice has become a treasured symbol of eternal life. During the sacrament of Holy Communion, the 'blood of Christ' is served from a chalice sanctified by prayer. As a boy, my family approached the front of the church sanctuary to receive symbolic bread and wine during communion services. Like everyone else, I sipped the Welch's grape juice and nibbled on a morsel of white bread. But when I took communion, something unusual happened. After the sacrament, my hunger typically vanished. This occurred throughout my teenage years, and as a result, I believed there was something magical about Holy Communion. But then, there are countless more profound stories associated with the sacrament than the pacifying of a voracious teenage appetite.

The search for the Holy Grail has been a metaphysical quest as well as a physical one. The cup itself is valued more as a symbol than a metal vessel buried somewhere in England. The ability to rejuvenate the physical system is discussed in age-old Vedic texts that describe a special substance that fills a chalice-like cup at the crown of the head. In the subtle brain there is a lotus flower that forms a chalice of light when the brain is awakened through deep meditation and yogic techniques. Once the lotus is open it can be filled with a substance of light and prana, the nectar of immortality called amrit, which, as a result of advanced yogic practice, flows into the top of the head enlivening regions of the brain that are dormant in the average person. Like a chalice, the lotus cup at the crown of the head has a stem that connects the cup to the rest of the body via a subtle canal in the spine. Through this canal, called sushumna nadi, the enervating influence of amrit passes along the spine from where it spreads throughout the body, producing immense bliss in the process. Although Vedic texts describe more than one method of producing amrit in the body of an advanced yogi, scientists still have work to do to verify its presence. A self generated elixir like amrit might explain how Devraha Baba and Tralanga Swami lived for hundreds of years. It is also significant that neither yogi ate food. It is said that when the body manufactures amrit, the intake of food becomes optional. It seems ironic that the quest for the Holy Grail ultimately doesn't require leaving one's own home as the elixir of life lies within each of us and not in some mythic location in a faraway land.

The hymns of an entire section of Rig Veda are dedicated to the praise of the nectar of immortality, in this case called soma. The green tinted soma juice is said to be a favorite of the gods. It has a delicious, sweet taste, like honey, and collects between the two halves of the brain where drops of it fall onto the tongue of the yogi, bringing him immense bliss and contentment. Along with the sweet taste, come magical powers and refined perception. Soma is said to bestow sidhis or supernormal powers that are described in the Yoga Sutras of Patanjali. A hymn from Soma Mandala of Rig Veda describes the soma elixir and the benefits it bestows.

Where light is perpetual, in the world in which the sun is placed, in that immortal, imperishable world, place me, Soma Pavamana.

The Union Of Siva And Sakti

Attaining immortality, as one might imagine, does not occur overnight. The scriptures that venture an opinion on the subject suggest that it is a long journey to the pinnacle of human evolution. The spiritual path presents two fundamental stages of development. The first stage is gaining Mastery of Self. The process of achieving Self Mastery utilizes all the tools and techniques that bring about mind-body-soul development. These include diet, yoga, meditation, breathing exercises, scriptural study, therapeutic massage, and so forth. Self Mastery is a two-step process involving the removal of impurities that block the flow of consciousness and the awakening of kundalini shakti, the primordial energy within. Removing impurities includes eliminating habits that restrict our progress while harmonizing energies that otherwise interfere with the healthy expression of thought and emotion. As the body, mind, and emotions are cleared and freed from blockages of stress and tension, inner awakening happens quite naturally.

During a talk on Deep Meditation given in Munich, Germany in 1963, Maharishi had this to say about inner awakening: "During meditation you hit the abstract kundalini five or six times. That brings the brightness. The method of kundalini evolves itself without strain or unnatural pressure. Kundalini Yoga states that as long as kundalini is sleeping, life cannot be perfect. With kundalini asleep, life is never complete. Kundalini is often explained in terms of certain glands in the body. The top of the head is the seat of Lord Siva. Siva is the god of death, or eternal life. The seat of kundalini is the bottom end (base) of the spine. Kundalini Shakti is the power of Siva. When the power is enlivened and unites with the Lord, then the Lord becomes fully capable of action. There is no end to our fortune to get such a thing as Eternal Life. For this wisdom, the children of India forgo all. They renounce all to get this blessed state."

The permanent union of Siva and Shakti in the crown chakra marks the establishment of Self Mastery, or Enlightenment, a milestone in evolution that is rarely attained in an age of spiritual darkness like the one now coming to a close. It is important to understand that awakening of kundalini should only be undertaken with the guidance of a qualified teacher who knows the time tested techniques necessary to prepare the physiology. Once the kundalini is awakened, the pace of progress accelerates and one is considered well along the road to Self Mastery. At this point, the second phase of the journey to immortality commences. The sidha cultures a body of light, a process of raising the individual's vibration through still more advanced techniques that have been practiced over the millennia by only the most advanced yogis like Buddha, Jesus, St. Germaine, Babaji, Ramakrishna, and Kwan Yin. The ascent becomes steeper at this stage, but the views must be breathtaking.

With the mature awakening of kundalini, the lotus cups in the subtle physiology are ready to receive the inputs necessary for ascension. These divine inputs now have a place to be deposited, and can flow directly from the heart of the Creator, filling the golden chalices with Divine Light, Love, and Grace. At this refined stage of development, intuition supersedes any formal technique of meditation one may have utilized at earlier stages on the path. Intuition on the road to perfection often involves direct guidance from the Masters, those beings of light called Perfected Sidhas, who have already achieved ascension and are dedicated to lending a helping hand to others.

Sidha Support

Throughout the ages man has always wanted to fly. Leonardo DaVinci and the Wright brothers devised crude wings to help them fulfill the deep-seated desire. Children often dream about flying. The reason for this is that deep within everyone is the desire to ascend, to rise into freedom, to soar through the heavens like a bird. Yogic flying, which Rishi Patanjali described in his treatise, The Yoga Sutras of Patanjali, is the fastest way to transform the body into a body of light that can fly. Patanjali describes the process of refining the physiology until it becomes the weight of a cotton ball through the power of the yogi's consciousness.

Twenty-five years ago I was giving a lecture in a college auditorium in South India. In the course of the talk I mentioned how the yogis of India had mastered supernormal powers such as levitation, omniscience, and invisibility. After the lecture, a man approached me outside and thanked me for explaining levitation. As a young boy, he and his family had attended a satsang (spiritual gathering) given by a saint who had come to Madurai. According to the man, the yogi had levitated from one end of the hall to the other, floating ten feet off the ground. For fifty years the fellow had been puzzled by what he had seen.

A Perfected Sidha is one who has reached the pinnacle of human evolution. In that state, one may choose to render service to those following in the same footsteps. For example, a Perfected Sidha can intervene to have an aspirant's personal karma lifted by appealing to the Karma Board. If the board is benevolently inclined, one's mountain of past karma can be erased. This is a boon that significantly speeds up one's progress. The perfected ones can also light the ascension flames for an aspirant, spiritual flames at the center of each chakra that appear like a pilot light in a furnace. Once these flames are lit, they burn away subtle impurities that restrict spiritual progress, and raise the vibrational rate of the individual.

The Perfected Sidhas also teach one to receive divine energies that get deposited in the lotus cups, creating a cosmic bank account to insure one has everything they need in life: prosperity, wisdom, joy, love, light, energy, the full package for living a life of contentment. The unimpeded flow of life naturally follows. The Masters often oversee the day-to-day activities of a rising sidha, serving as guru, guide, and friend. When he or she becomes mature enough, the aspirant, in turn, lends a supportive hand to others. This is a vital part of his training, because the commitment to become a Perfected Sidha is also a commitment to serve. The Perfected Sidhas have dedicated themselves to the task of assisting souls in ascension as well as ensuring that humanity as a whole receives the spiritual support it needs. The protection and guidance given by these great souls has preserved and advanced life on earth over the long cycles of time, but has rarely been more accessible than in recent years.

As one advances, one gains the ability to directly access the yogic techniques necessary for full mastery of the sidhis. This allows one to progress, even if a guru is not present on the physical plane. All the techniques provided by the Creator are available to be downloaded as 'shareware,' free of charge, on the condition that the user have the requisite purity of intent. Without purity of intent, one can't be given the password. In the lives of saints, east and west, there are examples of meditation and other yogic techniques being received directly through the faculty of intuition. Ananda Mayi Ma never had a physical guru and apparently didn't need one. Her spiritual guidance, which she called 'keyala,' came entirely from within.

Each individual has a unique set of spiritual aptitudes, and the techniques that are needed for the spiritual journey will present themselves at the right time. Shareware is always available, but Windows software would be of little benefit to a Mac user. A monk would have little use for a technique that unifies the hearts of a couple aspiring to become Perfected Sidhas, but he might like a technique to recalibrate his system. The saying 'deserve and then desire' applies to spiritual shareware. The Creator, like a loving parent, will do almost anything for her children. At the same time, a mother must protect the child from touching a hot stove or handling a sharp knife. There is no limit to the generosity of the Creator once the aspirant has demonstrated maturity in using Divine Gifts. Although there are those who claim the spiritual path is a lonely journey, no one is ever without support as they find their way back to Source.

SIXTEEN

Talks With A Himalayan Master

Angelic teachers cannot be sought out,
It is they who seek out the student.

—*Lao Tzu*

I had made a number of trips into the mountains, but I had never gone alone, so one autumn I headed for Joshimath and along the way stopped at the Glass House. The former vacation lodge of the king of the region was my favorite getaway. Set in a fruit orchard on a secluded bluff overlooking the river a short drive from Rishikesh, I could hear the roar of the Ganges day and night from my bungalow in the orange grove.

On a previous visit, while walking along the river one evening, a friend and I had noticed a faint light in the forest. The next morning we investigated, and found that a Bengali yogi lived in a cave on the hillside above the river. His name was Giri Baba, and, like many babas, he lived in seclusion. When not wound around his head, his matted hair reached the ground, and he wore nothing but a loincloth. The diminutive recluse was prone to fits of laughter, and was a highly charged personality.

At first opportunity I went to see Giri Baba on my return to the Glass House. As I entered his porch above the river, I was struck by his immaculate hideaway. From his grass mat he could watch the flow of the river for hours on end, or by shifting directions, he could worship at his altar.

"Namaste, Giri Baba," I called to the tiny recluse as I slipped off my chappals before stepping onto his porch. Giri Baba, who had been enjoying the sight and sound of the river below, jumped to his feet to greet me.

"Hari Bhagawan (hail the divine)!" he shouted, gesturing for me to join him.

"Hanuman Ki Jai," I shouted back, pressing my hands together, acknowledging the picture of the Ramayana hero pasted on the wall outside his cave.

"Friend good?" Giri Baba inquired.

"Teech (OK)," I replied. "Baba's swastic (health) good?" It amazed me that these hermits could sustain themselves without any visible means other than a friendly villager's kindness and the grace of God.

"Aacha swastic (health is good)! Bhagawan (God) good to me!" he boomed, smiling so broadly that his eyes shut.

His waiflike body wasn't a pound heavier since I saw him last, although the mound of hair piled on top of his head was even higher than I remembered. The Calcutta native stood just a couple inches over five feet tall when his hair was down, but was considerably taller with it wrapped in a beehive. Giri Baba had been living near the Glass House for a decade, and the local villagers had taken an interest in him, supplying him with food-stuffs, although I imagined he ate very little. He spoke Bengali, but not much Hindi. It wasn't easy for us to communicate, but what we lacked in common vocabulary, we made up for with volume and enthusiasm, shouting back and forth like geezers in need of hearing aids.

"Photos?" I asked, spotting the photo album he had shown us the previous year.

Baba opened the album to a photo of Randy and me standing next to him, and asked about my Iowa friend who was staying at a Himalayan ashram. On the opposite page, a five hundred-rupee note was wedged inside the plastic insert. The sizeable sum meant far less to him than the faded snapshots in the album. When Randy gave him the gift, Baba had laughed wildly, shouting. "Me Bhagawan! Me NOOO rupee! Me Bhagawan! Me NOOO rupee!" He then pointed in the direction of a wealthy ashram downstream, and shouted "Rupees! NOOO Bhagawan! Rupees! NOOO Bhagawan!" His comical outburst translated: 'I love God, not money! They love money, not God!' The tiny yogi was part free spir-it, part sprite, and totally content with what he was. He showed me his cave, which looked custom fitted for the little fellow, but was a challenge for me to even enter. I imagined my friend spending long hours meditat-ing inside his secret abode.

I had promised to bring Giri Baba a Rudraksha mala (beads) from Katmandu and handed him the strand of over-sized red seeds. He lit up at the sight of the gift and placed them carefully on his altar. Giri Baba lived in the present, and the smallest incident brought great peels of laughter that shook his entire body. Our clumsy efforts to communicate somehow added to his delight, and we laughed hysterically without knowing why. Baba had a child's heart, playful and charming, and I connected easily with him. He called the river Mata (mother) and the mountains Pitaji (father). Like most Indians Giri Baba was a heart person, and that is one of the culture's great strengths, for the heart is the gateway to Divinity.

After visiting Giri Baba, I bumped into Rajiv, the manager of the Glass House, and so I asked him about his odd neighbor. Rajiv was a Garwhal native who was familiar with yogis. "Baba is very good yogi," Rajiv said. "He never bothers anyone, but one strange thing is that every spring he leaps into the Ganges. We see him floating past the guesthouse, his long hair spread out like a helicopter propeller on the water. Very dangerous! We are afraid he will drown."

"Does he know how to swim?" I asked. The current was swift with rapids and boulders at the turn.

"No, he cannot swim. It is his way to surrender everything to God," replied the manager shrugging his shoulders. Giri Baba was a carefree soul, and a happy one.

Himalayan Gorges

The drive from the Glass House to Joshimath took me past deep gorges carved by the Alakanda River and its tributaries. Five holy confluences mark one's progress on the road into the Himalaya. My first stop was Deoprayag where the churning rapids could sweep one away in an instant. The mighty collision of water marks the spot where Ram performed a yagya 10,000 years ago. I made the long descent into the cavernous gorge on foot, passing a small village and crossing a dramatic footbridge as I went. A busload of South Indians and their priest were having ritual baths when I arrived. The wide-eyed pilgrims from Madras had never seen such ferocity in a river, and they looked on with great trepidation as their priest cradled and submerged a tiny infant in the swirling waters. For an instant, the waves engulfed the helpless baby, before the priest lifted his shiny prize out of the furious current. The tender gesture of the priest, as he wiped the waters from the newborn's brow, contrasted the fierce velocity of the raging waters at his feet.

I watched the sacrament from a rock, and then took my turn, making my plunge without the assistance of a priest. Clutching the heavy chains that disappeared like the tentacles of a huge iron octopus into the foaming current, the unruly waters pulled at my legs as I dangled from the end of the metal rope like a fallen water-skier still clinging to his line. The force of the whirlpools buffeted me about, testing both my grip and my resolve. The thrill of knowing that the slightest miscue would be my last, sent rushes of energy through my body as the savage waters swirled around me. My brazen method of bathing drew concerned looks from the pilgrims who approached their own baths cautiously. A local priest waited with red powder as I climbed dripping onto a boulder at river's edge. The old priest's shrine by the rapids was inside a grotto where an oil lamp burned in the dark. He had ventured out hoping to solicit my business. "Sir, very dangerous," he shouted above the roar of the river, but it was too late to issue a warning for I had already completed my watery rite. The red paste he applied to my forehead ran down my cheek like a red badge of courage for the daring challenge I had issued the tempestuous waters.

I was keen to reach Rudraprayag before nightfall for I wanted to meet an extraordinary yogini who stayed near the river. I went immediately to touch the feet of Mata Giri, the saint who had lived at the river shrine since she was a small child. Her loving eyes and youthful face disguised her advanced age, and she greeted me as I approached. Many times I had meditated outside her tiny temple above the converging rivers that cut a narrower, but equally dramatic gorge as Deoprayag. Each evening at dusk, Mataji emerged from the temple in her ochre gown, with bell and oil lamp in hand. After summoning the devas with a ring of the bell, she waived the lamp at the surrounding mountains and rapids below, greeting beings that only she seemed fully aware of. She smiled as she paid homage to the mountain deities and spirits of the river, and sometimes even engaged her friends in conversation. Arrivals from the city might think she was eccentric, but I knew that she was a rare soul who watched over the holy spot like a guardian angel. The locals knew of her spiritual gift and revered her as a saint. After performing her vigil, she sprinkled holy water on my head and promised me a fruitful journey. Light poured from her amber eyes, and I wished we spoke a common language so that I could learn more about her. Somehow I felt she was trying to tell me good luck lay ahead.

Emerald mountains framed the swirling eddies and I was held hostage by the endless pattern of fleeting impressions on the water. Swooping swallows and darting bats winged about the narrow valley, drawing my attention to the village on the opposite hill and the contoured green rising up from water's edge. The converging rivers, one channel clear and the other carrying silt, transported waters from inaccessible glaciers and snow peaks, and I filled my lungs with the pregnant air until blackness overcame the region, releasing me from my blissful bondage. Through the night, I listened to the roar outside my room, and when I awoke before dawn, I was eager to be by the river once more.

Mata Giri's Shrine At Rudraprayag

Sparky And His Gang

I lingered in Rudraprayag to visit the jal samadhi (water burial) of a saint whose shaded ashram lay on the far side of the river. The tenuous footbridge I crossed bounced with each step, and I wondered if it would hold me. There was no guardrail, and fifty feet below, the river was poised to engulf me should I fall. The force of the rapids below had carved a deep chasm between the rock ledges on either side. Having crossed the bridge, I stepped along a stone ledge leading to a mossy cave. Inside, marigolds had been placed on a dozen stalagmites. The conical pillars appeared like Siva lingams, and I wanted to sit and meditate, but the floor of the cave was soaked from the steady drip of water.

Saints are not cremated in India because the purificatory rite isn't necessary. When the mahatma who lived by the river passed away, his body was consigned to the river for the benefit of all living beings in the vicinity.

It was almost dark by the time I reached Joshimath, the village where pilgrims overnight on their way to Badrinath. Out of habit, I found lodging in Narasimha Bazaar above a cluster of small temples enclosed in a slate courtyard. The central shrine, a small, lamp-lit chamber the size of a large broom closet houses a statue of the man-lion Narasimha, a granite idol whose left arm has eroded away over ten centuries. According to legend, when the pencil-thin arm finally breaks off, the valley leading to Badrinath will seal itself off as the result of a massive earthquake. I hoped the cataclysmic event would wait a few days while I enjoyed the superb mountain scenery from the bugiyals (meadows) above Joshimath.

I chose a new trail to the hotel after visiting the Narasimha shrine. The path led through a cluster of stone cottages interspersed with vegetable gardens, fruit trees, and cow shelters. A huge magnolia by the path was dropping blossoms on the ground, and I stopped to collect one. The pitched slate roofs on many of the homes were covered with red chilies and pastel garments drying in the sun. As I climbed the stone trail, a shaggy dog blocked my way, but his wagging tail let me know he was someone's pet and not a hungry street dog. As I approached the friendly pup, heads appeared from behind walls and hedges on both sides of the path. I had inadvertently entered a fairy tale. No less than ten cherubic faces peered out from every angle; a most sociable creature looked expectantly up at me. Suspecting the children were simply curious to get a glimpse of the foreigner passing through their neighborhood, I stopped on the trail. With the curly-haired dog barking at my feet, the children lept out of their hiding places. Surrounded by giggling kids, I was taken hostage onto the balcony of a bright yellow house. Six of the children came from the cheery house; the others were cousins from the cottage next door. All but one were girls. The spunky gray Disney dog's name was Sparky, the perfect pet for any family. The mother of the friendly gang came out to greet me, and soon I was sipping tea and answering a hundred questions. The family's name was Bisht, and the father of the happy clan was the executive director of the Badrinath temple, one of India's holiest shrines.

A View Of Heaven

Above Joshimath, the views of Nanda Devi, India's tallest peak, are breathtaking. After riding the Austrian-built gondola to the ski village Auli, I climbed beyond an old oak forest into a highland meadow where sheep grazed. Blue poppies, yellow primulus, and crocus adorned the meadow where a shepherd serenaded his flock with a wood flute. His simple melody echoed faintly off the higher peaks. If there was a more agreeable alpine setting in the Himalaya, I hadn't found it. I watched the clever game of hide and seek played by wispy cloud and white massif for a long while, before entering another old growth forest where gnarled trunks and overhanging limbs magnified the silence on the mountain. The forest felt alive, and I half expected to meet a dryad or leprechaun on the trail.

I walked among the oaks, trying not to stumble over exposed roots as I went. A gray-headed parrot with a bright green body and long tail settled on a limb overhead. He took an interest in my presence, and flew from limb to limb above the trail ahead of me, waiting for me to catch up before flying deeper into the forest. I followed him, enjoying his graceful flight and friendly presence. Unlike his riotous cousins in the Kerala jungles that shot across the sky like iridescent lime flares, this parrot flew alone, which seemed appropriate in a region where reclusive living came naturally. He made very little chatter, but from his alert eyes I could see that he was clever, and would be quite trainable. After all, his relatives in the south had been taught to chant the names of the goddess Meenakshi. Before long, the bright bird had lured me deep into the woods, and I found myself surrounded by what appeared to be the oldest trees in the forest.

Sunlight scarcely penetrated the canopied woods; so dense was the ceiling of limbs and leaves. Dividing my attention between bird above and exposed roots below, I was paying little attention to the path itself when I looked up to find a youthful and extremely handsome yogi standing before me on the trail. His unexpected appearance would have startled me, if not for the unusual calm I felt from his presence. "Namaste," said the yogi as he touched his right hand to his chest.

"Namaste," I said instinctively, wondering where he had come from.

"I come in peace, my friend," he said in a voice filled with kindness.

"Where did you come from?" I had seen no one other than the shepherd since starting up the mountain.

"I live on that mountain you have been admiring."

Puzzled, I thought for a moment. "You mean Nanda Devi? I didn't know anyone lived there." His remark surprised me even more than his presence, but this was not the first time an ascetic had appeared out of nowhere.

"Sit," he said, pointing to a fallen tree.

"How did you know I was here?" I asked.

"Friend, I know much about you."

"Then you know I was just hiking in the forest, heading nowhere in particular."

"Nature is a faithful guide."

"But how did you know I was here?" I asked again.

"It is time. Deep inside you know it is time. So you came to Himalaya for diksha (initiation)."

"I'm not sure I understand."

"Your spiritual practice has opened a door. Allow me to guide you." He spoke with such tenderness that, although his words surprised me, I felt at ease with everything he said.

"Then I guess you know I've been seeking for a long time." I was beginning to suspect he really did know quite a lot about me.

"Yes. Whole life, isn't it? You've got it now. You are able to intend and receive divine union. There is still more for you." He said, pointing to the domed treetops above us.

"There is more. I know that. Yes, that is why I am drawn to these mountains."

"Freedom." He opened his hands and gestured as if making a big circle in the air. "Time for next step to freedom. You understand?"

"Not really," I said.

"Moksha is heart's rejoicing in Bhagawan (God). Life and all its needs become gifts."

"Moksha is enlightenment," I replied.

"Enlightenment yes. God Realization."

"I like coming to the Himalaya. Cities are crowded, but I feel at home here." If given the opportunity, I believed I could live happily in the Himalaya.

He smiled. "Yes, cities chaotic. Disharmony cannot be present in those who aspire for perfection. Prema is key." The yogi spoke softly, but with the authority of a mountain climber describing the view from a summit he had already conquered.

"Prema means Divine Love, doesn't it?" I asked, keen to know his secrets.

"Yes. Let us have taste of prema now. I'll guide you." He then proceeded to put me in a deep meditative state. I sank into my heart, which was already filling with an acutely satisfying substance.

He continued, "Allow prema to bathe your chakras. Everywhere it can go. No limit how wide one can open."

"I feel bathed in a liquid of love inside," I said. He listened, observing how I responded to the instruction.

"Now we will go within together." I closed my eyes and sank into a deep state again.

After a while he spoke, "Now, place your attention in the heart. Breathe into the heart. Center your awareness there. Breathe as if through the wall of the chest rather than through the nose. Feel yourself merging with the one dearest to you. Who would you like to merge with? Krishna? Buddha? Christ?"

"Krishna," I replied.

"Good! Merge with Krishna. Breathe and release, and then merge more deeply. Do this until all restrictions are lifted within, and you feel bathed in prema." I went deeper than I had ever gone. Time passed, but I had no idea how much, and didn't care. I could sit in this forest forever, I thought.

"Now bring your awareness back slowly," came a distant voice. He waited until I opened my eyes, and then asked, "You like?"

"That was great," I said.

"You can do much with this merging. Bhakti is in your nature."

"Can I do it every day?"

"Yes. Do it morning when fresh, before sun comes up."

"I felt a fabric of love I have never felt before. Should I always merge with Krishna?"

"Merge with any divine being you wish."

"I love the feeling," I said. I felt like a helium balloon about to float above the forest. "May I ask something?"

"Yes."

"I feel like I know you. How did you know I was here?"

He paused, looking deep into my eyes before speaking. "We have been together many times, sitting by the fire and dancing by the sea."

He continued, "You are ready for partial dose of prema. It is powerful. World is ready for prema. Time is coming when all unhappiness will be lifted from this planet."

"I may not be ready for a full dose." I was feeling quite intoxicated already. My comment brought another knowing smile to the yogi's serene face.

"Drink in prema. It is here supporting you so life is sweet like honey...balanced and easy. There is no limit how wide you can open.

"Prema will change the world. Old beliefs will go. No more 'us and them.'" I had never seen such compassion in a man's eyes.

"But 'us and them' is how the world is."

"Tired beliefs going now," he said, with a wave of his hand. "When love is everywhere around you, it is everywhere around creation." Not a trace of uncertainty betrayed his words.

"Time will come when people will be dancing in this energy, just dancing for joy. It is long awaited. Humanity has been like a thirsty man in desert crawling after water." Great expanses of time and space were reflected in his eyes, which sparkled like gems. "Know that there is more love than oxygen on this earth. It is for everyone."

"But, Master," (somehow the word 'Master' just came out), "many don't want change. They want things to remain as they are," I protested.

"Those that resist will perish spiritually. Not necessarily physically. What is not harmonious will perish." His words had a finality that convinced me of their truth.

"How does one perish spiritually?"

"By living only material life one self destructs."

"Is our world headed for cataclysm?"

"It can happen. Nothing is fixed. Future is like an ocean. Not solid. Currents, waves, temperature changing every minute." His gaze surveyed all the possibilities, and none of them fazed him in the slightest. "You are filling now with prema. This is 'old hat' for you. Don't be bashful about your wisdom." He seemed to know quite a bit more about me than I knew about myself.

"Does 'old hat' mean I've done this in the past?" I asked.

"Yes. We are simply talking while your system fills with prema."

"I feel light enough to fly."

"Friend, you came here in ski car?"

"Yes, I took the gondola."

"Better not delay. Gondola leaving soon, then finished. Come again. We meet in bugiyal (meadow) where the shepherd sat, Teech?" The yogi, who I was beginning to adore, smiled and folded his hands at his chest, and I did the same before starting down the trail to the gondola station. Strangely, this yogi seemed like an old friend, but I didn't even know his name. I would ask him when we met again on top of the mountain.

Clouds shrouded the upper half of Nanda Devi as the gondola glided above the treetops and ski runs below. Many questions were forming in my head. How had the yogi known I was in the forest, and how could he live in a cave on Nanda Devi peak, which was a good distance away even as the crow flies, not to mention the fact that the sanctuary was off limits to trekkers and climbers? And what did he mean when he said 'we have been by the fire together before?'

As the gondola reached the lower section of the ride, an old ashram came into view. On a ridge to the east, the Shankaracharya Math overlooked Joshimath. I would visit the two-story wood frame ashram built by Maharishi's master in the morning.

Shaŋkara's Tree

The hikes up and down the mountain from my guesthouse in the lower bazaar to the upper market left me breathless. The town sat precariously on several shelves in an earthquake zone, and served as both an army cantonment and an overnight halt for pilgrims on their way deeper into the mountains. The fledgling ski resort above Joshimath seemed out of place, a novelty that could have been developed elsewhere, but I was happy for the gondola that carried me above the clouds.

Maharishi's master, Swami Brahmananda Saraswati, was a lifelong recluse who left his family as a youngster in search of God Realization. After spending sixty years in forested seclusion, he was persuaded to accept the seat of Shankaracharya of Jyotirmath, a position comparable to the pope. According to literature at the math, the seat had been vacant for over a century before Swami Brahmananda Saraswati accepted the position.

The trail to the quaint ashram led past a massive mulberry tree under which Shankara is said to have attained liberation, just as Buddha had achieved it under the sacred Bodhi Tree, also a type of mulberry tree. I entered the ashram grounds through a creaky turnstile gate and followed the trail through a rose garden. The scent of the red, pink, and yellow blossoms was more potent than other gardens, which I attributed to the pure Himalayan air. Two old swamis looking after the ashram let me meditate in the second floor hall where Maharishi's master gave darshan fifty years ago. A pair of Swami Brahmananda Saraswati's wooden sandals graced the dais. Guru Dev, as Maharishi liked to call his master, was not inclined to give long lectures, but he looked deep into the hearts of people, and on that basis, he transformed their lives.

It is said that one day a wealthy man came to Guru Dev, and said, "I have been so happy whenever I have come to you. Would you allow me to donate something for your ashram?"

"No," said Guru Dev. "I do not want your money, but I want from you what is dearest to you!"

"Do you want my estates?" asked the man.

"No, your estates do not belong to you, you have so many debts." Now the man was frightened, but Guru Dev continued, "You have a little box in your pocket. What is in it? That is what I want, for that is dearest to you! For that opium you have been spending all your money and have made your family unhappy. If you have to make an offering, offer not your money, but your defects, so that you are redeemed and made whole."

Trembling, the man took the little box out of his pocket and handed it to Guru Dev. He then prostrated before the master for a long time and thanked him. As the man was about to leave the room, Guru Dev said, "Now go, and work, and make your family happy."

Rare is the master that can reverse misguided lives so readily. Guru Dev always cautioned people not to become ensnared by worldly trappings that are of no lasting value, for he knew how precious it is to have a human body. Guru Dev's own life was an example of a life spent pursuing the highest spiritual attainment. Once a great master was asked by his disciple: "Master, who should I worship, the guru or God?" Without hesitating, the master said, "Worship the guru, because without him, you will never find God."

Guru Dev said, "To get a human body is a rare thing. Make full use of it. There are eight million kinds of lives a soul can gather. After that, one gets a human body. Therefore, one should not waste this chance. Every second in human life is valuable. If you don't value this, then you will weep in the end. Because you are human, God has given you power to think and decide what is good and bad. Therefore, you can do the best possible kind of action. You should never consider yourself weak, or a fallen creature. Whatever may have happened up to now may be because you didn't know, but now be careful. After getting a human body, if you don't reach God, then you have sold a diamond for the price of spinach."

I pressed my forehead to Guru Dev's sandals. He had been a light illumining my way for thirty years, and I felt greatly indebted to him. Ultimately there is nothing one can do to repay the guru for his generosity, except to try to make every minute on the path count.

After departing the ashram, I stopped to admire the mulberry tree. Measuring over sixty feet around, the gnarled tree provided ample shade for meditation. As I sat at its base, my mind elevated easily. My yogi friend's instructions had guided me during each meditation since our meeting in the forest. Rather than sinking into the customary state, I was filled with an exquisite liquid-light that rapidly spread throughout my body. If this were a partial dose, surely a full one would be too much. Indeed, I had been like a man in a desert who had found water after a long search. I understood why Shankara and Guru Dev and my yogi friend reached down to give a hand to those willing to make an effort to reach up.

Once the container was full, the mind lifted into realms the yogi had shown me in the forest. It seemed so natural to soar above the valley, the churning Alakananda River rushing headlong below. I envied the Himalayan eagles whose keen vision saw every twist and turn in the river. Most of humanity was only able to see the next turn in the road. Touching the azure sky above the Alakananda was Nanda Devi, the mightiest of the Indian Himalaya. A white shroud cloaked the lower range, but Nanda Devi hovered above the clouds. I too rose up like a peak into the canopy of blue above. The higher I lifted the greater the bliss became inside, until there was no difference between myself and the space I floated in. Having soared into freedom like a bird in flight, I returned to my seat under the mulberry tree, content. I was ready to see my Himalayan friend again. I would take the first gondola up the mountain in the morning.

Bisht Hospitality

After dinner, I dropped in on the Bisht family to see the gang of kids and their dog who had befriended me the previous day. During the pilgrim season, Mr. Bisht was busy with temple administration and only visited his family two weekends a month. The children, with the exception of the boy, were a gregarious bunch. Ram seemed overwhelmed by his sisters, who smothered him with affection. Swati and Puja, the teenage twins, quizzed me about American pop stars and Indian cricket players, but neither topic was a specialty of mine. In the kitchen, Mrs. Bisht prepared milk from the family cow. The small living room doubled as a bedroom and the two beds were used as couches. It wasn't long before all six Bisht children, their cousins, and Sparky the dog had packed into the room. They sat in each other's lap and draped one over the other, a tangle of arms and legs. The group had been weaned on togetherness. Since meeting the yogi, I had become keenly aware of love wherever it appeared, and the Bisht family radiated it.

The first gondola up the mountain was scheduled to depart at nine, but it didn't leave until it was full. Pilgrims found the tram a novelty, but grew anxious when it stopped suddenly along the way, causing the car to swing precariously in the clouds. The bugiyal where I was instructed to meet the yogi was a good hike up the mountain from the gondola station. I was out of breath from the steep climb as a team of Indian soldiers descended the mountain in fatigues and polished black boots. The tourists riding the gondola ventured only short distances, content to enjoy the views from an outdoor café near the gondola station. Climbing required too much exertion for most. After passing through the old forest, I reached the edge of the high altitude meadow where sheep had been grazing on my previous visit. A sweet silence blanketed the magic mountain. Had I been with a companion, we would have conversed in whispers. I climbed to the top of the highest knoll in the grassy sanctuary, and leaned against the slope. Yellow and blue wild flowers peeked timorously at the sky. Feeling suddenly drowsy, I closed my eyes and drifted into a relaxed reverie. How long it lasted was hard to say, but when I opened my eyes I was not alone. Next to me sat my yogi friend.

"Namaste, my friend. Have you been enjoying prema since our meeting?" the yogi asked.

"Oh yes," I answered, sensing that he knew I had.

The morning sunlight on the meadow allowed me to see my guide in a way that hadn't been possible in the half-light of the forest. His almond eyes were deep pools of understanding; his jet-black hair was long and straight, and fell behind his shoulders. He wore white robes, attire ill-suited for the high Himalaya. I judged him to be about five foot ten. Youthfulness came to mind as I looked at him, but his age was cleverly disguised. I guessed him to be twenty-five, but having read accounts of yogis and their ability to defy ageing, I couldn't be sure. Still-he was beautiful to look at. His hands flowed gracefully as he talked. They moved about, yet they never hurried.

"Yesterday I visited the ashram of my Guru Deva and meditated under Shankara's tree," I said. "I've spent many hours in meditation since we met in the forest. I did merging each time."

"Aacha. Did you know your Guru Deva is still Shankaracharya?"

"I didn't know. His presence is strong in the math."

"You enjoyed under Bodhi Tree as you lifted in freedom above the valley?"

"Oh yes! I followed your instructions. There were moments when I couldn't contain another drop of love. But still I wanted more," I said.

"There is always more, always! Partial dose is potent. Like learning to ride bicycle. Soon tidal waves will wash over you. Know that it is grace that moves love. Now close your eyes and have taste of grace." I sat, eyes closed, as he gave me instructions that took me deeper and deeper.

After many minutes, he spoke again. "Grace is like delivery van. Human mind has no vocabulary for grace. Like air, it is everywhere, waiting to serve. This is the way of Universe. Grace is like butler. Here to serve you."

"Is this grace what Krishna taught?" I asked.

"All great masters teach same thing. Buddha and Christ taught this also. All great masters teach from deep understanding of nature."

"But many do not agree that these great teachers taught the same thing," I said.

"They have not studied with open mind. As you experienced on your soul flight, reality is One. Dogma blinds men to truth." The yogi looked away for a moment, as if assessing the situation. "World is changing, but still clouds hanging over humanity.

"Grace is at your fingertips. You can have everything you need on this earth for wellbeing and progress. Like riding a bike. Start with short rides. Soon always in state of grace."

"Master…is it alright if I call you Master?" I felt a great bond of love with this graceful yogi.

"Ever have I been, ever shall I be," he said with a finality that left me feeling like an iron filing drawn to a powerful magnet.

"Soon you will master grace. All masters are one with grace. Allow it to be your blood and breath." As he spoke, a separation occurred. My awareness floated above me, as if there were two of me. The snow peaks in the distance seemed insubstantial, and yet vividly clear.

"Good. See, you are floating in grace now! Be grateful for everything. Grace acts in your highest good." His words structured my experience as he spoke. I trusted him completely.

"Master, how did our first meeting come about, and how did you know I would be here today?" I wanted to penetrate the veil of mystery surrounding my yogi friend, but only if he was willing.

"Sidha (perfected one) is not bound by time or space. He can go anywhere at any time. Nanda Devi is not so far away. What a yogi needs to know, he can know. You know about sidhis (supernormal powers) already." He was stretching my limits, but I remained silent.

"Then you knew because of yogic powers?" I asked.

"Simple thing. Like riding bike."

"I guess I'm still using training wheels."

"Human life is training. Now, we will fill you with prema, until you say 'Uncle' (a familiar American expression meaning 'enough'). Prema is key to perfection."

"Does that mean we are finished with partial doses? I'm not sure I'm ready for a full dose yet."

"Enjoy blessings of Divine Grace. I am here. You are safe." Immediately, I felt a surge at the base of my spine and a swelling in the heart as light filled my head. The intensity of the experience grew and grew until I could have said 'Uncle,' but didn't. The container was overflowing, as if a hose had been left running in a bucket.

"Aacha. You are feeling happy inside? Notice that love is everywhere. Mind will not understand, but heart knows prema."

"Master, I see myself as a meditation teacher."

"Love has unlimited expression. It can express itself through meditation or hugging an elderly person. No one way to express love. Now close eyes and go deep with me."

As he whispered, I sank like a stone tossed into a lake. Deeper and deeper I plunged, until I reached that familiar region where thoughts are as meaningless as air bubbles. The mind centered, the spine straightened, and I entered the world the Master instructed me to explore. The world of intuition was my favorite realm. It was fresh, original, and deeply satisfying. The breath, although barely perceptible, guided me. Mind and breath moved together in a gentle motion coming up the spine, suspending briefly at the top, and then traveling back down as I exhaled. The easy flow of prana had a multi-dimensional quality, more like liquid than air, as it moved through the body. It was a delicious sensation. I felt this prana could heal anything from an injured knee to a broken heart.

The attention rested in the heart as the breath shifted again. It flowed directly into the heart through the wall of my chest, or so it seemed. I felt a presence in my heart as I inhaled. It was Master. I bowed and touched his feet, a gesture of gratitude that lifted me high above my body in a rush of devotion. 'This is merging,' an inner voice whispered. 'Now lift even more.' With that, another surge swept me still higher, until I felt a holy presence of such potency that I knew I was reaching my limit.

My awareness hovered in a realm of golden light; my heart was immersed in love. I felt goodwill toward everything on the earth below. Plants, animals, and humans were somehow under my protective care, the way I imagined guardian angels looked after children. Indeed, there was more love than oxygen in the world. I felt overwhelmed. It would have been easy to say, 'Uncle.'

"You did not say 'Uncle,' but you wanted too." Again he smiled knowingly.

"I was determined not to. I felt freedom and great compassion for the world."

"This is a simple truth that few understand. The more you share, the more will be given to you. I am pleased. You and I are ONE.

"I will go now. You have done well. As I said, this is 'old hat' for you. We meet again tomorrow. I will find you." Although he graciously allowed me to play the game, he was obviously calling the shots.

I pressed my hands together, and he did the same. "But Master, I don't know your name. Please, tell me your name before I go." I had almost forgotten to ask.

"I am known by different names. Remember, you and I are One. Namaste." Although I wanted to follow him, he waited for me to go. The mystery was building, but I would solve it only if he allowed me to.

I stumbled down the mountain, giddy from the time spent with him. I felt on top of the world, but the altitude, steep slope, and strong separation of awareness conspired, and I stumbled over a root in the oak forest, falling to my knees. Euphoria indeed needed humility as its ballast.

Men Over Forty Five

The following morning I visited Guru Dev's ashram again, and plucked a handful of roses before entering a small cave below the mulberry tree. It was vacant so I went inside and sat down to meditate. I had reached a quiet state when I sensed someone, and opened my eyes. Master stood at the entrance to the cave. I was happy to see him. The silhouette of his slender, well-proportioned body confirmed that he was in perfect health. Age is deceiving, but never more so than in the case of this mysterious yogi, who showed no signs of ageing. My physical state, on the other hand, was already on the decline. My hair was graying and my athletic build was past its prime.

"Cave is yogi's abode. Do you know why?" he asked, taking a seat beside me on the stone floor.

"Must be the silence. I always feel it when I meditate in a cave," I said in a hushed tone.

"Silence is strongest inside Bhudevi (mother earth). Gufa is best place for meditation." He looked completely at home inside the cave.

"Master, I am not yet fifty, and already the body is changing for the worse." I wanted to see if he would talk about health, since he was the healthiest person I had ever met.

"You are vegetarian, yes?" he asked.

"Yes."

"What is diet?"

"I eat subjii (vegetables), fruit, rice, dal. I like milk and fresh cheese. I also take a vitamin supplement." My diet was pretty simple, except for the occasional visit to the five star hotels, where we treated ourselves to rich Italian dishes and chocolate cake, but I didn't mention that.

"Your diet is good. Simple diet is best. What is supplement?"

"I take a supplement called 'Men Over 45,'" I replied.

As he repeated my words, he started to laugh. "Men over 45! But you're just a baby. The guys I hang out with are all over a thousand." I burst out laughing at such a preposterous idea and, at the same time, wondered who his friends were.

"How can I stay youthful like you?" He sensed my genuine request, and possibly my vanity.

"Laughter is best medicine. And eat living foods, whole foods." He paused for a moment, as if deciding what else he wanted to prescribe. "Time to go beyond the meditation you have been doing."

"How?" I asked incredulously.

"Perfection is easy. Just clear your awareness, and lift into light." It sounded so simple. Maybe it was.

"No 'efforting' is there. Allow nature." I understood him completely. Meditation was effortless. After all, Maharishi had taught me thirty years ago that the key to deep meditation was 'letting go.'

"Full expression of life is in two realms. Sidha has head in clouds and feet on earth. Not necessary to live in cave." He knew I had gone into the Himalaya many times seeking solitude, often meditating in caves and on mountain tops.

"But you live in a cave, don't you?" I protested.

"Cave is my home, but not yours. You are for the world." I guess my fascination with caves was just a passing fancy.

"Unexpected turns in river of your life coming. But boat is secure." What, I wondered was he referring to?

I wanted to know about his friends. "Master, who are the friends you speak of?"

"We are sidhas, and we have come to enhance your purpose and others like you. We want to protect you, to give a shield so you can work unnoticed." Work unnoticed? What on earth did he have in mind, intercepting terrorists? I had had enough of terrorist scares.

"Protection from being pulled down. Most people have bad habits," he explained.

"What is it that pulls people down?" I was sure he could see my bad habits if he wanted. Maybe he would mention my fondness for ice cream, or chocolate cake.

"Drugs make mind dull. Alcohol makes anger. Eating meat creates fear. Tobacco increases hate. Sugar makes lethargy and caffeine lust. Moderation is necessary, or better to abstain all together." He spoke with compassion, but a sense of authority was in his voice, as he identified humanity's favorite vices.

"Many people are addicted to the things you mentioned. How does eating meat create fear?" I knew the logic, but wanted to hear his reasoning.

"Animal feels death. Becomes afraid. Fear is passed on to flesh eaters. Karma is there. Remember, 'As ye sow so shall ye reap.'"

"Christ also said, 'Thou shalt not kill,' but most people insist he meant killing other people," I added. I loved Christ's message, but felt it had been badly interpreted.

"Ignorance no excuse," Master said.

"How can a person know when a habit is a good one?"

"If something gives lasting happiness, with no undesirable side-effect, then right direction. Heart is best guide." His simple advice rang true.

"Two directions in the world: toward light and toward darkness. We want those going to light to reach their goal. We want them to go further. Ascension is possible."

"Master, what quality do you appreciate most in a disciple?"

"Perseverance. " His reply was swift and certain. As we sat together in the cave, the power of his presence struck me in a way I hadn't recognized in either the meadow or among the shadows of the forest. Although sunlight filtered through the cave's entrance, we were enveloped in a cocoon of light originating within the cave itself. This was not my first visit to the cave, but the subtle currents of energy I now felt had not been there on previous visits.

As if he read my thoughts, he said. "Today we met in cave so you could experience a new level of oneness. When a dam is open, water level on both sides becomes same."

"You mentioned ascension. What is life like in ascension?"

"You will see light, clarity, world renewal. New world emerging. Clean oceans and forests, safety for all. World is a family. This is future."

"I believe this is our future, but humanity's problems are many," I said.

"We are here. No worry for the world. Two forces on earth. One pulling man down into animal nature. Other lifting him to freedom and God Realization." The master spoke with equal concern for those moving in both directions.

"How do the souls that are spiraling downward awaken?"

"Some will not respond in present incarnation. More chances will come. Soul comes and goes as easily as slipping on an overcoat. In time, he begins search. Bhagawan is patient."

"Master, who do you worship?"

"Siva," he said reverently. "We honor your courage. Be fearless like the warrior you are. You are a truth speaker. Tell those who have hit a ceiling in their practice that there is more." I felt his kindness washing over me like an ocean wave. "Teach those who come as I have taught you. Remember, you and I are One. To call me, simply have my name in your heart."

"But Master, I don't know your name."

He was quiet for a moment, and then he looked into my eyes with great affection. "Whisper Keshava in your heart, and I will come." I tried to move, but found myself riveted to the floor of the cave. I took the roses, and with great effort, I touched my head to his feet, placing the flowers there as well. He placed his hand on my head, and spoke softly, "Now you meditate. Remember, there is no limit to how wide you can open. I will go now." Sunlight framed his form at the mouth of the cave for a moment, and then he was gone.

SEVENTEEN

Appeasing the Gods

The gods approximate the depth and not the tumult of the soul.
—*William Wordsworth*

Siva's Shaft Of Light

I stood on a bluff overlooking the Narmada River, blinded by the late afternoon sun. From my vantage point on the precipice, the humpbacked Madhana Island rose out of the river's rapids like a stone fortress hovering at the center of a broad and churning moat. As we approached the island, a swift current swept our craft down river, but our boatman had aimed the pilgrim's ferry well upstream to ensure that we arrived on target. Although nothing could match the spiritual atmosphere of the Himalaya, we often retreated to India's holy rivers in search of seclusion and renewal, and the Narmada was central India's finest fresh water destination.

The Narmada emerges from the dense Amarkatank forest, a region inhabited by hermits and banjaras (tribals), and flows west across the state of Madhya Pradesh in the direction of the Arabian Sea. The two-mile split in the smooth flowing river turns into roiling rapids as the river squeezes between rock ledges and steep hills. The ferry ride to the island was a noisy one. The crude floating box with its diesel engine and tarp roof chugged toward the landing, where flower vendors stood ready to pounce. We selected our offerings and then walked a vendor's gauntlet past assorted stalls leading to the temple. It was never easy passing through an Indian market with its insistent merchants casting baited pleas from every side. 'Sir, this best brass bowl… Sir, see this fine shawl… Sir, you want coconut?'

The Om Kareshwar temple's white tower formed a series of shrines stacked one on top of the other. Inside the sanctum, a stream of milk cascaded over the Siva linga, but the throng of pilgrims was so tightly packed that we climbed four levels to a shrine directly above the main sanctuary. An opening in the tower filled our attic perch with fresh air and provided an expansive view of the island and river circling it.

Secluded in the tower, we closed our eyes to sample the temple atmosphere. Our intention was to sit for a few minutes, but whenever a place felt right, we stayed longer, sometimes for hours. Having found the prime spot in the tower, we settled in. It wasn't long before I felt like a powerful force, a sensation not unlike the time I parasailed on Lake Michigan, was pulling me up. Up and up my settled mind went on a brilliant shaft of light that beamed high into the sky. The column of light passed right through me and out the top of my head, seeming to originate in the sanctum below. We just happened to be meditating directly above the temple's main sanctuary, and were being swept upward by the powerful current. The deeper I went, the more I lifted, escaping the confines of temple and island altogether. The sensation felt like flying.

The Siva Puranas tell the story of the gods arguing over who is the supreme lord of creation. Vishnu was reclining peacefully on the cosmic ocean when Brahma appeared and demanded that Vishnu worship him. Vishnu countered, saying that it was Brahma who should worship him, and a battle ensued. Being the two most powerful gods in creation (along with Siva), the universe faced destruction as the fight raged, for the fire of the two gods was burning everything up. At a desperate stage of the conflict, Siva appeared as a great column of light that dazzled the two combatants, and said, "Whoever can find the end of this shaft of light is the greatest god." Vishnu and Brahma stopped fighting and agreed to seek the limits of the shaft of light. Vishnu traveled down the shaft in search of its bottom and Brahma went up seeking its top, but neither could find an end to the infinite shaft of light. Vishnu admitted that he had failed to find the bottom, but Brahma lied, saying he had seen its top.

At that point, Siva assumed a visible form and chastised Brahma for lying. Meanwhile, Vishnu reverently grabbed hold of Siva's feet. As a result, Brahma was cursed by Siva never to be worshipped. Siva explained that his form, the shaft of infinite light, should be worshipped in the form of a lingam. Purification of the soul is the primary purpose for visiting a Siva temple, its holy atmosphere removes the accumulated sin of wrong actions, bringing one closer to liberation from the cycle of rebirth. According to the Siva Puranas, the soul revolves lifetime after lifetime like a wheel. Siva, the Creator of the Wheel, is worshipped for the wheel to stop. Gradually karma comes under control by Siva's grace, and the soul achieves final liberation.

When we emerged from the temple, daylight was almost gone. The fading light altered the look of the river, and the red ledges that extended like shelves over the water now hovered in the air. A solitary saffron figure sat absorbed in contemplation on one of the outcroppings above the turbulent current. I also found an isolated ledge and spent the remaining minutes of daylight watching the swirling patterns of the water. Luminous experiences like the one in the temple tower occurred mysteriously, whether in the Himalaya, or by a river, or inside a temple, but I had no explanation for them. They were part of life's lila (play) just as the spinning current was part of the river's lila.

A devotional song from an ashram on the island wafted over the water as the transition from dusk to darkness was completed. Over a thousand years ago, in a lightless underground cave on the island, two of India's greatest sages were destined to meet. The great rishi Govinda was meditating in his cave when the child sage Shankara entered. Govinda, upon seeing the boy, asked "Who are you?" to which Shankara replied, "Sivoham (I am Siva)." Govinda immediately accepted the youth as his disciple, tutoring the young saint in Sanskrit and guiding his inner development, a process that ultimately led to the revival of Hinduism all over India.

Skyclad

The following morning we hired a small boat to make a parikrama (circumambulation) of the island. Circling Siva's island is said to be the equivalent of circumambulating the entire universe, and is a tradition at Om Kareshwar. The downstream sections of the journey were easy for the boatmen, but plying the heavy wooden craft upstream was nearly impossible. The men worked hard, but the boat struggled against the current. Twice the swift white-water pushed us backward, forcing us to portage, but the placid sections beyond the rapids made idyllic boating. Red cliffs and jagged rocks loomed overhead. A pair of black ibis and a painted stork shared a rocky section of the rapids. A water buffalo on the far riverbank appeared ambivalent about entering the water, like a child summoning the courage to leap into a swimming pool.

We docked halfway around the island where a trail led to a monument in the forest. Halfway there, we were mobbed by a gang of exuberant children who escorted us to our destination. The Jain monument honored Digambara (without cloth) priests, who are commonly called skyclad monks. Of all the sects in India, the Jains adhere to the strictest regimen regarding diet and personal habits. Many wear white and strap gauze masks over their mouths to prevent the accidental swallowing of insects. They take their vegetarian vows seriously.

The paintings of the skyclad monks reminded me of a Jain monk we passed on our way to our Delhi office not long after arriving in India. It was a December morning, and traffic was stalled on the Yamuna River Bridge. It was cold and motorcyclists were bundled up in wool sweaters and gloves. Traffic was backed up all the way from Outer Ring Road to the bridge. While we sat stalled in traffic, a figure moved along the shoulder against the flow. As he approached, I rubbed the condensation from the window to have a better look. A well-built young man with long black hair and full beard marched past the car. There was nothing extraordinary about him, except that he was naked. His athletic gait gave him an extra bounce as he passed, and I wondered where he was headed with such purposefulness in his step. Without pretense or self-consciousness, the man marched along as if he were a solitary soldier crossing the Thar Desert. That, of course, was not the case. The sadhu was a skyclad monk.

Jain monks reject all worldly possessions to live an ascetic life. Their nakedness supports the conviction that one should rise above feelings of shame and modesty. The skyclads live entirely on charity, allowing themselves only as much food as they can cup in their hands. Generally, they move about in groups, but the solitary figure by the road was obviously enjoying his freedom, and was quite oblivious to the traffic jam that ensnared the rest of us.

Vedic Engineering

Later that evening, a yagya (Vedic ritual) was in progress inside the Om Kareshwar temple. Indian families commission yagyas for health and longevity, marital happiness, fertility, education, and finances. Having obstacles removed is also popular. Yagyas have even been performed for world peace. In 1944, Maharishi's master, Swami Brahmananda Saraswati organized one of the largest yagyas in history. Vedic pundits from all over India gathered along the banks of the Yamuna River outside Delhi to participate in a World Peace yagya to end World War II. The yagya recitations continued for ten days, and a photo of the assembly of pundits appeared in Life Magazine. Not long after the yagya, the war ended. The following text appeared along with the picture in Life Magazine.

Near the end of WWII, 2000 Hindu priests and 10,000 of their follow-
ers gathered outside New Delhi by the sacred river Yamuna to pray for world
peace. For ten days the murmur of their prayers and the smoke of their fires rose
like incense from a great thatch and bamboo pandal built on the plain. For ten
days austere Brahmins under the leadership of His Holiness Shri Jagadguru
Shankarcharya chanted a master verse from the 3,000 year-old Vedas. "The
sun is the centre of the entire universe; all intelligence, all energy, all health are
derived from the sun." In all, during this Mahayagya or great sacrifice, more
than 10 million prayers of praise and supplication were recited. It was proba-
bly the greatest demonstration of mass praying in modern times, and, as rever-
ent Hindus believe, helped defeat the Axis powers.

In June 1988, India was enduring an unbearably hot summer with no
relief in sight. Drought threatened the nation. Day after day, Indians
looked to the skies hoping for a sign that a rain shower might bring temporary respite. But no clouds appeared, and the sun scorched the land mercilessly. Maharishi was in India at the time, and he, like everyone else, was
aware of the need for rain if disaster was to be averted.

One day a team of south Indian priests arrived at Maharishi Nagar.
They had been invited by Maharishi to perform a rain yagya. In an open
area in the ashram, the colorfully attired pundits invoked the gods in the
traditional way their ancestors had done. Three of the men formed a semi-
circle, pounding on three-foot double-sided drums as the head priest
danced and chanted under a cloudless sky. The dancer moved from drummer to drummer, his brilliant pink and turquoise costume in contrast to
the khaki ground. The priest's movements were not random for his hands
formed mudras (auspicious gestures) and his steps were carefully measured.
As he danced, the chanting grew louder and more intense. The pundit's
incantations formed a series of punctuated notes that became increasingly
rapid-fire as he chanted. The beat became stronger and stronger until the
ritual reached a frenzied pace as the dancer whirled about the field.
Mysteriously, man and nature were harmonizing as a result of the ancient
ceremony.

Clouds began forming overhead. The performance, as artistic as it was
purposeful, was witnessed by a number of ashram residents, including a
pack of stray dogs lying about in the dust. The sky darkened overhead,
looking increasingly ominous as the dance achieved a frenetic tempo. Then
the midnight blue and gray firmament flew into a rage and hail rained
down on the onlookers, sending the dogs yelping for cover. The dancer
continued his ornate rite, undeterred by the pelting of stones. The gods
responded with spirited claps of thunder before unleashing a deluge of

water reminiscent of the downpour that required Krishna's intervention at Govardhan Mountain. Indra, the lord of rain, must have been pleased with the rite as sheets of water soaked the entranced dancer and temperatures dropped. Relief had come at last.

Hailstones are rare on the Gangetic plain and storms of that intensity are common only during monsoon season, but the monsoon was still more than a month away. The success of the yagya pleased Maharishi, who referred to the ritual as Vedic engineering—the ability to apply the understanding of nature to bring practical benefits. Afterward, the weather remained unseasonably cool until the arrival of the monsoon at summer's end.

One day, I spent the last of my savings on a yagya to bolster my personal finances. As a volunteer working in India, I had little income, so I invited a pundit to my room to perform a yagya to Mahalaxmi, the goddess of wealth. The sublime feeling in the room during the ceremony was ample reward, but to my surprise some friends from USA stopped in Delhi on their way to the States a couple days later. Before departing, they slipped an envelope full of hundred dollar bills under my door, an unsolicited gift that eased my poverty.

The relationship between man and nature has become badly strained today. Having witnessed the power of Vedic yagyas to restore the balance between man and nature, I intensified my resolve to support every aspect of nature, seen and unseen. Worship in every religion is ultimately an internal experience. The highly respected Swami Sivananda wrote, "The greatest and highest worship is to pour the waters of pure love on the lingam in the lotus of the heart. External worship is intended to lead to internal worship, wherein there is a flow of pure love." The Bengali saint of saints Ananda Mayi Ma, when asked about temple worship, replied "If you don't find God in your heart, you won't find Him in a stone. And if you do find Him in your heart, you won't need to find Him in a stone." External forms of worship like yagyas are redundant for the adept, but they do it to set an example for the less advanced aspirant and because external worship enlivens spiritual vibration on the physical level, which is of great benefit to society.

Before leaving Om Kareshwar, I walked along the river where I came across a sadhu sitting outside his hut. He wanted some rupees for his meal. The man had the look of a Shaivite (Siva worshipper). A large strand of rudkraksha beads hung across his chest and bold horizontal lines were painted on his forehead. His orange cloth, matted locks, and begging bowl were all trappings of wandering mendicants. I had seen the sadhu smoking chillum (hashish mixed with tobacco) when we arrived. The glow from his short pipe flared red when he pulled on it. The man looked dazed as he got up to approach me, hoping for some rupees. I wanted to ask him where in the scriptures chillum was prescribed, but handed him five rupees instead.

Further along, it was a typical scene by an Indian river. Women beat wet saris against concrete, monks fingered prayer beads, and pilgrims made water oblations to the sun. An old woman touched the forehead of a cow and then her own. The gentle cow's eyes acknowledged the respectful gesture. Everyone depended on the river in one way or another. To perform a yagya near a holy river is said to increase its potency. Whether to invoke rain, create peace, or bring prosperity, the bond between man and nature needs nurturing.

Peace pervaded the river community of mendicant, pilgrim, and cow, and the serene environs reminded me of a dialogue between Yogananda and his western disciple who had been traveling about the country. When Yogananda asked the westerner, "What is your impression of India?" The disciple astutely replied, "Peace. The racial aura is peace."

EIGHTEEN

The Kumaon Hills

Only let the running waters calm down and
the sun and moon will be reflected on the surface of your being.

—*Rumi*

Local Talent

It was my first night in the Kumaon hills and the thunderous commotion outside my window wrenched me from a sweet slumber. I lay there half awake, thinking the Chinese had invaded. The din was deafening; bombs were exploding everywhere. Peering tentatively out my bedroom window I saw that a troop of thirty Hanuman langurs with black-masked faces, coiled tails, and silver fur had invaded the neighborhood, and not the Chinese. The army of apes descended from the forests, moving from tree to tree, leaping from limbs onto the corrugated metal roofs, and making an enormous amount of racket in the process. In response to the aerial invasion, the chained Tibetan bhutias guarding the guesthouses barked ferociously, an ineffective deterrent against the highflying acrobats that swung like trapeze artists through the conifers. The fierce bhutias' growls and barks echoed off the surrounding hills like great claps of monsoon thunder; their futile leaps cut off their breath as taut heavy chains restrained them. The first primate assault had come unexpected, but the battle raged on morning after morning, and I often watched the aerial spectacle from my balcony. Life is a lila (divine play), and with the first rays of light, the fun-loving simians wasted no time getting to their favorite playground.

Nainital, the picturesque hill station in the Kumaon Himalaya bordered by Nepal to the east and Tibet to the north, was our new home. Kumaon, with its gentle terraced hillsides and slate-roofed cottages built on angular terrain is a magical place to explore. Formerly a British hill station, Nainital grew up around a deep lake that is shaped like a foot at the base of forested mountains. The smell of cedar filled the air day and night, and the bark of our guesthouse dog was both thunderous and intimidating.

The large Bhutia dog chained to the balcony was among the fiercest in Nainital. His baritone bark and vicious growl kept everyone away. Mrs. Tewari warned me that his bite was as nasty as his bark, and so I entered the house from the other side, approaching the beast only in the company of his owners, for he had attacked guests in the past. The large metal chain around his thick neck tensed whenever the agile langurs passed overhead. These were the same large skulled brown mastiffs I had seen with the gujjars and shepherds in the Himalayan bugiyals herding sheep and buffalo. To protect them against attack from leopards, shepherds put broad metal collars around the dogs' necks, a vulnerable spot in a skirmish.

We were in Nainital to conduct retreats for teachers from 200 primary schools around India. Principals and teachers came to learn how to teach their students the Vedic disciplines, and our first group arrived from as far away as Rajasthan. Very few had been in the mountains before, and none had been away from their families for more than a few days at a time. Although our students were almost always cold and homesick, the spirit of the group was strong. Lines formed by the phone every evening to call home, and Mrs. Tewari handed out extra blankets.

Before our students could teach the Vedic methods, they needed to be trained in the curriculum. Our workshops taught them pranayama (breathing techniques), nadi vigyan (self-pulse diagnosis), yoga asanas, and graha shanti (recitations to pacify the planets), and how to conduct group meditation in the classroom. By the time the teachers boarded the bus at the end of a retreat, they had a tool belt full of proven methods to improve the health and spiritual well being of their students.

Our hosts, the Tewaris, owned the guesthouse where we stayed and conducted our classes. Mr. Tewari was a retired government accountant and his wife was an English professor at the local government girl's college. Mrs. Tewari was a devout woman and the backbone of a family that included a daughter and son at home, and two older daughters who were married. The boy, Ekesh, was a chubby twelve year-old who was overly fond of American television, and spent hours after school watching professional wrestling. Muscled men like 'Stone Cold' Steve Austin tossed their opponents around the ring, interspersing crude comments as they fought. There were many exceptional aspects of American culture, but 'Stone Cold' wasn't one of them. I didn't like seeing such poor ambassadors representing my culture, if only on television. On one telecast, when asked how he trained, Austin grunted like a Neanderthal, "I eat hamburgers and drink beer." The Tewaris didn't know the fights were staged, that the good guys were just oversized actors providing cheap entertainment. When he wasn't watching wrestling, Ekesh tuned into the cartoon channel. Once again violence was the message.

The multinational companies had come to India to market cultural values and lifestyles. Nike and Reebok sneakers were already on the feet of every boy whose parents could afford them and the first big purchase in the average Indian household was a color television. With the arrival of satellite and cable networks, American programming was wired into every middle class living room. MTV, Baywatch, Dallas, professional wrestling, cartoons; the package was a marketing dream for western companies.

But culture flows in both directions. Nose rings, bindis, and henna tattoos had found their way from India to the States, and I'm sure more than one American mom pushed the panic button when her fifteen year-old came home from school convinced she needed to have her nose pierced or body painted. Cultural exchange is healthy when it's genuine culture and not a here today and gone tomorrow fad, but maybe I was losing touch as the years sped past.

On the final night of each retreat, our students performed songs and folk dances. While the Tewari's watched American TV upstairs, downstairs our course participants sat in a circle on the floor, and when the spirit moved someone, a soul stirring song filled the room. Not knowing what to expect, we were staggered by the quality of the performances. With composure and naturalness, the participants sang songs from their childhood. Some were folk songs; others were devotional. After each heartfelt solo, the group roared its approval. When we were asked to take a turn singing songs from our culture, I felt impoverished by comparison; after having listened to their beautiful ballads, the best I could do was to stumble through a verse of Puff the Magic Dragon.

Gola Baba The Gurkha

One afternoon our host packed us into his jeep and drove us to the home of Gola Baba, a Gurkha from western Nepal. Gola Baba was a retired Indian air force officer living on a modest pension with his wife, daughter, and grandson. His son-in-law was serving in the Indian army, and had been away for six months. Gola Baba was not your average retired military officer for his reputation as a healer of rare skill brought scores of people to his house each day. On our way to see Gola Baba our hosts told us that the healer refused any kind of payment, but we stopped at a shop and bought some wild honey as a gift.

Gola Baba winced as I ducked under the low doorway of his adobe-walled room. "Careful, friends. Low ceiling!" He cautioned, as I bumped my head. The graying man seemed to be expecting us; his warmth and naturalness made us feel completely at home the moment we sat down. His young grandson toddled in and out as we listened to the former pilot explain how his gift of healing had come to him and leafed through a stack of photo albums of his patients who were both western and Indian. According to our guesthouse owner, the retired pilot could cure everything from serious physical ailments to family financial problems.

With the innocence of his three year-old grandson, Gola Baba pointed to a poster of Durga (Divine Mother who rides on a lion) taped to the wall, and gushed, "She is my Mommy, She is my Mommy." The goddess had appeared to Gola Baba in his youth, he said, and blessed him with the ability to both heal and intuit the needs of anyone who came for help.

Gola Baba saw patients from all over the world. His detailed records and photos supported his claim that over 300,000 people had come to him over the years. A European film crew had made a documentary about his life. Staunchly refusing to accept any form of payment for his services, Gola Baba waved away our jars of honey. We enjoyed the healer's company, and he seemed to enjoy ours. After all, we were quite healthy, a contrast to most who came.

Gola Baba's style was unorthodox. First he instructed his patient to light an entire pack of incense and place it under the tree where he sat. He then took two sticks from the pack, and waved them at the individual while blowing in their direction. Next, he instructed the patient to perform some exercises on the ground in front of him. Some of the stretches were difficult, but Gola Baba helped each person, often despite protests of pain. The old healer had a good sense of humor, but insisted his patients perform the exercises as best they could. Once the patient had assumed a contorted posture (mine was sitting on my heels, feet flat on the ground), Gola Baba slapped the patient hard on the back, a knock that had toppled me over. His unorthodox methods were famous for removing disease and even restoring mobility to paralyzed limbs if the patient was willing to come often enough.

"Gola Baba, you have a family to feed. Why do you refuse payment?" I asked.

"She who gave this gift has instructed me not to accept anything in return. That is the agreement," he replied with the firmness of a military officer.

"Why do you strike the patient on the back?" I asked, having just received a forceful blow.

"You see, the slap delivers the necessary karma to allow the healing," he explained as he prepared to strike yet another patient. Spending the afternoon in his yard, watching him help sick and distressed villagers without accepting gifts or payment of any sort was something I had not seen since the Philippines where faith healers often worked without expectation of compensation. Although his methods were different from the Manila healers, his results were equally impressive. Like the mother-daughter team that lived in a bamboo hut on the outskirts of Manila, Gola Baba went straight for my neck. He hadn't even waited for me to tell him what was wrong. These people knew instinctively what the problem was and went about their work efficiently. I was convinced that extraordinary compassion played a role in his treatments.

That night an apparition appeared in my sleep. I was surprised to see him standing by my bed. It was Gola Baba in his body of light. "I've come to finish the work I started," he said. "Your neck will be better in the morning." He then went to work, and when I woke in the morning, my neck felt better than it had for a long, long time.

Badrinath

As Mrs. Tewari told the story over dinner of how her mother spent four months walking the narrow and often perilous Himalayan trails on a yatra (spiritual pilgrimage), the image of a tiny woman walking from sunup until sundown with a minimum of food and water came to mind. The journey was so hazardous that pilgrims bid a final farewell to family and friends before departing. Resolute in her desire to reach the holy Badrinath shrine, Grandma Tewari reached her goal and considered it the crowning achievement of her life. The rough Himalayan trails cut through heavy forests and along rushing rivers, passing through regions inhabited by leopards, bears, and poisonous snakes. Tigers were once a threat, but they no longer roam the hills. Sometimes weary pilgrims were able to secure overnight lodging in villages along the way, but not always. It was a once in a lifetime journey that every devout Hindu of former generations wished to make, and Mrs. Tewari spoke with pride about her mother's achievement.

We were on our way to Badrinath, but not on foot. I was keen to make the trip because it would take us near the Nanda Devi region where I had met the Himalayan Master. Secretly, I hoped to meet him again. Ten minutes out of Nainital, the road switched back repeatedly as we traversed the face of a mountain. A speeding taxi with Delhi plates bullied past us, nearly forcing us over the escarpment. The two vehicles' side mirrors scraped as the thoughtless driver trespassed on our share of the narrow road. Then, five minutes later, a three-ton boulder crashed to the pavement just meters ahead of us. Was our trip ill fated, I wondered?

The road to the Badrinath shrine, one of the holiest spots in the mountains crosses the Alakananda River and then makes a steep ascent up a vertical mountain leading to a region known as the Valley of the Gods. As we were about to begin our climb, we passed a procession of soldiers walking behind a shrouded form on a bamboo bier. A soldier had fallen from a mountain and his comrades were taking the body to the river where it would be consumed in flames, its ashes consigned to the water.

The climb took us around switchbacks cut from the side of the mountain. The road was single lane in many places and we cautioned our driver to proceed slowly. There were few guardrails and the drop was one no one cared to think about. Waterfalls cascaded down the length of smooth rock faces and streams tumbled over stacked boulders, providing breathtaking theater at every turn. Conifers had rooted in the rocky clefts and crags. The peaks overhead were veiled due to haze caused by forest fires, the result of many months of dry weather. We were not optimistic that we would glimpse the high Himalaya during our stay. Frequent avalanches and rockslides made the Badrinath road a challenge to keep open, but its strategic importance for border security necessitated it. On the final switchback before reaching our destination, our vehicle waded through a stream that soaked its undercarriage.

The pilgrimage town of Badrinath is situated at over 10,500 feet. The winds that whip through the icy pyramids above the village cause temperatures to dip below freezing even in summer. As a result, I slept under a mountain of blankets and even lit a pack of candles in a failed effort to stay warm. A sleeping bag was all that was needed, but I didn't have one with me. The feature attraction in the valley is the Badrinath temple, which is painted in bright colors reminiscent of the stupas of Nepal and Tibet. In fact, Buddhists, after removing the 5,000-year-old statue of Lord Vishnu and submerging it in the Alakananda River, converted the temple into a stupa, which is how it remained until Shankara, the Hindu revivalist, recovered the stature and reinstalled it in the temple.

The blue, red, and mustard-colored temple overlooks the Alakananda River that flows furiously below its entrance. Heavy stone pillars define the small space in the inner sanctum. We squeezed inside the columns along with fifty peasants to watch the elaborate ceremonies performed by the chief priest, who added tasteful theater to the rituals. With brass oil lamps, baskets of flower petals, and holy basil cuttings as props, the priest flamboyantly performed while a team of pundits chanted in unison. They sat in pairs on either side of us, and their powerful voices set the pious mood.

The focal point of the ceremony was the black granite form of Vishnu at the center of a recessed chamber. The weathered statue had been retrieved from the river over a thousand years earlier. Time and a swift current had worn the deity's features, but the form of a yogi sitting in meditation was still visible. The silhouette in the stone was that of an ascetic retreating into the Absolute, melting into infinity. All eyes in the hall were fixed on the granite form as the priest waved a camphor fire in front of it. I soon fell under the influence of the Rawaal's (chief priest's) magic and closed my eyes. The image of the granite deity remained in my mind's eye, and I felt the urge to merge with it. I focused on Vishnu's image, drawing him into my heart. With each breath his presence increased until a sweet vibration filled me. Softly I breathed through the wall of my chest, feeling lighter and lighter as if I was being lifted on the wings of a great eagle. Perhaps it was Garuda, Vishnu's mount. Soaring through inner realms, a great cosmic ocean spread before me. In the vast sea of existence, I was no more significant than a drop of water, and at the same time, I was the ocean itself. Molten sands of consciousness rippled in all directions, alive and scintillating. Vishnu, Vishnu I repeated over and over to myself...and then there was nothing.

The chanting kept me faintly in touch with the sanctum. When the Rawaal finished the aarti ceremony, he handed an attendant a platter with the camphor lamp on it. As the holy flame was passed through the group, pilgrims tossed sprigs of holy basil and flower petals toward the idol, and took turns sweeping their hands through the fire and then touching their foreheads, as if inviting the flame to enter them. It is, after all, the fire god Agni who takes the offerings to the abode of the deity before returning with prasad (blessings) for the devotees. Before closing the temple for the night, the Rawaal removed the large blue diamond from the forehead of the deity, holding it up for everyone to see. The devotion on the faces of those inside the sanctum was apparent, and they were amply rewarded for the sacrifices they had made to be there.

Having visited with the Rawaal on previous trips, I knew him to be a shy man who took his work seriously. During the six-month season when the temple is open, the Rawaal is expected to perform every ceremony from sunrise until the temple closes each night. If, for any reason, he missed even a single performance, he would lose his position and his assistant would take over his duties as chief priest. While we sat with the Rawaal in his apartment, he talked about how the temple had attracted pilgrims for thousands of years. Until recently, those who journeyed to the Valley of the Gods braved perilous conditions to get there. Danger was imminent everywhere along the pilgrim trail. Wild animals were not the only threat to defenseless pilgrims; the footing on sections of the path was unsafe, and some tumbled to their death in places where the trail had washed away. I found it hard to believe that Mrs. Tewari's mother, who I imagined to be as devout as her daughter, had made it to Badrinath and back on foot.

Before the army built permanent river crossings, rope bridges were the only means of crossing the turbulent streams that carved deep gorges in the mountains. Freezing temperatures also threatened pilgrims who were unused to the high altitude. But none of this deterred the ardent seekers who came for a glimpse of Badri-Vishal. With the construction of the motor road, remote Himalayan temples like Gangotri and Badrinath are now accessible, and 400,000 pilgrims come annually. As a result, hotels and dharamshalas have sprung up everywhere in the valley.

As we were about to leave the Rawaal's apartment, I noticed a framed drawing on his wall. The sketch was of a Himalayan yogi deep in meditation. I was immediately attracted to the picture. "Who is this yogi?" I asked the Rawaal.

"The previous head priest drew that picture from a vision he had of a yogi who is said to be ageless and appears from time to time in these mountains," he said. It was time for the Rawaal to return to the temple, but for some peculiar reason I couldn't pull myself away from the picture on the wall.

The inner sanctuary of the temple was a favorite of mine, but unfortunately not everyone came in the spirit of community worship. One evening, the Rawaal was performing puja when a politician forced his way to the front of the packed hall. After jostling the tightly packed crowd, he reached the front. The Rawaal kept an eye on the intruder as he performed the puja. After finishing, he chastised the politician, reminding him that all have equal right to God's blessings. The chastened politician left quietly, but began plotting his revenge. When he got back to civilization, he created a storm over the Rawaal's behavior, and demanded censorship of the priest. By now the story was being reported in the papers, and the Rawaal found himself involved in a simmering controversy, knowing full well the power and pettiness of the Indian politician. But he stood firm, and demanded a public apology from the quarrelsome babu and he gave the man a deadline to do it. The politician promptly rescinded his accusations and wrote a letter of apology that appeared in the *Times of India*.

When I heard the outcome, I felt India's good guys had won a small battle against the corrupt public officials that have held the nation hostage for decades. It was gratifying to know that a thoughtful and reserved man like the Rawaal had stood up to an arrogant politician and triumphed.

To escape the chill temperatures outside, pilgrims sat near kitchen fires or sipped chai in riverside cafés. Snow fell on the footbridge leading to the temple. From the restaurant window, I could see the long row of mendicants huddled under blankets along the path, snowflakes collecting on their beards. I watched families experience snowfall for the first time. They danced about like children on the street. Inside, we sat at a table with a family that entertained us with bhajans. The children were good singers and the boy pounded a powerful rhythm on the table, his makeshift tabla. Although it was spring, the weather shifted with the whims of the wind.

After another arctic night, I peered out my frost-etched window to see if clouds still shrouded the valley, but the atmosphere was a portrait of Himalayan perfection. The cerulean sky above and behind the superbly contoured Mount Neelkanth provided a suitable backdrop for the snow-clad peak. After admiring the unspoiled beauty above us, we bathed in the hot springs near the temple, which are said to have curative powers. And healing it was, if only because it relieved the chill of a night spent in a freezing room.

After visiting the temple, we trekked to Vasudhara Falls, the source of the Alakananda River. By mid-morning, our Nepalese sherpa had led us into the heart of the Valley of the Gods. Mana, a Tibetan village stood vacant, waiting for its inhabitants to return with warmer weather. Mana was on the ancient trade route, the first village that Tibetan caravans encountered in India after crossing the nearby Mana pass. Beyond the village, we stopped at Bhimpol, a spectacular glacier-fed spring that foamed and roared between massive boulders as it funneled into a deep and narrow gorge that poured into the Saraswati River. The air at Bhimpol was misty, the force of the water so powerful that a massive boulder trembled under its relentless force. Hermits lived among the cliffs above the gorge, but I could see padlocks on the doors to their caves, for the yogis, like their

Tibetan neighbors, had not yet returned from lower altitudes.

The valley turned to the west as we climbed to our destination. Ahead of us loomed Kamet, a superb peak of dizzying height near the border of Tibet. The trail to the falls is described as the place where the Pandava brothers made their final walk before ascending into heaven at the conclusion of the epic Mahabharata. Only the eldest of the clan, Yudhishthira, remained on earth along with his dog, refusing to join his brothers in heaven unless the dog could join him. From my vantage point on the trail, I could see no reason to go anywhere to attain a heavenly abode, for we were standing in its midst already. Peaks in all directions enclosed the trail, their pointed tops looking like white wizard hats. Alpine flowers bloomed violet and yellow on grassy patches, and scree-covered the slopes above the trail.

The spraying twin falls came into view. As we approached the falls, we passed a cave with a large brass bell at its entrance. I sensed someone was inside the cave, but we passed without stopping. We then crossed a slick snowfield flecked with pebbles and shards of ice to get to some rocks between the plummeting streams. Sitting on the boulders, the spray cooled us first from one side, and then the other, as the wind shifted directions. Three sherpas shared our trail mix while we relaxed on the rocks. The mild fatigue of the trek soon evaporated in the vicinity of the falls. We were now ready to connect with the subtler energies of the region.

It was time to locate a spot for meditation. I stuck my head inside the cave with the bell and found a hermit warming himself over orange embers. He had a kindly but weathered look and motioned for me to join him. Sitting opposite him, I could see the clouds forming over his eyes. I was certain, the fire that warmed the recluse was the culprit just as it had been with Ram Baba in Gangotri. Occupational hazard, I thought. I stayed with the gentle man for a few minutes before climbing to the ledge above his cave where he suggested I meditate. The spot, he said, was a place suitable for a sage. Indeed, the hermit's craggy seat had a commanding view of the peaks, and I was pleased that he had directed me to it. But it wasn't easy looking within when such enormity loomed without. Wanting to fathom as best I could the inner landscape of the region, I was caught between two worlds, uncertain whether to close my eyes or bask in the awesome presence of the Himalaya. And so I solved my dilemma by meditating with eyes wide open.

Adding to the mystique of the angular obelisk, Kamet was falling under the spell of a white veil. An ethereal mood had come over the landscape, the result of the milky hue that now hovered above the valley floor. We were in the heart of a valley that is said to be home to the gods. It seemed an eternity from humanity, but the gods are said to do their best work in isolation. After watching the clouds cloak the upper portion of the peaks, I engaged my mantra with a few casual repetitions. In this pristine place it didn't take much before I found myself swimming in an ocean of aloof awareness. The heart absorbed each whisper of the secret word as it faded into the substratum of my mind.

The Himalaya transmitted the primal impulses of the mantra like a radio tower amplifying a signal. The reverberation within created an equal effect without, for no dissonance was present in the valley to disturb either the emission of sound, or the receiving of it. If anything, the primordial note was magnified, and its silent murmur assumed a life of its own, humming as if in resonance with infinity. Maybe this was how the sages beamed their telepathic messages of peace to the world from their hidden abodes. Although I had never been in a more isolated place, I felt that every impulse affected every other human being. Surcharged by the cosmic generator, I found it difficult to dislodge myself from the ledge.

It would have been easy to extend our stay, but the Indian army accounted for foreigners along the Tibetan border, and had advised us to return to Badrinath before nightfall. Gravity swept me along as we descended from the falls. On the return we stopped at Vyasa Gufa, a cave said to have been the abode of Rishi Vyasa who cognized the Vedas over 5,000 years ago. I was reminded of a TM course I had attended in an equally pristine atmosphere in the Swiss Alps in 1973. Maharishi had created a stir of excitement among our group of American college students when he came for a visit. Most of us were teenagers who had never seen him in person. The night Maharishi arrived we were in our seats, flowers in hand, long before the lecture started. Our expectations were stratospheric, but our special guest never came to the hall. Nor did he come the next day, or the next. After three days, everyone was totally discouraged, thinking Maharishi didn't like us.

But our inexperienced group knew little of the ways of our teacher. We had almost given up on the idea of even seeing Maharishi when he walked unannounced into the hall one evening, wearing a smile that lit the room. The first words out of his mouth were "I'm sorry I didn't come sooner. I didn't think you would mind if I spent some time with Veda Vyasa." What had he meant? Had Vyasa somehow been in our Swiss hotel.

We were dumbfounded. We had heard about the great seer who was said to have compiled the Vedas, a body of scriptures four times as large as the Bible. Rumors circulated through the group that Vyasa still inhabited a Himalayan cave, but no one could imagine how he could have come to the Alps. After Maharishi's opening comment, he spoke late into the night about Vyasa's cognitions, a lecture that continued for several days. For the most part the lecture went over my head, but decades later the talk is still considered one of Maharishi's finest.

Two images from that three-month stay near St. Moritz are still with me. Maharishi's infectious laughter and the crimson rose he fingered as he spoke remain etched in my memory. As Maharishi left the hall the last night, I handed him a rose, and he gave it back to me, smiling over his shoulder as he walked out of the hall. The rose kept its bloom for many days. I had hoped it would last forever. It didn't, but Maharishi's smile has.

Maharishi And Author In Switzerland, 1973

I had only one thing on my mind the rest of the way down the mountain: the hot springs at the temple. When we arrived in Badrinath, we headed straight for a bath. I paid little attention to the Indian men sitting by the side of the tank. No one was in the water, but it never occurred to me why. I quickly found out. The water was much hotter than it had been in the morning, far too hot to linger even for a moment, and I scrambled out as fast as I could, lucky to avoid being scalded. The men sitting by the tank had a good laugh as I cooled down, feeling like a lobster that had narrowly escaped the boiling pot.

Our return to Nainital kept us on the road late into the night. Drivers often refuse to drive in the mountains after dark because of the threat of boulders dropping onto the road. As we crept along, the eerie glow of forest fires lit the hillsides. Several villages were in danger of being consumed and we felt the fear of the forests. The ominous explosions of ignited wood alarmed all the creatures in the vicinity. It was an anxious situation that depended solely on Mother Nature for a solution.

The road was perilous and our driver Ganesh and I were navigating as a team when he suddenly shouted "Bhog! Bhog!" Bhog means tiger, but I couldn't imagine seeing one in this region, and was unsure exactly what Ganesh was trying to communicate as I scanned the terrain lit by our headlights. Then I saw it. Off the pavement to our left stood the cat. It was a leopard, not an uncommon sight in the mountains. The spotted predator, being a nocturnal hunter, was either searching for dinner or had come down the mountain to flee the fires.

The combined omens of forest fire and leopard seemed inauspicious, but the stealthy cat interested us since we had been reading a book by the famous tiger hunter Jim Corbett. *Man Eaters of Kumaon* is a compelling account of a British outdoorsman raised in the Himalaya who hunted man-eating tigers and leopards. Corbett, who grew up in Nainital where his father was postmaster, is said to have killed over a hundred known man-eaters. In the forward to his book, he explained that most man-eating cats attack humans because of injuries that prevent them from hunting their normal prey.

Old age or a paw infected by porcupine quills were the common reasons why the magnificent creatures resorted to preying on villagers. The Champawat tiger that had been chased out of Nepal and the Panar leopard had killed 836 Nepalese and Kumaon villagers before Corbett tracked them down. Predatory beasts like these would have posed a major threat to pilgrims on the lonely footpaths en route to Badrinath, but now their population is diminished. There are no tigers in the mountains anymore, and the leopards have retreated to less populated areas.

On my final day in Nainital, rain pounded the corrugated roofs in the neighborhood with the intensity of a Kerala drum festival. The pre-monsoon that would extinguish the forest fires upstaged the usual clamor of monkeys leaping from roof to roof and the chorus of Tibetan Bhutias that responded to the primate pranks. As my bus pulled away, raindrops dimpled the surface of Naini Lake without making a sound. It had been a magical ten weeks, and my departure for the dusty plains was a reluctant one. One became easily attached to life in the Himalaya with is fragrant forests, kindly villagers, and spiritual disposition, and I found it difficult to leave.

The Himalayan retreats had been training for us as much as they had been for our students.

NINETEEN

Balaji And The Babus

The soul should always stand ajar; ready to welcome the ecstatic experience.

—Emily Dickenson

The Liu

Somewhere in the sandy expanse of the Thar Desert, a devilish spirit mixed a potent concoction of dust, wind, and heat. Muslims call these mischievous spirits djinns, and ascribe to them an assortment of qualities: some good, some not so good. If, in fact, an ill-tempered djinn was whipping up the sinister winds from western Rajasthan, he was doing a fine job.

Delhi's insufferable summer heat holds the city hostage for sixty days a year. The ransom for one's freedom from the onslaught is the cost of a week's stay at a hill station. Those who can afford it, escape to Shimla or Nainital, the rest move about the city at half speed. The elderly and infirm lay lifeless on charpoys (string cots), praying for an early monsoon. Taxi and auto rikshaw drivers are testy and easily irritated. Shop owners doze in front of oscillating fans. Schools close. The elite, who work in air-conditioned towers around the city, slip away with their families to Europe and America. Government employees stay home, or produce less than normal, which is never much. Foreign diplomats return to their homelands. Fan salesmen and ice cream vendors are the few who benefit from the heat, but they too pay a price. The city is under siege annually.

As our vehicle headed out of the concrete inferno, we passed a cynical sign that read, "Delhiites don't trust the air they can't see." Add uncontrolled pollution to the Djinn's maddening mix, and it's easy to see why those who could, left town. My pretense for leaving was a meditation course in Shimla, the former summer capital of the British Raj. On the day we departed Delhi, angry winds swept litter about the roundabouts in Connaught Circus where two boys splashed in a fountain, the only sign of life outside our vehicle. I breathed a sigh of relief as we escaped the furnace.

Delhi natives refer to the punishing winds as The Liu (The Desert Wind), a menacing windstorm similar to those that periodically sweep through Europe, the Middle East, and southern California. In Switzerland and Austria, the Foehn whips hot, dry winds through Alpine valleys causing mountain sickness. Egyptians suffer from airstreams called Khamsin, which induces a form of madness. Crime and automobile accidents rise so dramatically that Egyptian judges sentence more leniently during Khamsin than the rest of the year.

The cantankerous winds contain higher concentrations of positive ions than normal air, a possible explanation for the increased depression, anger, and tension they cause. Indians are more resilient than most and endure the annoyance stoically, but the Djinns wreak havoc with everybody's sanity.

The Government Babus

Shimla's forested mountains, inspired vistas, and temperate climate proved the perfect antidote to Delhi's sweltering heat. It's easy to understood why the British packed up their files and woolens, and boarded the narrow gauge train for the steep ascent to Shimla when the Liu arrived. Our cozy guesthouse was positioned on such dizzyingly vertical terrain that taxis refused to venture down the drive. Our own vehicle lacked the horsepower to climb the steep gradient with passengers, forcing us to hoof it up the hill to lighten the load.

Shimla is near India's best fruit orchards and vendors at the ridge mall sold tree ripened ruby plums by the case and plump strawberries by the kilo. Exotic lychees were plentiful and delicious. Halfway through our stay, a hydroelectric company invited us to teach a meditation course at their facility deep in the Himalayan interior where glacier fed rivers washed over the feet of snowcapped peaks. No travel agent could have planned a better holiday.

We were busy packing for the remote region of Kinnaur when the guesthouse phone rang. A barely audible German voice at the other end of the line shouted instructions that we didn't want to hear; we were to catch the next flight to Hyderabad, a city at the opposite end of India. The instruction meant returning to Delhi immediately; an unappealing prospect at best. The news was so badly timed that we pretended to be unable to hear Immanuel over the scratchy line, but after cross-examining the German, we learned that the government of Andhra Pradesh had requested statewide programs, and that a million people were waiting to learn meditation. We were to meet with the state's Chief Minister (like a US governor) the moment we arrived in Hyderabad. And so our junket to the Himalayan interior was jettisoned and we found ourselves seated opposite the Chief Minister (CM) of Andhra Pradesh twenty-four hours later.

Chandra Babu Naidu was a legend of sorts and possibly the best-known Indian politician in the west. He was already on the radar of the world's movers and shakers, and two famous Bill's, Clinton and Gates, had recently paid him visits. A tall, well-built man with a trim and graying beard, his eyes had the focus of a man on a serious mission. He seemed the antithesis of the stereotyped Indian politicos who relish the spotlight and perks without concern for achieving anything. When we walked into his office, the CM dispensed with formalities, preferring to roll up his sleeves like a plant manager from Cleveland. Seated without pomp or pretense behind his desk, Chandra Babu reviewed our proposal thoughtfully. He then suggested we begin teaching the entire upper echelon of the state government the following morning. He apologized for the short notice, but confessed that his calendar was completely booked for the next nine months. According to an aide, the Chief Minister worked eighteen-hour days. After hearing that, I felt better about having aborted our latest Himalayan adventure.

At 8:00am the following morning, I addressed the delegation assembled in the white-domed Jubilee Hall built by the Nizam of Hyderabad. On the walls of the grand hall were life-sized portraits of Mahatma Gandhi, Pundit Nehru, and Dr. Ambedkar, the architects of Indian independence. Every seat in the hall was filled as I explained that everyone would have the chance to learn meditation in the coming days.

After my talk, two men and their assistants approached me from different directions. One was a television reporter from Star Network who wanted to do an interview outside, and the other was Mr. Rao, the number two man in the state government. The Chief Secretary was upset and didn't waste any time letting me know it. "Why are you doing this to us?" he asked accusingly.

"Doing what, sir?" I replied. He had caught me off guard. I had just stepped away from the podium and was feeling quite satisfied by the way things were going.

"Why must we all learn meditation?" he fumed. Mr. Rao was angry.

"Please, Mr. Rao. It will all be clear tomorrow." I could see that my answer was unsatisfactory, but that was the best I could do. The following day Mr. Rao and his colleagues learned meditation in our guesthouse. When the Chief Secretary emerged from his meditation, I barely recognized him. His frown was gone; a broad smile replaced it. "It's a miracle. This meditation is a miracle," he beamed. I was relieved to see that he was satisfied after the way he had accosted me the previous day.

If Andhra Pradesh were a nation, it would be among the twenty largest in the world. With seventy million people to look after, Chandra Babu and his staff worked overtime seven days a week. The CM's ironclad resolve appeared to be moving mountains, but time would tell whether his futuristic vision dovetailed with the needs of the people, especially the farmers. Chandra Babu had staked his political career on technology and the information economy, believing it to be the state's passport to prosperity.

Happy Vaidya

One day a newcomer came to my room. His name was Chari and if he stood up straight, he reached five foot two. The distinguishing feature about Chari was a pair of eyes that twinkled the way one imagined a wizard's would. They also penetrated deeply. Chari was from a village outside Hyderabad, the grandson of a shaman who knew the secrets of herbs and yogic practices. Like his grandfather, Chari was a skilled physician who had been schooled in forest retreats rather than a medical school laboratory. It became apparent that Chari had special gifts when a German friend of mine asked him to diagnose a health problem that had bothered him since childhood. Without any prior knowledge, Chari looked into Wolfgang's eyes and gave a detailed description of the problem. We were all dumbfounded by the casual way Chari went about his profession!

"Chari, where did you learn this?" I asked.

"As a boy, I spent all my time with my grandfather," he said. "He taught me the secrets of seeing and the inner realms." His eyes twinkled like lustrous stars as he spoke.

"Most vaidyas diagnose by feeling the pulse, but you didn't touch Wolfgang," I countered.

"Touching not necessary. Whole story is in the eyes. Even past life can be known from eyes."

"Were you born with this skill, or did you learn it from your grandfather?" I asked.

"Both. I was born with ability, but grandfather taught me how to use it."

"Do you practice meditation?" I asked.

"Yes. My grandfather sent me to live in the forest for two years when I was young. I did much meditation then, but now I want to learn from you."

"I can teach you," I said, wondering if he shouldn't be teaching me. "Will you have a look at me?" I was astonished at how easily he had diagnosed Wolfgang and wanted to see if he could do as well with me.

After looking into my eyes, he said. "Some neck pain. Otherwise health good." Of course he was right. My neck had recently started hurting again.

"What do you recommend?"

Without answering, Chari performed a swift maneuver, and the next thing I knew he was upside down walking around the room on his hands with the agility of a gymnast. When he finished, he said, "Handstand is good remedy for neck." Then he performed the feat again, this time laughing so hard I was afraid he would crash into the bed.

"How did you make your diagnosis?" I asked.

Chari chuckled, "You can know anything about a person from the eyes. They tell story of the soul. Past, present, and future." I did not doubt his words, or his methods.

As our jovial friend was about to leave, I dubbed him 'Happy Vaidya' (Happy Doctor) and invited him to come back soon. He liked the name, and repeated it as he bounded out the door. We would see more of Happy Vaidya.

In the days that followed the Jubilee Hall session, grumpy bureaucrats emerged from their meditations looking younger and happier. Within weeks, we were teaching meditation in virtually every department of the state government. Government ministers, rank and file bureaucrats, police officers, prisoners, students, and business executives were introduced to meditation. Even our guesthouse staff learned. 23,000 people had been initiated in the first eight weeks, and the numbers were growing daily. But if we were to teach a million, we would need reinforcements.

Not all government departments are created equal. I volunteered to teach in the Department of Social Welfare and Backward Classes, and my students were a sleepy bunch. There was no conference room in the building and so we gathered on the floor in the hallway. After teaching in Delhi's corporate boardrooms, it was a humbling experience, but I didn't mind.

{

After each course, the department director invited me into his office for tea, but he never had much to say, and I began to wonder if he was satisfied with our meditation classes. After a few weeks, everyone in the department had learned to meditate. As we met together for the last time, Dr. Garg said, "Dr. Steve, we are pleased with this meditation and want it for all of our residential schools. We have 60,000 students. They should all meditate." I was ecstatic. To have impoverished children given the chance to meditate pleased me, and I congratulated Dr. Garg for his vision.

Weeks later, just as suddenly as he had disappeared, Chari bounded into my room in the middle of my morning meditation. I was beginning to wonder if I would see him again. He placed a large bag on my bed and circled the room as he gave instructions.

"This is for your neck Steveji," Chari said, opening a bag filled with carefully wrapped powders. "It is special bhasma preparation made from crushed plants gathered in the forest. Powerful medicine. Take a pinch with ghee each day."

After handing me the medicine, Chari held my hand in his palms; once again, we were laughing like children. Despite his informal role as medical adviser, Chari treated me like an older brother. But he was the wise one. Chari was part wizard and part hobbit- intuitive, charming, and ever playful.

"Chari, do you have a job?" I asked. I wanted to know more about this baffling new friend who had mysteriously come into my life.

"No need!" he replied with a wave of his hand. "Father provide money. He wants me to follow his father's path." Happy Vaidya lived a charmed life, performing good deeds along the way.

Seven Hills In Heaven

Seven hills rise unexpectedly out of the dusty Deccan plains in the southeast corner of Andhra Pradesh. As our loose-jointed, faded blue Ambassador taxi carried us from Tirupati airport up the narrow twisting road, lush vegetation absorbed the mid-day sun overhead. Climbing to 3,200 feet, we arrived at the entrance to a well-kept garden community of tidy guest cottages, dormitories, hotels, shops, and eateries scattered among flowering bushes and massive mulberry trees.

I was prepared for a marathon effort, but we arrived at our destination in little over three hours from the time we walked out of our Hyderabad flat. As guests of the Chief Minister, we were given priority over politicians, industrialists, film stars, and even expat Hindus coming from the far corners of the globe. Our host, the executive director of the temple, served tea in his living room as he oriented us. A word to his assistant standing in the wings and our stay was swiftly and efficiently organized.

Excitement was in the air as VIP's and their coteries walked in and out of the Executive Director's bungalow. The Venkateshwara Temple atop Tirumala Hill is widely regarded as the most powerful spiritual atmosphere on the subcontinent, and our Hyderabad friends visited regularly, often returning with their shaved heads. It's customary to offer one's hair to the temple deity, and entire families walked about the hill having just had their jet-black locks shorn. When I asked the temple director about the practice, he explained that it was a symbolic act of renouncing the ego. Considering how little hair I had left, my shaved head would hardly qualify as ego surgery, and so we passed the sheering stalls without entering.

According to the Vedas, Kali Yuga is the Dark Age when suffering and unhappiness envelops the earth. It is a time when material desire and animal instincts usurp righteous behavior and spiritual aspirations. According to the Bhagavad Gita, the world is now in the throes of Kali Yuga. The scriptures also say that Lord Vishnu, the great preserver, incarnates in troubled times to restore righteous behavior on earth. Vishnu came as the famous avatars Ram and Krishna to defeat ignorance and restore dharma, but in the blackness of Kali Yuga, Vishnu is said to be unwilling to take human form. Out of compassion, however, he agreed to enter a stone idol atop Tirumala Hill so that his devotees could receive his blessings. Historians have determined that the Venkateshwara temple dates back to 400 BC. Balaji is the affectionate name given to Vishnu's black granite form. Literature outside the temple explains that Lord Vishnu's celestial heaven, Vaikuntha, is ethereally located above Tirumala Hill.

Balaji's temple is the wealthiest in the world with a collection of precious gems estimated to be worth seventy million dollars, and gold ornaments and reserves weighing 1,500 pounds. 40,000 pilgrims visit the temple each day, giving on average, a dollar each. Even the poorest donate what they can. Many Hindus offer family heirlooms. Villagers, to insure the health of a newborn baby offer the infant's weight in rice or sugar cane. The hair cut from pilgrims outside the temple is also offered to Balaji, bringing the temple a million dollars a year in the sale of natural wigs. These gifts support a hospital, schools, the training of pundits, and employ tens of thousands of people who work in the temple town.

It was 2:00 in the morning when the cottage doorbell woke me. I had been resting soundly, enjoying the soothing sounds of night crickets and leaves shuffling about the garden outside my bedroom window. Both sounds are commonplace enough in colder climates, but were a unique nocturnal melody on the subcontinent. Our considerate guide, Nagaraj, watched patiently as our untrained fingers struggled to fasten cotton dhotis at the waist. From head to toe we were attired in white, as we walked from guest cottage to temple. Appearing like spirits in the night, a shroud of fog enveloped the mountain as we moved phantomlike toward the temple. The hike was exhilarating; our loose garments flowed and fluttered in the breeze necessitating cautious steps.

It was our first darshan with Balaji, and our privileged status spared us standing in lines taking as much as twenty-four hours. To the devout Hindu, the wait is also darshan, but we were relieved to bypass it. Nagaraj escorted us through a maze of underground corridors, up and down stone staircases, and past waiting rooms, leaving me disoriented in the process. Because we were foreigners, we were asked to sign a form stating, 'I believe in Balaji.' Eventually we emerged from the underground labyrinth at the temple's main entrance. An automated system sent a steady stream of water rushing over every entrant's feet as they crossed the threshold to the temple. Horns and drums could be heard inside, and it sounded as if a king's coronation were about to commence.

As we moved purposefully toward the inner sanctum, a faint wave of piety swelled in my heart. We were joined in an antechamber by a handful of well-dressed Indians, men to the left and women to the right. A half dozen bearded, round-bellied pundits with prominent markings on their foreheads chanted in powerful tones. Their faces radiated affection. Ghee lamps flickered, creating a mystical half-light, and swirling incense mingled with the smell of burning camphor. Tulsi leaves strung above passageways looked like miniature olive flags. All eyes were fixed on the massive double doors, as they swung slowly open. We were witnessing a daily ritual called Subhabrattom, the "waking" of the lord from his slumber. Reed horns, drums, and bells intoned together. We were about to enter the sanctum sanctorum, the abode of Lord Balaji.

One by one devotees stepped over the brass threshold into a narrow, dimly lit corridor leading to a heavy, stone vault. At the end of the passage, a vague form was visible. As we drew near to the form, faint feelings of piety became thrills of blissful energy. I was overtaken almost forcefully by his power and presence. We stood wide-eyed against a brass rail in full view of Balaji's imposing eight-foot black granite form. Vertical white stripes covered his eyes and his broad form had massive hands plated in gold. His right palm opened to us in a gesture of blessing. Over his strong shoulder was draped fine silk studded with hundreds of precious gems. His chest and shoulders were massive and impregnable like the granite that formed them. Resting on Balaji's head was a cylindrical crown set with dazzling diamonds and a ten-centimeter emerald said to be the most valuable in the world. We stood in awe of Balaji, like infants at the feet of a mighty monarch.

One by one we passed in front of Him. With palms pressed together, we made our secret offering from the heart and basked in delightful waves of darshan, as ushers guided us toward the exit. The inwardly absorbed mood remained long after we were outside the chamber and all were compelled to look back as we exited. We were now standing in the night air. Subhabratom was over. The fresh, cool air brought me slowly back to my senses. No one spoke; all were immersed in personal reflections. Then two hefty bearers whisked past us, carrying an oversized basket of orange and white garlands; another ceremony was about to begin.

Again we were ushered into the inner sanctum. This time we were seated front and center, some ten feet from the feet of the granite king. We watched as two priests performed tholam, the offering of flowers to the lord. Bright, colorful garlands were carefully draped over Balaji's shoulders, chest, and waist, and a priest waved incense about the room as pundits chanted continuously throughout the ceremony. We sat spellbound like children listening to a fairytale being sung in a language we didn't understand. I felt drawn into the form in front of me and into myself simultaneously. It was a most pleasant sensation. The distinction between inside and out dissolved like a curtain made of mist. No thoughts disturbed the pervasive, tranquil feeling as serenity gave rise to bliss. Bliss turned into devotion and devotion was drowned in the ocean of Being. Devotion emerged again, swelling in great waves before receding into nothingness. A simple request found its way into my heart: 'Balaji, may this be my reality always.'

The flower offerings were now completed. They sweetened the atmosphere, scenting it with rose. After another wait in the dark outside, the third thirty-minute ceremony commenced. Archana, the offering of light was accompanied by the thousand names of Lord Vishnu, which were recited in a strong cadence. A dozen flames dazzled the eyes as a huge brass lamp circled clockwise round and round in front of Balaji. The final ritual was magnificent, and at the same time, it was nothing at all. Balaji was all that mattered, and by now we were feeling more intimate with his exalted presence. As we sat, a gap in time occurred, a period that was unaccounted for. Then, inexplicably, I found myself standing again after having been seated during the light offerings. The ceremony was now complete, and I watched the head priest turn and smile slightly as he carried a brass bowl in my direction. Instinctively, I lowered my head as he placed the bowl on the crown of the head. Pleasant sensations raced up and down my spine filling my head with light and my heart with love. Everyone in the room received the blessing in turn, a waterless baptism of sorts.

Again we were ushered from the smoky sanctum. Each person turned for a final glimpse of Balaji as they exited the surcharged chamber. It was still dark outside, but the sun would soon be up. Darshan was complete. Our faithful guide Nagaraj handed us prasad, baseball-sized ladhus, as we circled the temple. Carved beings on the temple roof kept an eye on us as the solid gold dome atop the temple caught the first faint rays of sunlight, glistening against the emerald hillside.

Despite the morning hour, sleep came easily at the guest cottage. Day and night atop Tirumala Hill ran together like diluted watercolors. Darshan continued round the clock. While we slept, tens of thousands would come and go. Again, the sound of night crickets serenaded the senses while fallen leaves danced lightly in the background. Again, the doorbell roused us. Once more we wrapped ourselves in white cotton, stepped into the clouds, and followed Nagaraj through the misty night to the vaulted abode of Balaji. A second visit would confirm that the first had not been a dream. On a Swiss mountain, Maharishi had once assured us, "There are many heavens on earth." Surely Tirumala Hill is one of them.

TWENTY

Siva's Abode

Out of a great need we are all holding hands and climbing.

—*Hafiz*

Slate-roofed houses dotted the mountainside and clustered together near rivers. Wisps of smoke rose from the quaint abodes. Mountain goats must live up there, I thought; the climb was so steep. On the road below, pilgrims sped past the Himalayan villages in sporty jeeps and sleek sedans, covering the entire distance to Kedarnath in a single day. The element of tapas (penance) that had been a part of the spiritual journey for generations had yielded to a new style of pilgrimage. Although a few still made the journey on foot (often barefoot), carrying nothing but a cotton bundle and a walking staff on the three hundred mile trek into the Himalayas, most modern pilgrims traveled with the entire family, often with their cook and grandparents packed into an SUV.

Our first stop, Kalimath, was hidden deep in a narrow canyon, and the poor condition of the road had our driver on edge. His fretting seemed chronic, but then that was typical of many 'hill drivers' who toured the Himalaya. Mudslides had rendered the road barely passable, and only our constant reassurance convinced our driver to proceed against his better judgment. After multiple crossings of a river on single lane bridges, the road ended abruptly at a stairway descending to a footbridge spanning the swift flowing stream. On the opposite side, a collection of dwellings was clustered near the river.

Hot and dusty from the journey, we watched with envy as a frolicking group of boys splashed about in the current. Our whimsical decision was a unanimous one, and we plunged headlong into the water to join the fun as our incredulous driver looked on, wondering if our watery diversion was the sole reason he had risked his vehicle in the quagmires. The boys' favorite trick was leaping off a boulder at a bend in the stream and then riding the quick current downstream where they were deposited on the opposite bank. We copied the maneuver, reveling in the joy of happy-go-lucky adolescence. The recreation reminded me of sultry summer days when I was the age of the boys we mimicked, although my Midwestern playgrounds paled in comparison to their Himalayan paradise.

The refreshing swim alone made our detour worthwhile. After visiting the open air Kali shrine at the center of the tiny settlement, we joined three sadhus who were relaxing under a canvas cover by the water. Not even teenage boys can match the nonchalance of a carefree sadhu. After all, wandering holy men make a career out of indifference.

We spent the night on an obscure mountain above a forest of gnarled oak and deodar off the main road. The collection of slate roofed dwellings was almost obscured by fog when we arrived, and a misty drizzle caused the gray stone to glisten in the temple courtyard. We found accommodations in a rustic dharamshala (rest house), arriving just ahead of a group of Rajasthani yatriks (pilgrims) who had come by bus. After cooking and eating their chapatis and rajma dal (red beans) in the hallway outside our rooms, the turbaned Rajputs and their wrinkled wives sat in segregated groups, slurping tea. The warmth from the hot drinks would hold off the cold night air until after they were asleep.

I awakened in the early morning to the sound of hens cackling outside my window and the clamor of pilgrims outside my door. Throwing open the wooden shutters brought a rush of scented air into the characterless room that I had shared with an extremely large and hairy black spider. My roommate looked more menacing than he was; at least, that was my conviction. I watched the mountain play hide and seek in the puffy clouds above the garden outside my window, and found myself half in heaven, half rooted in a potato patch. The gray clouds shrouding the upper section of the peak would soon be depositing more rain on us.

Stepping over the weathered Rajasthani villagers outside my door, I began my search for the bucket of warm water promised by the guesthouse manager, but was soon pouring icy buckets on my head instead. Communicating with the proprietor had not been easy. Had it not been for a Hindi lesson at the Pateriyas, we would have spent the night on the floor alongside our Rajasthani neighbors. When I inquired about rooms, the proprietor had pointed to the floor. Fortunately, the word I was searching for had surfaced in time.

"Palang (Bed)?" I asked.

"Ji, Ji-ha (Sir, yes sir)," replied the manager, who promptly unlocked three adjoining rooms furnished with wood beds, hard mattresses, and cotton quilts. Once again, the absurdity of contrasting cultures surfaced. We were three Americans, each in a private room, while thirty villagers slept in tight rows in the hallway, pressed together like asparagus stalks in a can.

Traffic brought us to a halt two kilometers short of our destination. Kedarnath temple is a twelve mile trek with an elevation change of 5,000 feet. As a result, many pilgrims opt to ride mules or sit on wood palanquins carried by Nepalese sherpas. We fueled ourselves with Chinese noodles and cabbage before beginning the five-hour climb. The trail out of Gaurikund was chaotic. Grazing mules were tethered everywhere, waiting while their owners negotiated favorable prices with the pilgrims. No one wanted to pay the inflated rates, and because it was late in the day our bargaining succeeded, as there were more porters than pilgrims seeking their services.

Once the haggling was over, the long climb began. From the look on the faces of those coming down, we were not embarking on a Sunday stroll. If coming down was exhausting, how difficult was the climb up, I wondered. The pilgrims, including those being carried on wooden platforms looked exhausted. For a short distance we made conversation with our fellow yatriks, joking with children seated in large wicker baskets that hung from porters' backs, but the rigors of the trek silenced everyone before long. One portly gentleman sitting on a palanquin had a transistor radio pressed to his ear. Four fit sherpas buckled beneath his weight as he sat listening to a world cup cricket match in England. Rivals India and Pakistan competed against one another and a small group of men trailed after him, eager to hear the play by play of the game. What did cricket have to do with spiritual pilgrimage aside from the fact that its stars were worshipped the way American sports figures were? The sociable phase of the journey ended as it became evident that our energy reserves would be needed if we were to arrive at the goal intact. The first few miles were severe. The stone trail, which was wide enough for a car, switched back and forth as it rose above the valley. Pilgrims stopped frequently to rest and snack at canvas stalls along the way. The Indian body, generally not as fit as its western counterpart, seemed ill-suited to climbing, but hidden behind the soft physiques was a resilient will.

The trail was crowded. Thousands were ascending with equal numbers descending. The mules moving downhill posed a threat to the pilgrims going up; the animals moved too fast to avoid anyone in their way. Sensing that a meal awaited them at day's end, they're homing instincts had taken over. It was up to walkers to remain alert for their own safety, but we were also on the lookout to avoid their fresh droppings on the trail. The routine was; look up to avoid oncoming mules, look down to avoid their deposits. I wanted to propose a ban on mules in the valley.

After an hour it began to rain, causing some to don bright plastic slickers, but mostly pilgrims scurried into the nearest tea stall or plodded ahead, unmindful of the elements. Everyone needed to arrive at Kedarnath by evening or risk spending a long night in the cold. We continued on.

Every age, size, and shape moved harmoniously along the trail. Elderly village women, belongings balanced tenuously on their heads, walked barefoot alongside teenagers in jeans and sunglasses. Overweight businessmen wheezed along. Children held younger siblings' hands, while their mothers kept a watchful eye on the entire family. The athletic few moved ahead of the pack. The collective energy of the shared mission was palpable. My energy supported the man next to me, and his aided some-one else. The rhythm of steps taken together was invigorating. Now I understood what it was like to be a leg of a millipede. We marched like an army, united in purpose.

The halfway point was over the next ridge. Although fatigue had set in, my heart was spared. Yet another heavy rain chased us to cover and refreshment. The wetness exaggerated the smell of rich soil. Fifty pilgrims were packed into a space for fifteen inside our tea stall. Rejuvenated by the pause, the mood of the group became friendly. A plate of spicy potatoes and a fresh lime soda fueled me for the second half of the journey, which began as the rain slowed to a drizzle.

I walked with two American friends, Tim Jones and Doug Rexford. Tim had come to India soon after I arrived to look after our management institutes, and Doug was a recent arrival, although all of us had been to India many times. Tim and I invested all our reserves in getting up the mountain, while Doug, the fittest of our trio, struck up conversations with anyone energetic enough to reply. With few exceptions, glassy stares were the norm now. 'Namaste' was muttered now and then, but the incessant bumping and bouncing taxed even those carried by porters, but the real strain showed on the porters' faces. Whether carrying children in baskets or adults on palanquins, their task was severe.

The final hour passed as a blur. Mental activity yielded to physical exertion. Angular rainfall, driven by a chilling wind, became an unrelent-ing theme in the late afternoon as we reached higher altitudes. The gray sky and steady showers dulled the pristine beauty of the valley, which was superb at every turn. My awareness turned inward as a matter of survival. When possible, we took shortcuts—alternate trails used by the more agile hikers. I followed a porter carrying a hip twelve year-old. Dressed in a black turtleneck and jeans ensemble, she smiled behind reflector sunglasses. Apparently she hadn't noticed the overcast skies. Designer styled hair disguised her innocence; her childlike expression seemed incongruous with her fashion.

The distances to our collective goal were whitewashed on trailside rocks at regular intervals, but I preferred not to know. The final hour was punishing. Cold moisture penetrated as we climbed a steep section in taxingly thin air. Pained muscles strained to keep me going. An element of madness now pervaded the mission. The odd mix of perspiration and freezing air confused my senses and I numbingly pushed on. A hot bath and soft bed would work wonders for my aching body; a hot chocolate would have helped too. Such luxuries were not part of the Himalayan experience. After all, this was a spiritual pilgrimage, with austerity playing a central part in a pilgrim's progress. The final moments of daylight hung around long enough to give stragglers time to cross the footbridge into the village of Kedarnath. Despite the near-freezing air and water, a group was bathing by the river. This was done more out of respect for the holy environs they entered rather than the need to bathe. With a shudder I bypassed the ritual in search of a room. Pushy hawkers at village edge hindered that task, each pitching his guesthouse as the finest in town at the best price.

God smiles on all his children, great and small, including our foreign delegation. We found a room in an anonymous cinderblock on the main path to the temple. No doubt it had a name, but I was so overcome by fatigue that, had it been the Himalayan Hilton, I wouldn't have noticed or cared. Nine cots filled the room and we used them all. A narrow aisle allowed passage to and from the bathroom, which had a gaping hole in the ceiling that brought blasts of freezing air inside. Each of us occupied three cots, one for the body, one for the bag, and one to be used as a dining room table. Too tired to want anything and too exhausted to sit, we were prone for two hours before a trace of life force seeped back into our aching bodies. Audible sighs of relief were heard now and then. No regrets were expressed, but whether we were willing to admit it or not, we were all beyond our physical prime.

"My next visit to Kedarnath will be by helicopter," I moaned, feebly attempting some humor. Tim, who was part rugged outdoorsman and part sanyasi, bore his soreness stoically. He, more than most, resonated with the wandering mendicants we met on the trail. Doug, who was weaned on St. Louis country clubs, still had some humor left in him, and was always cheerful and ready to assist anyone in need.

A cowl of clouds veiled the reward that awaited us. In the morning, we would experience the Himalayan abode of Lord Siva, but at the moment a hot meal and some rest were ample compensation for the journey. The latter came easily, but dinner was barely edible. It hardly mattered though as we were asleep in minutes, not waking until daylight filtered through the frosted windowpanes. Stiff but rested, I stumbled out the door and began another search for hot water, determined to avoid dowsing myself with a bucket of ice water in the frigid air.

The thought of hot water evaporated as I caught sight of the peaks above Kedarnath. The tiny village was set against a backdrop of magnificent massifs. Green meadows flanking the village yielded to vertical rock faces that supported sky-touching conical formations. The Mandakani River tumbled past the village to the west. High overhead, the gods sat on their respective thrones. The Hindu deities certainly knew exclusive real estate. Siva had chosen well when he selected Kedarnath as his mountain abode.

Kedarnath Temple

Siva's Darshan

I once heard heaven defined as one's highest consciousness, and Kedarnath pushed mine to heights I rarely achieved. No vehicles could come here; nor was meat or alcohol permitted. It seemed that no undesirable element could infiltrate this remote and pure place. Our good fortune was apparent despite the disorientation caused by altitude, cold, and improper food. Hot milk warmed us before we joined the morning darshan queue behind the temple. The line snaked around to the rear of the shrine, ending at a monument to Shankara. It was a pristine morning. Rest, breakfast, and the prospect of entering one of the Himalaya's mythical shrines buoyed my spirits. The line moved steadily, but somehow our progress was stalled.

I looked ahead and discovered that the old trick of line jumping applied not only to Indian post offices. Couples older than my parents were slipping in ahead of us. Although we were now alert to the situation, what could one say to someone who had spent a lifetime waiting for this moment? They were simply impatient to fulfill their dream. Not everyone who observed the ploy saw it that way, however, and one elderly couple was sent to the rear of the line by a uniformed guard.

Inside the temple, the scene was subtly energizing. The greater body of the crowd ushered us along when a bewildered woman shrieked as a boy made off with her camera. Temple guards failed to grab the elusive thief, and in an instant, he vanished, leaving everyone groping for their valuables. The unfortunate act was soon forgotten, and the pilgrims again focused on the inner sanctum.

We approached the three-foot holy stone with a pair of priests in tow. We had hired them to perform short ceremonies of worship. When my turn came, I knelt to touch the sacred stone. The field of energy around it was strong, attracting me like a magnet. As the pundits chanted, I went deeper, absorbed in the sublime atmosphere. Then, just as I made a clear connection to the temple and its power, something unbearably heavy landed on my head and I was crushed by the weight of it. My survival instincts lept into action and I pushed hard against the mass, trying to free myself, but I couldn't move. Then I realized it was just the woman behind me who had dived onto my head. She was trying desperately to touch the stone, but her short arms couldn't reach it. The load on top of me had undone my transcendent moment and I found myself pinned like a lineman at the bottom of a pile in a high school football game. My head, which was wedged beneath the thickset figure, found just enough space to wriggle free, but the weight of religious fervor was fully and literally on my shoulders.

The hefty woman was completely unaware of me as she spread sandal paste on the rock. When she finally got up, the pundit chastised the zealous devotee with a frown and shake of the head. At last I was freed from the impossible position. I made my way to the exit, having sampled the sublime and the ridiculous in the blink of an eye. A mantle of peace cloaked the temple and its commotion. Elevating vibrations permeated the sanctuary like pungent incense, lifting the consciousness of one and all. It was this *presence* that fulfilled our journey to the mountain abode of Siva where the sweet essence of spiritual nectar lingered in the air. The moment of communion with the Self more than offset the effects of the arduous trek and austere conditions. As we stepped into the sunlight, the woman who I had been trapped beneath glowed with satisfaction, and I was satisfied that she was happy.

Non-Attachment

Although we were not prepared to explore deeper into the region, we followed a grassy trail to a small community of sadhus that lived on the green slopes above the river. The elevated trail exposed crystalline peaks that glistened like inverted chandeliers in the sunlight. Small earthen shelters had been dug from the mountain where the hermits lived. It would take a monumental effort to live at Kedarnath year round, but those who succeeded were amply rewarded for it.

Our return trek went easily, aided by gravity and the company of a sadhu named Swami Hari, who had spent twenty-seven years moving about India barefoot. The soles of Swami's feet were as tough as any pair of hiking boots and never needed replacing. Before reaching the road head, we bought Swami Hari lunch at Gaurikund, the village at the base of Kedarnath mountain. When we offered Swami a ride to Rishikesh, he politely declined. Swami Hari reminded me of my master's response to a question about choosing the life of a monk. He had said simply, "You can travel faster alone." The walk was his path, and Swami Hari would not be denied his carefree wanderings through the Himalaya. He seemed the epitome of contentment and I thought for a moment that Tim might join him for he shared a special bond with these self-contained sadhus.

Detachment comes up in any conversation about holy men, for Indians view spiritual progress as demanding, believing that one cannot make much headway without renouncing the world. The old story of a monk riding on a train underscores their belief in the importance of non-attachment. Indian trains are always packed with people and luggage as they crawl along a diverse network of track, often taking days to reach their destinations. The typical family travels with bags filled with food and bedding in order to make the journey comfortable.

The mendicant in the story was traveling with a cloth bag that rested on his lap. As he sat quietly, a man across the aisle observed him closely. After watching the holy man for many hours, the man suddenly blurted out, "You are supposed to be a renunciate, but you also have possessions. You are as attached to your belongings as we householders, aren't you."

The holy man said nothing, but continued sitting peacefully. Time passed. Then, as the train crossed a river, the renunciate stood up. Leaning out the open window, he tossed his bag into the river below and turned to the passenger, saying, "I have tossed all my worldly possessions into the water. Can you do the same?" The chastened man sad nothing for the remainder of the journey.

The genuine Indian sadhu is like a bead of water on the leaf of a lotus plant. The water moves freely over the surface of the leaf, but remains separate from it as if the leaf were coated with wax. Frictionless is the nature of mature detachment. The world of renunciation is unfathomable to the majority, and that is how nature planned it. It's simply not a part of most people's DNA. The idea of walking penniless from place to place without home or family would cause most people to panic. Our trails parted and we wished Swami Hari well. I was relieved to find our driver waiting for us, for renunciation was not my chosen path.

Men like Swami Hari were role models for aspiring monks. He expected nothing from anyone, but was grateful for what came to him. The state of total non-attachment to worldly possessions was a state I hoped to achieve one day, but I still had a ways to go. On our drive back to Nainital, we passed many carefree sadhus along the road. All of them were following their inner voice.

TWENTY ONE

Dance of Karma

The earth braces itself for the lover of God about to dance.

—*Hafiz*

"Steev Uncle, please come to our home for Laxmi Puja. Love, Pateriya Family" read the Diwali card wedged under my door. India's favorite holiday had arrived, and I spent the day shopping for gifts. The centuries-old festival of lights varies from region to region, but families typically welcome Laxmi, the goddess of prosperity, into their homes by lighting rows of earthen lamps that burn through the night. The celebration falls in early November on the darkest night of the year. The lights and festive atmosphere brings optimism and hope, dispelling the darkness of the new moon and debilitated sun.

Merchants wanting their businesses to prosper are said to have been the first to celebrate Diwali. Pujas are performed to purify account ledgers and financial records. In addition to bringing good fortune to home and business, Laxmi is also worshipped as mother earth, and is honored during Diwali for bringing an abundant harvest. Fireworks are heard everywhere for a week, and gifts and sweets are exchanged with friends.

We spent the day shopping for sweets at the Bengali Market, and dropping them at our friends' offices around Delhi. Like Christmas in the west, shoppers were out in large numbers. The markets were decorated in sparkling gold and silver, and everyone was in a relaxed mood as they chose from dozens of sweets made in makeshift kitchens. The rich milk sweets were decorated with paper-thin silver foil, and we purchased milk fudge squares, pistachio diamonds, and almond paste ovals. The mood was festive, and we felt part of it.

As Diwali approached, plans were announced to curb the excessive use of crackers (fireworks) that exploded around the clock, but in the end, the unrelenting 'pop pop pop' went late into the night. Teenage boys were the culprits, and they engaged themselves in an endurance contest, igniting crackers and running for cover for hours at a time.

Abishek greeted me in front of his family's freshly whitewashed house. A cloud of incense engulfed us as we entered the living room. Laxmi Puja was in progress. A cushion was placed on the floor for me. Ever at ease, Pateriya paused to explain what he was doing. In front of him, offerings to the goddess Laxmi were in progress. Curd, vermillion powder, a coconut, and a new red sari waited to be offered. Pateriya's eldest daughter Kusum assisted with the puja, knowing just the right moment to present each item.

When Pateriya's puja ended, home-made sweets streamed out of the kitchen. Gulab jamin and saffron flavored golden pretzels called jelebis oozed cane syrup. Following dinner, we attended the ashram's Mahapuja (grand ceremony) in the rice field. We rode in Pateriya's Gypsy, which sat idle next to the cow shelter most of the time, its tank empty for lack of funds. But tonight Pateriya felt distinguished and jumped into the driver's seat. When he turned the ignition, there was no response, so we climbed out and gave the vehicle a good push. On the second try, the jeep lurched forward and off we went.

Night had come, and a chill was in the air. Fluorescent tube lights attached to wooden poles illumined the field and a diesel generator chugged in the background, keeping the lights burning brightly. Already hundreds of pundits were sitting in rows on canvas coverings. More than three thousand in all would chant at the open-air celebration, a tradition begun a decade earlier. It had been years since Maharishi departed India for Holland, but the autumn tradition continued as if he were present. Canvas walls had been erected to create a temporary hall, and behind the stage, marigold ropes cascaded to the ground like ochre waterfalls. Abundance was in the air. The pundits, dressed in new yellow robes and handsome Kashmiri shawls, chanted while baskets piled high with colorful fruits and brass platters stacked with sweets were offered to the goddess. Wives of ashram administrators wore stunning new saris in crimson shades with gold stitching. A gilded platter mounded with coins from every country in the world symbolized global prosperity. A second plate was piled high with gold coins. The puja was an embellished version of Pateriya's living room ritual, but rather than one voice, thousands recited in unison, while the purohit (officiating priest) tossed rose blossoms at Laxmi's picture, releasing the ruby petals with a reverse flick of the wrist. The ceremony had an enchanting effect.

The darkest night of the year felt brighter than most. When the chanting ended, a bhajan started up. No one wanted to let go of the warm internal glow generated by the puja. Finally the singing faded into poignant silence, and only the distant 'pop pop' of firecrackers could be heard from a neighboring village. Having waited patiently, the throng of pundit boys rose to their feet as prasad was distributed at the edge of the stage. The younger boys rushed forward, filling their hands and pockets with sweets and dried fruits. It was time to celebrate. Fireworks soon filled the sky above the field.

A decade earlier Maharishi had presided over the first Mahalaxmi Puja on the rice field where we now celebrated. The setting hadn't changed. Before the ceremony commenced, Maharishi had explained that it was our wish for Mahalaxmi to enter every home in the world, to bring happiness and prosperity to all. He then sat, eyes closed and motionless, throughout the two-hour ceremony. When the puja ended, he opened his eyes; slowly drawing in a breath the way one inhales the fragrance of a rose, and said, "She came. Did you see her? Did you feel her presence?"

Fog Sets In

The onset of winter that followed Diwali was a difficult time of year for Maharishi Nagar residents. Chowkidars (guards) huddled around campfires trying to hold off the cold night air. The friendly banter with the guards disappeared with the last balmy days of autumn. Taciturn moods prevailed; the battle to stay warm became the overriding concern of the day. The night watchmen in their second-hand coats stared at the embers of half-burnt logs, looking disheartened. We tried to ease their brooding by buying chai for the guards, thinking a cup of tea would lift their spirits, but they were committed to their doldrums.

The mix of dung smoke and fog that burned our throats shortened our nightly walks. The ashram vaidyas recommended warm oil baths in winter, but I gave up on the idea after an electrical fire blackened the bathroom wall and melted the fixture. Either I had electrical karma, or Indian appliances were poorly made. I decided it was a combination of the two, with emphasis on the latter.

I was in Connaught Place, the popular shopping center for foreign tourists and moneyed Indians. As I crossed the green park at the center of the circle of shops, a shoeshine boy approached, pointing down, "Sir, shoes dirty. I shine, OK?" I looked down at my freshly shined shoes. My left shoe was caked with cow dung. How did that get there? I wondered. I had the boy clean and shine my shoes, and thought no more of it.

Two weeks later, I was back in Connaught Place, and the episode repeated itself. But this time I was more alert, and saw the shoeshine boy's accomplice toss dung onto my shoe. Clever trick, I thought, feeling annoyed by the tactic. I let him do his work, but refused to pay, letting the boy know I was onto the prank. Meanwhile, another shoeshine boy was busy frisking two Italians who were fresh off the plane from Europe. He got 200 rupees for each shine, a job that Indians pay two rupees for and for which I paid five. I didn't mind paying a premium as a foreigner, but the unwitting Italians would run out of money if they didn't figure things out fast. Life on the street for these boys wasn't easy. The lack of real opportunity led them to cook up scams aimed at unwary tourists.

There was a boy in Connaught Place who shined my shoes sometimes. Shoeshines aren't needed much in America, but India was different. The dust and heat dried the leather, and soon they were cracking. I also kept them polished for the corporate image. Rajesh, the boy who did my shoes, was from Rajasthan. He was a nice kid, the son of a farmer who had left his parched plot for a fresh start in the city. When I asked him if he went to school, Rajesh said that he did, but the lack of conviction in his voice made me wonder. After a few shines, he approached me whenever I was in the neighborhood, which was quite often since we were visiting corporate offices in the vicinity. Rajesh shined my shoes without a box, using the sidewalk for his workplace.

One day Rajesh asked me if I would buy him a box. A box, he said, was needed to be a real shoeshine man, not just a boy taking business away from the professionals that had permanent spots staked out on the sidewalks. A box allowed the customer to put his foot up at the proper angle for a better shine. It also stored the tools of his trade; wax, brushes, and crème. So I gave Rajesh the rupees he wanted, thinking a box would help him in his trade. A month later, I saw my young friend again, but he still didn't have a box. "Where is your box, Rajesh?" I asked, remembering the deal.

"Mr. Steve, no box," replied Rajesh, looking dejected.

"But why?"

"My father take rupees. He use for liquor," said the lad. My God, I thought, this boy is out here hustling on the street to support a problem at home.

"Sir, please buy me a box." Rajesh pleaded.

"Yes, but this time I will buy you a box, instead of giving you the rupees. Understand?"

"But, Mr. Steve, I cannot buy box without rupees," the boy said, not fully understanding me.

"Yes, I know. Take me to the box maker and I'll get you a box. Otherwise, your father will end up with the rupees again." But Rajesh said it wasn't possible. He wanted a box, but there were issues involved. He had to go through proper channels to get the box, and deal with the guys who controlled the action on the street. And so, he said, it wouldn't be possible for me to go to the carpenter who made the boxes. It didn't work that way. I felt sorry for Rajesh. He had been in Delhi less than a year and had already picked up a lot of English, but his future looked bleak. In the years to come, I watched Rajesh grow into a man. I saw him hawking chess sets and toys, and later found him outside a Kashmiri shop, coaxing foreigners inside. Rajesh never got his box.

On our way out of Connaught Place that afternoon, we stopped for ice cream at Nirulas. Lane got his customary hot fudge sundae, Anil his Mango swirl, and I splurged on a banana split. The roads out of Delhi were already gridlocked with commuters; the rush of traffic that crawled out of the city each day snared us. The major intersections around Delhi were swarming with beggars and one particularly needy man approached my window. From his fingers I knew he was a leper. Although they were partially bandaged, he tapped the glass with stumps. His gaunt face told me that he had been hungry for a long time. I sensed his destitute condition as he gestured, slowly moving his hand from the window to his mouth and back again while I sat there with this enormous banana split in my lap. I never felt more uncomfortable in my life. The forty-rupees (one dollar) I had spent on the ice cream would have fed the man for a week or more, and I had enough rupees in my pocket to buy a hundred sundaes. It would be the last time I ate ice cream in the car, and marked the beginning of a more compassionate response to the folks who lived without hope under plastic and plywood on the streets of Delhi.

By early February, the fields surrounding the ashram had transformed themselves from lumpy plots to stunning gardens. The mustard crop was in bloom. The sea of delicate yellow buds set against the fresh azure sky reassured me that spring would regenerate the barren landscape and infuse fresh color into the insipid sky. It was the season for long Sunday walks along the dusty bullock paths outside the ashram. When I returned to my second floor room one Sunday afternoon, I found an unexpected visitor at my desk. The air conditioner had been pulled out for repairs, and an intruder had slipped in through the opening. A brazen, red-faced monkey stood on my desk trying to pry open a carton of mango juice. I grabbed my tennis racket and chased him around the room and onto the balcony, where he leapt to the grass below. Somehow he managed to hang onto the carton of juice as he made his bold getaway.

Holi Colors

Spring hadn't officially arrived, but ashram children were already climbing about the mulberry trees in the garden, filling their bags and mouths with juicy berries, and staining their hands and shirts deep purple in the process. The succulent berries enticed me as well, but I was tall enough to reach all I could eat from the ground. We spent our days conducting human development seminars in corporate towers and our evenings at the ashram village. We commuted between two cultures, one contemporary, the other traditional; one cosmopolitan, the other rural; one spoke English, the other Hindi; both were Indian. In Delhi boardrooms, we dressed the part of businessmen, but at the ashram we wore homespun cotton and chappals (sandals). I enjoyed the daily juxtaposition of cultures. After all, we were living in a multi-cultural subcontinent more diverse than Europe. I couldn't think of a better way to live the Vedic aphorism Vasudev Kutumbh Katam (the world is my family).

Holi had arrived. On the Indian calendar, Holi marks the seasonal shift to spring. I had been forewarned about Holi, India's most unruly holiday when social boundaries dissolve in a riotous game called 'colors.' Holi celebrates the goddess Durga's triumph over a nasty demon named Holika. In the morning, children chase after each other smearing pastel powders on one another's face and clothes. Social protocol is ignored during Holi. In theory, a pot washer is entitled to rub red or blue powder on a banker's cheeks and starched white shirt. The rule for Holi is that there are none. If you don't want to play, stay inside. The red dirt roads around the ashram were conspicuously vacant the morning Holi arrived, except for those playing colors.

I was deep in morning meditation when some ashram friends from Orissa dropped by. At first they knocked politely, but when they got no response, they banged obnoxiously, shouting, "Steve-sir, we know you're in there." Hesitantly, I cracked open the door and caught a glimpse of the five handsome faces painted royal blue. For the past three months I had been training the group to lecture and contact companies. My apprentices looked like half-crazed Scottish warriors on their way to battle. When they realized I wasn't about to let them in, they pushed hard, but my firmly planted foot kept the door from swinging open. Their normally languid eyes were wild with mischief and a touch of comic madness. Realizing they wouldn't get in without breaking down the door, they tried another tactic, pleading with me to come out, which I might have done had I not been settled in meditation. Not wanting to send them away unhappy, I negotiated with them, agreeing to exchange a spot of color on the forehead with each of the boys, but nothing more. After all, this was how mature folks played Holi, or so I had been told. The idea seemed to satisfy them, so I let them in under the condition that they not discolor my clothes or the room.

I loved these country boys from Orissa. None of them had ever ventured very far from their villages before coming to Maharishi Nagar, and the day after I checked them into their rooms I dropped in on them to see how they were faring. I had pulled some strings to get them private rooms, but when I knocked on their doors no one answered until I came to the last room assigned them. Raghuram, a former math teacher greeted me at the door, but when he invited me inside, I barely recognized his room. Cotton kurtas and bath towels hung from makeshift clotheslines crisscrossing the space beneath the ceiling fan and extra beds had been dragged in. All five trainees had slept side by side like quintuplets in a gigantic crib. I teased the men about the peculiar arrangement, not understanding that a westerner's need for privacy had no place in the Indian psyche. They moaned that a horrible loneliness had invaded their hearts from the moment they checked into their rooms, and so they had all moved into one room; the way they knew life in the village. They were quite happy with the arrangement, although they missed their families terribly. I had much to learn about Indian culture.

It was a small miracle, but my white kurta was still spotless when I entered Pateriya's living room that evening. I had successfully eluded the rainbow of colors on the faces and clothes of everyone I passed on the road. Pateriya was napping when I arrived, so I instructed the children not to disturb him. He typically rose at 3:00 a.m. to perform his devotionals before going to work in the garden. His naps were well earned. The children took turns placing a spot of vermillion on my forehead. Having received red markings from many hands, my forehead looked like an errant bullet had hit directly between my eyes.

Pateriya woke up just in time for dinner and eyed me suspiciously before reaching for a plastic object on the windowsill. Without a word, he sat up, pointed the plastic object in my direction, and fired a stream of lavender liquid that spotted and stained the entire front of my shirt. As if Zorro himself had left his mark, a large purple 'Z' was blazoned on my tunic. Then, laughing riotously, Pateriya emptied the water pistol's contents on my kurta as his children looked on in astonishment. My defenses were down and my new kurta ruined, so the kids took me outside for my first game of Holi. We chased about the yard smearing one another with powdered colors, and by the time we were finished, we looked like a motley troupe of hand-painted ghouls.

Colored green and purple, we joined many hundreds of Holi revelers for the grand finale of the day, the burning of the demon Holika that hung in disgrace from a tall pole in the center of the cricket field. The pundit boys, in their uniform yellow cloth, filled the field to witness the sacrifice, rainbows painted across their happy faces. A torch touched the paper devil and flames engulfed it as the crowd roared and chanted Mata Ki Jai, (Victory to Mother). The effigy was soon reduced to ashes that fluttered harmlessly to the ground. As the charred remains smoldered, I retreated to my room, looking like a clown returning from the circus. Holi was not only on my face; it was now in my blood.

Rooftop Dancing

Our management institute had recently opened in the ashram, and fifty urban students were thrust into a world unfamiliar to them: an Indian village. The newly matriculated MBA students were generally wealthy and shared little in common with the village pundits and illiterate laborers who lived at Maharishi Nagar. Dressed in blue jeans, leather jackets, and logoed sneakers, the class of '96 sped through the ashram on motorcycles and scooters, slipping off to movies and restaurants, and spending in a weekend what an ashram worker earned in a month. The incoming class included just one girl.

Our students represented a generation in transition. Traditional ways were on the way out in the Indian city, but the new ways were still being established. When one of our American professors entered a swanky clothing store dressed in traditional Indian clothes, the young shop clerks crowded around him, and asked, "Sir, why are you wearing Indian clothes?" He told them about ashram life, and then asked them a question in return: "Tell me, why are you all wearing foreign clothes?" A spokesman for the group replied, "Sir, because we don't know who we are." Welcome globalization!

Raised in affluent families with western standards, the students moved restlessly about campus in search of stimulation that was unavailable in our walled village. I had been asked to teach the incoming students' meditation class and noticed how eager the boys were to interact with me, trying to make a favorable impression. They wanted a western role model, but I was hardly what they sought, for my inclinations were closer to the Vedic pundits than the blue-jean students. One evening, several of the boys dropped by my room. They were planning a roof dance and wanted me to attend. I reluctantly agreed. My friend Tim Jones, our full time liaison at the institute, had also been invited.

Preparations for the dance were in the works for a week; great energy and focus went into the planning of the event. In addition to the usual snacks and decorations, a sophisticated sound system was set up on the roof of the three-story academic building. By nightfall, the building was vibrating. As Tim and I climbed to the roof, MTV soundtracks were already reverberating throughout the ashram. The speakers throbbed under the brash beat. I had barely passed the Holi test and didn't expect to fare much better at the dance. From the roof, the silhouette of neighboring villages and fields came into view. The villagers would already be asleep. The only sign of life I could find was a solitary cow grazing peacefully under a street lamp on the roadside.

"Are you ready for this?" I asked Tim, shifting my attention from rural India to a blast of high decibel music.

"Sure Coach, this should be fun," Tim replied optimistically.

To one side of the makeshift dance floor, we spotted Radhika, who was seated on a chair surrounded by a coterie of adoring classmates. Radhika was the only girl enrolled at Maharishi Institute of Management. I had sat in on her entrance interview and her English skills were impeccable. She was an only child, exceptionally bright, and quite comfortable being the center of attention. Her physician parents had left Srinagar when Muslim separatists began harassing Hindus in Kashmir a decade earlier. Her classmates had already crowned Radhika as their Queen Bee, but most of the boys were to shy to approach her.

It was my first Indian dance. In fact, I hadn't been to a dance since senior prom almost thirty years earlier. I wondered how the lopsided gender ratio would work, but the boys seemed content to dance with each other, a custom not borrowed from the west. As the volume increased, the frenetic pace of the dancing picked up while Radhika, Tim, and I sat like wallflowers, a safe distance from the gyrating jeans.

"Won't you dance with these guys?" I asked Radhika.

She smiled coyly, a condescending "No," slipped out as she exhaled. She was the queen and the guys out there on the floor were her worker bees. I didn't envy their odds for only one would rise to share the throne with Radhika in the coming months.

"But these guys are dying to dance with you," Tim protested.

"I don't know them well enough. What about you?" she asked. She was making the rules for the game.

"Us? Dance?" I asked in disbelief. "Maybe Tim, but not me."

"Tim, why don't you dance with the guys?" Radhika prodded.

"Where I come from, men don't dance with men," Tim replied with manly conviction. I smiled, knowing one would hardly find an all male dance in the Big Sky country.

Radhika, by maintaining her aloofness, only enhanced her diva-esque mystique. Her fawning classmates approached her, but she never stepped down from her throne. Tim and I hid behind our faculty status, making excuses for not joining in, but the truth was, single gender dancing didn't interest either of us. I was about to excuse myself when a group of students approached Tim, trying to coax him into the dance. Tim's excuses were drowned out by the music, and when the boys realized he wouldn't join them, they started pulling him from his chair, a tactic that amused Radhika. Tim was our sacrificial lamb. With him out there, no one would bother me, I thought.

The dancers cheered as Tim did his best to conjure up a few moves from the past. I was sure he hadn't been on a dance floor in decades, and his outdated steps were lost on everyone but me. After all, these kids were still in diapers when the Bee Gees were in. Tim had good rhythm; all he needed was a tube of grease and a pair of tight jeans.

They came for me next, and, like Tim, I soon realized that resisting was more agonizing then joining in, and so I got up, allowing the music to sweep me among the gyrating bodies. Another roar filled the night as the boys mobbed me. The mood of the group was peaking now. To leave would deflate the fun, so we danced on. The boys danced far better than Tim or I ever had, their rhythm animated by adolescent euphoria. Youth enjoyed stamina that, when fueled by music, was inexhaustible. I was participating in an ancestral rite disguised by denim and pop music. The boys danced into the night, but I slipped out. Radhika sat impassively on her dais attended by her adoring classmates.

Opalescent moonlight bathed the ashram; the rooftop din shattered the calm of the Indian night. Hours later, long after Tim and I had retired for the night, music still rocked the ashram. Soon the pundits would be chanting, but until then, the ashram danced to a different beat.

Ganesh's Miracle

One emerald morning, the peacock that visited our garden with his mates was performing at his flamboyant best. His harem of peahens and I watched the vain showman's dance. The proud bird circled like a Native American chief dancing at a powwow. His iridescent train and steel-blue breast was more stunning than the feathered headdress of a Shoshone or Blackfoot chief. The large black eyes and gaudy greens and blues of his feathers mesmerized his consorts as he paraded past. Perhaps the showiest bird on earth, the peacock is Krishna's favorite, and rightly so, for Krishna also cast an hypnotic effect on his adoring gopis (maidens). I would do well to copy the peacock's subtle steps should I decide to dance again.

Lane and I had been teaching in Bombay. It had been several weeks since I'd seen the Pateriya family. My Hero bicycle lurched about as I navigated the potholed dirt road leading to Pateriya's house in the far corner of the ashram. I was bringing my friends a framed picture of Krishna, but the lumpy road made it almost impossible to carry the gift and ride at the same time.

"Steveji, have you heard?" bubbled Pateriya as I walked into his living room.

"Heard what?"

"Ganesh drinking milk in temples all over India."

"What do you mean?" I hadn't heard the news.

"He's drinking. Come." Pateriya led me barefoot into his puja room where we sat in front of his bronze Ganesh statue. Pateriya prayed for a moment and then took a small spoonful of milk from a bowl and put it up to Ganesh's mouth. Then something amazing happened. The milk slowly disappeared as if the elephant god were drinking it.

"But that's incredible, Pateriya."

"Steveji, you try it," Pateriya suggested and so I filled the sugar spoon and put it up to Ganesh's mouth. Again the milk disappeared, except for a small amount, which Pateriya and I shared as prasada. "It's a miracle," enthused Pateriya.

"Only in India," I replied, shaking my head.

"No," countered Pateriya. "It happened in a temple in London and Hong Kong too."

"In a Hindu temple, no doubt."

The next day I read about it in the newspaper. Ganesh temples all over India were reporting the exact thing I had witnessed at Pateriya's house. Thousands lined up outside temples with jugs of milk to feed their beloved god, but apparently not only Ganesh was thirsty; Siva also drank the offered milk. The miracle was so widespread that the Indian government closed down, and the Bombay Stock Exchange stopped trading so everyone could visit the temples. Wealthy Delhi women with silver pitchers lined up alongside street urchins carrying plastic pouches of milk. Millions of people claimed to have seen what we had seen in Pateriya's puja room. The news was reported all over the world. A wave of inspiration swept India. For Hindus it was proof that their gods were here on earth.

Ganesh

As summer approached, Delhi braced for its annual heat wave. The signs were ominous. Winter showers never came and temperatures were well above normal. The fields were parched and cracking. By mid May, temperatures reached 115 degrees, sometimes higher. Our guesthouse generator was underpowered, leaving us without electricity during the heat of the day. Not even a fan moved the air. Health authorities warned citizens to take precautions, but those who lived outdoors had little recourse. Children cooled themselves in fountains around the city, and water wagons rolled through the streets, hydrating the thirsty populace. It was a battle for survival, and some were losing. The newspapers claimed Delhi was in the throes of the hottest summer in recorded history. Daytime temperatures soared for six weeks without respite. Over 900 people had already succumbed to the heat. I wondered if I would be one of them.

I Almost Made It To Heaven

Years ago I had decided that a technicality would determine whether I made it into heaven or not. According to what I was taught as a teenager preparing for Methodist confirmation, one had to 'accept Christ as THE only begotten Son of God' in order to pass through the gates of heaven. If St. Peter, who supposedly guards the gates, were to ask me, I might not be invited in, since I believe there are MANY 'Sons of God,' Jesus being one of the more illustrious. On the other hand, if St. Peter asked, "Do you accept Jesus Christ as a Son of God?" then I could comfortably say 'yes' and be welcomed into the fellowship of good Christians. But even if invited, I wouldn't do well in the Christian Kingdom; the thought of spending eternity with Jerry Falwell and his flock troubled me. Heaven, I mused, could be hell with guys like that wandering around.

I loved the golden rule and philosophy of forgiveness, and I also believe in the resurrection and ascension, the many miracles and healings, and especially Christ's message of peace. But if entry into heaven meant attending church regularly, I'd already failed, for I bristled at the liturgical passages that the congregation parroted each week. Responses like 'we are all sinners in the eyes of God' reeked of dogma that, as far as I was concerned, had nothing to do with the spirit of Christ's message. The concept of original sin never resonated with me either and the Biblical account of the Garden of Eden drew conclusions that I could never accept. It all seemed foreign, especially the idea of a vengeful God.

Maybe I'm a prodigal son, but I was never comfortable being told how to worship. I drew inspiration from personal discovery, finding the freedom to test my spiritual wings outside organized religion. I enjoyed the challenge of living in the present; a habit formed as a competitive athlete, and didn't understand why Sundays should be so different from the rest of the week. In that regard, I was more Buddhist than Christian. We would have to wait and see whether St. Peter let me inside the Pearly Gates. I was prepared for the worst.

My head spun wildly the day I checked into Sukdha Hospital in South Delhi's upscale Pomposh Enclave at the height of the city's record heat wave. I was suffering from severe dehydration. When I awoke, caring individuals peered down at me, looking concerned by what they saw. As liquids dripped into my arm, I drifted in and out of consciousness. In time, the room stopped spinning, and I found myself between fresh sheets with a team of nurses hovering over me. They checked my vital signs, discussed the results, and expressed optimism. The sight of five beatific nurses, all wearing crosses around their neck, buoyed my flagging spirits. I tried unsuccessfully at first to engage the group in conversation. Being a westerner, but not a westerner dressed like a Hindu, they assumed I was Christian, and I saw no reason to dispute that notion prior to Judgment Day. The attentive quintet was relieved that their patient showed signs of revival.

"Sir, are you feeling better now?" a sweet voice asked.

"Yes. I'll be alright."

"We were worried," said the head nurse.

"Sir, are you Swedish?" one of the others nurses asked timidly.

"Yes...and...no," I said slowly. "My grandparents came from Sweden...so, in a way I am...but actually I'm American," I said, surprised at how long it took to get the sentence out. I felt quite lame lying there in an open-backed medical gown with a tube dripping liquid into my vein.

"Sir, America is the best country," replied a second nurse, who could have passed for the first nurse's sister. Each of the five women had white wedges pinned to their coal black hair. Their white frocks gave them the appearance of nuns. All looked younger than their ages, and except for their vivaciousness, they could have passed for novices in a convent like the one Maria had joined in *The Sound of Music*. Their innocence certainly qualified them.

"Yes...America...is a great country...but no better...than India," I replied, waiting to see how they reacted to my comment. My mental fog was lifting and I could almost speak coherently, although the words came out slowly. "Where...are you from?"

"Sir, we are from Kerala, but we all want to go to America. My aunty is there. She lives in California. I saw photos. California is very beautiful." It was worth the dehydration to spend a little time with these sweet souls. Maybe I should reconsider that Christian heaven.

"California is a paradise...but then, so is Kerala...wouldn't you agree?" I wanted to portray the two countries equally.

"Yes sir, but Americans are Christians. They love Jesus! That is better, isn't it?" asked a third. I wished they would stop calling me 'sir,' but mentioning it would have thrown them off. They'd been raised to respect their elders, and I was as old as their fathers.

"America also has Jews and Buddhists...Chinese and Hispanics. Like India, America has many cultures."

"Indians are there too, sir!" added the nurse whose aunt lived in California.

The door then swung open and Dr. Gupta stepped into the room, and instructed the nurses to prepare an injection.

"How am I doing, Doctor?"

"You'll be fine. I want to keep you over night, but you should be able to go home tomorrow." Dr. Gupta had received his medical training in Scotland. He also owned the hospital.

"You have a fine staff...Dr. Gupta," I said, complimenting the nurses.

With a kindly look, he replied, "I'll check in on you in the morning," and left the room.

"Tell me, do Indian Christians believe Krishna is an incarnation of God like Jesus?" I probed. The nurses didn't respond so I rephrased the question. "What do you think of Krishna? Do you like him?"

"Many in our village worship Krishna," nurse number one answered. "We like him, but we don't worship him."

"But most Hindus revere Christ, don't they?"

"Yes. They love all the gods...except maybe Allah," nurse three answered.

"Did you study in Christian schools?" It was obvious they had all studied in English medium schools.

"Yes. Our training was at a women's Christian college." Kerala had the highest literacy rate in India and was half Christian. It also had the highest percentage of communists in the country.

"Do you know who Yogananda was?" I asked. I was about to test the limits of their convictions.

"No sir."

"Yogananda was a Bengali swami who came to America sixty years ago. He was a gentle saint who was much loved by his students, east and west."

"Sir, did Yogananda like America more than India?" nurse number three asked. For some reason these gals insisted on comparing the two countries.

"He loved both countries, and viewed both as his home, although when he returned to India he kissed the ground when he got off the ship. Yogananda had many spiritual visions. Once Krishna and Christ appeared to him, standing side by side. When he asked them if they were the same, the two personalities merged into one. As a result, he believed there was no difference between the two. The vision helped Yogananda, because most of his students in America were Christian. He taught that Christ and Krishna were one and the same."

"But sir, we are taught there is a difference," nurse number one said humbly.

"Forget what you've been taught for a moment and ask yourself, do you think Yogananda's vision was real? What does your heart tell you?" I was testing these kind souls. I was also challenging the tenets of the religion of my youth.

"Sir, we don't know what to say," answered number two.

"Not every question needs an answer. Thinking about some questions is enough. Which part of Kerala are you from?" East and west, people had been taught what to believe, but few had significant inner experience. It was as if humanity had been told how delicious strawberries taste without ever having eaten one. Yogananda was one who had actually tasted the strawberry.

"Sir, we three are from Cochin, and they are from Trivandrum," the head nurse explained.

"Then you're from the Malabar Coast. Such beautiful beaches." Interesting, I thought to myself, the Malabar Coast was where St. Thomas first brought Christ's message to India not long after the crucifixion. There were twenty million Christians in India, most of them in the south. Very likely, the ancestors of the nurses had been Christians long before mine.

Many Worlds

I had landed in the hospital having been unable to eat anything solid for two weeks. It was my first night ever in a hospital bed, but I didn't mind, especially with such a sweet team of nurses looking after me. The private room was clean and quiet, and I drifted off to sleep easily. As I rested, an inner light triggered a succession of visions. The first was of a region inhabited by souls who were suffering terribly. Closely quartered like chickens in a coop, they cried and wailed continuously due to the pain they inflicted on themselves. Their torment was obvious, and I felt compassion for them, but didn't want to investigate too closely. There seemed to be someone keeping watch, so I went on.

The scene then shifted. I was now viewing a region where souls were immersed in a sensual dream, gratifying their carnal desires again and again. They were less tormented than the first group, but they also seemed lost in their dream. The group was without joy or happiness, pressed the way they were, flesh against flesh. There was no sense of freedom in their world. Again I felt like moving on.

After observing the first two worlds, I soared upward to a world that was similar to life on earth, and yet it was not a physical realm. The inhabitants lived in houses with gardens and seemed content with their existence, although I could not call their world particularly spiritual. It was quite ordinary.

I left that scene, rising higher into increasing levels of joy, both inside and out. Enchantingly beautiful music now filled the ether. It flowed through me like water through a sieve. I saw a bridge leading to a city of light and felt the presence of loving souls, dear ones who embraced me in their hearts. I felt a great affinity for this realm. The souls here were bathed in light and lived in harmony. Contentment pervaded their world. I felt immersed in peace, and wanted to stay.

Then the dream journey ended, and I found myself at the crown of my head, suffused in a light that left me no wish other than to bask in its benevolent presence. I sat up and fell into a long, peaceful meditation. When it was over, I knew my body was repaired.

In the morning I tried to interpret the strange vision in the night, which was clearly no ordinary dream. It seemed there were many places we could go between lives according to our inclinations, and of course, our karma. Some were heavens, but not all. During the journey, I found no gatekeepers and no one asked about my faith. After experiencing the beautiful realm of light I knew there would be no questions. Everyone would find their way to the place where his or her destiny took them.

TWENTY TWO

Meeting Amma

Tonight is worthy music.
Let's get loose with compassion,
Let's drown in the delicious
Ambience of Love.

—*Hafiz*

A Blue Collar Yogi

Our good friend Shashi Ullal opened birthday cards as we talked. We were celebrating Shashi's sixtieth, and were relaxing in his office after taking him to lunch at a swanky south Delhi hotel. Shashi was in high spirits. Two years earlier, just months after Shashi had taken over the helm at Hughes-Escorts Communications (HECL), we had taught a meditation course to his managers. Of all the executives I had met in India, Shashi's management style impressed me the most. His down to earth approach to running a business was reflected in both his personality and dress. I never saw Shashi in a suit; he wore short-sleeve shirts 365 days a year, including the winter months when the rest of Delhi shivered in their woolens. Shashi credited his forty years of yoga practice for fortifying his body against even the coldest winter mornings. As a seasoned executive, he insisted his people make important decisions and implement them even though the company was less than a year old when he took over the helm.

HECL, India's premier satellite communications company is a joint venture between an American firm founded by Howard Hughes and Escorts, India's leading tractor manufacturer. After opening his greeting cards, Shashi leaned back in his chair and shared a story with us. The company had reached a crossroads in its growth and needed additional bandwidth on INSAT (India's largest satellite) in order to position itself in the rapidly expanding industry. After long deliberations with corporate directors in Delhi and Washington, DC, it was decided that the expansion move was too risky. If Shashi's engineers failed to re-position four hundred ground dish receivers in a timely manner, customers (banks, brokerages, and corporations) would experience a crisis in their operations. Shashi's superiors feared lawsuits. The result would be disastrous for HECL.

Shashi knew the stakes, and convinced his directors that his people could accomplish the job of repositioning the dishes, which were scattered from Kashmir in the north to Kanya Kumari in the south. Working around the clock, they accomplished the task in twenty-four hours, braving snow-storms and the attacks of wild dogs in the process. As a result, none of HECL's clients experienced any down time, and Shashi was praised within and without the company. Because of his trust in people, HECL went on to become the leader in the communications industry for all of Southeast Asia.

Shashi was compensated royally for his efforts and could retire any-time he wanted, but he told us there was much more he wanted to accom-plish. Shashi readily acknowledged that his spiritual practice had given him the inner strength he needed to achieve his goals. "My luck has increased dramatically since learning meditation," he told me. "I count on it and it never lets me down."

Shashi asked me to instruct his family in a private meditation course. His college age daughter, Smriti, was struggling with health problems and Shashi thought meditation would help her, so I agreed to teach a small course and invited a young golf professional I had met to join the Ullal women. Everyone in the class was finding gratifying benefits. Mrs. Ullal, a devout woman, was rediscovering her peace of mind and the young golf pro, Jyoti Randhawa, was convinced meditation was what he had needed to deal with the pressures of his competitive vocation (Jyoti later became the top-ranked Asian PGA pro). Although Smriti's progress was uneven, she showed signs of coming out of her depression. On the final day of class, Mrs. Ullal invited me to meet a saint that she had taken Smriti to see in Bombay a few months earlier. That same saint was coming to Delhi and so I joined the Ullals the following weekend at a gathering near the airport.

Hugging One And All

The open-air hall was full by the time we arrived for the morning sat-sang. A young man was giving a lecture in Hindi as we seated ourselves on the floor. After the talk, chanting started in the back of the hall and the crowd rose to its feet as a small procession made its way through the group, led by a short but solidly built woman in white robes. She beamed a brilliant smile at each person she made eye contact with, which included many in the human corridor through which she passed. I was too far away to have a good look at her, but an elevating energy flooded the hall as she seated herself on stage.

After sitting for a moment, the round-faced woman scanned the audience with a confident gaze, smiling all the while. She then turned to a member of the entourage, and a group of bearded Swamis in orange robes sang a series of bhajans dedicated to the deities of the Hindu faith. The music filled the hall as lines formed leading to the saint who sat cross-legged at the edge of the stage. One by one, individuals made their way to the blissful woman who embraced each person lovingly. I remained seated, content to watch as person after person was caressed and held in the arms of the sturdy middle-aged woman.

Mrs. Ullal told me her name was Amma, which means Divine Mother. The crowd that had come to be with Amma was a mix of villagers and middle class Delhi residents. Many wept uncontrollably after their hug as attendants led them away. As she hugged each person, Amma stroked their back, sometimes touching them on the forehead and looking deeply into their eyes before releasing them. Some shared personal heartbreak with her; others approached the saint in silence. Whatever the internal change, nearly every person seemed moved by the experience. The hugging went on for an hour before I decided to join the men's line. Something was happening up there on stage and I wanted to experience it too.

Mrs. Ullal and Smriti were near the front of the women's line by now. Amma's eyes widened when the Ullals' turn came. She spoke to them like old friends before clasping mother and daughter in a long, tender embrace. As the Ullals started to get up, Amma pulled them back into her lap for a second squeeze, then kissed them on the cheek and applied sandal paste to their foreheads. As mother and daughter walked away, tears streamed down their cheeks.

Amma gave each person equal care and attention. As she looked into a pair of expectant eyes, she opened her arms and accepted the person as if they were a son or daughter returning after having been away from home for a long time. The faces of those who had been hugged looked different. Some smiled, some wept, but all were affected by their moment in the arms of the 'hugging saint.' One man shook uncontrollably as he sobbed on the shoulder of his wife.

When my turn came, I leaned forward, placing my head on Amma's shoulder the way I had seen others do. Amma held me firmly as she whispered something into my ear in a language I didn't understand. After a moment I thought it was time to get up, but as she had done with many others, she pulled me back for another embrace, this time whispering, "my darling son, my darling son," as she massaged my back. Before I moved away, I looked into her eyes and saw the ocean of love and compassion, a moment that stayed with me for a long time. By now she had already placed a candy in my hand and was pulling the next person into her arms.

Then a gap in time occurred. The details of what transpired in the ensuing minutes blurred, but I remember hearing a voice from a great distance, as if the words had traveled through a tunnel to reach me. Someone was saying my name, but I had no interest in responding; I was absorbed in a state that was incredibly satisfying. Again, someone called my name as if they were trying to awaken me from a deep slumber. The next thing I knew, Mrs. Ullal was standing in front of me. She said she had called my name several times before I recognized her. From my years of meditation, I knew that my mind had plunged into its innermost depths, a transcendence that came only during the deepest moments. I followed Mrs. Ullal to our seats, where Smriti was sitting with a peaceful look on her face. She looked radiant. It was a beautiful expression, something I hadn't seen even after Smriti learned to meditate.

Mrs. Ullal told me their story with Amma. Smriti had been struggling for some time. Several months earlier, Mrs. Ullal had discussed her daughter's problem with Amma, who had assured Mrs. Ullal that she would take care of it. When the Ullals went for their hug, Amma recognized them immediately, saying, "Daughter, I have taken care of Smriti. You need not worry." This astounded Mrs. Ullal because she knew Amma had hugged hundreds of thousands of people since their first meeting in Bombay. As we were leaving the hall, I turned to Amma for a final look, and knew without question that she was no ordinary person. The poster we passed on the way out described the woman in white as the Universal Mother. I didn't know who this remarkable woman was, but I hoped to find out.

Devi Bhava

I was deeply moved by Amma, and decided to see her again. According to one of her people, an all night affair called Devi Bhava was scheduled for her last day in Delhi. A sprawling tent was already filled beyond capacity when I arrived, but with the help of a volunteer, I located a seat on the canvas-covered ground near the front. After a lamp-lighting ceremony and a short talk, Amma led a group meditation. Then the stage curtains closed around her for ten minutes. Bells and chanting could be heard, but what transpired behind the curtains remained a mystery. The person sitting next to me said that Amma was entering a divine mood called Devi Bhava.

When the curtains opened, Amma was wearing a deep purple sari and had a tall silver crown on her head. She had apparently entered the mood of Divine Mother. Assistants began bringing over nine thousand people one by one to be consoled and uplifted. She embraced families together and placed babies on her lap, cuddling and kissing them on the cheeks. Many sobbed as personal trauma was expelled when Amma stroked their head and back. Her expression was filled with understanding and concern as she comforted the distressed and disturbed. A disfigured child near me was carried to the stage by his mother and placed in Amma's lap. She gazed compassionately into the boy's eyes, kissed him several times on the cheeks, and then sprinkled flower petals on him. His face glowed as his mother carried him back to his place. Biblical stories of Christ ministering to the sick and lame came to my mind.

The hugging continued for sixteen hours. During that time, Amma never left her couch. On two occasions she sipped water from a metal cup. By early morning, Amma's right cheek was bruised from having heads press against it all night. An assistant alternated massaging her back and feet. Amma embraced ten people per minute with assembly line precision, yet each hug was custom-fit for the individual, bringing smiles to some and evoking fits of emotion in others. Her endurance alone was superhuman; her energy never waned, nor did her enthusiasm, and she smiled and chatted with helpers as she hugged. All night long bhajans were sung by a group of devotees. The last in the tent to be hugged was greeted with the same tender smile and heartfelt embrace as the first. I was told Amma repeated this ritual virtually every day as she circled the globe on a personal mission to eradicate suffering. While traveling, she embraced people in airports, even hugging passengers on international flights, including pilots and flight attendants. By 2002, when she received the Gandhi-King Award for non-violence, she had already hugged twenty-one million people.

After hugging everyone in the tent, she stood at the front of the stage. An assistant stood next to her holding a bowl filled with flower petals. Amma's divine mood was different now. She appeared more abstract and less approachable as she stared at the audience. Her intensely personal style of interacting one to one with people was gone. She rocked from side to side as if possessed by a cosmic personality too great to be accommodated in a human body. As she swayed, my perception underwent a bizarre change. Everything dissolved around me, including the noise of the crowd, which faded to a faint drone. Although the singers had increased the volume to extreme levels, I barely noticed. No matter how I adjusted the focus of my eyes, I couldn't see Amma. I looked intently as she stood there, but she looked different. I no longer saw Amma. Instead, the mystifying Kali that I had seen in the Calcutta temple a few years earlier stared with intense eyes at the audience, but the all-powerful gaze of the black goddess was tempered with immense kindness. Disheveled hair formed a mist around her head, and her scarlet tongue stretched beyond her chin. As I stood there amidst the crowd of thousands, it was evident that either I was hallucinating from the combined effects of sleep deprivation and sensory overload from the music, or what I saw was real. The goddess possessed the power to destroy anything that displeased her. Kali was, as the scriptures described her, unassailable and intent on destroying suffering. I felt safe with her as a protector, but would never want to encounter her displeasure. She was both benevolent and uncompromising.

I tried to hold onto the specter as it faded, but it was hopeless. The vision of the black goddess vanished as mysteriously as it had come. A sort of mist now shrouded the stage, and when it cleared, Amma was standing there, throwing flower petals at the audience like a shortstop in a baseball game. With an almost casual sidearm motion, she tossed handfuls of rose petals as the crowd scrambled to collect them with the zeal of a beggar chasing ten-rupee notes. As the beat of the tabla intensified I looked for signs of reassurance that I was not the only person that had seen the awesome sight, for confirmation that I was not losing my mind. Was it real, or had the lack of sleep and earsplitting music induced the strange vision?

Maybe others had seen it too. I looked at the faces near me, but I wasn't sure until I saw the same crippled boy who had been carried to Amma earlier. I had looked at him from time to time, but his expression hadn't changed all night. He had appeared completely out of touch until now. But now his eyes were open wide, as if he had seen a ghost. He was staring at Amma. More remarkably, his tongue extended from his mouth to his chin as if he were mimicking someone doing the same thing. It was the only time all night I had seen his tongue. I wondered if he had seen what I had seen.

After a superhuman length of time onstage, Amma climbed down and walked briskly through a human corridor with the enthusiasm of a youngster on her way to visit friends, smiling at anyone and everyone. A van outside was poised to take her to the airport for a flight to Calcutta, where even greater numbers were expected. In the sudden wake of her departure, tears streamed down the cheeks of many. Others looked bewildered. With her hands pressed together in the traditional gesture of reverence, Amma stepped into the van and was gone. I glanced again at the crippled boy. His tongue was still stretching to touch his chin. I wanted to ask him what he had seen, but what did it matter? Numerous miracles had been attributed to this tiny woman from the Kerala backwaters, but the feats she had performed in the tent that night were miracle enough for me.

TWENTY THREE

The Brahmin Ideal

All history points to India as the mother of science and art.

—*William Macintosh*

Palm Leaf Predictions

The millennium ended on a bold note of personal insight. I had heard about an unusual system of Indian astrology called Nadi Palm from a friend, but had only gotten around to making an appointment for the last day of the year. Excitement, and some trepidation, was in the air as the millennium drew to a close. Y2K seemed to be on everyone's mind. It was a time of both uncertainty and anticipation, as the world was poised to leap into the future. A cynical Internet joke read, '80% of Indian banks are computerized, the rest are Y2K compliant,' but in reality, Indian programmers were doing the lion's share to prepare a computer dependent world for the new millennium.

When I arrived at the second floor apartment of a south Delhi residence, shoes and sandals blocked the landing. Inside, the waiting room looked like a doctor's office, minus the magazines and music. After a few minutes, a man approached me with an inkpad. He pressed my right thumb (left thumb for ladies) first on the pad and then on a slip of paper. Although I had never been fingerprinted, I imagined the process to be similar. After twenty minutes I was escorted to a back office and told to wait.

The dhoti-clad astrologer who entered the room wore unstitched cloth, a tradition among Brahmins. He had with him a stack of thin strips of brown wood, which he explained were palm leaves. Each leaf, according to the Brahmin, contained someone's life story. Although the leaves looked as regular as the wooden rulers we used in elementary school forty years ago, they had been fashioned from palm trees, and rounded Tamil script was meticulously etched all over the surface of each leaf.

The pundit inspected the stack of leaves, before stopping to scrutinize one more closely. Reading from the slender strip, he said, "Father's name is Olive and mother's name is Dolores. You have one brother and one sister, both married. Moon is Cancer. You are single and have PhD." Every detail was accurate except for my Dad's name, which was Oliver, not Olive. The rest of the information on the leaf was accurate to the detail. I hadn't said a word about my family or educational background and sat there marveling that a piece of a palm tree could contain such accurate information.

The confirmation of my parents' names satisfied the man, who said, "This is your leaf. The story of your life is preserved on this ancient leaf." Then he left the room, leaving me to sort out the strange sensations I was feeling in my solar plexus. I was intrigued by the possibility that the major events of a person's life could be recorded on a palm leaf long before they were born, and was anxious to know what the elegantly carved script had to say. At the same time, I felt ambivalent; the disturbing encounter with the astrologer, who had predicted my death soon after I arrived in India, had left some residue in my psyche.

After fifteen minutes, the Brahmin returned with his translator, who read what was purported to be the story of my life. His opening statement got my attention. "This is a dialogue between Lord Siva and Parvati (Siva's consort) as recorded by Rishi Kaushika (a sage who lived some 3000 years ago). Parvati asks Lord Siva about the incarnation of Steve Briggs, who comes for the reading at age 47." How was it possible, I wondered, that one's life could have been recorded on a leaf thousands of years ago? After all, no one, not even my friends, knew the names of my parents. Where was this information coming from? This could only be happening in unfathomable India, I thought. I had no choice but to suspend all judgment and listen.

The predictions pertained to the future and included the year of my death. I was relieved to find that there was no mention of an imminent heart attack, however as predicted earlier, the heart would be the ultimate cause of my passing. The second part of the predictions pertained to a previous life. Time would tell if the predictions were accurate or not. The leaf indicated that I would be teaching meditation abroad for many years, and that there would be visions of important saints and gods. Publishing was mentioned and many pilgrimages were predicted, especially visits to the Divine Mother along with wisdom received from a spiritual teacher that I would meet unexpectedly. I would die at age 72. I was relieved to know that I still had a few years left.

The leaf also claimed I had been a Buddhist living in a village in Ceylon in a previous life. This information intrigued me, and I was able to confirm that at least the village existed. As for the character named Bussyo who I was reputed to have been, he remained a foggy mix of enigma and imagination. Recommendations from a second leaf advised me to travel to the coastal region of Tamil Nadu to four ancient temples to propitiate the planets and gods that I had in some way offended. The entire session was fascinating, although I had no way to verify the accuracy of it all.

Later I found out more about the Nadi Palm tradition. The Chola kings of south India had patronized the system 2,000 years ago. The word Nadi means 'destined to come of their own accord.' The collections of leaves are extensive and include knowledge of herbal cures, alchemy, kayakalp (methods to increase longevity), and fortune telling. The British had negotiated with the Brahmin family in charge of the library of leaves, but the family refused to give them up for they had been part of their ancestry for centuries. From sub-lines of the thumb impression, 1,008 categories of leaves had been created, which allowed an expert to narrow his search until he found the right leaf, a process that often took hours, and in some cases, even weeks. Not everyone's leaf was found.

Appeasing The Planets

When the Birla Group booked us in Bangalore a few months later, Lane and I pulled out a map along with our Nadi Palm prescriptions and booked flights into Madras. From Madras we traveled by car to Kumbakonam, a town at the heart of an area where most of the prescribed temples were located. The night of our arrival, a procession honoring the avatar Ram paraded through the streets, led by a lumbering elephant with the symbol 'OM' painted across its forehead and crimson kum kum rubbed on the upper half of her trunk. Devotees marched behind the deity as drummers pounded a strong beat and a pair of horns trumpeted. Being back in south India was a homecoming of sorts; I had spent four months in Tamil Nadu fifteen years earlier, and the Dravidian culture hadn't changed much.

Waking up to a south Indian morning is a treat. A languid feeling envelops the body upon rising, and the pace of one's heart slows a beat or two as it adjusts to the unhurried ambiance. Cocks crowed robustly outside, leaving me little option but to rise with the villagers who were preparing for a day in the fields. The smell of red soil and tropical flora was strong, and agreeable. While an outdoor bucket bath had been my nemesis in the Himalaya, it suited south India. An old Brahmin had advised me that pouring well water over my head in the morning sun would ensure good health. It was wisdom that I didn't understand, but appreciated.

It was therapeutic being away from Indian cities, and my mind entertained fanciful thoughts of retiring to a Tamil village the way urban Americans dream of moving to Crested Butte or Telluride while camping in the Rockies. The knock on the door was breakfast. Rice cakes had arrived. Uttapam, a south Indian staple, is a rice-flour pancake made for coconut chutney the way buckwheat pancakes are meant for maple syrup. The sambar (soup), on the other hand, burned all the way down, a sensation I disliked anytime, but especially in the morning. One needed to be on constant alert for chilies, which floated around in soups like red devils.

Our astrological missions had separate itineraries. The planetary prescription for Lane's horoscope was different from mine, except for Jupiter, the planet of spiritual knowledge, which we had both been advised to visit. The Brihaspati (Jupiter) temple was in a village called Alangudi, a fair distance from Kumbakonam. The journey took us past peasant lifestyles that had changed little over the millennia. As we crept along the single lane road, cuttings from bushes spread across the road caught in the undercarriage of our taxi. The villagers had placed the cuttings on the road to help crush the vegetation, which somehow eased their harvesting task. Our cooperation was acknowledged by bobbles of the head as we passed the sinewy farmers, who kept a close watch on their harvest.

A good-natured old Brahmin at the temple guided us through the propitiation ritual. We were to light a ghee lamp, place it in front of the planetary deity, and then circle the temple clockwise. We were to repeat the procedure ten times. The only witness to the arcane custom was a monkey who watched from the overhanging trees. He was looking for a snack, but seeing that we had no food, he lost interest before our final round. When we finished, the priest performed a more elaborate ceremony, waiving a larger lamp in front of the oiled statue. The entire process was a sincere gesture to the planet of wisdom.

By late evening my planetary duties were completed and I returned to Kumbakonam. Again, a parade marched around the terra cotta streets led by the elephant. It was spring and the Tamil people were celebrating before putting seeds in the soil. I followed the procession to a pillared mandap (hall) outside the Ram temple where I watched the mahout tether the elephant to an iron stake. The gentle elephant's forehead, upper trunk, and ears were painted with bold designs. I offered her prasada, and in exchange for the sweets, she raised her trunk and sprayed me with a blast of saliva and hot air. I wasn't sure how to interpret the shower, but as I wiped my face with the sleeve of my kurta, the mahout assured me that I had received the blessings of the hati and Ram as well. I was grateful, but took another shower when I got back to the hotel.

My final karmic obligation was at a Siva temple built by the same Chola kings who once patronized the Nadi Palm tradition. The temple was located in a small seaside village named Chidambaram. Chidambaram means consciousness as expansive as the sky, and Nataraj, the divine dancer, is the principal deity worshiped within the imposing walls of the temple.

The temple towers are carved with images of the 108 poses Siva assumes during his divine dance. Inside the temple are five enclosures, a hall with 1,000 monolithic pillars, and an inner sanctum where Nataraj stands at the center of a ring of fire. The statue, which is crafted from five metals, is the prototype for Nataraj statues seen all over the world.

It was time to settle my debt with the great cosmic dancer. I sat in the center of the stone courtyard as a priest impaled a coconut on an iron stake and a team of Brahmins launched into Rudrabishek, the traditional recitation to Lord Siva. The four priests formed a square, each sitting in a corner while I sat in the center. The chanting continued for a long time, gathering intensity as it progressed. I became restless and opened my eyes to have a look around, but I had no choice but to stay put while my karmic debts were settled. Fortress-like walls surrounded me on all sides. There was no escaping, and for the next two hours I squirmed and shifted positions in my self-imposed incarceration. As the ceremony progressed, an invisible fire burned inside me, wetting both brow and chest. I hadn't been this uncomfortable since spending an hour in the middle school principal's office for playing my baritone too loud during band practice.

The Hindu scriptures explain that the seeds of one's karma need to be roasted so they will never sprout again. By the time the ceremony ended, I was thoroughly baked. After the ritual, liquid offerings were poured over a crystal linga in the temple's inner sanctum, and the internal fire cooled down. A great lightness now pervaded my being. The journey into India's ancient traditions was complete, and I felt peace within. The palm leaf prescriptions had been filled, the medicine taken, and the debt repaid. It was time to head for Bangalore.

The Garden City

Bangalore is unlike other Indian cities. Once a sparkling emerald in a salubrious climate, a major influx of people has forever tainted its allure. The city's lush gardens and parks, tree-lined streets, and handsome red stone government complex, conjure up images of affluence and sound city planning. But Bangalore has not escaped the ravages of growth. It once enjoyed the title The Garden City, but the moniker no longer applies. At an elevation of 3,000 feet, residences and offices once shunned artificial cooling, but with a population swelling to five million, climatic changes have occurred. Commuters wear masks over their mouths to protect against sulfurous clouds on the streets. Still, Bangalore is the envy of every other Indian city.

Bangalore's latest incarnation has been dubbed the Silicon Valley of India. While playing a round of golf at the upscale Karnataka Golf Club, my caddy advised me to take aim at various glass-plated corporate towers on the horizon. One of the towers housed Microsoft, a target I would have preferred aiming at with more than a golf ball, considering the recent spate of system crashes on my laptop. The software giants have invaded Bangalore to employ the city's techies who perform at a fraction of the cost of their western counterparts.

It is projected that over three million jobs will be outsourced to India from the US alone in the coming decade. Megabytes of opportunity lie ahead for India's educated youth. With over a half billion Indians under the age of twenty-five, there are plenty of young people preparing for careers that didn't exist for their parents. Even Santa, according to an Internet cartoon, has been outsourced to Bangalore.

Brahmin Traditions

India's contributions to knowledge have not been as widely recognized as those of ancient Rome, Greece or Egypt, but they are arguably more impressive. The world's first university was founded in northwest India and was attended by 10,000 students who studied Grammar, Mathematics, Philosophy, Medicine, Surgery, Politics, and Astronomy. Students came from Babylonia, Syria, China, and Greece to study at Takshashila University. 2,700 years later, the affinity Indians have for science, engineering, and mathematics can be seen by their employment at NASA, IBM, and Microsoft, where about one third of all employees are Indian.

Although India's contributions in mathematics are not as well known as the Greeks, they are equally impressive. Indians discovered the zero, without which there would be no binary system and no computers. As Albert Einstein wrote, "We owe a lot to the Indians, who taught us how to count, without which no worthwhile scientific discovery could have been made." Geometry may be credited to Euclid, but Indian geometry predates the Greeks by 700 years. The Indian treatise, Surya Siddhantam, introduced trigonometry in the 4th century, 800 years before it was introduced in Europe and a decimal system flourished in India by 100 BC. Indians seem to have a knack for abstract thinking, which has given them an advantage in the computer age.

Indian astronomers postulated that the earth was round and that it rotated on its axis a thousand years before Copernicus published his theory of the earth's rotation. An Indian treatise on gravity was written long before it was discovered by Newton. In the field of medicine, the physician Shushruta practiced advanced methods of surgery in 600 B.C., performing dozens of surgical procedures like plastic surgery, amputations, brain surgery, cataract, and caesarean surgery. Anesthesia was also used in ancient India. Advances in physics, grammar, genetics, navigation, physiology, and anatomy were all made in India at very early dates. According to one British historian, many of the advances in science that we consider today to have been made in Europe, were, in fact, made in India centuries earlier.

The educational antecedents contributing to India's scientific acumen can be traced, in part, to Brahmin traditions of learning. Nowhere is this in greater evidence than in south India. Say the word 'Brahmin' on the street today and you may be met with a frown or worse. The idea of caste in India, with its 3,000 sub-castes evokes images of discrimination and government quotas. Brahmins, who have remained at the top of the archaic caste structure by maintaining an aura of intellectual superiority and exclusivity, are widely criticized.

On the other hand, the traditions of knowledge passed down through the centuries within the Brahmin community deserve recognition for fostering unique intellectual abilities. In ancient times, Brahmin boys studied and memorized the Vedic scriptures while leading contemplative lives prescribed by Manu, the first lawgiver. As a result, Brahmins excelled at abstract thought. Children became familiar with the concepts of infinity and eternity at a young age as a consequence of what they were taught in their philosophical studies. Today, although it is no longer fashionable to adhere rigidly to caste; marriage, cultural gatherings, and residential enclaves still revolve around caste to a great extent.

Among the routines followed by the Brahmin community were a vegetarian diet, daily worship, and strict rules regarding hygiene. These fundamentals of Brahmin life were meant to promote clear and insightful thinking, a tradition that began at the dinner table. Food is considered sacred in the Hindu religion, and the vegetarian diet, which is lighter than most, was believed to produce an alert and pure mind, one that is more attuned to the spirit. Until recently, Brahmins ate only in the home, avoiding restaurants because they believed food prepared by outsiders was inferior. And this may well be true, when one considers that profit is the motive behind commercial establishments, whereas love and devotion form the core of a good home-cooked meal.

Traditionally, Brahmin families followed a disciplined routine in order to ensure a calm mind and healthy body. Polluting agents such as nicotine and alcohol were scrupulously avoided. Marriage contracts were made with other Brahmins to preserve genetic purity, and disciplines like meditation and worship of the family deity were followed to further attune the awareness to the divine. It was these precepts that fostered the academic genius appreciated by early Greeks, Romans, and other cultures that exchanged ideas with India.

In 1982, I spent two weeks in a Brahmin colony near Cape Comorin. The ancient Tamil ways were observed in the community, although the videshis (foreigners) staying in the neighborhood violated some basic rules. Each night we listened to readings of the Ramayana from our roof just like the Brahmin families who relaxed on charpoys in the moonlight as they listened to the annual reading of India's favorite epic poem.

Brahmins staffed temples, and they were also teachers. They administered religious rites, led philosophical enquiry, and engaged in abstract thinking; they steadfastly avoided manual labor. The methods they used to instruct their own children were often adopted in schools. To a great extent, this is how the Brahmin way filtered into academic life, and today, India's burgeoning technology industries owe a debt of gratitude to the Brahmin community, however unpopular the caste concept.

The Indian economy moves like a clock with three hands: an hour hand, a minute hand, and a second hand. India's agriculture sector moves at the speed of the hour hand, its progress is as slow as the bullock cart. India's industrial sector moves at the speed of the minute hand, growing at a healthy pace. But racing ahead is technology, which moves at the speed of the second hand, keeping up with the pace of globalization. Although it takes all three hands to tell the time, India's economic prosperity lies with technology. The country enjoys a competitive advantage over nations that don't have intellectual traditions preserved by the Brahmin ideal.

Mysore

Bangalore serves megabytes of fast food. Favoring custom cuisine, we avoided the popular franchises lining the commercial districts. Locals, who flocked to McDonalds and Pizza Hut, obviously didn't share our point of view. Again, the irony of westerners in search of Indian food while Indians lined up for American cuisine was not lost on us. After our final meeting with the Birla managers, we splurged on a meal at Bangalore's Oberoi Hotel. The hotel's paneled dining room with its lush tropical gardens took me back in time to the Bangalore that I remembered when it was still The Garden City.

After lunch, I boarded a train bound for Mysore, a city that has preserved its heritage more fastidiously than Bangalore. The journey passed idyllic villages and temple towers that rose above verdant paddy fields. The clarity of colors in the countryside—azure sky, chartreuse field, and ivory tower—was more vivid than in the city, whose colors were dulled by pollution.

A family of four sat across the isle on the second-class coach. I played a game of cat and mouse with the little one who stood on her father's seat, casting shy glances in my direction and quickly diverting her eyes whenever I looked her way. Outfitted in yellow lace dresses, the adorable little girl and her sister were on their way to visit their grandparents and the Mysore zoo, a perfect weekend for any young family.

Trains have an hypnotic effect on the mind; their fluid motion is soothing. Swaying side to side, the train moved majestically, like the enormous elephants that lumbered along Delhi boulevards. As kids, my brother, sister, and I traveled on the Rock Island Rocket to Chicago from our home in western Illinois to compete in tennis tournaments. Traveling on our own, we felt like aristocrats in our reclining seats. The fact that we saw nothing but corn and soybeans didn't diminish the magic at all. A uniformed coachman served us sodas at a white linen table in the club car, and when we were restless, we stood on the platform between cars, our heads stuck out the window. For a ten year-old, the Rock Island Rocket was the ultimate adventure.

We got our first tennis rackets when we started school, and spent our summers learning the game on the public courts near our house. Before long, we were traveling to tournaments around the Midwest. By the time

I reached junior high, I had already been thrashed a few times by a talented Illinois native named Jimmy Connors. We loved the game, the competition, and the travel.

The brakeman pulled the lever and the train came to a stop in Mysore station. Although I had burned Mysore incense for decades, I had never seen a sandalwood forest until my taxi driver took me through a grove of the sacred trees on my way to a hilltop temple outside the city.

Nature's Best Incense

India's trees are almost as holy as its rivers. The banyan, with its flying buttress root system and uncanny ability to send roots from its limbs down to the soil to spawn more trees is my favorite. One famous banyan has rooted so many times that it covers several acres of land. All over India you'll see grand old trees with a flower or sweet left at its base. Equally common is the sight of a massive trunk wrapped in red or white string, an indicator that the tree is being worshipped. Sandalwood, banyan, neem, and deodar are all mentioned in the Vedic scriptures. Some of these trees possess medicinal properties. Esoteric beliefs maintain that benevolent beings of light inhabit the trees, offering protection to those who approach with devotion.

The sandalwood tree is valued not only for its scented oil, but also for its wood, which is ground into a powder by rubbing a block of it against a stone. Yogis mix the powder with a drop of water to form a paste that they smear across their forehead. Chandanam (sandalwood) is said to cool the mind and is beneficial to those who practice long meditation. Hindus believe that celestial beings are attracted to scents, which explains the use of incense in religious ceremonies the world over. Sandalwood incense is among the most popular, although the resin from cedar, juniper, and frankincense also make potent aromas believed to attract the attention of the devas.

Chamundi Hill is dedicated to the goddess Chamundeshwari. Her hilltop temple stands on a foundation that is 2,000 years old, and is home to the goddess that slew the demon Mahishasura. The goddess was once the family deity of the Maharaja of Mysore, which explains how the temple came to be endowed with a solid gold statue of the devi. Most pilgrims climb the steep hill on foot, but I settled for a ride in the taxi.

The temple priests offered me a seat close to the brilliant golden goddess. They worked efficiently, placing offerings at the feet of the goddess and dispensing holy water into the hands of devotees from a brass spoon.

The shimmering presence of the goddess filled the small chamber.

Outside, I circled the temple along with Indian families before stopping to sit in the shade of a small grove behind the temple. Leaning against one of the trees I watched the pilgrims pass at a leisurely pace. I sank into meditation and before long, I was as rooted to the earth as the tree that propped me up. The chatter of birds held my attention for a while, but their sounds soon vanished. As I settled, energies percolated, and soon a golden thread stretched the length of my spine and out the top of my head, producing a fountain of light above me. Sweet rushes of delight flowed along the filament like messages along a fiber optic strand. A switchboard behind my eyes directed the flow of energy, and whenever my awareness rested there, an involuntary command generated another intoxicating surge. Then the switchboard shut down, and the jetsam of my thoughts dispersed like fallen leaves in the wind. Recharged by the interlude beneath the leafy grove, I bounded toward the taxi on my way to visit Mysore Palace.

The Maharaja's magnificent residence, a stately Indo-Sarcenic palace graced by handsome arches, colonnades, and domes tells a story of enormous wealth. Like its counterparts in Rajasthan, the palace reflects eclectic tastes ranging from sublime to impulsive. The Wodeyar family were descendents of Vijaynagar kings, and they ruled benevolently for hundreds of years, playing a significant role in the advancement of Mysore state, now called Karnataka. The Wodeyars built colleges and hospitals and supported agriculture projects. They also created beautiful cities with public parks and gardens. Their foresight may ultimately have drawn too many to the Garden City. Mahatma Gandhi once referred to the Wodeyar dynasty as Raam Raj, the highest tribute one could pay a kingdom.

The Maharaja's 450 pound jewel-studded solid gold throne, although more suitable in size for a child monarch than a grown man, must have dazzled his constituency. I wondered how a peasant family would react to the overt opulence of the palace, but poor Indians have long been reconciled to the extremes of class inequity. Belief in fate plays a larger role in the eastern psychology than it does in the west. After land, gold is India's most cherished commodity, and her feudal kings amassed copious amounts of it. The stained glass ceiling of the palace foyer was a novel notion, casting a cool light the way the sun does when filtered through a jungle canopy. The Mysore palace stands as one of India's most elegant architectural achievements, a monument to the good governance of the former Mysore state.

Breakdown

It was time to return to Bangalore to catch the evening flight back to Delhi. I hoped to see the adorable sisters on the return trip; I wanted to quiz them about the animals at the zoo, but they were not on the train. I was deep in travel trance when the train rolled to a stop in the middle of nowhere. For a few minutes, no one thought anything of the delay. After all, stranger things happen on Indian trains all the time. Then the announcement came that the train's engine had broken down, and we would be delayed until another engine could be brought from Bangalore. This was a first for me, but the businessman sitting next to me wasn't at all concerned. I asked him how long he thought the engine exchange would take. It would be an hour before we were moving again, he thought. If the delay were longer than an hour I would miss my flight. "What are my options?" I asked.

"You can climb down and hail a bus, but it's a risk," said the man, pointing to the road running parallel to the tracks.

Feeling venturesome, I got off, leaving the comfort of a cool coach in search of adventure and a faster way. The green of the fields and clattering palms were even more brilliant without dusty windows in the way. The thatched houses along the perimeters of the irrigated paddy were clean and cared for. Whatever the inconvenience of the stalled train, it was my good fortune to be stranded in rural Karnataka. I had been standing by the road for a few minutes and no vehicles had passed, so I made a small prayer to the golden Devi on the hill in Mysore, soliciting her help. Shortly, a local bus came lumbering along. I waved, and the vehicle slowed to a stop. I took the empty seat opposite a peasant with a caged chicken on his lap. The seats were full of introspective passengers. I was no stranger to Indian busses, but this one stopped any time a passenger approached the front. I began to wonder if I would make my flight.

As we slowly passed a bicycle, a passenger train overtook us. It was my train. My calculation that it would take two hours to change the engine was wrong, but we were already at the edge of Bangalore, so no time had been lost. As the bus pulled into the station, I searched for an auto rikshaw with an engine capable of reasonable speed. I found one and instructed its driver to take me to the Oberoi Hotel, a drop that doubled the driver's fare.

The rikshaw deposited me in front of the landmark establishment, a world apart from the barnyard bus. Handsome men and beautiful women staffed the marbled palace, speaking flawless English. The staff was graceful, even elegant, and I would have lingered in the lobby, but there was not a minute to spare if I was to catch my flight, so I handed the concierge my card, and said, "Sir, Ravi Bhootalingam is a personal friend of mine. I'm late for my flight. Can you help me?" Ravi was the president of East Indian Hotels, the corporation that owned and operated the Oberoi chain. I had taught Ravi to meditate a year earlier, and I was gambling that his name would evoke a helpful response, which it did.

"Dr. Briggs, what can we do for you?" asked the courteous employee.

"Please call the airline to see if my flight is on time, then order me a cheese sandwich from the coffee shop and have a vehicle with a senior driver ready in ten minutes. I need to clean up." It was no time to be bashful.

"No problem. Here's a key to our executive spa where you can freshen up. Your sandwich will be waiting for you. Our best driver will be out front. His name is Sunil." This was Indian service at its best: competence with flair. But I also appreciated the easygoing bus driver who had picked me up by the road. The peasants and the hotel staff were from different worlds, but they had kindness in common.

"Sir, your sandwich," the concierge said, handing me a bag as I crossed the lobby. "Your driver is out front. Your flight is on time, but the airline knows you're coming." I handed the good man a well-earned tip, climbed into the Japanese sedan, and promised to mention his name to Ravi.

Sunil knew what was expected of him, and sped through traffic like a formula one driver. It being Sunday, we were spared the workday congestion that the best driver couldn't overcome. Within minutes we were in front of the Jet Air terminal. A woman from the airline approached the car. "Sir, here is your boarding pass. I'll escort you to the gate." The attentive employee worked for arguably the finest domestic airline in the world. I was glad there had been time to shower.

When I called Ravi Bhootalingam the next day to tell him how helpful his people in Bangalore had been, his secretary informed me that her boss was on spiritual pilgrimage to a remote region in Tibet. When I asked if that meant Mount Kailash, she confirmed my suspicion. Ravi, an Oxford graduate, was an exceptional executive who was fond of British blazers and imported ties. Although he had taken to meditation immediately, I never expected to find him trekking over 18,000 foot passes in remote Tibet in search of spiritual merit. When I called Ravi again six weeks later, his secretary told me that upon returning from the pilgrimage, her boss had taken an extended sabbatical to 'reflect.' Pilgrimage was making a comeback in India, and I wanted to hear Ravi's story and tell him that I had visited his home state to have my planetary affairs put in order. After reading his fascinating diary account of Mt. Kailash, I suspected Ravi had undergone a profound transformation on his pilgrimage too, and I made a note to save three weeks for the trip to Tibet in the spring.

TWENTY FOUR

Holy Cows

*Man is the only animal that can remain on friendly terms
with the victims he intends to eat until he eats them.*

—*Sam Butler*

I had forgotten about the shrewd coolies at Delhi's Paharganj railway station. When they spotted our trunks stacked high on the roof of the taxi, they demanded more rupees to transport our belongings from the parking lot to our sleeper car than the cost of my passage to the far west of India. We had no alternative but to employ the scoundrels, as the trunks were too heavy for us to carry, and there wasn't time to make multiple trips to and from the train. I wished the uncouth workers could have a week of training under Ravi's supervision at the Oberoi Hotel, and hoped more reasonable people awaited us in Ahmedabad.

My new assignment took me to the state of Gujarat, accompanied by my eclectic friend Will Fox. Having grown up on the Gulf of Mexico, Will wasn't bothered much by heat, which would serve him well in the arid region by the Arabian Sea. Will had been teaching in India for five years and enjoyed exploring the local way of life wherever he went. Will had an interest in archaeology, and we had dubbed the affable Texan the Raja of Rubble on an earlier trip, and he was committed to living up to the title. With a fresh batch of corporate houses waiting for us, we boarded the Ashram Express at Delhi's main train station, a troop of coolies in tow.

I knew little about Gujarat, except that it was the birthplace of Mahatma Gandhi and that our flat was on Judge's Bungalow Road. We arrived at a tall, modern apartment complex that stood on concrete stilts above ground level parking. It was a relief to find that everything in our sixth floor apartment worked perfectly—plumbing, electricity, phone, and kitchen appliances. All passed repeated tests so routinely that I wondered if there wasn't a hidden catch somewhere. When even one or two fixtures worked properly at the ashram, I was elated. Even the lift showed no strain under the weight of our load, but I almost passed out on the floor when the security guard refused a tip for the trunks he had carried. If our first hour in Ahmedabad were any indicator, our new assignment would be to our liking.

Maharaj Is King

Cows are omnipresent on the subcontinent, and they generally mingle easily with humans. Being sociable creatures that love attention, they congregate in public places and even seek out medians and busy boulevards where they stand or lie unperturbed as traffic roars by day and night. When a safe place at road's edge isn't available, they will lie right down in the middle of the road, blocking traffic and forcing scooters to swerve to avoid them. But their indifference worried me, and more than once I came across a lame cow that had been sideswiped by a car. Plenty of bovines rummaged about our Judge's Bungalow neighborhood, which was a safer haven than the congested thoroughfares in other parts of Ahmedabad.

A few days after we arrived, I noticed a man and a cow waiting for a bus by the road one morning. Somehow the man and long-horned cow standing side by side at the bus stand conjured up images of a Far Side Cartoon. As I passed the odd couple, the cow moved behind the man. I sensed something was up, and watched in amazement as the cow lowered its head under the man's seat and lifted him off the ground. I could hardly believe my eyes. For a brief moment the bewildered man sat between the cow's horns as if seated at his desk, still holding his brief case. But before he knew what hit him, with a twist of its head, the cow spun the man in a complete loop and the fellow landed hard on his bottom in the dust, looking dazed by the cartwheel he had unwittingly performed. The poor guy never quite knew what had picked him up. As he dusted himself off, the guilty party stood there meekly as if nothing had happened.

The unexpected occurred inside our flat as well as at the bus stand. Our cook's name was Maharaj (Great King), and the white-haired raja ruled our kitchen with a self-confidence bordering on arrogance as he prepared meals with great aplomb. Although Maharaj didn't speak much English and we knew even less Gujarati, he intuited our tastes flawlessly.

As the weeks passed, the only complaint against Maharaj was his habit of disappearing for days at a time without informing anyone. We soon

discovered that his truant spells were spent creating elaborate wedding ban-
quets, a lucrative sideline that supplemented his modest income. We would
not have minded the moonlighting had he informed us, but Maharaj operated in secrecy, since other employers had penalized him for his absen-
teeism. Maharaj was an artist whose flamboyant disposition matched his
formidable talent. His creations were as mouth-watering as his moods
unpredictable. Like many Indians, Maharaj had learned his trade appren-
ticing at his father's side as a boy. Maharaj came to work in handsome
handspun tunics made from a fabric called Khadi, a material made popular by Mahatma Gandhi.

The Mahatma

I couldn't help noticing the orderly way Gujarati people moved about
the city, and the fact that the fleets of motor scooters flooding the streets
were driven by women as often as men. This was unheard of in other parts
of India, and it suggested liberal mindedness. Historically, Ahmedabad was
one of India's most affluent cities; its economic legacy closely linked to the
manufacture of textiles, an industry that has largely died out in recent
times. The old city on the opposite side of the Sabarmati River was once
home to the prospering industry. Today, the slender smokestacks of abandoned mills sever the skyline, bleak reminders of better times. At its zenith,
a quarter of the world's textiles were manufactured in India, but sadly that
is no longer the case. The inability to keep up with changing methods ultimately undid the family owned operations. Mechanization, which meant
better quality cloth, also meant replacing the mill workers that operated
the handlooms, and socialist governments stepped in to prevent job loss
and modernization, dooming the industry in the process.

Gujarat is the home of Indian independence and the birthplace of its
founder. In a sleepy, sun-soaked port on the Arabian Sea, Mohandas
Gandhi was one of six boys born into a bania (merchant) family. After
studying law in England and practicing it in South Africa, the great social
reformer returned to Ahmedabad, where he plotted the liberation of his
countrymen. The former headquarters of Gandhi's freedom movement is a
tranquil setting shaded by trees and dotted with spartan but well-main-
tained buildings overlooking the river. The Sabarmati has since all but
dried up, but Gandhi's legacy hasn't.

Textile manufacturing has always been an honored tradition in India,
and Gandhi sought to preserve that custom by spending his days at his
Ahmedabad ashram operating his spinning wheel in the hope that others

would follow his example and that the cottage industry could be revived. It was Gandhi's dream that India sustain itself by weaving khadi cloth.

Nowhere in the world are textile applications as varied as the tapestries, wedding gowns, wall hangings, and everyday apparel found in India. Exquisite designs employ needlework, brocade, hand painting, tie-dye, and appliqué, using color schemes rivaling a peacock's magnificence. The incalculable hours spent handcrafting garments is mind-boggling, but then time consuming endeavors are savored in India like a slow developing sitar raga. Jamavar shawls incorporating three hundred shades of vegetable dye, Sherbati fabrics, exotic muslins, and gossamer scarves with hand-painted flowers are all endangered traditions that once flourished at the hands of artisans.

Ikot Weaving

Over the years, I had seen women wearing the ubiquitous sari in a variety of ways from the stunning gold embroidered wedding saris worn by princesses and industrialist daughters to the simple wraps of peasant women as they waded about paddy fields, but I had no idea there were eighty-five ways to wear a sari, and as many ways of weaving them.

On a Saturday morning we set out for Patan. The medieval town, with its Jain temples and narrow footpaths, lay hidden behind tall perimeter walls. At the village's main entrance, a sprawling shade tree arched over the gate leading to a network of stone walkways. At the heart of the village unaltered by time, a family of weavers has labored for generations, creating exquisite wedding saris for the daughters of wealthy Bombay banias.

The Salvi family invited us into their home for tea and an informal tour of their unpretentious studio. We entered a work area where several frameless looms hung from the ceiling. Behind one of them, a middle-aged man with a round, cheerful face leaned over his work. Mr. Salvi was the senior member of one of two families in all of India still producing Double Ikat, one of the most demanding textiles woven anywhere in the world. As we chatted, his hands moved with the dexterity of a lute maestro. Appearing to possess a consciousness all their own, his fingers moved from task to task with precision and certainty, manifesting birds and elephants from thread as if by slight of hand. Mr. Salvi's fingers had been performing the intricate process of interlacing thread since he was a child. His sophisticated weaving methods required an aptitude for geometry and an artistic sense as well as unerring attention to minutest detail. He followed no pattern, but wove by intuition, the sure sign of a master artisan. After we had watched the deft movements of his hands, he stopped to show us a finished garment. To our amazement, both front and back of the double-sided cloth displayed the same beautiful figures woven into the garment, which is why Mr. Salvi's technique is called Double Ikot.

We marveled how the extraordinary saris were woven. The patience, focus, and dexterity necessary to craft these heirlooms demanded great dedication and discipline. To produce one sari, two expert weavers alternated ten-hour shifts on a single loom for five months. Although the weavers worked industriously, the Salvi family produced just a handful of saris each year. When I asked Mr. Salvi about his unusual vocation, he said, "Weaving is my passion. I am devoted to weaving."

The Salvi family has been honored with national awards, and their work has been exhibited in Moscow, Paris, and Washington, DC. An Indian postage stamp in recognition of the Patan weavers was proudly displayed on the Salvi's studio wall. The Salvi family was indeed fortunate to wake up each morning, knowing that their day would be spent doing what they loved most. In an age of automation, to see a family producing heirloom saris, I better understood my Himalayan Master's instruction, "Let prema (love) guide your life." Having visited the Salvi studio, I better understood the cultural sentiment that cloth is a sacred vestment worthy of the gods.

Hands At Play

A handicraft fair manifested like a desert mirage one day on a vacant field a few blocks from our flat. Craftsmen from the Rann of Kutch, a sparsely populated desert region in the northwest corner of Gujarat, were in the city to exhibit their creations. Since their soil was ill suited to farming, the villagers had become artisans, and were widely recognized for the handicrafts they fashioned in their homes. After work one day, we spent the evening admiring the handmade silver, chaklas (wall hangings), appliqué and patchwork quilts, wood carved spice boxes, and paintings in the tented stalls, and watched the craftsmen go about their work; creative collaborations of hand and heart.

One family of artists in particular caught my attention. Their favorite motif was the animals of India. Father was the master artist and his young daughter the budding apprentice. Although the father's technique was the more expert, both teacher and apprentice had an uncanny knack for endowing the animal kingdom with childlike qualities, a trait I felt was accurate for many species. Camel, tiger, elephant, monkey, and parrot were colorfully depicted as friends and playmates rather than predators or beasts of burden. The innocence of the artists entered their creatures, and the daughter's work called to mind the stuffed animals that a child would cuddle. I visited their stall a second time to watch them paint, and bought one of the girl's designs, which brought smiles of satisfaction to both father and daughter. I found these simple folks far more fascinating than the pharmaceutical executives we met with around the city each day.

Although our culinary needs were modest and didn't demand the dexterity of a Rann of Kutch artisan, the agile hands of Maharaj moved impressively about; chopping produce, sprinkling spices, and stirring concoctions with the flair of a symphony orchestra conductor. With paring knife as his baton, he waved it through the air with great panache, and if we unwittingly entered the kitchen at the wrong moment, a gesture of the makeshift baton stopped us in our tracks. Maharaj's culinary creations were command performances that, when interrupted, soured his mood, causing his music to go flat.

Sacred Cows And Unhappy Endings

My childhood exposure to dairy cows amounted to a story my dad told from time to time. As a teenager, he liked to ride around his friend's Iowa farm on the back of a motorcycle. One summer afternoon, he and his buddy were speeding about the homestead when they came around the corner of the barn and spotted a large cow standing directly in their path. Unable to avoid the collision, the boys were sent hurtling headlong into a pile of hay. Miraculously, no one was injured, including the cow, which continued grazing as if nothing had happened. Cows are unflappable creatures.

I also recall my somewhat eccentric Uncle Cecil exclaiming "Holy Cow" in his Alabama twang whenever the Crimson Tide scored a touchdown on television. The peculiar expression puzzled me, but I wrote it off as a quirk in my uncle's personality. A decade later, I learned about 'Sacred Cows' at management school. Again I wondered about the origin of the saying, but it wasn't until I came to India that I learned that cows were indeed sacred to the Hindu religion, and were worshipped in colorful autumnal festivals in villages across the country. I witnessed cows with horns painted purple and vermilion dots on their foreheads, and noticed that temples often kept a cow or two.

While studying meditation in the Alpine valleys of Switzerland, I noticed that the Swiss also took special pride in their cows. Handsome outsized bovines paraded along cobblestone streets each spring on their way to high pastures, wearing embroidered flannel jackets, flower garlands, and huge bells tied around their necks. Folk festivals with yodeling competitions and alpine horns were staged in their honor. The respect given cows in these cultures is understandable, considering the nutritious role their milk plays.

In a lecture given by Maharishi in India years ago, I gained a fresh perspective on the significance of cows. Maharishi one day got the attention of his young western audience when he said, "You can judge the quality of a culture by how it treats its cows." The remark sounded ominous for America, England, Argentina, and other countries that consumed large quantities of beef. He explained that it is vital for a cow to live a full span of life and be allowed to die a natural death in order for it to become the most fully developed human possible in its next incarnation. Those in the audience who had grown up eating MacDonald's hamburgers fidgeted as he spoke.

Maharishi went on to say, "Cow becomes a Brahmin (priest) and therefore it is vital that the cow should grow as a cow to the fullest value before it terminates its period as a cow."

"If the seed is not ripe, the tree that is going to grow out of the seed will not be fully developed. The tree will grow, it will have leaves, it will have flowers and fruit, but they will not fully develop. The cow is the seed of that class of people who are competent to preserve the Vedas. And therefore the basis of all well being and progress of anyone and everyone in the world depends on the full growth of a cow. Traditionally, those that feed the cows in India do all sorts of worship and show adoration to the cow." The popular practice of honoring of cows in India is known as Govardhana Puja.

Maharishi then answered questions about cows and reincarnation.

Question: "Can a cow become something other than a man?"

Maharishi: "A fully developed cow will die and become a man. It's written in nature. A half-developed cow becomes a half-developed man, and a half-developed man is like a fruit coming out of a half-developed tree.

Question: "What are your thoughts on a man that eats beef?"

Maharishi: "He eats a dead body. That's all he is doing. How can you afford to do that?" (Laughter from the audience). "What will be the level of consciousness that eats a dead body?" (More laughter) "Who can think of that? If one eats something that is deteriorating rather than growing, what will happen to the system?

Question: "Don't vegetables decay also?"

Maharishi: "When they decay in the stomach, they help us grow. The thing is if you have to survive at the cost of someone, better use least evolved life for your survival. Rather than use highly evolved state of life (cow), use least evolved state of life. If you have to eat somebody, then eat the smallest life." Not long after hearing about Maharishi's Rishikesh lecture I became a vegetarian.

Fifteen years ago, I attended a lecture by the foremost expert in Ayur Veda, India's indigenous health care system. Dr. B.V. Triguna, longtime president of the All India Ayur Veda Council and one of the most gifted physicians I have ever met, shared his insights on the subject of a vegetarian diet. He began his talk by telling a story. While touring Germany, he had spoken to a group about the value of a vegetarian diet. A man in the audience insisted that non-vegetarian diets were healthier. Dr. Triguna listened patiently, then said to the man, "If I cannot convince you that the vegetarian diet is healthier and more natural than eating meat, than I myself will eat meat. But, if I do convince you of its merit, then you must agree to become a vegetarian." The man was confident and agreed to the terms of the debate.

Dr. Triguna's logic was compelling; he pointed out that the strongest animals in the world are vegetarians. Elephants, horses, and oxen all graze on grasses, and the largest dinosaurs were herbivores. On the other hand, he said, animals that rely on meat as their staple are often dull and lethargic, requiring much more sleep than their plant-eating neighbors. Lions, who eat nothing but meat, sleep twenty hours a day and dogs lie around a lot of the time too, especially after a big meal of meat. On the other hand, orangutans that eat exclusively plants and fruit sleep only six hours a day. It is interesting to note, he said, that gorillas subsist on plants and fruits except when living in captivity, where they are fed meat.

According to Dr. Triguna, carnivores like the lion and tiger possess a radically different digestive system than humans. Their intestinal tracts are only a few feet in length, whereas the average human's small intestine measures twenty-two feet and its large intestine is over five feet long. This is an important factor in determining what one should eat. True carnivores digest meat much faster than humans because their abbreviated intestinal tracts are designed for it. Thus they avert putrefaction, or rotting of the meat they ingest. Man's digestive system requires a longer time to process its foods, as it passes through a lengthy digestive system. Putrefaction of meat in the digestive tract can lead to intestinal and colon cancer. Consequently, vegetables, fruits, and grains, which move through the lengthy digestive tract of the human body more rapidly, are the foods nature intended man to eat.

Dr. Triguna also pointed out that the psychology of an animal about to be slaughtered must be considered. Animals know when they are about to die; they feel it instinctively, and it causes great fear. This fear causes powerful chemicals and hormones to be secreted into the blood stream, which circulate throughout an animal's nervous system prior to being killed. Some call this the 'death hormone,' a chemical reaction that triggers the decaying process of the body. Dr. Triguna argued that when humans eat meat, especially red meat, feelings of fear and impending death are ingested along with the meat itself. This, in turn, increases fear and anxiety in a person's life, which disturbs the mental-emotional balance of the individual. Having listened to his compelling arguments, the German man agreed to become a vegetarian.

Those who eat meat might reconsider their dietary preferences after observing what goes on in a commercial slaughterhouse. The horrific methods employed to kill and carve up innocent animals are to be condemned on a humanitarian basis alone. Stunned by hammer blows and electric shocks, the animals are often still alive when the carving commences. Obviously these animals feel pain as their heartrending screams can be heard before they fall unconscious. If Dr. Triguna's assertion is correct that an animal's emotional state at the time of death is transferred to those who consume it later on, then one wonders how eating meat can possibly be a healthy option.

In their popular book, *Fit For Life*, Harvey and Marilyn Diamond discuss the issue of strength, a topic of concern for parents who are weighing the pros and cons of a vegetarian diet for their children. The Diamonds write, "Have you ever seen a silverback gorilla? The silverback gorilla physiologically resembles the human being. It is incredibly strong. Even though it is three times the size of a man, it has thirty times a man's strength! A silverback could toss a two-hundred-pound man across the street like a Frisbee. And what does the silverback eat? Fruits and other vegetation! What does that indicate about the necessity to eat meat for strength?"

The Diamonds go on to say, "All nutritive material is formed in the plant kingdom; animals have the power to appropriate, but never to form or create protein's source, the eight essential amino acids. Plants can synthesize amino acids from air, earth, and water, but animals, including humans, are dependent on plant protein—either directly, by eating the plant, or indirectly, by eating an animal that has eaten the plant. There are no 'essential' amino acids in flesh that the animal did not derive from plants, and that humans cannot also derive from plants. That is why all the animals of strength have all the protein they need." Given this understanding it is disturbing to learn that 47 million cows, plus 9 billion other land-based animals and 17 billion aquatic animals are consumed in America each year according to PETA, presumably for the protein as much as the taste.

Seventy per cent of all corn grown on 400,000 farms in the U.S. is dedicated to animal feed. 145 million acres of American soil is used for corn and soybean crops, the majority of which feeds livestock. The inherent inefficiencies are staggering. Whether from an economic, health, or spiritual point of view, the meat-based diet is destined to become obsolete in the coming decades as people become better informed. Mahatma Gandhi summed it up quite well when he wrote, "I do feel that spiritual progress does demand at some stage that we cease to kill our fellow creatures for the satisfaction of bodily wants."

Prominent vegetarians from western cultures include history's greatest novelist, Leo Tolstoy, Wagner the composer, Henry David Thoreau the transcendentalist, Benjamin Franklin who became a vegetarian at age sixteen, Greek mathematician Pythagoras, Roman author Plutarch, and St. Benedict, who founded the Benedictine Order of monks in the middle ages. These enlightened minds chose vegetarianism during periods when fresh fruits and vegetables were unavailable out of season and hard to get in season. It's much easier being a vegetarian today than it was even thirty years ago. When I stopped eating meat in 1972, the vegetarian options on a restaurant menu were few. Most offered three choices: grilled cheese on rye, whole wheat, or sour dough bread. But before adopting a meatless diet, one should understand the basics of food combining to insure a balanced diet, and be mindful that those preparing your meals may not agree with your approach to diet.

Most of us simply continue to eat what our parents fed us as we were growing up. It is understandable that we have acquired the taste for meat, but that doesn't mean it's too late to reconsider the effects our diet is having on us. Conscious eating goes hand in hand with spiritual wakefulness. The risk of heart disease is 50% for meat eaters compared to 5% for vegetarians. Considering that 1.3 million Americans succumb to heart disease, cancer, and strokes each year, and that diet is a proven contributor for each, our food choices could be a matter of life and death; ours as well as the animals we consume.

What You See, You Become

The food on the dinner table is not the only food we consume during the day. The objects of all our senses, not just those of taste, feed us constantly. Literary classics and mindless sitcoms are food too, nourishment taken in through the ears and eyes. Well-written prose might be compared to gourmet cuisine; a sitcom, on the other hand, is junk food for the senses. The smell of jasmine, the embrace of a loved one, or the sound of our children laughing is potentially more nourishing than our favorite dish of pasta. For the enlightened lama, the air he breathes or the water she drinks may be all the body requires complimenting a simple bowl of steamed rice.

Each nervous system responds to inputs differently depending on one's level of awareness. As we grow, the needs of our mind and body change. Just as spoiled food can upset our stomach, damaging sensory inputs can upset our internal equilibrium. A family argument or a gripping horror movie can result in a fitful night's sleep. Noxious bus fumes or high-decibel music are examples of sensory foods we would do better without. There is a saying in India, 'What you see you become.' In the west, we like to say, 'We are what we eat.' These sayings apply to all the senses, not just our taste buds. With that in mind, can one afford to be indiscriminate about entertainment and behavioral choices any more than we are about dietary preferences? The menu options on cable television and at the multiplex cinema are tempting, but we need to ask ourselves, 'Do I want that in my (or my child's) sensory diet today?'

According to Ayur Veda, the formula for a healthy meal depends on three things: quality ingredients, caring preparation, and a harmonious atmosphere in which to consume it. Most of us are beginning to appreciate the importance of healthy ingredients, but the disposition of the cook is as important as the ingredients that go into a good meal. A lovingly prepared meal will nourish us better than an expensive dinner prepared by a gourmet chef who is upset or unhealthy. And what about those rushed meals we eat on the way to the soccer match that are assembled from processed ingredients, and then handed to us at the drive up window of our favorite fast food outlet? While on a tour of the west, Dr. Triguna was asked what he thought of America. He had traveled the country, visiting Niagara Falls, Disneyworld, and the California coast along the way, but the impression that stuck in his mind were America's eating habits. "Why does everyone eat their meal while riding in their car?" he asked.

The Pulse Tells All

I've been fortunate to know Dr. Triguna for twenty-five years. He is now in his late eighties, but he still sees three hundred patients a day in his Delhi clinic while looking after India's Prime Minister. Dr. Triguna's personal dynamism and robust health astounds everyone. One year, while living at Maharishi Nagar, I grew frustrated with the electricity in my bathroom that was short-circuiting all the time and decided not to bother with hot water for my morning shower. After all, eight months out of the year, the water came out of the tap warm with or without the water heater. That winter I took cold showers before my morning meditation. I liked the invigorating effects of the cold water; it stimulated me the way mountain lakes do on a camping trip.

That spring I visited Dr. Triguna's Delhi clinic for a checkup. Dr. Triguna's method of examination is simple. He uses no diagnostic tools: no stethoscope, BP sleeve, or any other medical equipment. He simply places his fingers on your wrist and feels the pulse for a moment, and then describes your health with mind-blowing accuracy. Having said nothing other than "Namaste" to Dr. Triguna, I sat next to him while he felt my pulse. After a moment, he looked up, and said, "Your health is fine, but joint stiffness. No more cold showers." Then he beamed a knowing smile. As always, he hit the mark perfectly. I had been feeling increasing stiffness in my spine and hips over the winter. My yoga exercises were not so easy to do anymore, and even my tennis game felt restricted. Apparently this was the result of the daily cold showers I had been taking. No amount of allopathic tests would have diagnosed the cause of my stiffness, and yet feeling my pulse for thirty seconds did the job.

People all over the world have experienced the genius of Dr. Triguna. His diagnostic skills are virtually flawless. He treats most health problems by recommending herbs and dietary modifications according to the constitution of the individual. He often advises aggressive, easily angered people to eat cooling foods like fruits, grains, and sweets. Worried and anxious individuals are prescribed calming diets that include milk and fresh cheese. Lethargic personalities are advised to add more spice to their meals. The science of diet, according to Ayur Veda, is a tool that can help restore balance and maintain good health for any individual. It simply requires a basic knowledge of the effects of food and its preparation on the mind and body. Contrary to allopathic medicine, Ayur Veda treats the patient rather than the disease.

The Milk Man Of India

After seeing their eye-catching billboards around Bombay, I wanted to know more about Amul, India's ubiquitous dairy cooperative. When we were invited to speak at Amul's headquarters, we hardly expected to be treated to one of history's great success stories.

In 1946, a year before Indian independence, a group of Gujarati farmers formed a small cooperative for the purpose of supplying milk to Bombay. The collective effort began as a protest against India's exploitative middlemen who profited at the expense of the poor farmers. Until they organized, the farmers had been without any bargaining power because their milk would spoil if the unscrupulous middlemen balked at purchasing it. Thus, the farmers were hardly able to realize any profit at all from the sale of their milk.

The cooperative worked so well that the dairy union, known as Amul, caught on elsewhere around Gujarat and ultimately swept the entire nation. From being a major importer of dairy in the 1950's, India's dairy output grew under the visionary leadership of a man named Dr. Kurien. By 1999, India had surpassed the United States to become the largest milk producer in the world, producing a whopping 748 million tons of dairy annually.

In 1970, Dr. Kurien spearheaded an ambitious national program called Operation Flood. The snowballing success of Operation Flood resulted in over ten million farmers supplying milk to 81,000 cooperative societies, which distributed dairy to urban markets nationwide, setting the stage for India's prominence in the world's dairy industry. Fifty million liters of milk are collected daily by the local societies, which are owned and run by the farmers. These figures are staggering considering that the average cooperative member owns only a handful of animals that contribute to the total daily milk production. When one understands that India represents 16% of the world's population, and that two out of three Indians earn their livelihood through agriculture, the impact of Dr. Kurien's miracle is better appreciated.

The man often referred to as the 'Milk Man of India' claims cooperatives are ultimately about faith and passion. Dr. Kurien's career, which began as part of a protest movement, in many ways, paralleled that of Mahatma Gandhi. Dr. Kurien is a champion of the people, motivated by the ideals of reform and selfless service. Gandhi, when asked why he applied his formidable talents to the betterment of his compatriots, replied, "Man becomes great exactly in the degree in which he works for the welfare of his fellow-men." The name Amul means 'priceless' in Sanskrit, and over the past half century, the co-operative has earned its name in service to its country.

The Salt March

While a string of Ahmedabad companies were reviewing our proposals, we departed on a four-day pilgrimage to the Arabian Sea. Long stretches of salt marsh reminiscent of western Utah stretched to the horizon on the Saurasthra peninsula. The uncannily straight road we traversed skirted archeological ruins believed to be part of the Harappan civilization, dating back 4,500 years. Villagers clad from head to toe in homespun cotton and mounded turbans called to mind Mahatma Gandhi's legendary protest march, which took him across these same salt flats seventy years ago.

Gandhi, who believed he was guided by an inner voice to lead his countrymen out of the clutches of the British, was relentless in his search for ways to expel India's foreign rulers. In March of 1930, as Gujarat's temperatures soared above 100 degrees, the Mahatma launched a protest against the unfair taxation levied by the Salt Laws. These arbitrary laws gave a salt monopoly to the British and served no purpose other than to generate revenue for an imperialist government that already enjoyed a higher standard of living than its counterpart back in England. In addition to taxing salt, a common mineral available in most parts of India, the laws made it illegal to collect it from surface deposits, filter it from the sea, or mine it. The unreasonable legislation affected rich and poor alike, for everyone from royal to peasant needed sodium in their diet in a climate such as India's. Common laborers who had easy access to salt deposits were barred from gathering it for fear of fine or imprisonment. It was a cruel and hard-hearted tax.

Gandhi shrewdly assessed the situation, believing the Salt Laws to be a vulnerable spot in the British armor, because the laws struck a sensitive nerve in every Indian. His Satygraha (firmness in truth) march from his Sabarmati ashram to the Arabian Sea covered almost 250 miles in twenty-three days. Accompanying Gandhi were seventy-eight men who possessed the will to defy not only the British, but the sun as well.

Vast stretches of uninhabitable salt marsh looked sun baked and bleak. As I scanned the landscape, searching for shade, it was painful to imagine the diminutive Gandhi, trademark staff in hand, leading his weaponless army clad in their homespun cotton uniforms across the salt flats, but the strategy proved brilliant. Entire villages turned out to offer food, water, and encouragement to the renegades who roused the nation's spirit of civil disobedience. The effects of the salt march were felt in every district of India.

The British responded to the insurrection by incarcerating sixty thousand people, but it was a futile gesture, for Gandhi's iron resolve to liberate India was now shared by his countrymen, and his message had reached the attention of the world. Of his capacity to overcome the insurmountable, Gandhi wrote, 'Courage has never been known to be a matter of muscle, it is a matter of the heart.'

The Sweet Taste Of Somnath

The road took us through Rajkot where Gandhi spent much of his childhood. From Rajkot, we headed for the Orchard Palace Hotel, the former residence of the Maharaja of Gondal. At the entrance to the Maharaja's estate, in the center of a circular drive, a pair of granite mermaids gurgled water. The voluptuous aquatic maidens seemed out of place in the arid environs. Our spacious second floor rooms, furnished with brass beds and art deco collectibles, looked onto a citrus grove.

As the era of the Maharajas came to an end with Indian independence, many of India's regional rulers, having accumulated enormous wealth during their reign, traveled the world. The Maharaja of Gondal was no exception. In his carriage house was a collection of thirty-five mint condition automobiles from Europe and America dating back to the mid-fifties. While having breakfast on the veranda, a BBC crew arrived to film the collection of shining Cadillacs, Austin Healys, and Jaguars. I wondered if Gandhi should have included the Maharaja of Gondal in his boycotts, for he too must have taxed his subjects severely in order to afford such extravagant toys.

From Gondal, we headed for Somnath on the Arabian Sea. We arrived in Somnath just before nightfall, having stopped to survey a sun-baked fortress along the way. A police barricade obstructed our progress on the main road into Somnath and so, bags in hand, we joined a throng of pilgrims walking into town. We had arrived by accident at the onset of a major Gujarati festival. A Ferris wheel spun above the town as the fair grounds came into view. Smaller rides, food stalls, and makeshift shops were already open for business in anticipation of the evening's festivities.

When we emerged from our rooms, a circular moon filled the sky. The carnival grounds and surrounding streets were packed with tens of thousands of villagers celebrating Kartik Purnima Mela, the harvest full moon festival. As rides filled with screaming occupants spun along geometric paths like brightly lit toys against the evening sky, music blared from scratchy speakers. Vendors selling sweets and trinkets competed vocally with one another as families strolled about the grounds. We moved through the carnival atmosphere, beneath the mela's principle attraction, a luminous harvest moon. We were headed for the temple of the moon.

Somnath Temple occupies the land where Soma, the moon god, is said to have worshipped Lord Siva. The temple blends perfectly with the sand it stands on; only blue sky above and foaming sea behind the temple set it apart from its surroundings. Set on a bluff above the Arabian Sea, the temple is surrounded to the south and west by ocean expanse. No landmass lies between Somnath and Antarctica.

Somnath Temple

Families were picnicking on the grounds as we approached the temple. The compactly built Chalukya-style shrine is multi-faceted and beautifully crafted; fine sculpture, densely packed pillars, and studded roofs shown in the moonlight. Inside, a curious mix of power and peace filled the spacious hall where priests moved to and from an enormous egg-shaped stone. The lunar influence suffused the area with scintillating energy as if there were no roof at all on the temple.

In former times, Somnath Temple housed priceless gems and exquisite ornaments made of pure gold, but it became a favorite target of Mogul emperors who sacked and removed vast treasures from the sanctum on six different occasions, destroying the temple each time. After one sacking, the Siva stone was removed and crushed into small stones to make a walkway into a Delhi mosque. The hardhearted gesture fueled great animosity between the two religions. Each time the Somnath temple was razed to the ground, it was rebuilt on the same seaside land where legend says the moon god prayed in ancient times.

Outside, a trance-inducing moon hung above the shoreline, illumining an endless procession of white-tipped waves. Below us, broad stretches of foaming tide gave way to freshly churned sea as waves rhythmically rolled ashore and withdrew. Above, an incandescent autumnal moon rose, the principle cause for celebration and symbol of hope to Indian farmers everywhere. The perpetual renewal of nature by the sea was reassuring. Life rolled on season after season, generation after generation.

It was estimated that 100,000 were in attendance for the fall festival. Many were peasant women clustered on the ground in groups wherever space permitted. The women, costumed in tribal attire, were fasting, only families were picnicking on the bluff overlooking the ocean. Although we were not a family, we sat near those clustered on blankets. Several families offered to share their meal with us, their faces glowing in the moonlight.

It is the sacred duty of a Hindu wife to propitiate the gods for the well being of her family, home, animals, and crops by performing puja to the harvest moon at the auspicious time. In this way, she insures a wave of good fortune and health each year by honoring the moon god, Soma. I first witnessed the ceremony in Pateriya's front yard not long after arriving in India. Mrs. Pateriya fastened a strand of straw around each family member's index finger, before offering grains of wheat to the yellow harvest moon. Hers had been a tender offering made with a full heart.

In the Mahabharata epic, the noble Yudhisthira approached his family priest, Dhaumya, in search of the key to sustaining health and vitality. The wise priest thought for a moment, then advised Yudisthira that the health of a person is dependent on the moon, for it is the moon that converts the vitalizing effects of the sun, reflecting that influence onto the plant kingdom during the auspicious phases of the lunar cycle. It is the moon that nurtures the sprouting seeds and growing plants into vegetables and grains suitable for consumption. For Hindus, Kartak Purnima is the most auspicious day in the lunar calendar for making offerings, and Somnath is the most propitious spot on earth to do it.

Although we saw no holy men at the festival, ascetics honor the moon as well. They can be found taking holy baths or meditating during lunar eclipses, and honoring the moon as the bestower of the nectar of immortality. Himalayan yogis, possessing secret knowledge of the plant kingdom, harvest the rare soma plant for use in potions that restore youthfulness and awaken hidden stores of consciousness. The rays of the full moon, when reflected off the water, are believed to be infused with soma. Participating in the celebration of the harvest moon altered my perception of the celestial body, raising it to the stature of a god.

The ancient Sanskrit texts declare that the full moon is the cosmic counterpart to the mind, that it showers wisdom onto earth, and therefore the sages honor the moon. Over the decades, twice I had been initiated by Maharishi during the full moon. Over the years, my best meditations in India consistently came on the full moon.

The festival continued late into the night, long after we had retired. When I stepped out of the hotel the next morning, a congregation of coffee brown cows was sifting through debris strewn about the mela grounds. As I approached our taxi, a black bear blocked my way. After six years in India, I believed I was prepared for anything, but the big beast caught me completely off guard. With a gentle poke of a stick, the trainer prodded his leashed pet, and the dusty fellow performed a jig worthy of a county fair. I watched the not so nimble creature dance, shifting his weight from leg to leg as his leathery forepaws did their best to imitate the graceful gestures of a prima ballerina. The dancer's name was Jambavan, the king of bears. The preposterous parody was not without its fee, however, and I forked over five rupees for the private show.

It was time to journey up the coast to Dwarka, the northernmost point of the peninsula. As we drove along the coast, the unhurried seaside villages were still suffused with the vitality of the previous night. Coco palms dappled the road and tropical seascapes beckoned us. From time to time, we crossed narrow bridges spanning aquamarine estuaries, home to fragile waterfowl. Ibis, Dalmatian pelican, heron, and painted stork inhabited the coastal lagoons. Calm coves sheltered wooden fishing vessels preparing for launch. A long stretch of isolated beach looked inviting. Instructing our driver to pull over, we splashed in the rolling surf. Pirate vessels once patrolled the coastal waters, plundering merchant ships and making off with precious cargos of spice and textiles; on this cloudless day, only a handful of rough-cut fishing boats patrolled the watery Eden.

By evening we reached Dwarka, the celebrated city where Krishna ruled 5,000 years ago. The Puranas say 15,000 palaces once housed Krishna's devotees in the vicinity of seaside Dwarka, but the ocean has long since claimed the avatar's kingdom. Archaeologists have discovered five former cities near Dwarka, all at the bottom of the ocean. As we approached, a handful of temple towers were the only edifices rising above the simple fishing village.

Although the moon now waned, Kartik Purnima celebrations continued as we walked along narrow lanes through the temple district of Dwarka, one of the seven holy cities of India. I entered an old Krishna temple through the Moksh Dwara, the Door to Salvation, wishing liberation could be gained as easily as walking through an open door; for some it would be. For me, I knew it would take a supreme effort. A festive atmosphere in the temple courtyard drew us into the moonlit space where devotees were serving bowls of prasad to worshippers seated among the columns at the edge of the yard. A friendly man invited us to sit next to him on the stone floor. Moments later bowlfuls of a milky concoction were put in front of us. The man explained that we were being served Krishna's kheer (sweetened milk), a dessert charged by hours of mantra recitation and then left in the courtyard overnight to absorb the 'spiritual vibrations' of the full moon. I could see by the look on the affable man's face that he couldn't wait to taste the milk pudding. Judging by the anticipation in the air, we were lucky to be sharing the sweet, which was prepared just once a year.

It was time to return to Ahmedabad. As we drove into the night, the taste of nectar lingered on my tongue. The road crossing the salt flats nearly qualified as a superhighway. We had hired a good vehicle and our driver raced along at high speeds, slowing down when we cautioned him, but speeding up again while we slept. I was asleep in the front seat when our driver slammed on the brakes, throwing me against the dashboard. Why had we stopped so suddenly? Despite the fact that thousands of acres of empty fields surrounded us on all sides, a cow had decided to bed down for the night in the middle of the road. Our driver had swerved sharply, missing the sleeping animal by inches. Indian cows are lovable but quirky creatures that enjoy complete freedom to roam about, exempt from all rules because they are holy. As Pateriya put it, "Cows are our second mothers."

India has been criticized for holding its cows in such high regard, for not consuming them during times of famine, but common sense says that a cow will produce a lifetime of nourishment when allowed to live. After enjoying the small bowl of Krishna kheer, I had never felt more nourished from anything I had eaten in my entire life. How was it possible that simple milk pudding could have made such a satisfying meal? I could only assume that its preparation played a key role. If a bowl of pudding ever had consciousness in it, this kheer did. The recipe was equal parts milk from a temple cow, Vedic recitation, and Kartik Purnima moonbeams with

Krishna's blessings as a sweetener.

Prasad is food that has first been offered to the Divine. Every good Hindu has some prasad in his or her diet. Prasad also means clarity or brightness. Food lovingly prepared with Divinity in mind and then reverently consumed should be a part of everyone's diet because it nourishes the soul as much as the body. Gandhi once said there is always a cure for something that has harmed the body, but there are few cures for a damaged soul. At times, India has struggled to feed its masses, but it has always strived to nourish the soul of its people.

Everywhere we went in Gujarat, hands were skillfully engaged creating works of art. Whether nimbly at work weaving a wedding sari, preparing a gourmet meal, painting happy animals, or stitching a patchwork quilt, it was an awesome sight to watch the hands of gifted craftsmen. It would have gratified Mahatma Gandhi to know that fifty years after his passing, the artisan traditions he hoped to build India upon are still honored in the state where he was born.

TWENTY FIVE

Kumbha Mela

Heaven will be inherited by every man who has heaven in his soul.

—*Henry Ward Beecher*

The sun hadn't reached the horizon, but the city of Allahabad stirred. The chill in my unheated room sent a shiver through my body as I slipped from the warmth of my sleeping bag, stepping tentatively onto the cold concrete floor. I dressed quickly that wintry January morning, eager to have my first bath at a time and place prescribed by a council of Indian astrologers. A white dhoti tied at the waist was followed by a cotton kurta, and then a layer of woolens to complete the insulating ensemble. The holy bath I dressed for would be no ordinary scrubbing, for it would occur in the morning hours at the confluence of three rivers in the company of five million pilgrims. It was the first auspicious day at the Kumbha Mela.

Every resident of our guesthouse was awake and performing a similar ritual. Dawn greeted pilgrims from Switzerland, Italy, Germany, Israel, India, and USA in the garden outside my room. Sleepy-eyed westerners carrying daypacks and water bottles, and armed with cameras and video cams, wedged themselves into a rented sport utility. Two Italians, the last to emerge from their room, opted to sit on the roof despite mild protests from our driver.

In a wine-red SUV, we were on our way to the world's largest religious festival and probably the largest gathering of humanity in history, the 2001 Maha Kumbha Mela. Held every twelve years in Allahabad at the confluence of rivers Ganges, Yamuna, and Saraswati, eighty million pilgrims were expected to bathe over a three-week period in the sacred waters at Sangam, the point where the three holy rivers joined. The numbers expected were staggering.

Kumbha Mela means 'Celebrating the pot of nectar of immortality.' According to Vedic lore, the gods, in the process of transporting a pot filled with the ambrosia of immortality, spilled some of the nectar when a group of demons tried to steal the precious liquid. During the struggle for possession of the pot, several drops of ambrosia fell to earth at Sangam. According to legend, the journey of the gods transporting the cherished elixir took twelve days to reach heaven, the equivalent of twelve years in the human calendar. Thus the Kumbha Mela is held once every twelve years, at which time it is believed a small amount of nectar falls to earth for the liberation of the religious minded. Millions were assembling at the Mela grounds in case a drop of the nectar should fall from the heavens.

The Kumbha Mela, celebrated in India for over two thousand years, attracts pilgrims from all corners of the globe, including those wedged inside and on top of our vehicle, as it moved along the tree-lined lanes of the still sleeping army cantonment near Allahabad's civil lines. As we entered the city's market district, our odd appearance attracted the attention of locals unaccustomed to seeing westerners perched atop transport vehicles the way Indians adhere like barnacles to the roofs of busses and trains. As we drew near to Sangam, traffic increased. Most pilgrims journeyed on foot, bedrolls balanced on their heads. Bicycles, auto rickshaws, and horse drawn tangas jockeyed for position on the crowded streets.

Our arrival at the Kumbha Mela fell on the first of several special bathing days on the Vedic calendar, which were determined by the mathematical computations of knowledgeable pundits. The astrologers proclaimed this Kumbha Mela to be the most auspicious in 144 years.

The motorized leg of our journey ended abruptly at a police barricade near a train bridge spanning the Yamuna River. Our progress toward Sangam continued on foot as we moved with thousands of villagers who arrived in every imaginable conveyance. A dozen additional trains from Delhi alone arrived daily at Allahabad station, and hundreds of tour busses were corralled on a nearby field. Oxcarts, jeeps, vans, and bicycle rickshaws carried twice their capacity, as they inched along clogged arteries in the direction of sangam.

I found the walk along the Yamuna refreshing. Cramped limbs stretched as sunlight shimmered on the placid waters. When we reached Saraswati Ghat we discovered boats were still operating. Our Indian friends, after negotiating for a large boat with two oarsmen, waved us to a wooden craft commissioned to take us to our final destination.

Space on the boat was ample. The curtain of vapor veiling the river allowed enough warmth from the sun to take the chill out of the air as our boatman's oars moved easily in and out of the water. Smiles appeared on faces for the first time as the river cast a spell over its guests. We were only a few strokes away from shore when another craft approached. The mysterious occupants of the intruding vessel wore olive uniforms. The man nearest our boat reached out as the boats touched, seizing the boatman's oar. A discussion ensued, after which our distressed oarsman produced a tattered paper, which the uniformed man examined before putting in his pocket.

The police patrolling the river had decided that our boat had too many onboard. We would be allowed to proceed, but our hapless boatman would endure a trying encounter with the authorities if he was to retrieve his license at day's end. The episode was suspicious, as our boatload of fifteen was fewer than many other vessels plying freely up and down the river. As a veteran of police encounters, I knew the issue would ultimately be settled by a payment of baksheesh to the officials who viewed a boat full of foreigners as one whose owner would earn much more than other boats on the river. We would make sure our forlorn boatman received an adequate tip so that he could pay the 'foreigner tax.'

The rhythmic motion of our vessel eased the confusion. Some of the passengers closed their eyes to meditate, others found the river a meditation in itself. A near collision with another craft moving upstream failed to fracture our collective calm as we approached our goal. I was enjoying the spiritual outing; the haze casting an ethereal blanket over the region put me in an expansive mood. I could think of no place in the world I'd rather be on this chilly January morning.

We floated triumphantly into the Mela grounds where an extraordinary sight met our eyes. Stretching as far as the eye could see, khaki tents and a sea of humanity blanketed the sandy banks. It was as if an entire nation of nomads had converged to bathe in the river together, pitching their tents in the neighborhood for convenience. Five million pilgrims had come with a common purpose and the spiritual feeling in the air was strong.

Dozens of boats of various shapes waited their turn to dock at makeshift temples decorated by colorful banners and flags atop wooden poles. The wooden platforms appeared to float, an illusion created by the shallow waters. Pandas (priests) on the platforms performed short pujas for pilgrims according to their gotra (spiritual lineage). Pilgrims from various regions recognized their panda by the pendants, which bore the symbol of the temples from their district.

On average, a boat needed thirty minutes to give its passengers time to disrobe, wade into the waist-deep water, make offerings, submerge three times, dry off and dress before boatmen began the task of extricating their craft from the congested dock. The bathing process took into considera- tion the modesty of Indian women. It was an awkward procedure to bathe in a sari, but that's how most women did it, including Sonya Gandhi, wife of the former Indian Prime Minister, who bathed nearby. The men plunged in with their young sons and daughters clutching their shoulders. To their great distress, tiny infants were also submerged. The shock to their sensitive systems brought wails and shrieks as parents dried the little ones before the chill penetrated too deeply.

Our boat wedged itself among those already docked. Scrambling across the decks of other boats, the members of our group reached the aus- picious spot where the ambrosia of immortality is said to have fallen into the holy waters. A panda hoping to perform a perfunctory ritual approached me, waving his arms, but my attention was elsewhere, and I was relieved to see him retreat quietly.

Flower garlands bobbed about as I lowered myself into the chill cur- rent for my first Mela bath near a sandbar formed by the converging rivers. Cold shot through me, sending shivers up and down my body, but the ini- tial response to the water temperature soon gave way to a less physical reac- tion. Exhilaration filled me as I submerged the traditional three times, and then sat on the sandy bottom, content to linger in the gentle current like a water buffalo resting on a river bottom, my chin suspended on the water's surface. A community of bathers in the vicinity bobbed up and down like buoys in the open sea, absorbed in their moment of reverence.

Surya, the solar deity, the golden hued giver of life, shimmered on the water as cupped handfuls of water were offered up to the sun. Satisfied that my oblations had been received, I emerged from my submerged state and was greeted by the broad smile of a man who had just completed a similar ritual. The contentment on his face mirrored mine as we silently greeted one another, hands pressed together at the chest. Although we were total strangers, we bonded like brothers in the euphoric atmosphere.

The devout believe that a bath in the Ganges washes away sin. Maharishi was once asked whether this belief had any merit or not, to which he replied, "Yes, one's sins are removed when one dips in the Ganges, but we don't know what is waiting for us when we return to the shore." The Puranas, the ancient scriptures of India, say, "Heaps of sin accumulated during millions of births are destroyed by the mere contact of a wind charged with the vapor of Ganga." I needed every benefit the gods were willing to grant me and decided to bathe at every opportunity.

Throughout the ages, water has been the great healer of body and soul. Every religious tradition employs water in its rituals as a symbol of purity and purification. As I retraced my steps to our boat, stepping tentatively across the bows of rough-hewn vessels, an elevated feeling pervaded the scene. Lightness permeated my being, as if old burdens had been removed. I would know better when we returned to shore if my euphoria was to be short-lived. The boatmen worked their long poles to extricate us from the tangle of craft. Broad smiles and clear eyes appeared on the faces of our international delegation. I felt like an infant freshly baptized in the waters of a glacial Himalayan spring as the craft moved easily up the Yamuna River. While we bathed, the sun had entered the constellation Makara (Capricorn), the auspicious moment selected by the astrologers.

The Sahi Family

The following morning, our Australian friend Peter arrived from Delhi. From the bench of a bicycle rikshaw he searched for our guesthouse in the neighborhood near the high court. After riding around Allahabad's cantonment, an enclave of garden bungalows built by British bureaucrats at the turn of the century, Peter spotted what he thought was our hotel. As he approached the gated entrance to the spacious estate set among flowering gardens and lofty trees, a boy emerged from the shadows of the bungalow's front porch, and asked if he could be of assistance to the lost foreigner. When the youth learned that Peter was searching for a hotel, he retreated into the house before reappearing with a woman wearing a welcoming smile.

Peter asked directions to our hotel, but was invited in for tea instead, and to his astonishment, by the time he got up to go, he had been invited to stay with the family. As we learned later, inviting strangers into the home, an unheard of practice in the West, was a family tradition in the Sahi household. Kaju, the friendly teenager who had spotted Peter at the gate, explained that his grandfather searched the Allahabad train station during the Kumbha Mela, inviting weary foreigners to stay in his home. In keeping with their grandfather's tradition of kindness, the family insisted that Peter be their guest while in Allahabad. Little did anyone know that the Sahi residence would become the scene of its own festival in the coming days.

The following morning a shining green sedan pulled up outside our hotel. Peter and his host, A.P. Sahi, had come to invite us to stay with them, and before we knew it, we had been whisked off to the Sahi home. Allahabad schools were closed during the Kumbha Mela and so the entire family gathered in the courtyard to meet Peter's American friends. My friend Ramprasad, who had come down from Katmandu, Peter, and I were treated to Indian hospitality at its sweetest as we feasted on a banquet grown in the Sahi family's two-acre organic garden. The shaded veranda attached to the historic bungalow, built by a British railway commissioner, was filled with laughter as servants paraded to and from the kitchen, keeping us supplied with fresh breads and spicy curries.

Two calves were tethered under a fig tree in the courtyard; content to be a part of the idyllic setting on the sunny January day. As dessert arrived, the conversation turned to the amla tree shading our gathering. The amla fruit is used in many Ayur Veda formulas and is considered the best of medicines. A.P. Sahi, our lighthearted host, instructed his young servant to bring some of the fruits, and soon the nimble boy was dangling from the top of the tree, dislodging green balls from roof level limbs. A barrage of the pale green fruits pelted the ground. After corralling the fruit, the boy proudly presented his harvest for everyone to see. Kaju, and his thirteen year-old cousin, Elsa, watched with interest as their guests sectioned the amla with a knife. Amla is traditionally sweetened with plenty of sugar and never consumed the way one would eat an apple, but Peter was keen to taste the fruit in its natural state.

Unwittingly we bit into the fruit as the curious children suppressed smirks and giggles. The extreme sour taste turned my mouth upside down and the servants rushed off to get water to wash the tart taste away. Everyone at the table, including grandma, burst out laughing at our foolishness. The spontaneous fun that would result in a deep bond of affection between the Sahi family and their foreign guests in the coming days had begun.

A.P. Sahi was a man of considerable intelligence and position in the community. Along with his father-in-law, he was a senior partner in the most successful law firm in Allahabad, the seat of the state's high court. After lunch, A.P. showed us around his home with its cavernous cathedral ceilings.

"A.P., how long have you lived here?" I asked.

"My grandfather bought the bungalow from a British railway commissioner," A.P. said, pointing to a portrait of a man bearing a strong resemblance to our host. "That's my grandfather, the last Maharaja of Gorakhpur. He purchased the house when the British left India. At the time of Indian independence, we were feudal lords with 2,000 villages under our jurisdiction. We ruled the region from the Ganges to the border of Nepal."

"Did all those villages pay taxes to your ancestors?"

"Yes. In fact, I am the first Sahi in 114 generations to work for a living." The name Sahi means royal. After India gained independence, the rule of the Maharajas came to an end, resulting in enormous loss of property and assets that were appropriated by the newly formed Indian government. Today, most descendents of royal lineage support themselves in businesses or professions, much the way A.P. does.

"The British found Allahabad's heat unbearable," A.P. said, pointing to an archaic system of ropes and canvas flaps, "so they devised clever methods to cool their houses. This room has twenty-five foot ceilings so the heat can rise up. Servants pulled the ropes, which turned the canvas flaps to keep the air moving, but we spend our summers at the Gorakhpur farm where the climate is milder." At the Sahi family's insistence, we moved in with Peter as houseguests. Kaju offered me his bedroom, which, like the rest of the house, was exactly as it was when the bungalow was built.

I was intrigued by the family's background. They were such unassuming people, so completely devoid of pretension, that I wondered if they cared to talk about their royal lineage. The faint remains of aristocracy, however, were present. Outside, on a plot beside the nursery, a collection of British sports cars gathered rust, the names MG and Austin Healey were barely legible under the accumulated dust. The collection belonged to A.P.'s older brother, who now operated the ancestral farm in Gorakhpur.

One afternoon Mrs. Sahi opened a trunk, and one by one displayed dozens of heirloom shawls handed down over the generations. The ring shawls, both pashmina and shahtoosh, were exquisite, many were embroidered in real gold. The shahtoosh shawl is now illegal, since the gathering of the hairs that are woven into it has endangered the Tibetan antelope. According to Ramprasad, who had spent two years in the cashmere business, the contents of the trunk were worth a small fortune. After showing us the buttery garments, Mrs. Sahi carefully rewrapped each, inserting sections of newspaper between the folds to prevent mildew.

On a sunny afternoon, A.P. took us to his country villa for a picnic. He called the former family estate his farm, because a large cultivated acreage was attached to it, but the house was really a small palace. A.P. had an obvious affection for the old place and he proudly showed us all the nooks and crannies where he had played as a youngster. After lunch, he ushered us into a heavily secured room. He kept the only keys to the vault where his personal heirlooms, the Sahi men's equivalent of the ring shawls, were kept. Weaponry was carefully stored there-scimitars and knives with ivory handles, equestrian gear, handguns and armor, coats of arms, antiques-remnants of a benevolent dynasty that had ruled for a hundred generations. Each article in the Sahi family's personal museum held a memory for A.P.

That evening, A.P. took us out for sweets. Having seen the glossy, glass enclosed shops near the Internet café that lured a steady flow of foreigners off the street, I expected A.P. to take us to one, but, being a native of Allahabad, A.P. knew the authentic spots. He took us to many stalls; the way people go bar hopping in the west. By the time we reached our final shop, a tiny hole in the wall in an unlit alley, I was fully under the influence of Allahabad's famous caramelized milk sweets.

As we sat each morning for our meditation, curious children peered through latticed partitions and around open doors to catch a glimpse of their peculiar guests sitting eyes closed for hours at a time. Soon everyone wanted to know about meditation, and so we taught the entire clan. Each evening, after a day spent at the Mela grounds, we conducted satsang, lively spiritual discussions on topics like meditation, Vedic astrology, and Ayur Veda.

The Tent City

In the sea of Kumbha Mela pandals (large tents), satsang was also in the air. Five thousand camps hosted spiritual discourses and devotional song, and thousands received the darshan of Shankaracharyas and swamis from all over India. An articulate nine-year-old from Madhya Pradesh presided over one of the more popular satsangs. Richa Goswamy's tent overflowed with curious onlookers and devotees. Reports circulated that Richa had been delivering scriptural discourses since age three. When asked how she obtained such profound knowledge at such a tender age, the young adept joked, "Maybe my Mother read scriptures during her pregnancy."

At the heart of the tented camps was a yagya-shala, a large building spewing great volumes of smoke through its vented roof. The smoking structure appeared to be on fire. Inside, the chanting of scores of pundits was loud and so I peered in. Pairs of priests making offerings into the flames attended long rows of fire pits evenly spaced across the earthen floor of the hall. In unison, the pundits tossed a grain mix into the fires and chanted as one indomitable voice. In all, there were 108 fire pits. Maha Rudrabishek, a Vedic ceremony traditionally performed for world peace, was in progress. Had the hall not been inundated with smoke I would have entered. It was a mystery how the priests could breathe, but the effect they created was awesome, and I felt great blasts of energy and light wash over me as I stood at the entrance.

Swamis with colorful titles were scattered among the camps extending as far as the eye could see. Kali Baba (an African swami), Pilot Baba (a former air force officer), and armies of sparsely clad Naga Babas with names like Mahanirvana and Niranjana drew crowds wherever they went. The Naga Baba akaras (groups) captured center stage on parade days at the Mela. Originating during the Middle Ages as warrior tribes assigned to protect India's saints and sadhus, the Naga Babas' fierce demeanor was exaggerated by bodies covered with ash and matted locks that extended to the ground. Crowds numbering in the millions gathered along the parade route to watch the Naga Babas lead the processions of holy men on auspicious bathing days.

Foreign photographers used telephoto lenses to photograph the Naga Babas, but I questioned the fairness of wiring photos of these tribal-looking characters around the world. One needed to be in the Mela atmosphere to understand the role the Nagas played. Some of the more aggressive photographers had their equipment smashed or confiscated for their indiscretions. Wielding tridents, swords, and other medieval weapons, the primeval figures appeared as apparitions on their way to an imaginary battle. The power of the festival filled the air: Vedic pundits chanting for peace, swamis presiding over satsang, processionals of Naga Babas, millions bathing from sunrise to sunset. I was awed by what transpired at the festival, but the rest of the world had no idea.

According to the council of astrologers, Mauni Amavasya is the most auspicious day of the Kumbha Mela and thirty million people were expected to bathe in a twenty-four hour period! No one knew exactly what to expect, but organizers planned for every eventuality, and closed all roads to the Mela grounds for three days in an effort to reduce traffic. The specter of the already swollen crowds growing ten-fold was impossible to conceive. I only knew I wanted to be among the multitude.

The Sahis planned to enter the Mela grounds the eve of Mauni Amavasya and bathe during the auspicious hours in the morning. A.P. took his mother and the other adults to a tented camp where the women sang kirtans (devotional songs) late into the night, but they didn't risk bringing the children, who would bathe on a less crowded day. A child could easily disappear in crowds expected to be double the population of Bombay.

Bollywood, Bombay's other name, is home to the largest film industry in the world, and it's directors have used the Kumbha Mela theme effectively over the years. One story revolved around a family traveling the length of the sub-continent by train to attend the Mela. In the crush of the festival crowd, the young son is separated from his family. For years his mother mourns the loss of her boy until decades later, with hope nearly extinguished, the family is miraculously reunited in a gripping climactic scene.

Mauni Amavasya

At three in the morning we began a five-mile walk toward the sangam. Villagers were already moving along the path leading to the Mela grounds in such density that the crush of humanity looked like one enormous body with countless arms and legs attached. The men wore white cotton and the women wore mainly red, but also greens and blues. We flowed along like one great river of harmony, and I felt like an extra in an epic saga. All five of the westerners I was with were a head taller than the masses we moved with. Our height was the only thing that prevented us from getting separated.

Some pilgrims were actually connected at the wrists by ropes; others held hands. Small children were leashed to their parents like house pets. Newspapers reported that on Mauni Amavasya alone, ten thousand people got separated from their families. On public speakers all over the tent city, distraught mothers pleaded for their lost children to find their way to police posts. Most families were happily reunited by nightfall.

Kumbha Mela organizers deserved recognition for the Herculean efforts of thousands of volunteers, community service organizations, and police forces. Preparations for the Kumbha Mela begin years in advance. Pontoon bridges were constructed for pedestrians and cars, and 20,000 portable toilets and 35 power centers were installed. 13,000 tons of flour and 8,000 tons of rice fed the hungry masses. 20,000 police officers were on duty to insure the safety of the participants. In spite of long shifts and a spate of emergencies, security teams were courteous and helpful.

A gathering the size of the Kumbha Mela is unfathomable. The biggest day at the Mela had seventy times the number of people that attended the 1969 Woodstock music festival in upstate New York, which was attended by 400,000 people. The Mela also had twenty times the number of law enforcement agents. Ironically, Woodstock surpassed the Kumbha Mela in one category that no one would have guessed. As it turned out, 450 cows attended Woodstock, while the omnipresent Indian cow was not permitted on the Mela grounds. Woodstock lacked refuse bins; the Mela grounds lacked refuse. Miraculously, it was one of the cleanest places I had seen in India, or anywhere else for that matter.

Many villagers at the Mela had never ventured more than thirty miles from their home. For millions, visiting the Kumbha Mela was a lifetime ambition and they saved for years to afford a train or bus ticket. Upon arriving at sangam, pilgrims spent the night on the sand banks, huddled near a small fire or wrapped under a wool blanket while they waited for the appointed hour to bathe. After dipping, villagers enjoyed the parade of holy men before making the long trip home.

Villages on the outskirts of the Mela grounds welcomed weary travelers. One village train station, a five-mile walk from the rivers, received trainloads of pilgrims day and night for the duration of the six-week festival. Local businessmen kept roadside fires ablaze and served tea to insure that pilgrims would pass through their village without feeling the effects of the cold north Indian night.

Describing the Kumbha Mela as the largest assembly of humanity in history is no exaggeration. In particular, Mauni Amavasya draws more than any other day, as it is the most auspicious day to offer oblations to the pitris (family ancestors). Although thirty million were expected, I was surprised to see pilgrims six abreast already homeward bound as we headed for Sangam several hours before sunrise. The path was well lit, allowing a good look at the humble peasants who had come to honor their departed ancestors and dip in the sacred waters. The Kumbha Mela was both a triumph of the spirit and an astonishing expression of cooperative effort. Why the rest of the world failed to recognize the achievement puzzled me.

At the river, we secured a boat and two oarsmen for the short ride to the spot where millions would dip during the auspicious window in time. The cold air and colder water washed away my drowsiness as I waded through knee-deep water to our craft. The Yamuna sparkled like a thousand gems as lights from the tented city reflected off its indigo surface. The atmosphere at the confluence was charged, and I felt certain myriad devas (celestial beings of light) were on hand to receive the prayers from all over India. Our turn to bathe came after a short wait. We had identified a favorite spot where the currents mingled, creating a healthy flow of water, and we were relieved to find adequate space. We had been warned that bathing on Mauni Amavasya would be shoulder to shoulder at best, but the early morning hour spared us.

In the moonless night I unwrapped my dhoti and plunged into the watery blackness, experiencing the odd sensation of physical discomfort and inner exhilaration. I could not have felt better, or worse, depending on the point of view. The darkness enveloping the rivers made my bath a private affair, but only because one could see just a short distance. Fellow pilgrims in the river lacked substance, appearing like water nymphs in the night. Submerging three times, I shot into the air after each plunge like a kid on a pogo stick. Although my body shivered like a Buddhist prayer flag in the wind, I was aglow with warmth and inner light.

Still freezing from the 4:00am submersion, we searched for the Sahi tent among hundreds of identical shelters. When we finally located their overnight abode, we found the Sahi men and women huddled together under blankets, waiting until it was warm enough to bathe. The women sang their devotional songs while the men made reconnaissance missions to survey the scene and purchase chai. I meditated under blankets until my body temperature returned to normal. No one minded the physical privation, all were happy to be at the festival on its most auspicious day.

Tent City

Pateriya was also huddled in one of the thousands of Mela tents that night. I wanted to find him, but it was hopeless, the rows of tents sprawled for miles. He had attended a previous Kumbha Mela when Maharishi had explained how the auspiciousness of the Kumbha Mela is the result of the sadhus (holy men) who come from all parts of India, bringing the devas with them. At the holy confluence, a brilliant aura permeated the atmosphere, and one couldn't help but be swept up in the great union of spirit, both human and divine. Even if one never dipped in the holy river, one still bathed in spiritual radiance at the Mela. It is the community of devas that renders a place auspicious, and they were all in attendance, celebrating the immortality of the soul.

A stiff wind dented the canvas walls of the Sahi tent. The sun was on the horizon now; my day was strangely complete before most of India had finished morning chai. Rarely had I hiked five miles, ridden in a boat, bathed and meditated before sunrise. I moved with the sea of civilian soldiers retreating to villages near and far. If bathing with millions was a once in a lifetime experience, finding my way back to the Sahi house equaled the blockbuster epic in other ways. I moved silently with the villagers, the wind whipping sand into my eyes and stinging my face. Everywhere, colorful green and orange and red saris were stretched out to dry. The gusting wind wrinkled the river and forced women to fasten their cloth to a tent or clasp it in their hands.

We moved as one colossal body headed for the train bridge spanning the Yamuna. The crush of humanity in my small section of the Mela grounds alone was many times greater than a New Year's Day crowd in Manhattan. If every college football fan attending every game in America on a given Saturday were to gather along the banks of the Mississippi River, they would total but a fraction of the number at the Mela on its biggest day.

Slowly pilgrims funneled into narrowed arteries leading to bus and train stations around the city. The average person leaving Woodstock walked many miles, but no more than departing pilgrims on their way to crowded transportation terminals. I had been walking for two hours, and still the crowd was shoulder to shoulder. Finally, I reached a street that allowed bicycle rickshaws, so I hired one with a wooden platform and instructed the driver to head for the High Court, the nearest landmark to the Sahi residence. I lay back basking in the warm winter sun on the worn planks that still carried loose cabbage leaves and a bruised potato or two from a previous run. My charioteer pedaled through the bedlam and traffic, passing smiling vendors and a few traffic cops along the way. For a hundred yards, three curious boys trotted along behind my carriage, giggling and pointing at my prone form. It was a humble but triumphant ride, a processional suitable for a warrior returning from a noble conquest, and no one dared assess my panting driver a 'foreigner's tax.' It was mid-afternoon by the time the Sahi's sprawling estate came into view. Festival goers never reached our shaded neighborhood, but the celebration itself easily reached the Sahi home. From the front gate, the towering trees, spacious grounds, and gardens appeared out of place, having just returned from sangam's vast and dusty throng.

By now the children's academic tutorials were finished and they were in a playful mood. Peter and Ramprasad were still at the Mela grounds; I was the only videshi in the house. The children wasted no time attacking me with chocolates, stuffing one after another into my mouth as if to prevent me from telling more Mela tales. Having been confined to their books all day, they were ready for a game on the lawn. I was instructed to chase after the entire gang of kids while Simba, the vegetarian German shepherd, chased after us. Although the long march home was exercise enough for one day, the lighthearted play was great fun, and more than once we found ourselves in a pile on the ground, tickling each other while Simba barked encouragement.

The principle bathing days were now over and our remaining days in Allahabad were spent in playful diversion. The family masseuse administered oil massages and gave haircuts; we picnicked at the Sahi farm and A.P. took us for another round of sweets. The extended family of thirty gathered for a birthday. Begam and Chotiwali, the family cows expected snacks when they saw us coming. The young servant children insisted that I chase them whenever I stepped outside. We were in heaven, the guest of a family of angels.

A Vedic scholar from Varanasi dropped by the house for tea and tested my scriptural understanding in the courtyard one afternoon, but my intellect had been drowned in the holy waters and I made no pretense of understanding anything derived from a text. Defending myself with the quote, "Knowledge in the book stays in the book," I ran off chasing the staff children. The scholar must have found my behavior peculiar, but I refused to engage the intellect any more than necessary. Each evening, we gathered for satsang and group meditation followed by a candlelit feast in the courtyard.

Western friends arrived at the Sahi bungalow nightly for a final taste of Indian hospitality, and sometimes a meditation or nap before joining the mass exodus at the train station. The Aussie delegation showed up in a mirthful mood, their heads freshly shaved after visiting one of the Mela's renowned saints.

Our day of departure had arrived. When we gathered on the lawn for snapshots and hugs, sad eyes appeared on cherubic faces. A beige jeep waited to take us to Allahabad's air force base for our flight to Delhi. We had arrived as strangers, but had been treated like princes in a palace where the heart flowed as gently as the Yamuna River. I had never met more kind and loving people. The tradition of Kaju's grandfather had been faithfully preserved as we passed one last time through the gate that had been so graciously opened to us a fortnight earlier.

TWENTY SIX

Hovering Around Heaven

Chanting is no more holy than listening to the murmur of a stream,
counting prayerbeads no more sacred than simply breathing.

—*Lao Tzu*

Structural Damage

After returning to Delhi from the Kumbha Mela, we waited to hear about our work in Ahmedabad. We were uncertain in the wake of the massive earthquake that rocked the state of Gujarat on India's Independence Day, sending tremors all the way to the Mela grounds hundreds of miles away. Entire villages had collapsed. Tens of thousands were injured and left homeless. Sadly, the state government's response to the disaster was ineffective. Our apartment building suffered structural damage, forcing our neighbors to leave their homes. Built on concrete pillars above a parking garage, cracks in the foundation left the structure unsafe. While waiting for word about Ahmedabad, I accepted an invitation to speak at a defense seminar in the Punjab.

The Invincible Shield

General Kulwant Singh stood to greet me in his Golf Links office. He struck a handsome pose in his navy blazer, his head wrapped in a matching turban. His warm smile welcomed me into the office. General Singh was a retired army officer with a Ph.D. in Philosophy and a heart of gold.

"General, how did a career military man like you latch onto meditation?" I asked as we got acquainted in his office.

"You see, I lost my wife two years back," he told me. "It was a blow more painful than anything I experienced in my forty years in the military. I was lost without her. Then I came across this meditation and it helped heal the wound."

"So now you're working with us." I was impressed that he had taken over our military programs so quickly.

"I'm retired now, but I want to serve, to do something worthwhile. I was feeling a void in my life." I was immediately struck by the sincerity of the general.

A few weeks later General Singh asked me to help with some military presentations. The first was a lecture to a group of retired generals and the next a presentation at the defense college at Punjabi University. General Singh owned a comfortable bungalow in Chandigarh, the Punjab capital, and invited me to spend the weekend with him prior to speaking at the university. His home was filled with memories of his family. Framed pictures of his attractive wife and their two daughters covered the walls. Military accolades and a remarkable assortment of Hindu statuary were displayed on tables and shelves.

"Where did you get these fine pieces, General?" I asked. I knew the statues hadn't come from craft shops.

"While being stationed around India, I used to visit the ancient temple sites, where I found them just lying about. 800-year-old treasures lay scattered, so I collected the statues. Now the government has put these pieces in museums and is trying to account for the rest. I sold part of my collection to the government and built my house down the street with the proceeds. This little bungalow was built with leftover materials."

"I imagine you fought in both wars with Pakistan," I probed, shifting the topic to the military.

"Oh yes. I also commanded in the peacekeeping efforts with the Tamil Tigers in Sri Lanka. War is hideous, you know. I hope our military leaders catch on to the idea that peace can come without war." General Singh had too tender of a heart for a military leader, I thought as I admired his collection of family photos.

"You know, General, my dad fought in WWII. He was with the 10th Mountain Division in Italy."

"Quite a celebrated outfit. He must have seen a lot of combat."

"Yes, but he never talked about it much. He went to Italy as a teenager. Dad was selected for the ski troops because he was athletic. He once told me the men (most were teenagers) he was with were the finest bunch of guys he ever met."

"War bonds men," agreed the general.

"My dad's troop was young and self-assured when they arrived at the front lines, but their confidence was short-lived. In one bombardment, their commanding officer and dad's two closest friends were killed. Dad caught shrapnel; when he returned to the foxhole things weren't the same. The Germans were positioned high up in the Apennines and were inflicting heavy causalities." Living in the cold and mud, and eating rations out of tin cans, made the young GI's homesick to be with their families back in the States.

"It's almost impossible when the enemy is positioned above you."

"Dad's most haunting memory was a German sniper they captured. He was just a kid, maybe fifteen, a few years younger than my dad. The officers interrogated him through a translator. It turned out that he was a junior Nazi party member, and when they asked him what he would do if they let him go he said coldly, 'More sniping.'"

"That's a difficult decision for the officer in charge," General Singh said, anticipating the conclusion of the story.

Not long before my dad had gone off to boot camp, he and his family had posed for photos at the church parsonage. Life Magazine had assigned Alfred Eisenstadt to do a photo essay on the life of a typical American pastor and his family. My grandfather was pastor at the Methodist church in Newton, Iowa at the time, and the celebrated photographer spent a week following the family around. The article was titled, "Practical Man of God," and one of the photos showed my dad and his sister Margaret playing a duet at the piano. On the cover of the issue were Nazi officers saluting one another, their swastika armbands prominently on display. When I was growing up, dad used to sit down to the piano and pound out the tunes he had learned as a teenager. His God given talents lay elsewhere.

Punjabi Masala

The general's loyal cook and household supervisor served delicious meals on the patio. After breakfast, the drive to Patiala took us past some of India's most fertile farmland. Punjab means 'land of five rivers,' and a network of irrigation canals had transformed the state into India's breadbasket. The enterprising Sikh community strived hard after partition and succeeded in India's agricultural and transportation sectors, as well as maintaining a strong presence in the armed forces. Their success in farming has not been limited to India. They've been equally successful in California agro business.

The dean of the department and an assortment of professors and students attended the presentation, but the audience couldn't easily grasp the connection between meditation and defense. I pointed out that military intervention, peacekeeping forces, and summit meetings have failed repeatedly to create peace. As an example, I cited the summit between Indian and Pakistani leaders, when just weeks later, Pakistani terrorists had boldly attacked the Indian parliament hoping to assassinate the prime minister. Indian security forces averted the disaster, but the vulnerability of the nation became a hot topic around Delhi. My reference to the unfortunate event hit a sensitive nerve, but I felt it needed to be said.

A fresh angle on peace is sorely needed, and I argued that peace begins with the individual, that the enemy outside the nation isn't the cause of war; that violence against the Self is the real source of conflict. I even quoted India's peaceful warrior Mahatma Gandhi, who wrote, "Be the change you wish to see in the world."

The Punjab lay directly between Pakistan and India, and would suffer inordinately should the two countries go to war again. India and Pakistan had been at war twice since partition and a possible conflict loomed on the horizon when one million troops gathered on the border amidst nuclear threats by Pakistan a year later.

Ancient India was a peaceful society because India's sages knew how create a national armor called rastriya kavach, which was based in consciousness. Since World War I, the 'War To End All Wars,' there have been hundreds of armed conflicts and over sixty million civilians have died due to military aggression. Peace treaties typically last less than a week before violence erupts all over again. My impassioned talk was my way of honoring the fact that my dad and soldiers everywhere have spent prime years of their life in combat.

I hadn't thought much about my dad's WWII experiences until that weekend with General Singh. Once I had pulled the bronze Stars and Purple Heart out of his dresser and asked him about them, but he didn't say much. It wasn't until I saw 'Saving Private Ryan' that the reality of war hit home. All the major themes in the movie lived in my dad's memory. Brothers dying, a commanding officer killed, a sniper captured and shot, shrapnel wounds, medals of honor… it all happened to GI's fresh out of high school and stayed with them for the rest of their lives.

The Levitating Rock

Will and I boarded a plane for Bombay to teach a course for Indian Oil executives at a picturesque resort overlooking the placid Vasistha River Valley, four hours south of Bombay. I couldn't imagine a more suitable location for a meditation course. The executives were in heaven and spent their days walking around with their heads in the clouds. The tension they brought with them was gone after a day or two.

On our return to Bombay, we stopped at a small village where miracles have been reported for centuries. Our journey took us to the village of Shivapur, site of the Levitating Rock. Many centuries ago, a gymnasium stood where a small courtyard and Sufi shrine now stand. Boys from the surrounding villages visited the gym daily. Two heavy stones (one weighing 150 pounds) were used by the boys to increase their strength, much the way body builders use free weights today.

The parents of a slightly built Muslim boy named Qamar Ali Darvesh insisted their son go to the gymnasium to develop his strength the way other boys in the community did. But Qamar's inclinations lay in other areas. From an early age the mysteries of Sufism and matters of the soul fascinated him. The young Qamar showed a predilection for supernormal abilities like clairvoyance and telepathy, but because he was small, the others mocked him whenever he came to the gymnasium.

Qamar put up with the abuse for a long time, but one day he had endured enough. After being mercilessly ridiculed by his peers, he responded to their cruelty by announcing, "From this day forward no one will be able to lift these exercise stones unless he repeats my name." In addition, he proclaimed that the bigger of the two rocks could only be raised if eleven fingers were touching it while chanting his name in unison. Mysteriously, from that day on, no matter how strong the man, no one has been able to lift the rock without following the formula laid out by Qamar eight centuries ago.

Will and I arrived at the shrine with differing attitudes toward the peculiar legend. I wasn't much interested, but since the shrine was on the road to Pune, I was happy to join Will in his latest effort to unearth another of India's inscrutable stories. I was prepared for whatever he turned up next, including rocks that could fly.

The forest green shrine confirmed that indeed this was a Muslim place of pilgrimage. A crowd of men milled around a small courtyard where two large round stones lay in the dust. Will was familiar with the lore surrounding the levitating rock, and immediately set out to enlist ten men to help him raise the rock while I paid homage to the Sufi saint's tomb. Having visited Sufi shrines in the past, I knew they possessed a subtle power, which was the reason thousands came for pilgrimage.

Garlands and wreaths blanketed the burial place. A pair of mendicants sat nearby murmuring mantras. As I stood near the tomb, the chant 'Qamar Ali Dervesh, Qamar Ali Dervesh' grew louder and louder. The noise was Will and his group who stood in a small circle invoking the Sufi saint. They chanted and chanted, waiting for a response from the rock. What happened next astonished me. After repeating the saint's name over and over, the large rock rose slowly above their heads on the tips of their index fingers, and for a brief moment, the collective will of the men seemed to levitate the stone before it fell hard to the ground. Will, who was a head taller than the others, was also the most enthusiastic member of the group. He was excited about his first 'miracle' and wanted me to try it.

Having placed a flower on the Sufi saint, I joined Will who was keen to perform the 'miracle' again. He tried to describe the experience, but couldn't. "Coach, you have to try it," he enthused in his Texas twang. So I joined Will and nine others, each man placing the tip of his index finger under the rock. We chanted in unison, but nothing happened and soon the chant broke down. Then we rallied for a second try. At first nothing happened, but then a thrill of energy surged through the group and the rock raised three feet off the ground before falling. On the final try, the group's resolve was strong. Over and over we chanted, "Qamar Ali Dervesh. Qamar Ali Dervesh," as if we were invoking a genie in a bottle. Suddenly, miraculously, the rock felt weightless as it rose into the air. Higher and higher it went until it hovered at eye level. For a fleeting moment we were captivated by the feat and then the rock crashed to the ground.

"Did you feel it?" Will pleaded, hoping I too had felt the thrill of energy that had surged through the group.

"Yes, of course," I replied as the others cheered and danced about like excited children. I was now a believer in Qamar Ali Dervesh and his levitating rock, yet another of India's enigmas.

Osho's Racket

Dusk covered Pune as we headed to the Osho Meditation Resort. The forty-acre facility, founded by Bhagwan Rajneesh, the Indian guru who made headlines for the town he founded in Oregon and the fleet of Rolls Royces he owned, is well known around India. Before visiting the Osho center, we checked into a nearby hotel. As the hotel clerk showed us to our rooms, a huge commotion started up outside. It sounded like a rock concert as the walls of the hotel began vibrating to the techno tunes from the party next door.

"Is that coming from the Osho ashram?" I asked.

"Yes, they're having music assisted meditation now. The noise will stop in forty minutes," explained the attractive young clerk.

"Music assisted meditation, what's that?" Will asked.

"I can't say, sir," said the polite young woman, "I've never gone inside. But I think there is dancing." The Osho scene had a reputation for being different and from the sound of it we might not fit in too well. The ashram rooftop dance had been more than enough for me.

Handing the room key back to the desk clerk, we headed out the door in search of a quieter place. After checking into a hotel a safe distance from the Osho campus, we indulged in our less flamboyant meditation practice.

"Will, meditation has changed since we learned thirty years ago, hasn't it," I joked, but Will was already too deep to reply. He certainly didn't need music to assist him with his practice.

We were hungry, having traveled all day, so we headed for Zen, a popular restaurant catering to Osho interns. My impression as I scanned the packed dining room in search of an empty table was that we had entered a movie set of a sci-fi flick. Han Solo must have had a similar reaction when he entered the Mos Eisley Cantina in Star Wars. The restaurant's eclectic clientele included diners from the far corners of the globe, possibly further. Petite oriental women with shaved heads shared tables with hulking, broad-shouldered Germans wearing black leather, also with shaved heads. The predominant attire was a burgundy acolyte's robe, the official garb in the ashram and not unsuitable apparel for a federation starship. Everyone was superbly cast for his or her role, except possibly us.

After dinner, we dropped by the Osho retreat, our curiosity having been sufficiently aroused by the music meditation and Zen's ET crowd, but when we were told at the front gate that we would need blood tests to enter, we opted for a walk in a nearby park instead.

That night we received an email inviting us to join some friends for a trek in the Nepal Himalaya, and so the following morning we raced down the concrete superhighway connecting Pune and Bombay to catch a flight to Delhi and another to Katmandu to join our American friends for a pilgrimage to Muktinath, Nepal's most sacred shrine.

Muktinath

The Nepal Himalaya, often referred to as the 'rooftop of the world,' is home to seven of the ten tallest peaks in the world. Our February trek to western Nepal brought us tantalizingly close to these magnificent pyramids rising to dizzying heights of over 25,000 feet. The night's blackness hadn't lifted as we jammed six backpacks into a pair of rusty taxis idling outside our rooms at a guesthouse overlooking Fewa Lake at the edge of Pokhara. The fireplace in our room still smoldered as I stepped into the brisk night air. The spectacular Annapurna range loomed above, but it would be another hour before we would glimpse its awesome contours.

By the time our gear was weighed and checked for the sunrise flight on Shangri-La Air, our first glimpse of the western Himalaya was at hand. Machapuchare stood in solitary splendor as we boarded the twenty-seat twin-engine plane and taxied the runway. Naturalists hail Machapuchare, popularly known as fishtail mountain, as the most beautiful mountain on earth. Its upper section spirals like a marlin's tail in mid-flight. The flawless pyramid stood against a powder blue sky as the morning sun edged over the horizon.

We were airborne moments after buckling into the cramped Beechcraft. Banking hard as we climbed, our pilot followed a line parallel to a range of magnificent peaks forming the centerpiece for one of the most renowned trekking routes in the world, the Annapurna circuit. Beneath the lofty Annapurna Range surged the tempestuous Kali Gandaki River, a willful and wild waterway raging through the world's deepest gorge. The holy river is said to be older than the Himalaya. Nothing was remotely mediocre in this rugged paradise.

Flights into the mountains depart in the early morning hours to avoid the unpredictable winds that whip up later in the day. Every seat was full on the thirty-five minute aerial adventure suitable for an Indiana Jones sequel. With saw-toothed peaks rising above us to the left and right, our tiny craft appeared as a buzzing insect in the vicinity of white giants that showed little interest in our presence.

Nepalese pilots have superb flying records and are intimately familiar with the navigational nuances of the demanding mountainous region. Our flight through the cloudless sky posed little problem for the leather jacketed men in the cockpit. As we rose above lower peaks, angling first left, and then right, the plane plotted a course above a terraced valley dotted with villages and stone farmhouses. Sudden updrafts repeatedly tossed our winged box about as we clutched metal armrests, sending our flight attendants scrambling to their seats.

Daulagiri and Nilgiri framed our passage as we moved beyond the Annapurna massif. The challenge each passenger faced was deciding where to look, for we had flown into the center of a three dimensional postcard of immense proportions. As stunning scenery swallowed our craft, our eyes grew wide with wonder. The Nepalese villagers living in the valleys below venerate these icy citadels as the abodes of their gods, and as a result, mountaineers are forbidden to climb many of the peaks. The approach to Jomsom airport came into view through the cockpit's open door. The narrow runway appeared no wider than a sidewalk. It was uncertain if we were about to land on an airstrip or a strip of flypaper. Descending rapidly, the pilot zeroed in on the 9,000-foot valley in the distance. After a final adjustment, the plane came in line with the landing strip and the wheels touched, bouncing along a runway cut from the mountain.

Stepping onto the plane's ladder, we were greeted with a slap on the cheek by a chill wind sweeping through the valley. The village of Jomsom, tucked beneath stately peaks, glistened with the first rays of morning sun under a cloudless sky. Disoriented by the change in altitude and awesome environs, I managed a snapshot of the plane and surroundings as a group of weary westerners boarded our craft for their return to Pokhara. Grabbing our packs that had been piled on the airstrip, we made our way to a stone and mud road flanked by teahouses and provision shops catering to western trekkers. A pair of drowsy yak, their long black hair touching the frozen ground, was tethered outside the one room airport in the heart of downtown Jomsom. Had they been horses, one could have easily mistaken the scene for a Colorado mining town. I wondered if the prehistoric-looking animals were Jomsom's taxi service.

The owner of Hotel Snowland stood at the entrance to welcome our group of six. Within minutes of deplaning, we were gathered around a large table, ordering breakfast. A grinning girl of ten arrived with a clay pot filled with glowing embers. We hadn't ordered red-hot coals for breakfast, and I wondered what she planned to do with them. Crawling under the table, she placed the hot bucket between our feet. Before long, our legs were as warm as the steaming cups of milk tea we sipped. A mother and her look-alike daughter busied themselves preparing our breakfast. Plates of steamed momos soon arrived with Tibetan bread, porridge, and more tea, a murky, milky drink called chia. The tasty deep fried Tibetan bread was the size of my plate, and I considered squirreling one or two away for the trail.

By 9:00a.m. we were on the trail heading out of Jomsom. Our

destination was Kagbeni, an easy five-hour trek up the Kali Gandaki River valley. It was the end of winter and still too cold to attract the large trekking groups that pour into the region during the fall and spring seasons. Insulated by down vests and windbreakers, we were delighted to be on the sun-drenched trail as pristine skies afforded us superb views of the lofty Himalaya. Traffic was sparse as we exited the north end of Jomsom by crossing a wooden footbridge spanning the river. During monsoon, the riverbed overflows its boundaries, flooding the wide valley. In winter, however, the river is nothing more than an alpine spring winding through a broad gravel bed of small, rounded stones. The locals call some of these stones shaligrams, and guesthouses along the way sold the fifty million year-old black fossils sacred to Lord Vishnu.

The legend of the river our path followed is the story of Gandaki, the daughter of a prostitute who had no choice but to adopt her mother's profession. The virtuous young woman believed in her heart that each suitor who came to her door would become her husband. One day an exceptionally handsome young man came and paid her well, but hardly noticed her. In keeping with her loyal disposition, she surrendered to him completely, believing that the suitor would become her husband before sunrise.

The young man died in the night, and the distraught Gandaki resolved to join him on the cremation pyre. But, as she prepared to enter the fire, a change came over the corpse, which appeared as brilliant as gold and had four arms. The god-like figure spoke, "Gandaki, I am Vishnu and I came to test you. You have passed my test. You may have three wishes." Gandaki had only one wish, and that was to be with her beloved forever, which pleased Vishnu.

Vishnu then explained to Gandaki that a saint had put a curse on him, causing him to turn into a stone. He told her, "Gandaki, you will turn into a river, and in the shape of a black stone (Shaligram), I will forever remain in your lap."

As we walked along the snaking Kali Gandaki River leading to Muktinath, the story of another prostitute came to my mind. There was a swami who lived across the alleyway from a prostitute. Every day while the swami was chanting and performing puja he thought how wretched the prostitute was, carrying on her unclean business nearby. His mind became obsessed with what was going on across the street. 'How despicable, how immoral this woman is,' he muttered to himself from his balcony one day.

Meanwhile, as the prostitute carried on her profession, she was filled with remorse that this was the only way she could earn her living and was always thinking about the great swami across the street. 'How pure and pious his life must be,' she thought. Then one day both the prostitute and the swami died. The swami was shocked to see the prostitute being escorted to heaven while he was dragged off to hell.

"Why this great injustice?" he cried. The reply came, 'Because your mind was filled with the filth of the prostitute's world while her mind was ever dwelling on the purity of yours. Remember, what you think is of greatest importance.'

Our ultimate destination was the ancient temple complex at Muktinath, the 12,300 foot abode of Lord Vishnu in the Nepal Himalaya. Muktinath is sacred to both Buddhists and Hindus, and receives pilgrims from Tibet, Nepal, and India who brave the elements to come and pray for liberation. Muktinath means 'place of liberation,' and those who make the journey to the hallowed spot are said to gain the favor of the gods, who grant the devout release from the wheel of karma and rebirth.

The legends surrounding Muktinath make suitable lore for this extraordinary region. Unseen yogis with supernormal powers are said to congregate on the mountain to meditate and shower blessings. A Buddhist manuscript called 'The Clear Mirror' describes Muktinath as the heaven where sixty-four deities of Supreme Bliss came into being.

The arid highland desert accommodates only the heartiest vegetation. Blue pine and craggy cyprus appeared now and then, but the barren environs offered little to sustain life. The rocky soil and inhospitable weather discourage both flora and fauna. The carefully stacked cairns that we passed along the trail stood as the sole reminders of humanity. By mid afternoon, the headwinds roaring down from a remote region at the border of Tibet known as the 'forbidden kingdom' were in full force. We had been advised to trek in the forenoon to avoid the howling winds that raced through the valley, bringing with them changeable weather, but our casual pace extended the hike into the late afternoon, giving us firsthand experience of our guide's forecast. But we didn't mind; we wanted to savor the intriguing lunar landscape as we moved along a dirt trail above the river that had been reduced to a gurgling stream by the dry season.

Amala's Inn

Our overnight stop was Kagbeni, an old Tibetan settlement located on the trade route connecting upper Mustang and Pokhara. Caravans have traveled the timeworn salt route connecting the Indian plains with the remote Tibetan plateaus of Central Asia for thousands of years. Kagbeni offered the yak caravans and their gritty guides respite from the strenuous

journey and erratic elements. The town centered on a carrot-colored
Tibetan monastery perched on a knoll near the ruins of a medieval palace.
After taking rooms in a tidy teahouse, we explored the stone walkways of
the town. The hodgepodge of crumbling walls and dwellings stood deserted. A nostalgic wind whistled lonesome notes in the narrow alleyways.

A small stupa obstructed our progress to the gompa. Its raised structure forced us to pass beneath it. Bent at the waist, we continued on our
way while looking up at paintings depicting Buddha's life. Except for a
handful of shops and guesthouses, the town was secured by heavy padlocks, awaiting its inhabitants' return from lower altitudes with the arrival
of spring. The palace ruins, partially renovated as family dwellings and
shops, were eerily devoid of life. Kagbeni was not your average tourist destination.

After stumbling through confusing alleys and passageways, we arrived
at the entrance to the gompa. A solitary figure robed in maroon greeted us
as we approached the monastery gates. The close-shaved llama invited us
to have a look around after accepting a donation for the upkeep of the
gompa. A row of barrel-shaped prayer wheels engraved with Buddhist
mantras lined the outer walls of the box-shaped building. No doubt members of Tibetan caravans had spun these wheels vigorously while muttering
their chants in the hope of gaining protection for their journey. We also
sent the wheels spinning as we circumambulated the monastery, although
our three-day hike was a benign Sunday stroll compared to the perilous
thousand-mile journey along the salt route.

As we entered the inner sanctuary a golden Buddha in teaching posture observed us from the opposite end of the hall. Colorfully painted
murals depicting scenes from the avatar's life were well preserved. From the
main sanctuary, we entered an adjacent room, a dimly lit library lined with
shelves of aged books. Our host carefully removed one of the heavy leather
bound volumes. A dim light filtering through a dusty window lit the faded
pages. The thick, black calligraphy was legible only to those who know the
language. Having survived the brutal attempts by the Chinese to demolish
Tibetan culture, these books preserved the teachings of Tibetan Buddhism.

Gingerly, we climbed a rough-hewn log ladder to the rooftop of the
monastery where tattered prayer flags fluttered ceaselessly in the gusting
wind. The horned head of a yak was speared on a south-facing pole. It had
been placed there to ward off evil influences and possibly to keep the
Chinese army away as well. Above us, a large griffon vulture searched for
rodents in the fruit orchards and barley fields at town's edge.

The view from the roof was expansive. Kagbeni serves as the gateway to more isolated regions leading into Tibet. We stood above the intersection of two river valleys. To the north the Kali Gandaki River cut an impressive gorge flowing down from the upper Mustang region, an area off limits to foreigners for decades due to its proximity to the border of China. To the east, a river valley rose dramatically in the direction of Muktinath.

Along a ridge to the northwest, a row of abandoned caves once housed reclusive monks who spent their days in meditative solitude, but I wondered how the monks got to the caves since they were carved half way up a steep escarpment. To the south, a green field would produce barley by early summer. Wheat was also grown in the patchwork fields around Kagbeni. The apple orchard at town's edge had not budded, but I would have made a special trip for the chance to pick a basketful. Above the valley, cathedral peaks served as silent sentinels aloofly overseeing the ancient trade corridor.

The elements played a formative role in molding the culture and personality of the people of the region. The Tibetans we met were called Thakalis. They were sturdy, resolute creatures possessing an abundant respect for, and dependence upon, nature. I had no doubt that their steady eyes took in more than their counterparts in other parts of the world. Simplicity of purpose backed by an inner calm guided their behavior. I imagined there wasn't much leisure time in a place like Kagbeni, where kindling was needed and bread dough kneaded, yaks milked and butter churned, fodder and eggs to be collected. The chores would be endless, but they served the family well.

Our guesthouse hosts were delightfully reserved. The owner's wife beamed when we called her 'Amala,' the Tibetan word for mother. Amala made every effort to see that her guests were well taken care of, and our accommodations exceeded our modest expectations. Hot water came into each private bath, and every guest room was freshly painted and carpeted. A potent silence pervaded the village, and we settled easily into meditation while our Tibetan mother prepared dinner. The simplicity of the lifestyle in this remote region encouraged introspection. Household duties were performed silently. The roar of winds sweeping down from towering peaks carried a message of silence, and I felt a deep resonance with it. Tired limbs recovered as the mind explored inner realms in this primordial place.

After dinner, a family of Tibetans arrived on foot from Mustang. The old women looked severe in their black gowns, fur boots, and wrinkled skin. But their smiles were warm and genuine. Like dried figs, their physical appearance didn't do justice to their sweetness. Our hosts and their friends spent the evening huddled around the kitchen stove sipping chia and exchanging news while we sat in our rooms comparing impressions of the day.

My friend Ramprasad and I shared a room at Amala's inn. Ramprasad was a Californian who had been working in Katmandu during the pashmina rage that had captured the New York fashion scene. He had shipped thousands of shawls and scarves to upscale American department stores during his two-year stay, but his sojourn in Katmandu was extended by his love of the Nepalese culture and he considered Nepal his second home. Whenever I came to Katmandu, Ramprasad took me around the ancient city. We were fond of walking about the old city after the tourists and locals had gone to bed, which wasn't very late. Once the shops were shuttered, we had the whole city to ourselves.

One night Ramprasad was reciting Hanuman Chalisa in Durbar Square when a drunken man trudged over to beg rupees, but when he heard the chanted prayer, the man froze like an ice statue in a Himalayan blizzard. By the time Ramprasad was finished, the fellow had completely forgotten why he had approached us in the first place and wandered off into the night mumbling bits of the chant to himself.

When our trekking party arrived in Katmandu, Ramprasad and I paid a visit to Bhagala Mukhi, the ancient goddess at the heart of a labyrinth of cobblestone alleys in a medieval part of the city. Past military checkpoints we drove, sandbagged fortifications with automatic guns pointing at the specter of defiant Maoists should the insurgents enter the capital city. One by one villages in eastern Nepal were falling into the deceiving hands of the Maoist rebels. Nepal was under attack, and tourism, its lifeblood, was drying up as a result.

We lit 108 butter lamps in the old stone courtyard of the pagoda as offerings to the Tantric goddess. Three dirt-smudged waifs assisted our lamp lighting that resulted in a golden glowing display, which we hoped would bring good fortune to our pilgrimage. Ours was the final offering of the evening. The priest closed the doors to the yellow robed goddess behind us, and the lamps burned brightly against the satin blackness of the night.

The Field Of Liberation

The second day of trekking began with a steep climb over the ridge behind the inn. I was breathless in minutes as the thin, chill air heaved my lungs. It took the better part of an hour to overtake the hill before we fell into an easier rhythm as the trail leveled. Vegetation was even sparser now.

Thorny bushes patiently waited for warmer weather. In fact, patience seemed to be a requirement in this far-flung place. The desolate landscape of the high altitude desert encouraged the eye to discern subtle variations in texture and color as rust, khaki, olive, slate, and brown wove a muted mosaic. Above and beyond the dessert terrain, Himalayan giants stared unblinking as our insignificant troop tread single file on the trail below. The sentient nature of rock, stream, and awe-inspiring peak compensated for the lack of more obvious life forms. My senses were alert, listening for messages at every turn in the trail.

From time to time we passed small villages. Communal clusters of stone and wood situated along the trekking route reflected an affluence not enjoyed by villages even a short distance from the flow of trekkers. A village on a far ridge had been abandoned altogether, its inhabitants having migrated to more affluent communities. We were hungry and stopped at a guesthouse along the trail in one of the more prosperous hamlets. The second floor dining room had handsome views of the valley and surrounding peaks, and a balcony where those better acclimatized than us dined. The sun coming through the large windows created a passive solar effect. The room was warm, and I wasted no time removing my jacket.

A second group of trekkers, a team of attractive young Scandinavian women arrived at the same time we did. One of the gals wore a heavy Tibetan sweater, the type sold around Katmandu. Before sitting down, she removed her backpack, sunglasses, and wool cap. A full head of flaxen hair fell to her shoulders. Next she pulled the sweater overhead, but with the sweater came her underclothes. I was not expecting the undressing in the dining room. Realizing the situation she quickly adjusted her clothes. Whether the change in temperature from chill outside air to toasty dining room was the cause, I can't say, but my Oakley's fogged over, and my buddies noticed.

"Coach, a bit warm in here for you?" ribbed my friend Sandy, who had witnessed both the sweater removal and my fogging glasses.

"Sudden change in temperature. Happens with these glasses all the time," I protested, smiling, but there was no hope of avoiding the barbs.

"You're looking a bit red in the face, Coach. Forget the sunscreen?" one of the others added.

"Yeah, must be the ultraviolet," I agreed. I was no stranger to self-deprecation. It was, after all, a monk's best protection. On a whole, my friends were a compassionate bunch, and we all enjoyed a good laugh.

Our group of six had come to Nepal to celebrate Sandy's fiftieth birthday, and Ramprasad had organized the trek on short notice. All of us were professors teaching at our management institute in Delhi, and were part of a larger group of monks that lived in the Smoky Mountains in North Carolina. In the past, we had boarded planes on a moment's notice for meditation projects in places like the Philippines, Thailand, Australia, Central Europe, and the Middle East; at times not even knowing where we were headed until the plane landed. We were like brothers; everyone in the group could be counted on, no matter what the situation.

Spaghetti for six arrived. Although Italian cuisine was not the special-ty of the house, the carbs would help us make it to our goal. The final hour to Muktinath, like the first hour in the morning, was difficult. Heavy legs trudged wearily uphill. Overtaking ridge after ridge, resolve prevailed upon tired limbs to advance one step at a time. The thin air grew thinner as we climbed. I didn't mind bringing up the rear with the birthday boy; my legs were leaden and Sandy's sandals slowed him.

"Sandy, we're almost there," I said, pointing to a cluster of buildings at the base of the mountain ahead. Sandy was a courageous fellow who I admired for returning to India after a close call a few years earlier. He had become ill after spending an evening in a Bengali village. The doctors had diagnosed it as Dengue fever possibly mixed with cholera. For weeks Sandy struggled with high fevers and delirium in his room at Maharishi Nagar. I had been in Bombay during much of his illness, but by the time I returned his condition had deteriorated badly. His face was bright crimson, his eyes glassy, and he had lost so much weight. It was touch and go for our friend, and we were all concerned. I had seen illness strike suddenly before in India. One agonizing night Sandy told one of the guys he thought the end had come, and so the friend stayed with him the entire night to ensure that it hadn't. Then, inexplicably, he took a turn for the better and eventually made a full recovery.

Our destination was in sight. Muktinath was situated on a slope at the base of a massif beyond a small settlement of guesthouses and shops. A sprinkling of snow wafted about as we climbed the stone steps leading to the temple compound. Somehow, gnarled cyprus and stunted poplar, which we had not seen for quite awhile, survived well above the tree line in the vicinity of shrines that were scattered about the sacred ground called Mukti Kshetra, 'the field of liberation.' Legend says these barren trees grew from the staffs planted by accomplished yogis who reached there with the aide of their walking sticks.

A wizened Hindu priest instructed us to make offerings at four altars before we proceeded to the main temple higher on the hill. After perform-ing the ritual with his help, we approached the central shrine, Lord

Vishnu's abode, a small three-tiered pagoda that stood near a row of water-spouts pouring out of the mountain. Exactly one hundred and eight icy streams flowed like taps—each issuing from a stone carved mouth of a cow. Pilgrims typically bathed under every spout before entering the main shrine, but the wintry weather prevented us from observing the custom. Snowflakes mingled with fluttering prayer flags above the temple as we splashed the holy water over our heads, but by the time I completed the cycle I was wet anyway, and curiously relieved from the fatigue of the day's trek.

Legends about Muktinath abound. In ancient times, eighty-four accomplished masters from India journeyed on foot to Lake Manasrovar, the holiest body of water in Tibet, each returning to Muktinath with a gourd full of water to propitiate Mukti Nath (Vishnu), the Lord of Salvation. Hindus believe that making the pilgrimage to Muktinath excuses them of great mountains of unwanted karma. According to Buddhists, who refer to Muktinath as Chumig Gyatsa (The Hundred Springs), the holy ground is one of twenty-four Tantric places and the earthly abode of the naga, or serpent deity. By practicing meditation and reciting mantras at Chumig Gyatsa, Buddhists believe the inner secrets of life are revealed and enlightenment is secured in a future life. The Tara prophecy says that fierce nagas live at Chumig Gyatsa and that Chakrasamvara and his consort reside there together. By going on pilgrimage to the holy site it is believed there will be no regression along the path to full understanding.

It's rare to find a sacred site venerated by two religions not at odds with each other. Hindu priests and Buddhist nuns at Muktinath show mutual respect and support for each other. Although the Hindu priest oriented us when we first arrived, a Buddhist nun living on the grounds was sweeping the central shrine when it was time for me to enter the pagoda. Hindus worship the deity as Vishnu while Buddhists worship him as Avilokiteshwara, but the deity is said to respond to either name.

While my friends were completing the watery rite, the nun permitted me to enter the main shrine, where I bowed before the image of Avilokiteshwara/Vishnu while she prepared the shrine for evening worship. It was a moment of good fortune at the feet of the Lord of Salvation. Clutching his ankles, I made pranam by pressing my head to Vishnu's feet, opening myself to the Divine Power streaming through the sacred form. I prostrated, fixing my mind on the goal of liberation as an illuminating current shot through my body, causing me to stiffen momentarily. Only a soft, distant voice retrieved me from my reverie as the kindly nun gently motioned for me to withdraw from the altar. My friends were ready for their moment of grace.

Red and yellow prayer flags were attached to bushes and strung from tree to tree above us. Tibetans believe that messages inscribed on the flags are carried by the wind throughout the region, dispelling personal obstacles and purifying the atmosphere. From Vishnu's pagoda we moved tentatively down an icy trail to the Jwala Mai temple where a blue flame burned on the surface of a small pool of water. Shepherds from nearby Jharkot village had rediscovered the perpetual flame fueled by natural gas, symbol of the union of opposing elements. The small shelter housed each of the elements, said to coexist in perfect harmony as they will again when the 'good age' on Earth dawns.

We meditated near the flame that burned on the waters symbolic of transcendent knowledge. Blue light filled my forehead as we sat on cold stones. As I repeated my mantra, the rarified air enhanced its power. Each repetition took longer than normal and created a subtle resonance in my chest that spread in concentric ripples across a luminescent ocean. Like a Tibetan singing bowl when struck, the rich vibration of the mantra slowly faded, yielding to a fresh repetition that produced another round of internal harmonics. Eventually my mind was swallowed by a boundless void and the repetitions ceased altogether. Washed out fabrics of thought scattered across the snow peaks like supplications inscribed on faded prayer flags. Dissolved into nothingness, a small oval of light was all that remained of my individuality. Our efforts to reach the remote refuge of the gods were being amply rewarded. If it all ended now, I would have no regrets.

By the time we reached our lodging, nightfall obscured the cluster of teahouses. My limbs were fatigued, but I felt light and free inside. Each in his own way had experienced the power of Muktinath; some had been overwhelmed by it.

As we slept, a soft, white blanket spread over the region. Our morning journey down the mountain traversed a trail hidden beneath a crystal garment woven in the sky. Once we lost our way and an impassable wall stopped our progress before we discovered the trail opposite a frozen plot. The entire valley glistened, shimmering in the translucent warmth of the sun. The snowfall had so radically transformed the landscape that it seemed we were trekking a new route.

By noon we were lunching outdoors at a teahouse in the Kali Gandaki Valley, enjoying the service of two beautiful Tibetan girls from a nearby village. Before departing, I picked out some shaligrams in the shop and our hostesses tied white scarves around each of us, a Tibetan gesture of hospitality and protection. As we hiked in the direction of Jomsom, a storm chased us down the valley. We hoped the silk scarves would help hold off the blizzard, but the storm overtook us an hour outside Jomsom. It was a wet, driving snow that reduced visibility to a few feet, sometimes less. Bent almost in half by the storm, we sought shelter among the rocks, trying to determine a strategy in the sudden onslaught of harsh weather. Far from any settlement, we huddled in the rocky enclosure, hoping the storm would pass. Judging Jomsom to be within reach, we headed into the howling wind that tested us even more than the snow. It blew forcefully and continuously as we stepped from rock to slippery rock along the river. There was a reason why the locals traveled in the forenoon. Our progress was slowed to a crawl, but our respect for the elements amplified by the time Jomsom came into view. The mountain storm passed, and our reentry into Jomsom took us past a stand of willows bent on touching the stream beneath them. A lonesome Tibetan partridge scratched about in search of food. It was not the only hungry creature on the trail.

Securely quartered once again inside Snowland Hotel, we gathered in the dining room with pots of chia in front of us. Our host informed us that all flights from Jomsom to Pokhara had been cancelled due to hazardous conditions caused by the storm, but to be waylaid in heaven was not a disagreeable prospect. After discussing our options, we contracted a helicopter since several members of our group had flights to catch back in Katmandu.

The following morning the clapping sound of our transport echoed through the valley as a blue and white helicopter appeared overhead. A dozen trekkers scrambled toward the craft as it settled onto the runway. Anxious foreigners, including a BBC camera crew, surrounded the transport; all hoping there would be an extra seat available. It seemed ironic that the same folks who had traveled great distances to encounter this out-of-the-way paradise were now desperate to be airlifted out, but of course they too had international flights to catch. Our group filled the chopper as it rose above the parka-clad trekkers. The thrill of the flight three days earlier was an experience not easily duplicated, but here we were moving through the Kali Gandaki Valley in slow motion, practically hovering among the world's tallest peaks. Having reversed our direction, we now viewed the awesome Annapurnas through the craft's transparent oval. If time could be suspended, I wished it would happen in the presence of these immense gods. Like great white-haired wizards, the gentle giants had lived for eons, the sedimentary strata of their bodies were yardsticks to measure time itself. Silent observers of the cycles of evolution. Serenity filled me as I gazed wide-eyed at our earth's everlasting monuments.

Fewa Lake, at the heart of Pokhara valley, came into view as we cleared a ridge decorated with blue-roofed cottages. Altitudes and seasons changed in the course of our flight. Alpine blossoms soaked up the brilliant sunlight and villagers toiled in the fields as we floated into the emerald valley. As the helicopter settled onto the tarmac, I felt like a child returning from an enchanted land where snow peaks are deities and their inhabitants, devout servants. The view from the rooftop of the world had changed my vision forever. I understood now why the elite climbers of the world approached their profession with such reverence and passion.

Muktinath Friends And Mount Machapuchare

Back in Katmandu, still stiff from three days of high-altitude hiking, I wove my way past the stealth vendors that stalked the muddy streets of Thamel at the heart of the city's tourist district. A dozen young men enticed me to buy everything from Tiger Balm to hashish as I slipped past them into a back alley, following signs leading to a shop advertising Ayur Vedic massage. Inside, I was escorted to a small room with a solitary table covered by a shabby sheet. I was handed a towel and instructed to strip down and wait. After a few minutes, a masseuse entered the room. Her name was Krishna, and she was the most beautiful woman I had seen since coming to Nepal. Krishna's cerulean blue eyes, delicate cheekbones, and finely sculpted nose were the work of a gifted artist. She was not shy like other Nepalese women, flashing a confident smile as she looked directly into my eyes and held out her hand, a gesture that would reveal her purpose. With my left hand clutching the towel around my waist, our right hands met. I knew instantly that hers were not hands trained to knead tired muscles, nor had they dug in the earth, formed flatbread, or scrubbed children. I imagined her long, slender hands to be those of a pianist or a potter. Before withdrawing her hand, Krishna allowed her fingertips to dance lightly on the palm of my hand. It was the clue I was looking for.

"Krishna, how old are you?" I asked, fully conscious that I was standing in a tattered bath towel in a room with a stunningly beautiful young woman who had come to do more than rub my aching limbs.

"Twenty," Krishna replied unconvincingly. Nepalese people have a youthful appearance, but I was quite sure she was not a day over seventeen.

"How long have you been giving Ayur Ved massage?"

"Three years, sir."

"But your hands are so soft. I have sore legs and a stiff neck. I'll need a deep one."

"Sir, I give best massage."

"I believe you. I'll have a massage later."

"But sir, I must give massage or you will not pay." A look of concern cast a shadow of doubt over her confidence.

"Don't worry, Krishna. I'll pay for the massage. Why did your parents name you Krishna? Isn't that a name given to boys?"

"Because of my eyes, sir." Krishna is a blue god and the name suited her, for her eyes matched the hue of the deity's skin.

"And because of your beauty, I think." Krishna blushed and lowered her head slightly, a gesture that betrayed her tender age.

"Sir, why don't you want massage from me?" she asked, her self-assurance waning. I didn't answer; but listened instead to the flurry of messages flashing within me. I was surprised to see my monk hood so easily challenged, but was equally surprised by the swell of parental concern welling up inside. A strange mix of emotion flooded the corridors of my heart. I waited for the internal waters to calm, remembering how easily the tidal waves of passion had engulfed some of the greatest of sages. Finally, a dominant voice in the crowd emerged and I recognized my course of action. Although other voices called out, the voice of compassion was the one I heard.

"Does your family come from the village?"

"Yes sir. We are Newars (artisans) from Bhaktarpur."

"Your father is a wood carver?"

"Yes sir. My family has very little. I am the oldest. The money I send is needed. My brothers and sisters are still small. Soon my oldest sister will join me in Katmandu. You can pay, sir?" An invisible hand wrenched at her heart as she talked about her family. An almost desperate expression now creased Krishna's lovely forehead. I sat on the edge of the table, listening, moved by her appeal, by her intelligence and honesty and responsibility. Compassion had been the right voice to listen to.

"I understand. Don't worry, I can pay." Krishna's face relaxed; she was smiling again. Still stiff, I pulled a handful of rupees from my pants pocket and reached out to shake her tender hand a second time. Her touch now had the feel of a friend; her smile, though still beguiling, beamed on behalf of her family. Krishna then left and I dressed to begin a fresh search for someone who could unknot my aching muscles, half expecting to settle for a jar of Tiger Balm from one of the vendors the street.

As our pilot charted a course parallel to peaks almost touching the wings of our cramped planeload of climbers and trekkers, I longed for this wondrously unspoiled and unparalleled land to remain untainted by foreign money and Maoist insurgents, hoping the sons and daughters of the Himalayan kingdom would continue to live in the purity and protection of their magnificent mountains.

TWENTY SEVEN

The Kingdoms Of Hyderabad

I asked a child walking with a candle,
"From where comes that light?"
Instantly he blew it out. "Tell me where it is gone
Then I will tell you where it came from."

—*Hasan of Basra*

With each sublime meditation in the lap of the Himalaya, I felt more and more like I wanted to make those magnificent mountains my home. And so I applied to live at a remote Himalayan ashram. By the time we returned from Nepal, a group had been selected to go to the retreat, but I was not among them. Instead, Will and I were asked to fly to Hyderabad to instruct several hundred software engineers at a company called Satyam Infosys. This was the second time I had been snatched away from a Himalayan sanctuary to go to Hyderabad, and I was beginning to wonder if I had unfinished business with the former city of Nizams (Muslim rulers). Off we rushed to catch a plane for south India instead of settling into the timeless Himalaya.

I hadn't been back to Hyderabad since the state government project four years earlier. The presence of western brands was the most obvious change in the city. International labels like Citibank, McDonalds, Sony, Nike, and Levis flashed on billboards and atop office buildings, and domestic brands sought to emulate them. The congested state capital had become still more crowded, but the local government was managing the city better than most. Chandra Babu had successfully courted Silicon Valley's InfoTech giants, and Bill Gates had visited again with a plan for a Microsoft university. Hyderabad strived for a glossy image, a direction that meant little to the farmers who made up seventy percent of the state's

population. Their perennial struggle against drought and poverty continued, but received less attention than the ambitious technology projects that
were being funded internationally.

It was evening when we arrived at Satyam's new campus in Banjara
Hills, a posh suburb overlooking Hyderabad's city lights that spread across
the Deccan plateau. Banjara means tribal, but our computer savvy students
were anything but tribal. On the first night, a roomful of talented young
software engineers listened as I explained the nuances of meditation, and
then quizzed me thoroughly after the talk. Many wanted to know why the
mantra needed to be kept a secret and so I offered an analogy, comparing
the mantra to a seed that, once planted, should not be dug up. Like that,
I said, as the mantra grows inside a person one needs to have faith in the
process, especially in the early stages. Since the deepest subconscious levels
of the mind are influenced by the mental repetition of the mantra, if it is
spoken out its potency can be diminished. This is why the student is asked
to keep the mantra private, I explained.

The Bengali saint Swami Ramakrishna used a variation of the seed
analogy to describe the role of the mantra. "Illumination," he said, "is hidden in a mantra like an oak tree in an acorn. To the ignorant, the mantra
is meaningless jargon, but the mantra is an open portal to Supreme
Reality." A traditional Sanskrit definition of the mantra is, "That which,
when meditated on, brings liberation."

One of my Satyam students, a young woman with large brown eyes,
approached me privately after her first meditation. She wanted to tell me
about her experience. She said she saw a beautiful goddess in a white sari
whenever she repeated her mantra and wondered if this was all right. I
could only reply, "How fortunate, you are doing everything just right."

The Satyam programmers were India's new generation. Unlike the
managers we typically worked with, the new generation was bold, inquisitive, and not afraid to challenge what they were told. In the final meeting,
the group peppered me with questions about their new practice. "Sir, how
does meditation take you to a state of Being each time?" asked a man sitting in the middle of the group of fifty.

"Being is like a cinema screen. The images of a movie are projected
onto the white screen, which doesn't change no matter what the film's content, whether comic, full of adventure, or tragic. We get so involved in the
drama of life that we forget about Being, which is the deepest level of our
existence. Meditation connects us to Being by reducing the mental activity until it dissolves into silence."

"Is experiencing Being during meditation the same as

Enlightenment?" asked a woman near the front.

"The never changing cinema screen is called Atma, or soul, which we glimpse during meditation. Transcending occurs naturally. There's no effort involved. It's like slipping on a banana peel. One minute we're standing and the next minute we're flat on our back. At first we don't know what happened, but over time we experience the process of falling. Eventually we realize Being fully."

"How long does that take?" an eager fellow asked from the back.

"That depends…"

"On what?" the same fellow fired back before I could reply.

"That depends on how far from Athens you are and how you plan to get there."

"I don't get what Athens has to do with Enlightenment," the guy shot back. He was impatient and wanted answers.

"Let's assume Athens represents Enlightenment. Moksha. Nirvana. Both the type of transportation we choose and the distance to our destination will determine how fast we reach Athens. Right?"

"I don't understand," the gal who asked the original question, complained.

"If you want to get to Athens and you're living in Barcelona you'll probably get there faster than someone living in Rio de Janeiro, but not necessarily."

"I don't get it," replied a well-built guy in the back row. "How could you get to Athens faster from Rio than from Barcelona?"

"It all depends how you travel. There are many options. You might want to go slowly and savor the journey. In which case you might cycle across southern Europe. It would be an intimate experience, but the journey will be long and endurance is necessary. Cycling would be unsuitable for most, but an athletic guy like you might enjoy the challenge."

"What if I was in a hurry to get to Athens?" the same guy asked.

"Then you'd want to book a seat on an express train or even better, a commercial airline. You see, there are many options, but if you chose to bicycle along the Mediterranean then someone flying from Rio would arrive in Athens ahead of you."

"But this is not a race, is it?" asked a calm man in front.

"There's no deadline. Enlightenment is there for all and we should have the attitude that we want to help each other along the way. If we see a friend struggling on the journey, then lend him or her a hand."

"You said that each person begins the journey from a different place. You mean we don't all start the journey from Barcelona?" asked the woman.

"Evolution is a long process and no two souls are at exactly the same place on the path."

"Are you saying that the growth to Enlightenment spans lifetimes?" asked the composed fellow who knew more than he was letting on.

"Evolution involves many lifetimes, but once we've got a ticket on a non-stop jet to our destination, we can get there very rapidly."

"In one lifetime?"

"Yes."

"But what's the hurry?" quizzed a fellow who had missed two meetings. "I'm enjoying my life and don't have time to meditate every day."

"We all have free will. I can recommend that you go by plane, but you might decide to backpack instead. I can only remind you that Enlightenment is your birth right and that you'll never regret making it a priority in your life."

"What's so special about Enlightenment?" asked the same guy.

"Enlightenment is about inner bliss, which comes from the knowledge that you are one with God. How many of you have children at home?" About half the hands went up. "You've all watched your children play with a ball and then become bored with it after awhile. What do you do when that happens?"

"I give my little girl her stuffed bear," said a woman who spoke for the first time.

"She plays with the bear, but if she begins to cry, what do you do?"

"I pick her up and hold her."

"Exactly! You hold her in your arms and she's happy. It's the loving embrace of mother that the child wants. You see the point?"

"I get it," the calm guy said. "We get caught up with our toys and forget what really brings us happiness."

"God Realization is like a child in the arms of Mother. But we have to cry for Mother before she picks us up. That's where free will comes in. But why delay being in the arms of our Mother?"

"But you haven't told us how long it will take to reach the goal?" countered the impatient one in the back.

"I can't tell you because it's not up to me. It's up to you. It's up to your free will. But I can say that it's attainable, even as we speak."

"If there are many ways to get to Athens then there must be many paths to God Realization. Buddha advised the Middle Way," observed a middle-aged man.

"That's right. Buddha was born a prince, but he abandoned the kingdom he was born to rule and chose a path of austerity. Ultimately, he abandoned that path and attained nirvana via the Middle Way that you mentioned."

"I don't like the idea of austerity," replied a chubby guy who was wedged into his desk.

"It's up to you. A travel agent can only make recommendations and book the flight. The decision is up to the individual," I had done the Enlightenment talk hundreds of times, but I always enjoyed it. Satyam's software engineers were brighter than most.

"You've told us you're not a guru, and yet Hindus believe its necessary to have a guru to gain Enlightenment," mentioned the oldest man in the group.

"A travel agent can book your flights and get you on the plane even if he hasn't been to Athens himself. But only someone who resides in Athens can honestly call himself a guru. Those who claim to have achieved the highest state of Enlightenment are really announcing to the world that they still have a ways to go. Fully enlightened souls are rare, and those who have the tools to teach another how to reach the goal are even rarer. Saints don't go around telling people that they're a saint."

"But you speak as though you know all about Enlightenment. Aren't you Enlightened?" asked the impatient one.

"I leave it up to you to decide if what we've talked about is true or not. It's not important whether I'm Enlightened or not. More important is what you experience inside."

"But how do we know if what you've said is true?" asked someone in the back.

"I can describe how sweet and juicy a strawberry is, but you have to taste it for yourself. No description can compare to the experience itself. Discussing the taste is not the taste. It's the same thing with the scriptures. Reading about Nirvana does not produce Nirvana. I leave it to you to dive into Being and know for yourself. You're fortunate. You now have the technique."

"Then you are not a guru?" asked the man in the back.

"Not at all. But the Master who we honored at the beginning of the classes is one. Remember Guru Dev? His was an amazing life and we can learn something about a true guru from his story."

"Are you talking about Maharishi's teacher?"

"Yes. At age nine, young Raja Ram left home in search of a guru. He looked long and hard, interviewing accomplished yogis along the way before he found the one he believed could lead him to the goal. The young seeker's criterion was three-fold. He wanted a master who was a life celibate, free from anger, and God-Realized. One day he approached a respected guru and asked him, 'Do you have fire?' The master was angered by the impertinence of the upstart youngster because he was of the order of monks that didn't use fire for cooking. Seeing the man's anger, little Raja Ram replied, 'If you do not have fire, then where is this anger coming from.' The man realized immediately that a rare soul sat in front of him and he pleaded with the boy to stay, but the boy left the guru's ashram to continue his search. Few have the patience or discrimination to search for years (he spent four years searching for his master) the way young Raja Ram did, but the point is well taken. The old adage, 'well begun is half done' applies to spiritual guides as well as the techniques they espouse."

"I don't understand the cinema screen analogy," a man with bright eyes said.

Guru Dev, Shankaracharya Of Jyotirmath

"Atma, or soul, is like gold which can be fashioned into beautiful jewelry. But when it's melted down, it resumes its unadulterated state and can once again be crafted into a stunning ornament. The gold never changes. Only its appearance changes. Same thing with the cinema screen. No matter what is projected onto it, the white screen remains the same. The guru comes along to remind us that we're made of pure gold, that our primordial nature remains the same. Once we've been taught the process of alchemy its up to us to turn ourselves back into gold."

"But sir," said the almond-eyed young woman in the front that had described the goddess to me the night before, "Aren't you Enlightened?"

"I am and I'm not," I had never given that answer before and wondered how the group would react. "From my thirty years on the path I'm more enlightened than when I started, but I won't celebrate my awakened self while part of me sleeps."

"But sir, if you're not enlightened after thirty years than what hope is there for us?" asked the woman in the back.

"It just means that I started in Rio and had a long way to go to get to Athens. You might be starting your journey from Piraeus, a town near Athens. You could arrive in Athens tomorrow."

"Sir, what about psychic powers like knowing the future?"

"Capture the fort. Once you own the fort all the diamond mines and gold mines in the territory are for your enjoyment. Pure Being is the fortress you need to capture. Without it, life will always be a struggle." The programmers were off to a solid start, and I would check in on them from time to time. Satyam had already booked more courses along with Citibank and Airtel, India's number one cellular service. There was little time to think about the Himalaya.

The Return Of The Rajas

We moved into a comfortable flat in a quiet neighborhood with a swimming pool, and a driver and car. I was awakened each morning to the rhythmic litany of street vendors repeating "Vada, idli. Vada, idli." I was often tempted to sample the breakfast they carried in baskets on their heads, but the comfort of my bed stopped me. Our taciturn driver was named Krishna, and our two domestic helpers included a cook and a sweeper. It wasn't long before we lost our cook, but rather than hire another, we promoted our sweeper to cook and asked her to clean as well. After shrewdly negotiating her new salary, Jaya took over running the household. Under Will's tutelage, Jaya blossomed into a fine cook with a solid repertoire of dishes. The fact that Jaya was from the lowest of castes didn't bother us, although we later found out that it meant quite a lot to our infrequent dinner guests, who barely touched their food. Nonetheless, we liked everything about Jaya; she was hard working and went about her business quietly, never disturbing our meditation. Once her husband sent false receipts with her, but when we caught on to the ploy Jaya admitted that her husband was up to mischief.

Dr. Raju and his family had recently returned from a visit to Holland. The Hyderabad natives are some of Ayur Veda's most skilled physicians, coming from a long line of gifted vaidyas that have developed hundreds of effective herbal formulas. These carefully guarded family secrets include cures for gallstones, liver ailments, high blood pressure, drug dependency, and many of other ailments. Whenever the Raju family conducted a free camp, thousands came for treatment.

In everyone's favorite epic, the Ramayana, a heroic warrior named Laxman lay dying on the battlefield, having been wounded by poison arrows. The army despaired and even his brother Ram lost his will to fight, seeing Laxman's grave condition. Determined to save Laxman, the monkey god Hanuman flew to the Himalaya in search of a rare herb called Sanjivani, which was the only hope of bringing Laxman back to life. The devoted Hanuman found the rare plant, and brought it back to Lanka. The herb worked its magic, Laxman was restored to health, and Ram's army rallied to defeat the demons.

Recently, Dr. Raju's elderly mother was stricken with a serious illness and there seemed little hope of recovery. Mataji Raju was slipping, and she passed away in her sleep one night. In the morning there were no vital signs and the family thought she was gone. Then the Rajus put an herb under her tongue and in a few minutes she regained consciousness and opened her eyes. Grandma Raju is doing fine now. When I heard this amazing story, I wondered if the Rajus hadn't administered Sanjivani. Surely there can't be many herbs with such power.

The legacy of India's herbs is an ancient one, a tradition that is being revived in the world today. Ayur Veda is one of the most popular and effective systems of indigenous health care, east or west, and even large pharmaceuticals are now patenting herbs and formulas that have been used as household remedies in India for generations.

One of the more remarkable features of Ayur Veda is a rejuvenation 1 Kaya Kalpa, which restores youthfulness. Kaya Kalpa a patient withdraw from society for from ninety days to six ing this time, the patient lives in a wood hut and is attended by an assistant who administers rasayanas (restorative preparations), as well as feeding the patient fresh milk in the morning to sustain the body. The patient spends his days resting and meditating while the herbal formulas repair the body and generate new cell growth. During seclusion there is no reading, conversing, or listening to a radio.

The results of Kaya Kalp, according to Dr. Raju, are nothing less than miraculous. A white-haired man of eighty, who has poor vision and is hard of hearing, can be restored to a youthful thirty year-old with shining black hair, healthy teeth, excellent vision, and supple muscles. According to Dr. Raju, the patient will look and feel like a young man with full life expectancy ahead of him. Unfortunately, very few vaidyas have the knowledge of Kaya Kalpa.

The account of a Punjabi saint named Maharaj, who twice underwent Kaya Kalp is chronicled in a book written by Anantha Murthy. During Maharaj's treatments, the first when he was about ninety years old and the second when he was 150, he experienced a full restoration of his youthful appearance and vitality. In Murthy's book, the amiable swami says his success with Kaya Kalpa had much to do with what he called, God's Grace. He spent three months sleeping and meditating inside a hut in Assam in his first rejuvenation and was interned in an underground cave at age 150 while another saint looked after him. According to his biography, Maharaj underwent the unique treatment when he was about to pass away so that he could progress further on the spiritual path. Maharaj finally died at age 185. When I asked Dr. Raju if he would perform Kaya Kalpa on me, he replied, "Not now, you don't need it yet."

Will and I once took the Raju clan for a holiday to the Himalaya. Grandma Raju and the children joined us and we stayed at a place called The Deodar above Mussourie. One night we were sitting outside our guesthouse under the biggest Deodar tree I had ever seen. It must have measured ten feet in diameter. We were roasting paneer (fresh cheese) kebabs over a wood fire when Dr. Raju gazed up into the overhanging limbs for a long time. He then whispered to me, "Steveji, this tree has great healing properties. We are fortunate. It is helping all of us tonight." Although I wasn't sure exactly what he meant, I too felt the healing presence of the benevolent tree.

The ancient sages knew that consciousness exists in everything, from a molecule to a rock to a galaxy. They were well aware of the plant kingdom and the crucial role it played, not only for health, but also for spiritual development. Plant biologists know that the plant kingdom transforms sunlight into life force through photosynthesis. Without the support of plants, humans and animals alike would be unable to draw the nourishment they need from the sun. The sages intuited the intermediary role played by the plant kingdom and venerated it for that very reason. They knew that plants absorb light and that light is what triggers spiritual awareness. For this reason indigenous peoples like Native Americans and Tibetans relied on plants to keep themselves healthy and spiritually attuned.

The sages say plants and trees possess psychic abilities and can transmit their healing energies when needed. According to the adept, plants are devoted to humanity and were placed on earth to support man's spiritual development by transmuting the energies of the sun and absorbing the moon's light, and also by drawing out the influence of minerals in the ground.

One of the world's greatest authorities on the plant kingdom was a modern sage named Balraj Maharishi, a senior colleague and friend of Dr. Raju, who was said to communicate directly with the plants, which he claimed were more than willing to tell him how they should be used. Balraj, who lived in Hyderabad, knew the uses of thousands of plants and made field trips deep into the Himalaya to collect rare plants for his medicines. On one such expedition, he came upon a cave, and was attracted to go inside. From the cave's entrance, he saw a yogi deep in meditation. Amazingly, the yogi's hair covered his face and extended all the way down to his knees. Balraj didn't want to disturb the ascetic, and was about to leave when the sage moved slightly. Very slowly, he lifted his hair up and flipped it behind his head so that he could see. He then gestured for Balraj to sit near him in the cave.

"Who are you?" asked the stunned Balraj.

"I am Ashwattama," replied the yogi. "Are you thirsty?" Ashwattama is described in Puranic literature as one of the seven humans destined to live to the end of time.

"Yes," said Balraj, and the yogi picked up a copper bowl and held it up to the wall of the cave. To Balraj's astonishment, a spout of water sprung from the cave's wall, filling the bowl.

The two wise men talked about plants and nature. After their visit, Ashwattama asked Balraj, "Would you like to return now to your home in Hyderabad?"

"But how is it possible? We are deep in the Himalaya."

"I will take you to your home under one condition; you must promise not to open your eyes until I say so. Otherwise I cannot be responsible for what might happen." Balraj closed his eyes as instructed and felt a surge of energy and then a wind rushed past his body. After a moment, he heard the words, "Now you can open your eyes." To his utter disbelief, he found himself sitting in his bedroom back in Hyderabad.

Mango Mania Time

Summer arrived in Hyderabad, and with it the markets were flooded with mangoes. As temperatures soared, India's favorite fruit ripened almost overnight in rural groves and cultivated orchards across the land. Each region boasted its special issue. A bumper crop was expected in Andhra Pradesh, and, if the streets were any indication, we were in for a treat. Positioned on nearly every corner were flat bed trolleys, mobile markets whose vendors stacked the golden fruits in tall pyramids.

The mangoes' exotic names—Alphonso, Himayat, Sundari, Zakir—equaled their exotic tastes and textures. Eighty varieties of mango, some small enough to fit in the palm of a child's hand while others weighing more than a pound flooded the outdoor markets. We were on our way to the AP Mango Center.

By the time we climbed out of our car, the shop's boys were busy preparing samples. One youngster carved up Himayat and Rassala, another pair of hands pressed a Sundari, a smallish mango relished for its honey-eyed juice. Sundari means beautiful, and after the boy had kneaded the fruit like a ball of bread dough, I squeezed the pulpy nectar into my mouth through the hole where the stem had been removed. I could have devoured a basket full of Sundari. We were lured into narrow aisles lined with circular straw baskets. The heady aroma was overwhelming. Even the bees flew in uncertain patterns, weaving left and right as if weighing their options before lighting on a pearl of nectar on a fruit bursting with flavor. We filled our bags with Himayat and Sundari.

As kilo after kilo was weighed and priced, I reeled from the scent sensation of the golden fruits. Twenty-five pounds of fruit were stuffed into the front seat of our car. On the kitchen table, I counted forty-eight mangoes, but Dr. Raju had recommended we eat as many as we liked during the hot season, saying mangoes pulled heat out of the body. During mango season we lived off the fruits, and it was just a few days before we were back at the AP Mango Center, sampling the latest arrivals.

Neither Man Nor Beast

We continued exploring on weekends the way we had in Gujarat. After completing a string of corporate courses with Airtel, India's top cellular company, we headed for a wish-fulfilling hill that Will had read about. Apparently, the unassuming place attracted peasants from near and far.

According to Vedic scriptures, Lord Vishnu, the great preserver, will incarnate ten times on earth. He has already taken nine births, including incarnations as Buddha, Ram, and Krishna, but his Narasimha avatar isn't well known since he came for one specific event. A powerful demon had been granted a boon by the gods that no human or god could kill him either during the day or at night, nor could he be slain inside or outside a building. The demon believed he was invincible.

Having secured the boon, the demon terrorized one and all, including his pious young son, Prahlad. The demon insisted that everyone worship him and forbade his son to worship his beloved Lord Vishnu. He became furious when his son disobeyed him, but Prahlad continued praying to his Vishnu, despite the repeated threats of his father. Infuriated by his son's insolence, the demon decided to kill the boy, but Vishnu intervened to protect his young devotee by taking the form of a creature that was half man and half lion. With the demon in his grasp, the fierce Narasimha killed him at twilight while standing on the threshold of the demon's house. In doing so, he negated the boon granted the evil being. Narasimha was neither man nor god, and the deed was done neither during the day, nor at night. The moral of the story is: arrogant demons seeking immortality should speak to a good attorney before entering into contracts with the gods.

Outside Narasimha's cavern, Will and I removed our sandals under a bamboo shelter. A young girl with lifeless legs struggled across the hot stone courtyard, hoping we had a rupee for her. She was not at all menacing in her need, and despite her disfigurement, the expression on her young face was one of hope. In the brightness of her amber flecked brown eyes was the light and joy that most children feel coursing through their entire bodies. This young one's heart beamed trust from her radiant face. I wanted to hug her, but without words, Will and I reached into our pockets to help.

Inside the hill, we climbed down a steep stairwell into the cavern housing the man-lion avatar. The cave was cool and dark, and only the ghee lamps burning in the recessed grotto gave us a glimpse of Narasimha as we squeezed into the small space along with others. This was the spot where wishes were said to be fulfilled, and bodies healed. The young girl was still on my mind as we stood at the wish-granting altar and so I made a small appeal that she be taken care of and that her life not be too difficult. Then we followed the stream of pilgrims climbing the stairway back into the sunlight.

On our way to Narasimha's hill, we had passed a batholith, a bulbous bubble of rock that appeared like a huge boil on the earth's surface. Geology was yet another of Will's interests, so we climbed the igneous rock formed by volcanic activity hundreds of millions of years ago. Exploring the ten-story rock under a strong sun would have been foolhardy, so we waited for the final hour of daylight to examine the geological oddity. The stone was still hot to the touch from the sun as we climbed.

Steps carved into the smooth rock angled up the side of the batholith leading to the summit. Up top, I spun around in a circle taking in the panorama. Will was already among the pillared remains of a small pavilion. Unable to keep up with Will, who was examining the ruins with the enthusiasm of an archaeologist, I sat at the edge of the batholith, watching the sun fall from sight. A hawk soared regally above green fields, eyeing the peaceful landscape. Few settings are as serene as an Indian countryside at sunset, especially from my vantage point on the rock. As twilight approached, a religious chant began in the village below. An imam's plaintive prayer blanketed the village. I too listened to the compelling appeal to Allah. His song reminded me of the loon's solitary call across a Canadian lake. As the light was extinguished, religious longing hung in the air like mist over a field at sunrise. Like the shennai (Indian oboe) that combined joy and sorrow in a single eerie note, the imam's call penetrated deeply.

Candles now flickered in the windows below. Electricity had lapsed. The imam's minions would be on their prayer rugs, facing Mecca. Then the prayers stopped and there was only silence, and darkness. The transition to night was complete. Transcendence lingered in the air like fine aloes wood incense. Then Will found me, and we were faced with the daunting task of faltering down the batholith in the blackness.

On our return to Hyderabad, Will had yet another hilltop diversion in mind. How he knew about these out of the way spots mystified me, and I teased him about it all the time. The Deccan plateau surrounding Hyderabad is full of odd rock formations. Villagers have a tradition of worshipping their gods on the highest spot in the area. After diverting again from the main road, we found ourselves surrounded by thirsty soil. Another climb up carved steps brought us to the edge of a small pond. A village wedding party was also on top of the hill, and they watched with interest as we invaded their remote place of worship. A storm was following us; it brooded over the fields, moving menacingly in our direction.

The priest looking after the holy pond handed us a bag of bread dough scraps and advised us to toss them into the water as we circled the pond that was no larger than those found in Japanese gardens. To our astonishment, when the scraps hit the water, a mad frenzy ensued as whiskered fish fought over the morsels. According to the priest, the catfish were sacred and had been worshipped by his ancestors. I wondered how the fish found their way to the hilltop pond in the first place; even the most determined trout would have had trouble climbing the stairs.

The ominous steel-blue storm clouds that threatened now hovered overhead. As the catfish battled for the final scraps, raindrops tapped the pond's surface, forming concentric circles. The calm was broken by a great gust of wind that swept a loose paper into the air. Then the impending downpour struck. Heavy drops fell from the shattering sky as claps of thunder boomed with such force that I felt the concussion inside my chest. The wedding party sought cover inside the shop, avoiding the deluge that came as a solid sheet of water. We found space under the corrugated roofing, but the torrent blew sideways, soaking our legs while sparing the wedding party. The timorous bride and groom sat, eyes downcast at the center of their group, looking bewildered by the storm and gravity of the occasion. Dressed in handsome ceremonial outfits, the pair looked more like life-size dolls than living beings. Possibly it was their first meeting, and their shyness showed.

Powerful gusts lashed at the shop. At any moment the roof would take flight. More thunderous booms followed blinding flashes of jagged light that streaked across the sky toward us, causing me to question the wisdom of standing under a metal roof on the highest point in the area. The tempest charged the atmosphere with electricity and parched fields drank as the downpour battered plant and tree. The newlyweds looked pleased; rain is always auspicious in India. Finally the storm passed, leaving behind the rich smell of rain, dung, and fecund soil as we stumbled down the mountain.

Everyone prayed in this pious land. The imam implored Allah to save his people, pilgrims wished for the health of their children, and the farmer prayed for the monsoon to wet his thirsty soil. I prayed for a home in the Himalaya. Although the gods were petitioned by a thousand names, I felt sure each prayer was heard.

Citicorp's Vacation Package

Monday morning meetings in the stylish offices of Citicorp and GE were a world apart from the hill temples and paddy fields of rural Andhra. As we waited for security clearance at the entrance to Citicorp's suite, gifted minds hid behind a sea of computer screens. This was not just an ancient land where villagers depended on wish-fulfilling shrines; it was also a land that provided professional services all over the globe. India exported software to ninety countries and her expatriates were making their mark in the global economy. In America, one out of three Microsoft employees and 38% of all physicians were Indian. 36% of NASA and 28% of IBM's employees hailed from India; figures that eclipsed every other country in the world.

Many of these professionals remained close to their cultural and religious roots. Our seminars at Citicorp had been postponed for a month while the head of the office made a religious pilgrimage to a remote region of Tibet. His mission was to circumambulate Mount Kailash. The manager would participate in arcane Tibetan rituals more outlandish than feeding holy fish, and forego a shower for two weeks for the privilege to do so. Despite his unconventional holiday, the senior manager was wide-eyed and smiling when we arrived for our seminar a day after his return.

Chari's Charitable Disposition

We had been in Hyderabad for several months, but we had not heard from Chari, the happy vaidya who had treated our ailments four years earlier. No one seemed to know his whereabouts, except that he had married a girl from his village. Then one morning the doorbell rang. In the hallway stood Chari, wearing a smile as broad as the doorway. The mercurial wizard bounded into the flat, talking on his cell phone. His inscrutable ways continued.

Chari had become a TM instructor since we last saw him, and was now in charge of an academy outside Hyderabad where he was training meditation teachers. He wanted us to see the academy, so we drove out to the facility located at the edge of a large reservoir that was Hyderabad's principle source of drinking water. In former times, Hyderabad was renowned for its healthy air and curative water. As we drove through a wooded area, we came upon two men by the road holding out a branch with a gray sphere attached to it. Chari tapped Krishna's shoulder, instructing him to stop. I couldn't imagine what this was all about.

"These Banjara men...Tribals," he explained. "They live in forest and collect honey."

"Then let's buy some," Will said eagerly.

"Wait! Honey may be fake. If good, then it is best honey and we buy." Chari's playful mood had become authoritative. "I will test."

Chari rolled down the window and a rapid-fire exchange in Telegu ensued, after which one of the men cut open the gray hive and poked a stick inside. When he withdrew the stick, it was covered with thick, golden honey that was about to drip on us as he pushed it through the car window.

"Aacha!" exclaimed Chari after putting the honey to his tongue. "You taste!" The rich flavor was superb, so we bought the entire branch after yet another flurry of words between Chari and the tribals. One never knew what to expect with Chari in charge.

"Chari, how could honey be fake?" I asked.

"Banjara man may remove honey and insert sugar water with syringe," Chari explained. Having Chari as our guide kept things interesting. After all, he had lived in the forest as a child.

Chari instructed the men to break away the branch, leaving us with a twelve-inch oblong hive that we put inside a plastic bag. We had purchased about a kilo of honey, or about 40,000 trips by the bees to and from flowers.

As we drove off, I asked Chari, "What about the bees? This was their home."

Chari shrugged his shoulders, and replied, "Bees already making new home in forest."

"Chari, is wild honey better than other honey?" I asked.

"Wild honey best medicine. Good healing properties. Wild honey is rasayana. Good for eyes and kills bacteria..." Chari was obviously pleased with the purchase, and we planned to give him most of it, which he would mix with his herbs to increase their potency.

Chari's English had improved since our first meeting, and we were engaged in animated chatter when he stopped in mid-sentence to observe a tiny insect on the window next to me. With great care, Chari rolled down the window and ushered it out. The insect was no larger than the head of a pin.

"What was that?" I asked.

"Very dangerous! If bug goes into ear it goes into brain. You die!" Chari explained as he shook his head, pretending the bug had gotten inside his ear. Everything seemed to amuse our friend.

A whirlwind of activity enveloped Chari, and at the same time a calm sea was behind his antics. After he finished with the bug, he pulled out his cell phone and called his friend in Amsterdam. He chatted casually for twenty minutes without the slightest interest in the cost of the call. Chari had just bartered with the Tribals over paise (pennies) and then spent a small fortune on his mobile. Even our industrialist friends weren't so extravagant, but Chari was not your average person. The more I was around him the more I recognized that there were no boundaries to this gregarious wizard.

Vijaynagar

Hyderabad was once part of the Vijaynagar dynasty, India's last great kingdom. It was a long drive into Karnataka to get there, but the skeletal remains of Vijaynagar lay before us, scattered among rolling hills, rock out-croppings, and paddy fields made green by the meandering Thunga Bhadra River. Hidden among colossal granite boulders, banana planta-tions, and coconut groves, we climbed over a World Heritage Site that cen-turies ago represented the pinnacle of human civilization. Vijaynagar's tem-ples, palaces, fabled bazaar, and graceful pavilions appear today as if some preternatural force had wreaked destruction on everything in its path. Reduced to bits and pieces of its former glory, the fractured palaces and halls are all that is left of what was once the world's richest empire.

Five hundred years ago, India was the wealthiest nation on earth, and Vijaynagar was at the center of that prosperity. If not for its remote loca-tion in northern Karnataka, the ruins would be among India's most popu-lar tourist destinations. At the peak of their 250-year reign, the rajas of Vijaynagar presided over a South Indian empire that extended coast-to-coast, from the Bay of Bengal to the Arabian Sea, and included the mod-ern day states of Andhra Pradesh, Karnataka, and Maharasthra.

From a vantage point atop a massive boulder, we surveyed the undu-lating terra cotta landscape where the kingdom's capital once stood. In vain, I tried to imagine the magnificence of the empire that had been so abruptly reduced to skeletal remains by marauding Mogul armies. A glimpse of the mighty fortresses as seen through the eyes of travelers who chronicled what they saw gives one a sense of the civilization. A Persian ambassador, who was no stranger to extravagance, claimed that his eyes had never seen anything like it and that there existed nothing to equal it in the world. The city was built with seven citadels and the same number of walls enclosing them.

The Portuguese traveler, Domingo Paes, road on horseback through the capital city and was dumbstruck by what he saw. Paes described the king's palace, coterie of wives, and 12,000 attendants and wrote in his diary that he went along with his head turning from one side to the other so fast that he was almost fell off his horse. In the main bazaar lived many merchants, and there one could find gems of every type and the finest silks. According to Paes, the common women sported jewelry fit for a queen in any other land. So great was the weight of the gold and jeweled bracelets worn by these women that servants had to support their arms. It didn't take long for tales of Vijaynagar's riches to circulate beyond the shores of India. The treasures that inspired commerce with China, Arabia, Egypt, and Persia also attracted the attention of Europeans like Columbus and de Gama, who solicited support from their kings for their voyages to the land of untold riches.

During festivals, the Vijaynagar kings were weighed against precious gems and gold, and then the treasure was distributed to the residents of the capital. The queen lived in a private palace that looked like a Persian dollhouse, if such a thing exists, and she bathed in a tank the size of a swimming pool. Even the royal elephants that wore precious gems were quartered in palatial stables built in grand Mogul style. Was it any wonder that enemy troops camped on the opposite shore of the river, waiting for an opportunity to invade?

But time and destiny have forever altered Vijaynagar. We were lunching at an outdoor café in the main bazaar when a destitute man refused to let us enjoy our meal. He came for rupees and the waiter chased him off. He returned again a minute later. After lunch, we walked among the stone colonnades that once separated shops overflowing with precious stones and metals. Shopkeepers now stocked their shelves with peanuts and chapati flour.

We wandered among the ruins half returned to the red earth where they once stood. As we scrutinized the sculpted forms of gods and kings whose granite heads had been smashed by invaders, I was reminded of Rome and Babylon, both ruined by their excesses. It took just six months of pillaging to reduce Vijaynagar to the condition in which we found it (it was worse before recent renovations). The allied armies of several sultanates killed 100,000 people before marching away with spectacular spoils of victory. "The plunder was so great that every private man in the allied army became rich in gold, jewelry, tents, arms, horses, and slaves," wrote the historian Robert Sewell. "Never perhaps in the history of the world has such havoc been wrought, and wrought so suddenly, on so splendid a city; teeming with a wealthy and industrious population in the plenitude of prosperity one day and on the next day seized, pillaged and reduced to ruins amid scenes of savage massacre and horrors beggaring description."

What were the excesses that led to the empire's collapse? Surely the ostentatious display of wealth had roused Mogul armies to form the alliances necessary to sack the city. Modern history would have the world believe that India's legacy is one of abject poverty, but nothing could be further from the truth. During the reign of Vijaynagar kings, the adventuresome from other parts of the world sailed the open seas hoping for a share of India's untold wealth.

Many of the world's greatest treasures come from India. Cotton, silk, and spices from the subcontinent filled the trunks of merchant ships returning to Europe, China, and the Middle East. Some critics say Vijaynagar rivaled a declining Rome for its decadence, but the secrets of its demise lay forever buried among the fallen plinths and columns scattered across the terra cotta landscape.

The Nizam And His Jewels

In the 17th century, during the height of Mogul rule in Delhi, a Baghdad descendent came to power in Hyderabad. His title was Nizam, and six generations of his offspring governed the Deccan, an area larger than England and Scotland combined. The seventh and last Nizam of Hyderabad was named Osman Ali Khan, an eccentric ruler considered to be the wealthiest man in world during his time. He ruled the Deccan for thirty-seven years as a reclusive despot who allied himself politically with the British. Under his rule, railways, roads, hospitals, libraries, and colleges were built in Hyderabad, but the Nizam, despite inheriting five marble palaces, countless trunks full of priceless gems, truck loads of gold bullion and currency, and a staff of 10,000, was somewhat of a miser.

The Nizams of Hyderabad amassed perhaps the world's greatest fortune via a taxation system called Nazranna. Whenever a subject looked at the Nizam, he was expected to offer a gift as a show of loyalty. Over two centuries, plenty of loyal subjects gazed at the Nizams and the Nazranna piled up, especially when the Golconda diamond mines began producing the world's first supply of high-grade diamonds. It was customary for the best gems to be presented to the Nizam, which led to one of the greatest gem collections ever amassed. Despite his outrageous wealth and retinue of 1,800 wives, children, and servants, the Nizam was a reclusive man who rarely left his personal quarters.

Although he owned gold place settings for a hundred, his fastidiousness compelled him to eat on a tin plate on the floor in his bedroom. His cellar was full of sapphires, rubies, diamonds, emeralds, and pearls piled like coal, and he kept the only key to the vault in his vest pocket. One day the Nizam found a massive diamond stuffed in the toe of a slipper and used the egg-sized gem as a paperweight, unaware that the Jacob was one of the most valuable diamonds in the world. The Nizam and his subjects surely would have benefited from a more generous outlook. Despite possessing the wealth of nations, he lived a cheerless life dependent on opium. It's incomprehensible that a ruler with the means to improve the lives of millions allowed rodents to gnaw at his stashes of currency rather than use it for the benefit of his citizenry, but probably that was the result of his addiction.

The Nizam's gem collection came to Hyderabad one day, where it was exhibited amidst intense security. Will and I went to see the magnificent display. We had waited outside the exhibit with a family of four. The well-behaved children stood passively with their parents, but the moment they entered the gem-filled room, they bounded about the room like toys wound too tight. I too felt the powerful currents of energy in the room and felt like joining them. I had no explanation for it other than the immense energy came from the gems themselves. Unless one has been in a room full of exquisite gems, their radiant effect is difficult to imagine.

Although the central attraction of the exhibit was the Nizam's former paperweight, the 184-carat Jacob diamond, the superb craftsmanship of the jewelry exceeded anything I had ever seen. Indian lapidary is unsurpassed. Combining intricate detail with exotic motifs, master craftsmen created stunning designs. A pair of gold bracelets was studded with 270 diamonds, a peerless necklace was strung with 380 pearls on seven strands, and a total of 173 pieces valued at two billion US dollars filled the viewing cases. The highly secured room was a cat thief's dream come true. Many of the pieces had never been seen by anyone other than a Nizam before being put on display in Hyderabad. One piece of jewelry that caught my eye was a navaratna ring containing gems representing the nine planets. According to Indian astrology, a navaratna setting harmonizes the astrological influences of all the planets, preventing the wearer from suffering from ill health or misfortune.

The scintillating energy in the vault emanating from the flawless rubies, emeralds, diamonds, and sapphires reminded me of a mountain cave I had visited at the opposite end of India. Both cave and exhibition room housed a rare and benevolent presence. An industrialist friend had suggested that we make a pilgrimage to the cave abode of Vaishno Devi on a mountaintop in the terrorist-torn state of Jammu-Kashmir. To enter the cave, we had to get down on our hands and knees to crawl through a three-foot opening in the mountain. That feat accomplished, we shuffled along single file in the dark, contorting this way and that as we squeezed through fissures in ankle-deep water. Halfway through the passage, the woman in front of me panicked, calling ahead to her husband for help, but he could do little. She had no choice but to continue shuffling along; there was no turning back. The convoluted passage continued for fifty tentative steps before the tunnel widened, allowing us to stand upright again. I could not recommend the passage for claustrophobics. Having navigated the obstacle course, I breathed easily again as I stood before the goddess in a small chamber at the tunnel's end.

The feeling in the cave was extraordinary; immediately I was hit with a spiritual energy that stopped me in my tracks. The priest allowed me to stand to the rear where I peered over the procession of pilgrims that passed in front of the Himalayan goddess, pausing briefly in a space big enough for only a handful of people. I was held spellbound by a spiritual presence in the surcharged confines of the cavern. Her presence was unmistakable. As I stood there, a golden flame ignited in my heart. The sensation felt better than the day I won my first tennis match. The fire, which began as no more than a pilot light, spread to other centers of my body, expanding as radiance throughout the entire physiology. As the spiritual fire engulfed me, pathways of inner light carried sublime currents until innumerable hair-like filaments formed a grid that glowed blue, a sort of holographic representation of my physical form. But strangely enough, the fire had no heat; to the contrary, a cool presence filled me with peace.

I looked at the pindi (sacred) stones on the natural altar, but they looked ordinary enough. Where was this awesome energy coming from? Was it coming from the cave itself or the priest's chants or the steady flow of the devout? In any case, it came from a deep place, and I groped inwardly, hoping to find the bliss-inducing source. Unwilling to relinquish the moment, the priest had to whisper instructions a second time before my wet feet shuffled along a second passageway leading to the night outside. I understood why a million pilgrims each year crawled through the tiny opening in the mountain to pay homage to Vaishno Devi. I would never know for sure what benevolent influence resided in that cave, but her presence rang clearer than a temple bell and richer than an egg-shaped diamond.

Diamonds Aren't Always Forever

Indian mines were the only known sources of diamonds in the world until South Africa began production a little more than a century ago. India's mines were located in the Deccan, a part of the Vijaynagar Empire. In the 13th century, Marco Polo visited the diamond mines and reported that diamonds not found in any other part of the world were both plentiful and good there.

The Hindu kings who controlled the Golconda mines didn't stuff their finest diamonds into slippers or use them as paperweights; instead they offered them to their gods, ornamenting Vishnu and Siva with lustrous diamonds, many of them blue in color. Experts have different opinions regarding the ten most celebrated diamonds in the world, but on everybody's list are six or seven priceless diamonds from India. The Hope, Koh-I-Noor, Idol's Eye, Orloff, Regent, Great Mogul, and Nassak diamonds, which are among the world's most coveted, were all mined in India. Some are privately owned; others are on exhibit at the Tower of London, Smithsonian, the Louvre, and the Kremlin.

The Koh-I-Noor diamond was found along the banks of the Ganges almost 700 years ago. The Mogul Emperor, Babur, wore it prominently on his turban. When it was first found, it was appraised at the value of one day's wages for the entire population of the world. The Koh-I-Noor diamond is now part of Her Majesty's Crown Jewels. Two other renowned diamonds, the Orloff and Idol's Eye, are believed to have been stolen from Hindu shrines where they adorned idols. One popular account claims that a French soldier removed the diamond eye from the Ram statue at the Srirangam temple in south India and made off with what later became known as the Orloff diamond. According to the story, the Frenchman was terror stricken at the thought of retribution, and fled over the temple's walls without removing the other eye of the idol. During the heist a storm raged in the temple city.

At least four of the most famous diamonds in the world are believed to have been stolen from Hindu temples, never to be returned. Some of these diamonds are said to carry the curse of Hindu deities. It is widely assumed that some of the spectacular gems that disappeared from India were smuggled out of the country and re-cut into smaller diamonds. Magnificent gems still decorate the deities at the Himalayan shrine at Badrinath and the Tirupati temple in south India, but security measures now taken to protect them are better than in centuries past.

India's diverse legacies fill the pages of history: from herbs that restore life and youthfulness to kings that offered their prized gems at the feet of deities to cities of incalculable wealth that now lay in ruin. The many kingdoms associated with Hyderabad—the gem kingdom, the plant kingdom, and Vijaynagar—are part of the glory of ancient India that surrounded us during our stay in the south Indian capital.

TWENTY EIGHT

Little Tibet

The color of the mountains is Buddha's body,
The sound of running water his speech.

—*Dogen Zenji*

Bound for the remotest part of India near the border of Tibet, our early morning flight soared across a cloudless sky, an endless sea of motionless whitecaps below. For an hour we headed north above vast uninhabitable regions until a verdant valley came into view out my window. At its center, the meandering Indus River bisected the broad basin. Ladakh lay below. The plane banked sharply, splitting the peaks on either side of the valley, and we glided easily into a culture that is among the oldest on earth. In a moment we were taxiing the landing strip at Leh, the capital of Ladakh. As we deplaned, our flight attendant reminded us to rest for a day or two until our bodies acclimatized to the Tibetan plateau, India's highest populated region.

A blast of brisk, dry air surprised us as we stepped off the plane. At almost 12,000 feet, I was already noticing the thin air by the time I reached the baggage claim. An elderly woman in a black garment that covered her from neck to ankles approached, gesturing for us to follow her out of the airport. She had come to greet us on behalf of the guesthouse I had booked on the phone the night before. Somehow the wrinkled woman had guessed who we were, and uttered just one word, "Jigmet," the name of our guesthouse.

Shimmering poplars and weeping willows shaded the lane separating our accommodation from a small monastery opposite us. Our sundrenched rooms faced a well-tended vegetable and flower garden. I sunbathed from my bed. At the far end of a wing of guest rooms, a cow mooed inside a lean-to. Two teenage girls turned the garden, collecting root veg-etables. We could not have been happier with our lodging, which made our self-imposed quarantine easier while we waited for our bodies to adjust to the altitude.

The Jigmet family was busy with chores when we arrived, but Mr. Jigmet stopped to welcome us and help with our bags. Each member of the family contributed to the efficiently run operation. Mr. Jigmet handled bookings and purchasing while his wife looked after the kitchen and their daughters kept the rooms in order, tended the garden, and waited tables in the small garden restaurant. The Jigmet family's days were long, but they went about their chores cheerfully. When winter arrived, they would retire to the warmth of the kitchen hearth, spending leisure days with friends.

We sat in our rooms reading about places we wanted to visit, but soon restlessness got the best of us and we headed for town. We walked along shaded footpaths of a living museum preserving the traditions of Buddhist culture. Ladakh had become a Buddhist culture centuries before Tibet and only later adopted Tibetan Buddhism as its dominant faith. Because Ladakh is part of India, it was protected from the widespread destruction of Tibetan culture when Mao's ruthless army marched into Tibet fifty years ago; a genocide that claimed over a million lives. Because the Chinese never entered Ladakh, it remains the purest Tibetan Buddhist culture in the world.

Ladakhis live with the geographical predicament of being sandwiched between the two largest populations in the world. India keeps 30,000 troops posted in the region to protect its border with China, but because Ladakh is a Tibetan culture, its people have traditionally owed allegiance to Tibet, which the Chinese now rule. As a result, the Chinese contend that Ladakh should be under their jurisdiction. The Indian government coun-ters by noting that the Dalai Lama, the supreme authority of Tibetans, resides in India. It's a sticky situation. To add to an already complex con-dition, the state government of Jammu-Kashmir, which administers Ladakh's affairs, is predominantly Muslim. Consequently, the people of Ladakh are left without a political voice and are discriminated against in schools and public services. But the fact that Ladakh falls within India's borders has been a blessing; India's willingness to adopt exiled peoples has helped preserve one of the great cultures of the world. The Ladakhi people have not only overcome a challenging climate, but have withstood politi-cal and cultural adversity.

We found Tibetan Buddhism at every turn. Multi-tiered medieval monasteries crowned hilltops, odd little chortens (shrines) protruded out of the sandy terrain like inverted white mushrooms, claret-robed monks ambled along willow-lined walkways at a pace unfamiliar to the west, and the soothing Tara mantra wafted about the town. I immediately felt at home with the Ladakhi people who struck me as peaceful, humble, and well connected to the earth.

On a hill above the town, the Ladakhi royal family's former palace slowly eroded, aided by biting winds that sweep through the Indus valley from the higher Himalaya. Portions of the abandoned brick and poplar beam edifice were crumbling. Patola palace in Lhasa was modeled after the old edifice, which was built thirty years before the former residence of the Dalai Lama. We wandered about in the shadow of the palace, observing the town of 10,000. Leh, once the most important trading post between Tibet and India, was a stopover for merchant caravans making the punishing journey from the Gobi desert to the Indian plains. Their yak and mule teams carried silk, gems, dried fruit, and musk, among other things for trade in the famous Indian bazaars. I could easily imagine a caravan hitched outside one of Leh's general stores while nomadic Tibetans and Mongolians smoked bidis or shared a bottle of bang.

The bright sun and dry August air were invigorating, but temperatures plummeted as the sun dropped behind the peaks. Two young monks, their heads shaved, sat on a bench conversing with the Jigmet women as I entered the guesthouse kitchen. By their cherubic faces, I judged the monks to be in their mid-teens. Mrs. Jigmet invited me to join the group for tea. One of her attractive daughters translated for me. The head-shaved pair had come from a monastery outside Leh to solicit donations for building renovations. According to the duo, cracks had formed in their monastery walls and they felt the freezing arctic blasts all winter. The maroon robed lamas shivered in jest as they described the austere conditions, but by mid-November the situation would be no laughing matter. Everyone gladly gave some rupees and the young mendicants departed, having duly recorded the contributions in their donation log.

"Does every family send a child to the monastery?" I asked.

"Not all, but most do." explained Deskit, Mrs. Jigmet's oldest daughter. "Both boys and girls go."

"How long have those boys been in the monastery?" I asked. For some reason, my innocent query caused a stir among the women, who giggled and smirked, trying to hide their amusement behind their teacups.

"Sir, those are not monks," said Deskit politely, correcting me as her mother and sister broke into another round of muted laughter.

"Not monks, you mean they're nuns?" I asked blushing.

"Yes, they're friends of my daughters," explained Mrs. Jigmet, a handsome woman with warm, compassionate eyes.

"How long have they been nuns?"

"Our friends have been in the convent for five years, since age twelve. They come around in summer to do service in the community and collect donations, but we never see them during the winter."

"The girls seem quite happy." They laughed the entire time they were in the kitchen. "Was it their decision to go to the convent or their family's?"

"The parents send their children, and we are happy to do what our parents think is best," explained Deskit's sister. I was amazed at the simple explanation and the way these people viewed life.

"Where is your brother?" I asked, eyeing a photo of the family on the wall, wondering if he too wasn't cloistered away somewhere.

"He is studying in Chandigarh," replied Mrs. Jigmet.

"Do you see him often?"

"He comes home twice a year. He's studying at the engineering college."

"Will he return to Leh when he graduates?"

"We hope so," Mrs. Jigmet replied as she refilled my cup. "We shall see."

Ladakh has enough ruins to keep a team of archaeologists occupied for more than one lifetime and Will would have welcomed the invitation to join the excavations. Whenever we ventured away from the irrigated greenbelt along the Indus River, the landscape was as barren as the ground the astronauts stepped onto when they first set foot on the moon; the rocky crags, scree, and shifting sands was an inhospitable moonscape. In contrast, the Ladakhi people were warm and friendly, and made us feel like we were their own.

The fading sun cast long shadows as I climbed a wooden ladder to the meditation room on the roof of the Jigmet's house. After lighting earthy joss sticks in front of their Buddha, we closed our eyes as the Jigmet family silently came for evening prayer. Mr. Jigmet caught me slumping over in meditation and suggested I amend my posture with a straighter spine. The vastness of Ladakh was seeping into my psyche, loosening my already flagging connection to civilization. Our rest was over, the journey about to begin.

A Dalai Lama From The West

Our first outing took us to monasteries outside Leh where Will romped about with the enthusiasm of a hairy-chinned anthropologist. Across the Indus River, the road twisted up a canyon where Hemis Monastery stood sequestered against an escarpment. As we passed a row of chortens containing religious relics, our driver told us the shrines were built on a grid to facilitate the flow of spiritual energy from the monastery to the village and farms below. Although these concepts were new to me, I found them intriguing and not totally implausible.

Hemis, one of Ladakh's oldest gompas, was built four centuries ago near a cave where a lama attained Nirvana. The pinnacle achievement inspired the construction of the monastery. Inside the courtyard, the complex was undergoing renovation as we entered. In fact, repairs were underway at many of the monasteries. Ladakh's gompas have been the beneficiary of Tibetan Buddhism's immense popularity in the world, which has fueled the restoration of the old bastions.

Stepping out of the brilliance of the high altitude sun, my eyes adjusted slowly to the monastery's poorly lit hall of worship. Oil lamps burned at the altar, augmenting the faint light filtering through smoky windowpanes. The residue of centuries of prayer and chanting lingered in the air, moving us to speak in whispers. I was particularly interested in the story of the nineteenth century Russian adventurer Nicolas Notovich. The Russian had fractured his leg while in Ladakh and the compassionate Hemis monks took him in. While convalescing, Notovich learned from the chief lama that the monastery had copies of ancient manuscripts about the life of a man they referred to as 'the Dalai Lama from the west.' The man behind the mysterious title had traveled and studied in Tibet and India two thousand years earlier. According to Notovich, the account of the man called Issa was none other than that of Jesus Christ.

As the weeks went by, the Hemis monks gained confidence in their Russian friend and permitted him to study the ancient manuscripts describing the life of the mystic that had visited their land. With the help of a translator, Notovich transcribed the texts with the intention of publishing them when he returned to Europe. According to the forward of his book, *The Unknown Life of Jesus Christ*, Notovich's plan to publish his findings was not well received by church officials in Rome. A Roman cardinal offered to buy the manuscript from Notovich, saying, "Nobody will attach much importance to it, and you will create numberless enemies thereby…If you need money, I can obtain some compensation for these notes." Notovich refused the cleric's offer, being justifiably suspicious of the cardinal's motives. A year later, he presented the manuscript again, this time to a cardinal in Paris, who also tried to suppress its publication.

Christians are taught that Jesus left his home in Nazareth as a boy and began his teachings around age thirty. The missing years have been the subject of research and speculation over the centuries, but the church has never acknowledged that Jesus received a portion of his spiritual education in Tibet and India, a fact that would undoubtedly upset church dogma. The archives in Lhasa once contained authentic documents indicating that Jesus did, in fact, spend approximately twelve years studying and meditating in Asia, but apparently these documents are no longer in the Potala monastery.

Although the church views Notovich's book with skepticism, the Christian establishment has little reason to be threatened by the manuscript. After all, Tibetans viewed the man called Issa as an extraordinary individual possessing miraculous powers and the highest spiritual attainment. The following are excerpts from the manuscript that Notovich studied at Hemis, which Buddhist monks had recorded.

"When Issa had attained the age of thirteen he clandestinely left his father's house, went out of Jerusalem, and, in company with some merchants, traveled toward Sindh (western India) that he might perfect himself in the divine word and study the laws of the great Buddhas (Buddhism was prominent in India at the time).

"(He) visited Juggernaut (Jaganath Temple in Puri) in the province of Orsis (Orissa on the east coast of India), where the remains of Vyasa-Krishna rest, and where he received a joyous welcome from the white priests of Brahma (Hindus).

"They taught him to read and understand the Vedas, to heal by prayer, to teach and explain the Holy Scripture, to cast out evil spirits from the body of man and give him back human semblance.

"He spent six years in Juggernaut, Rajagriha, Banares, and the other holy cities; all loved him, for Issa lived in peace with the vaishyas (merchant caste) and the sudras (low caste Indians), to whom he taught the Holy Scripture."

Notovich's translation of the Tibetan texts contains many of the same stories and parables known to Christians. It seems unreasonable that the cardinals would suppress the manuscripts, but politics have a way of corrupting organizations, and possibly the clerics feared others would think the Hindu and Buddhist practices Issa learned were unsuitable. They chose to keep his early training a mystery. Had the church fathers been more open-minded, they might have embraced the Tibetan manuscript and even used it to endorse Christ, noting that the Tibetans revered Issa like a god.

One day religious leaders will appreciate the profundity of other faiths rather than trying to convert those with differing beliefs. In comparing the great religions of the world I have found their similarities to far outweigh their differences. After all, every religion believes in a Supreme Being, the immortality of the soul, and the intrinsic goodness of man. As we go deeper into our faith, we will recognize the unity of religions rather than their differences.

Cradle Of Civilization

Ladakh's lifeline is the Indus, a river originating near the base of Mount Kailash that makes a long, winding journey through central Asia. Numerous streams flowing down from the Ladakh ranges join the Indus, which irrigates the fertile plains of western India and eastern Pakistan. The British adventurer William Moorcroft described the Indus as 'The great drain by which the snows upon the lofty ridges of Tibet are the means of fertilizing the plains of the Punjab.' On its journey, the Indus irrigates Ladakh's wheat and barley fields, and apricot and apple orchards, spinning prayer wheels and powering mills along the way.

By day's end, we had visited half dozen monasteries east of Leh, and were ready to explore the remote moonscapes to the west. Before departing, I tasted my first bowl of tsampa in the guesthouse garden. The roasted barley meal was not nearly so interesting as the impromptu fashion show I was treated to in the garden. A Dutch family had become friendly with the Jigmets, and their blond-haired, blue-eyed teenage daughter emerged from the house wearing a stunning perak, a turquoise studded heirloom cherished by Ladakhi women. Although the perak covers a woman's head and extends down her back, it's considered jewelry. The headdress, worn at weddings and festivals, is one of the largest pieces of jewelry anywhere in the world. The beautiful brocade ornament worn by the comely Dutch girl was covered with uncut turquoise and silver pieces. The girl's parents, who were seated at the next table, admired their beautiful daughter, but the goatskin ornament was extremely heavy and she was uncomfortable wearing it for long.

As we drove off in our Sumo SUV, the Jigmets waved from the gate. Their winsome smiles reminded me of the Tibetan proverb, 'Birds that live on a golden mountain reflect the color of gold.' Our journey west took us past otherworldly rock formations, into deep canyons, through quaint villages succored by the Indus, and beneath hilltop lamaseries in various stages of restoration. The landscape never seemed satisfied with its complexion; it changed colors as often as an actress donned costumes in a stage play. Subtle shades of rose, sapphire, and amethyst clothed the mountains. Long shadows spread across the valleys late in the day, and depending on whether one stood in the sun or shade, the temperature ranged from perfect to unpleasant.

Ladakhi homes are sturdy structures made of thick, whitewashed bricks. The typical two-story structure narrows slightly as it rises to a flat roof fortified to withstand heavy snowfall. Wood beams reinforce the house shared by a family and their animals. It is not uncommon for the family and their yak to sleep in the same room since the animals produce plenty of warmth. One can imagine that any additional heat would be welcomed in a house without central heating when temperatures plunge to minus fifty degrees. As we passed the sturdy homes, apricots were drying on many roofs along with piles of fodder.

Ladakh's lunar landscape was once the floor of a shallow ocean. As we drove west, the land became increasingly arid, and soon we found ourselves at the heart of a vast but vacant high altitude desert surrounded by mysterious mountains whose 20,000-foot peaks seemed nearer than they actually were because of the absence of humidity and dust in the air. After passing through a tiny village whose apricot orchards were ripe for harvest, we stopped to pick the fruit from a roadside tree. Bees sipped the beaded nectar of the sun-ripened apricots, but didn't object to our sharing their meal. The fruit was sweet and succulent, lacking the dry tartness of most apricots.

For much of the day we encountered no one, as Ladakh is sparsely populated; it is spread over a 100,000 square kilometer region, but only a quarter of the land is cultivable. The Tibetan agricultural method, however archaic, is undeniably effective, and I never saw a tractor in use in Ladakh. The yak and its relative, the dzo, perform the domestic chores around the farm. The dzo is half yak and half cow. Both animals not only give milk high in fat content that is ideal for making butter and cheese, but they're also steady plow animals and sturdy beasts of burden. The caravan traders that traveled from Mongolia to India relied on the yak.

By western standards, Ladakh is backward, but my personal indicators of quality of life are at odds with western standards. Friendliness, selflessness, community spirit, spiritual awareness, and respect for sentient beings, including rivers and streams were present everywhere we went. During planting and harvest seasons, Ladakh's valleys are filled with villagers singing folk songs and sharing stories as they help one another in the fields, ensuring that everyone gets their crops planted on time and harvested before the long winter sets in.

Ladakhis rely on their animals more than most cultures. The almost comical process of winnowing grain is a good example. I watched a group of yak, cows, and dzo hitched in a line to a horizontal pole that was connected to a post at the center of an area covered with grain. The smaller animals were positioned at the axis of the circle and the larger ones further away. As the animals moved in a circle around the pole, they trampled the grain, cracking the chaff, making it easier to separate the kernels of grain. Round and round they went like a living merry-go-round moving in slow motion. The primitive method of threshing has been in vogue as long as animals have been domesticated in Ladakh, which I imagined was a very long time.

Along the asphalt road running west to Srinagar, military convoys moved to and from border positions. The road shadowed the winding Indus River much of the way, but a long section cut straight across the desert. After a steep ascent, we arrived in the late afternoon at Lamayuru. Perched atop a precipice, the monastery looked precariously positioned, like a house of matchsticks that could collapse at any moment. In some places, the crag on which it stood had eroded out from under the structure. The monastery had recently opened a guesthouse, complete with modern plumbing and bed mattresses still wrapped in plastic. The night air was cold, but not unbearable, and the flutelike song of the wind as it swept through the monastery broke the silence.

We were the only visitors on the prowl at the fabled lamasery that once housed four hundred monks. In the courtyard, three elderly women approached. Their weathered faces and thick spectacles looked out of place in a yard full of novice monks romping about like children at recess. Clad in black dresses caked with dust, the women were endearing caricatures of Ladakhi culture. After posing for snapshots, they expected their fee, and proved to be skilled veterans that easily outwitted us. Agra's famous snake charmers could have apprenticed under these wily grandmothers, but we supported their charade, and everyone parted ways with smiles on their faces, appreciating the absurdity of the exchange. We had our snapshot and they their ten rupees.

A rosy-cheeked miniature monk wearing a sleeveless yellow shirt and burgundy robes that dragged on the ground waved a heavy brass bell outside the monastery kitchen. It was time for tea, and the boys came running from all directions at the signal. The young lamas invited us to join them. The boys, whose ages ranged from eight to eighteen, poured into a kitchen

specially equipped to brew tea. Cauldrons simmered beneath shelves housing pounded brass pots and pitchers. Each young lama held a cup that an
older boy filled, and they all sat together in the courtyard, sipping their
mid-morning snack.

I didn't see a single boy that wasn't enjoying his assigned role in the
monastery. All looked bright, energetic, and happy. Not a trace of severity
showed on any of the faces. In fact, the opposite was true. The younger
boys were mischievous and playful, mugging for snapshots with comical
expressions on their faces one minute and scrambling down an embankment to join in a fresh prank the next. But the young lamas' days were not
solely devoted to merriment. Later, we found them sitting among the
poplars with their teacher, reciting the ancient texts.

In the afternoon, we visited with a monk who appeared to be about
twenty-five. "Dorje, how long have you been a monk?" I asked.

"Since ten."

"Did you choose to be a monk?"

"My family sent me to this monastery. My two older brothers look
after our farm."

"Do you visit your family?"

"Yes. I go regularly. We are very close." His tidy room was furnished
with a Tibetan carpet, a wood-framed bed, desk, and chair. A thermos of
butter tea was ready whenever he needed the extra warmth, which would
be often on this mountain.

"You have a superb view of the mountains and canyon," I said, admiring the panorama from his window.

"Yes. This region was once a crystal lake. Watermark still on rocks.
See." Dorje pointed to the lines on the opposite hill. "Legend say that
nagas (serpents) lived in the lake. We believe this is holy place." In all eastern religions the serpent is considered auspicious because it represents the
spiritual energy, or kundalini, that fuels spiritual consciousness.

"Dorje, have you seen the Oracle?"

"Yes. Oracle is very popular at our festivals."

"How is he chosen?"

"Only pure lama is chosen to be Oracle. Must be pure so divine spirits can enter him on special day. Lama goes into deep trance and then pre-
dicts future. Like fortune teller."

"Do villagers ask the Oracle questions?"

"Yes. My brother asked once about family problem and he got good answer." The Oracle, according to Tibetan culture, is a spokesman for the divine. Able to predict the future, bless the community with abundant crops, and answer difficult questions for the villagers, the Oracle is much venerated. The Oracle also dispenses punishment from time to time to those who have incurred karma through their actions. The Oracle employs skillful theater and the spectacle of a costumed Oracle dancing wildly around the courtyard, wielding weapons and leaping about, is both frightening and hypnotic, and is an integral part of Tibetan religious festivals.

"Are you happy here?" I asked.

"Yes. Lamayuru is good place." I couldn't have agreed more. The lamas we had met were not conversationalists, and that is how it should be. Their task was to let go of words and thoughts, anchoring their minds in the Buddha's eternal Oneness.

Lamayuru Monastery

From my second floor window I observed the monks in the courtyard below. Young ones darted about while the meditative silence of senior lamas was preserved in less accessible parts of the complex. Others tended to shrines or were involved in renovation. Above the main building, compartments without windows had been dug out of the hillside. Monks lived in total isolation in this area. Each cell had a wood door with a slot in it, so food could be passed to the inmates. We were told that these advanced monks were observing silence. They started with three weeks of isolation and, if that went well, increased their seclusion to three months. Those who found the routine to their liking continued for three years. The reclusive monks occupying the cells were guaranteed success in observing the four virtues of a Buddhist: speaking truth, never speaking offensively, never engaging in frivolous conversation, and never defaming others.

The silent section reminded me of the story about the monk who was allowed to speak just two words a year. After the first year, the lama came out of his cell, and said, "Room cold." When another year passed, he said. "Bed hard." After the third year, he went to the head lama, and said, "I'm leaving." When the head lama heard this, he replied, "Good, you've done nothing but complain since you got here." I had no complaints about either bed or temperature, but the hilltop monastery would test even the strongest monk in winter when venturing outdoors would be impossible.

The self-imposed silence of the monks would bring them nirvana one day, but somehow the vigil didn't strike me as the Middle Way. It seemed fitting that Lamayuru should have a row of austere cells with invisible inmates, for the monastery still accepts criminals into its flock. But the monks feel secure on their craggy perch where they are guarded by an eleven-headed Chenrezi (Buddha of Compassion), who has a thousand eyes, making it extremely difficult to pinch something of value without being noticed.

Inside their place of gathering, the senior lamas began a chant to bring a good harvest for the village folk under their care. The deep, resonant chanting went on at such an even cadence that I had little choice but to fall inward and soon I was responding to the chorus of voices that set a frequency in motion that spread far beyond the monastery walls. I loved these keepers of harmony; simple monks who chanted, drummed, and rang bells for days at a time. When the morning ritual was complete, their round faces looked up from their scriptures and I saw the fullness of many benevolent moons in their expressions, their balanced hearts and minds ever ready to serve. These were peaceful warriors and had been for lifetimes.

Buddhist Culture

The three jewels of Buddhism are Teacher, Teaching, and Community: the Buddha, the Dharma, and the Sangha, respectively. The Sangha, or community, dominates life in Ladakh. Tibetan Buddhism is more a way of life than religions in the west, and at the heart of the Tibetan community is the monastery. The community relies on the lamas for guidance in matters of importance. Senior lamas are consulted in practical as well as spiritual affairs. Performing a function not unlike a civil court judge, the lamas settle disagreements and domestic disputes. The monastery also functions as a focal point for seasonal festivals when monks don colorful costumes and animated masks to enact plays conveying religious themes, not unlike the passion plays of medieval Europe. Skits and dances featuring monks wearing grotesque masks satirize undesirable human qualities stemming from the ego. Few aspects of Ladakhi life are not connected to religion.

The interdependence of life in the Tibetan culture is the result of Buddhist tradition that teaches that each individual, whether human, animal, or plant, is part of the One. This belief is reflected in day-to-day Ladakhi life, which places greater emphasis on the collective than on the individual, a principle that is reversed in most 'developed' societies where individual rights and personal achievements are given precedence.

Polyandry, the principle of a woman having more than one husband, would never work in the west. The western male would bridle at the thought of polyandry, but its practice was commonplace in Ladakhi culture for centuries and still exists in remote regions to this day. The practice of two or three brothers sharing a wife was an effective way of keeping ancestral properties within the family. All offspring of a polyandrous arrangement were considered the children of the oldest brother. Indian law has made polyandry illegal, which has reduced the practice today.

Alchi was our next stop. Alchi is nestled against a river, hidden at the back of a gentle valley and so it escaped the savagery of Muslim armies. An odd collection of stupas housed thousand year-old murals and woodcarvings portraying the Buddha's celestial realms. Weightless clouds, tumbling brooks, fire breathing dragons, floating monks, gods granting boons; all played a role in the soul's journey. The open window in my room framed a blooming mustard field. As the sun set, the Stok range was cast in lavender in the distance. I soaked up the pastoral scene while keeping an eye on an amusing drama that reenacted itself throughout the day.

A slow moving yak grazed on the blossoms; her blackness seemed out of place among the delicate yellow buds that blanketed the field. The wooly beast chewed and chewed, but never had her fill. An old woman, also attired in black, threw stones and hissed whenever she caught the yak on her garden. The woman's antics had little effect on the beast, so she resorted to swatting the beast on the rear with a stick to preserve her crop. I imagined the droll routine to be like a long running soap opera; both creatures were too stubborn to submit to the wishes of the other.

The apricots near Alchi were sumptuous and abundant. I was convinced they were the best in Ladakh. At one heavily laden tree, I filled a bag with fruit without asking permission from its owner. The fact that the ground beneath the tree was covered with freshly fallen apricots led me to believe that the owner didn't have much interest in the harvest. But just as my bag reached full, an old man in a gonda hat came out of his house to observe my boldness, catching me standing on a boundary wall with a bag of his plump apricots. The old fellow greeted me with a cheery "Jhuley," and I greeted him back. I offered him something for the fruit, but he had not come to investigate, but to invite me inside for a round of tea. I was touched by his kindness. If good will ruled the world, these simple Tibetans would be kings, I thought.

The Ladakhi Women's Festival was underway when we arrived back in Leh, and the Jigmet daughters invited us to attend as their guests. Along with their cousin, a tall, striking young woman whose mother was the president of the women's society, we spent the afternoon sampling Tibetan delicacies at the tented stalls. It seemed most of the treats were derived from some aspect of the apricot: juice, oil, pit, and dried fruit. After the crafts exhibition, the women performed a traditional Tibetan folk dance. The queen of Ladakh was the guest of honor, and at her side was a Swedish author who had written an authoritative book on Ladakhi culture. Sporting colored stove pipe hats with red bat-winged brims, richly embroidered silk capes, turquoise and silver jewelry, and white sashes tied at the waist, the costumed women performed a meticulous, trance-inducing dance, moving in a mandala at a pace only slightly faster than the second hand of a pocket watch. Their hands gestured thoughtfully; their movements were disciplined and introspective. The dance was as restrained as the Oracle's was flamboyant. The subdued pageant calmed the senses and awakened the inner mind rather than exciting it. The women's performance captured the essence of their ancient culture, which, after all, should be what a folk dance strives to achieve. Having witnessed their meditative performance, I concluded that Ladakh was a land of old souls that had been returning to this high plateau for many lifetimes.

Buddha's Message

The Buddha's eightfold path consists of right understanding, right thought, right speech, right action, right livelihood, right effort, right mindfulness, and right concentration. I found each aspect of the eightfold path as abundant as the apricot in this land. To find a religion so positively reflected in a culture was unheard of and I felt uniquely enriched by a people seamlessly stitched together by spiritual values and a palpable sense of humility. One of the great lessons of Ladakhi culture is the utter absence of ego and the supportive behavior that results from that endearing attribute.

Sunlight flooded the room the morning of our departure. Our neighbor was already weeding her garden and pulling root vegetables when Mr. Jigmet came to take us to the airport. The hospitable Tibetans called to mind the story of Buddha's passing. The Master gathered his disciples together one last time, sitting silently in their midst. He held a simple flower in his hand, but didn't speak. Of the hundreds of monks present, only one understood the Buddha's subtle message, and he was chosen as the Master's successor. The Buddha's message was the flower itself, which shares its fragrance and beauty for all to enjoy by simply being what it is. Being is more profound than doing. That seemed to be Ladakh's message. Just Be (happy)!

The plane angled above and then beyond the Indus valley. The sea of snowcapped peaks appeared again. We had glimpsed Ladakh, but another visit would be needed to savor this ancient culture. A return trip, we decided, would take us to a remote valley where the monks were said to practice levitation. Maybe we would even explore far-flung Zanskar, a desolate region where the Middle Way might not be an option. We wanted to experience the culture when it was collectively turned to the expanse within while the snow piled up outside. The vast simplicity of Ladakh supported the search for the inner Buddha; in fact, it demanded it.

TWENTY NINE

The Car Festival By The Sea

Deep in the sea are riches beyond compare
But if you seek safety, it is on the shore.

—*Sufi Mystic Saadi*

A big creamy cow with spiraling horns stood in our path, oblivious to our honks as she chewed her cud. Our driver wanted to move on, but the bovine had other ideas. Growing impatient, the driver signaled to a villager by the road, who came over to the car. In response to everything our driver said, the villager wagged his head from side to side, saying, "Ji Ji." I had never seen such a loosely connected head; its motion reminded me of a Chinese doll. Everyone used the gesture in conversation, and from time to time I found myself wiggling my head too. The gesture meant almost anything: yes, no, maybe, and half the time I wasn't sure how to interpret it, but it was pure Indian.

The village man nudged the cow and it moved ever so slowly out of the way. We were on our way again, heading to the temple town of Puri on the coast of Orissa. We were at the opposite end of India, and the climate and culture of Orissa was as different from Ladakh's high Tibetan plateau as Arkansas is from the Arctic Circle. On our journey to the Bay of Bengal, we passed through a string of small villages. As we entered each village, our progress slowed to a crawl to avoid the mayhem in our path. Sharing the road with us were sleeping dogs, boys playing, peasants winnowing grain, men in conversation, and even a band of furry pigs rummaging about with their snouts to the ground. Any one of the motley characters was likely to step in front of us, oblivious to any danger, as if the road were their private property. The scene was a typical Indian village.

One after another we passed clusters of one-room mud and thatch huts with a cow or two tethered outside. The tidy abodes hid from the sun beneath palm groves that provided easy access to building materials whenever roof repairs were in order. To have a pukha, or paved road, was a symbol of status, for it showed the state politicians cared about the village; it was also a feather in the cap of the village panchayat (council of elders). But more importantly, a paved road didn't turn into a quagmire during monsoon.

Traffic lights have no place in the Indian village, nor would they be obeyed even if there was reliable electricity to operate them. The roadside was where men, boys, and dogs loitered, but the village bore well was the gathering place for women and their daughters. One by one they filled their earthen pots and copper vessels before returning home with containers precariously balanced on their heads. With perfect posture, they moved deliberately along the trails before disappearing through low doorways.

Jaganath Puri

After many stops at the villages, we arrived in Puri, one of Hinduism's four dhamas (places of divine power). A dhama is a place permeated with divine radiance, the result of unusually concentrated spiritual energy. Puri's famous Jaganath Temple is said to be the place where the last rites for Lord Krishna were performed, and is a sacred spot for Hindus like Mecca for Muslims, Jerusalem for Christians and Muslims, and Bodh Gaya for Buddhists. The Jaganath Temple is also where Issa studied with the Brahmin priests and practiced yogic techniques. Later he taught and healed the low caste shudras who were not allowed inside the temple. According to the Tibetan text, the Jaganath priests ultimately rejected Issa for helping the untouchables, an act they deemed impure.

Puri's beach was bustling. Bengali families ambled about licking ice cream cones, and a group of boys played cricket. India's favorite pastime bears some resemblance to American baseball, and when one of the boys offered me a turn at bat I readied myself for the pitch. Having never swung a cricket bat, it seemed reasonable to take a cut at the ball the way I had in sandlot baseball as a kid. The boy delivered his pitch with a windmill motion and I swung hard, striking the ball solidly. The sensation of bat and ball colliding sent an adolescent thrill through my body, one I knew all too well. The ball sailed toward the rolling surf and the boy standing behind me gasped for fear that it would disappear into the sea. But a middle-aged couple near the water stepped into the path of the speeding ball, and it slammed into the woman's solar plexus. Her pain matched my vexation; I had no idea how the equipment would respond to a baseball swing. I knew the sting of the ball hurt—tennis balls had struck me many times—so I waved apologetically to her as a fielder retrieved the ball at her feet. It was my last at bat on Puri's beach, but not my last on the sub-continent.

I thanked the boys for the turn at bat, and went in search of a coconut vendor. Coconut water was always a safe and healthy drink. As I returned to the beach, the path took me through a vacant lot enclosed by crumbling walls on three sides. Passing through the property, I noticed some smoldering piles of ash and a small group of men sitting away from the dying fires. As I surveyed the scene, it dawned on me that I had entered a smashan, a Hindu cremation ground. The dhoti-clad men were doms, untouchables that performed the cremation rituals. One of the priests spotted me and gestured for me to join them. As I approached the men, I noticed a half empty bottle of brown liquid, a type of home brewed liquor called bangla. With the wildness of intoxication in his eyes, the dom waved the bottle at me. He wanted me to have some. Bangla is made from fermented animal entrails and the thought of anyone drinking it by choice seemed inconceivable to me. I declined, but asked if any of the men were Aghoras, the ascetic yogis who meditate in smashans and eat rice from bowls fashioned out of human skulls. "I good Aghora," the drunken man boasted, waving the bottle at me again. "Yes, I'm sure you are," I replied insincerely.

It wasn't the liquor that chased me off as much as the charred remains of the fires. I was no Aghora, and the cremation ground was not my kind of place. Puri, being a holy city, had ordinances banning alcohol, but the outcaste doms paid little attention to laws. After reaching the beach, I dove into the surf for an informal cleansing in case I had inadvertently disturbed the inhabitants of the smashan.

In a blaze of fiery coral, Surya slipped behind a palm grove. The sunset beach was calm, noticeably more serene than it had been just moments earlier. According to Indian scriptures, dawn and dusk are the best times for meditation. Nature's sandhya (point of transition) occurs daily at sunrise and sunset. The purpose of meditation is to enter nature's gateway within, and the yogis knew how to cross the threshold to the transcendent by closing their eyes during the transitions from night to day and day to night. I intended to do the same. The breeze tossed off the ocean was decidedly cooler with the onset of evening. As I sat secluded among the palms, away from meddling vendors and curious tourists, the waves washed over my awareness one by one, and soon the sandcastles of my mind dissolved. A clean canvas remained, and in that infinity of space, new creations emerged from the sands of primordial matter as I play-acted the

Creator the way a child fashions fantasies with its hands on a sun-drenched beach. With the doors to outer realities sealed, an inner portal opened, and I found myself shaping destiny from the molten sands of quantum consciousness like a potter shaping moist clay at his wheel. The sound of the sea itself was a suitable mantra, which, along with the fading light, assisted me as I dissolved into deep bliss.

Will Disappears

We had come to Orissa to witness the Jaganath Rath Yatra that drew 700,000 to the beach town for two weeks of worship and celebration. Puri's annual car festival is one of India's more colorful pageants. We selected our hotel carefully to be near the isolated beaches and clean water north of town. It was monsoon season and a steady rain fell from a low ceiling of gray. Having been on the dusty Deccan plateau for seven months without beach access, we ignored the drizzle and dreary sky, and headed for the ocean. Indians rarely swim even on calm days, so the resort's beach became our private playground. Signs along the trail warned of dangerous currents, but Will's childhood on the Gulf of Mexico and my preteen years in competitive swimming caused us to ignore the signs as we plunged headlong into the foaming surf.

The turbulent current kneaded my body like a massage. The ocean swirled and swelled under the spell of a strong wind that blew waves sideways along the shoreline. Will is a lap swimmer, but I am a corker. A corker is a bobber, one who rides waves like a block of driftwood, weightless and free, surrendering to the whims of the sea. Will challenged the ocean by cutting through the waves and against the current, his size fourteen feet propelling him effortlessly through the water. Beneath the misting blue-black sky, Will looked like a white whale in the swells. He plunged into his watery recreation passionately while I buoyed about, rising and falling with the surf. Corking is a type of meditation for the body, a liquid therapy that rejuvenates. The key to corking is surrender. There's no mission to go here or dive there; one just lets go in nature's ultimate mineral bath, allowing the body to respond like the child it wants to be.

Will, whether hiking in the Himalaya, scrambling over Mogul ruins, or shopping in a local bazaar, always outlasted me, so it was no surprise that I was the first one out of the water. Will had this knack for gliding through the water with the ease of a great aquatic creature. But when I scanned the choppy waters, the Texan was nowhere in sight. No head bobbed or arms flailed as I searched the coastline. I wasn't worried, but I hoped he would appear soon. Fifteen minutes passed, and still there was no sign of him. My mind began entertaining the possibility that we had lost Will. It was a thought I rejected, knowing my friend was a fine swimmer, but even the best swimmers can find trouble in turbulent waters. The sign we had passed on the trail with a large X painted over the symbol of a swimmer now haunted me, and I had given up searching the water when I caught a glimpse of a tiny form on the beach in the distance. Could it be Will? Had the current carried him so far away?

As I watched the figure grow in size from a speck on the horizon to an outline of a man, I recognized Will's walk. His huge feet pointed out like a penguin as they pounded the wet sand, heels first. But Will's body was anything but a penguin's. His lumbering gait and overall size looked like a Himalayan bear out for a stroll on the strand. Like the Lone Star state he hailed from, Will was extra large from head to toe. It was a long time before his untamed smile came into focus, but it was a broad one and I was glad to see it. Nothing made Will happier than the sea. Although the current had carried him far up the beach, he had been oblivious to any danger, and probably there was none.

Will Fox And Small Girl

A fine mist filled the air as we walked on the sand enjoying cool, moist air for the first time in months. Our beach was hidden from the resort by a stand of trees. The skies now threatened more than mist, but afternoon showers were expected during monsoon. Two pencil thin boys rummaged about looking for objects on the beach; Indian beachcombers I mused. One tried halfheartedly to sell us some small shells that were as plentiful as sand on the beach. Will was giddy from his latest aquatic adventure. Even the best hotel swimming pool was too tame for his care-free spirit. Seeing Will swim laps at a Hyderabad hotel was like watching Shamu the whale in his Sea World habitat. He needed the entire Indian Ocean; a pool amounted to a watery prison for Will.

The Parade

The Puri car festival attracts Krishna devotees from all over the country who come to view the colorful spectacle on Grand Road, which cuts a straight and broad swath through the heart of town. Pilgrims filed along the narrow walkways leading to the Jaganath Temple the way football fans converge on stadiums across America for a homecoming game. A festive mood was brewing by the time Will and I arrived at the parade route. The street was already packed with hundreds of thousands of onlookers. As more and more people poured out of the alleyways, a juggernaut formed. The crushing force of the crowd pressed us tighter and tighter together, and a shift in one section of the multitude caused a reaction thirty yards away.

Will and I stood a head taller than the severely compressed crowd. Wild-eyed young men jostled one another, shifting entire sections of the crowd in the process. The elderly couple near us had anxious looks on their faces. After considerable effort we reached an area cordoned off for ashrams. Groups of Krishna devotees stood beneath large banners with pic-tures of their gurus painted in bright colors. We slipped under the ropes and stood in the corner of their section. Near us, a group of girls danced like gopis in a Vrindavan forest. Holding hands, they circled round and round as they sang, oblivious to the crush of humanity on the street. Several of the kumaris had already slipped into a bhava of prema (state of divine love). The innocent girls moved gracefully about singing to Lord Krishna as they danced. A security guard soon noticed us and asked us to stand outside the roped area. We agreed to move, but when he walked away, we stayed inside the protected area where we had an excellent view of the pageant, but more important, space to breathe.

One beautiful Indian girl danced alone. Her white skirt fluttered as she spun about, unconscious of her surroundings. She moved silently, her feet barely touching the ground. Her docile brown eyes were clear, not unlike a fawn peering out from a stand of conifers. There was little doubt that the innocent one danced in ecstatic devotion for her beloved Krishna as she spun round and round, arms extended. Her head was thrown back from time to time as she gazed longingly into the sapphire sky. I had been to Vrindavan and witnessed the evenings of song and dance in the ashram courtyards, but the mood at the Rath Yatra (car festival) was exceptional, exceeding anything I had seen in Krishna's childhood village.

At the far end of Grand Road, outside the temple entrance, three enormous cars (raths) waited for the parade to begin. The forty foot-tall vehicles looked like oversized floats, but their occupants bore little resemblance to a homecoming queen and her court. The largest car rested on sixteen wooden wheels, each measuring seven feet in diameter. This was Lord Jaganath's (another name for Krishna) chariot, and it was wrapped in bright yellow cloth. The other two chariots were only slightly smaller; they were the conveyances of Jaganath's brother and sister, Balaram and Subhadra. The three cars had been fashioned from a thousand logs by a hundred carpenters who worked for two months on the vehicles. 2,000 meters of bright blue and yellow cloth decorated the cars. A pair of eight inch-thick ropes were attached to each cart. As the procession readied itself, the King of Puri climbed onto the cars to touch the feet of the gods, and then conches and drums sounded. The parade was about to begin. A teeming mass of 4,000 men tugged on ropes attached to the cars. At first it appeared to be a tug of war between the men and their gods, but when the massive cars moved, the multitude on the street cheered wildly, calling out the name of their beloved Jaganath Krishna. Balconies and rooftops were packed three deep, but the main body of the crowd shared our vantage point from the street.

As the men pulled the enormous cars, the crowd shifted, causing a ripple to pass through the throng, further compressing the onlookers. But no one seemed to mind; the holy procession was officially underway. The car festival hasn't always been without accident, but the organizers made every effort to prevent mishap. The vast majority of the crowd was calm and reverent; they had come for Lord Jaganath's darshan.

The Rath Yatra celebrates the two-mile journey of the three youthful gods to their summerhouse outside the city. The procession moved at a snail's pace and made frequent stops. When it reached the gopi dancers, Krishna's chariot paused long enough so that he could enjoy the ecstatic dancing of his devotees. It was our best opportunity to view Lord Jaganath, since westerners are forbidden inside the temple. We enjoyed his darshan although I was too self-conscious to join in the dancing.

India has as many festivals as days in the year and most are tributes to the gods. Jaganath and his siblings passed us seated high above the teeming masses. It was deeply satisfying to have a glimpse of the divine trio as they were pulled along at the pace of a minute hand by a team of bare-chested men who were engaged in a perpetual tug of war with the massive wood and cloth chariots. It was time to plunge into the ocean again, and Will planned to swim in deeper waters, while I would be content to cork in the waves.

Bhakti And Divine Love

The ecstatic expression on the young Hari Krishna girl's face stayed with me as I walked the beach. I had read sage Narada's Bhakti Sutras and knew about the exalted moods of Ramakrishna, but bhakti had never been a formal part of my spiritual training. "Bhakti is the easiest of the yogas," claimed Narada, friend and devotee of Lord Krishna. I believed that to be true for an egoless Indian girl inclined toward devotional surrender, but how effective would it be for westerners trained since childhood to favor the intellect? The training in the west has taught us to trust the mind over the heart, to celebrate ego over humility, and to pursue material goals rather than spiritual ones. Although western traditions are slowly beginning to honor the heart, the training from parents, teachers, coaches, leaders, and society in general are not easily reversed. I admired the innocent girl, whose devotion must have been nurtured by loving parents.

Maharishi was once asked why so few western students achieve spiritual heights. "Because you were not loved properly as children," he replied. Stress has overshadowed the ability to nurture and be nurtured within the family, the natural place for love to flow. To draw on Divine Love, which is of limitless supply, one simply needs to open the tap, to flip on the switch.

According to Narada, one can study religious scriptures and become learned, but the process doesn't necessarily bring one closer to God, because God's sphere is the realm of the soul, and logic, analysis, or scientific investigation simply aren't tools for accessing the soul. The intellect is not an effective instrument for exploring the realm of the spirit. Divine presence must unfold within the heart, and the guidance of a master is needed to nurture that process. The scriptures provide guidelines for spiritual living. The Bible, Upanishads, and the Tao give tantalizing descriptions of the 'Kingdom of Heaven,' but spiritual awakening occurs in the inner domain of the heart, and not in a book.

It takes courage to go within, because it often means swimming against the current. Society flows in a material direction. Spiritual life is a personal and sometimes lonely journey, one the Gnostics, medieval monks, Buddhist lamas, and yogis understood. Organized religion can't bestow spiritual experience any more than a well-written book can, although both can shed light on the path through the accounts of those who know the way. Study of the scriptures can even be counterproductive when one believes he has arrived at the goal through intellectual study alone. Without deep inner experience, Mohammed likened the study of scriptures to an ass carrying a load of books on its back. It becomes a burden.

Ramakrishna preached "You cannot make any dent with nails on a rock, howsoever you hammer on it. The nail will break. Similarly, there is no use in trying to teach a man about God if he is steeped in worldliness." We need to charter a new course, and can't afford to let our responsibilities suffocate our spirit. Soccer games, sales quotas, and mortgage payments go on, but they needn't impede our spiritual progress. Narada advised dedicating all activities, secular as well as sacred, to God.

One who practices bhakti (devotion to God), according to Narada, is one whose whole soul goes toward God, which means giving up every other refuge and taking refuge in God. To many, this sounds hopelessly idealistic. But no benefit comes from worrying about or fearing anything in life for negative emotion places new obstacles between our spiritual goals and us. I never played a good tennis match when I worried about the outcome. My triumphant moments came when my mind was unfettered and intuitive, and not all of those moments resulted in victory. Athletes strive to reach the zone by surrendering to their natural athleticism while maintaining high levels of inner alertness. Concern for the outcome of a match rarely enters a mature athlete's mind because he is totally immersed in the present moment and the principle holds true in every area of life. As a coach I used to tell my pupils, "Tennis tournaments are won one point at a time."

It takes courage and commitment to let go of our fears, but letting go is a significant step in the right direction. The girl who danced in ecstasy could not have whirled about with an anxious heart, but she felt free to express her love in a simple and direct way. Ramakrishna described a perfected soul this way, "Sometimes he will act like a five year-old child, or he may seem intoxicated or mad. Or he may remain silent and motionless. He is not bound by any law or code, but he does nothing immoral and unethical. His actions are selfless without trying to be selfless, just as a flower emits its fragrance."

Letting go of the fear associated with a negative outcome like debt or conflict is easier when one is immersed in the positive possibilities in life. The mind, until it attains an enlightened state, constantly searches for objects in the outer world to satisfy it like a monkey searching for a banana. We need to culture the habit of resting the attention in the lap of prema, divine love. With time and sincere effort, meditation will open a door, allowing inexpressible bliss to find its way into the heart. At first, a trickle of nectar comes, but with time, the floodgates will open and the soul will soar. Divine Love requires no object of devotion. No beach bungalow or club championship or year-end bonus affects prema. Divine Love is self-sufficient and yet it shares itself with family and community. Whatever the activity, whether it's shoveling snow in January or mowing the lawn in July, any action is joyful with prema in the heart. My Himalayan Master had said, "Love is the Divine on earth. It will not lead you astray. The heart is the gateway to heaven, it bypasses ego."

Lord Krishna said, 'cravings torment the heart,' but those cravings evaporate when the heart is filled with self-sustaining love. The sages council, 'Be drunk with the wine of Divine Love.' That is ultimately the only offering worthy of the temple of the heart. If one is intoxicated with Divine Love, relationships will take care of themselves because the intoxication is contagious. The light of prema easily dispels the shadow of loneliness. People are naturally drawn to those whose hearts are full. As the Himalayan Master said, "We have been like a man crawling in the dessert looking for water when there is more prema available than oxygen in this world." Investing time culturing the inner heart through meditation and service is a commitment worth making for Divine Love is a magnet that will attract the hearts of all the way Krishna did.

Dissolving The Ego

In the West, the ego is competitive. It revels in a Saturday golf game, a political debate, and even a disagreement at home. Ego is, without rival, the greatest obstacle to Divine Love. Ego is the off position on a light switch. It works in the shadows where light can't expose it. The ego gratifies itself, loves only itself, and can't tolerate anyone who contradicts it. Collective ego is the cause of war and suffering among humanity. Religious ego, political ego, and personal ego; all are divisive facades that divide and conquer rather than cooperate and team build.

The male ego is the principle culprit, although women also enjoy playing the power game. Vanity takes many forms, but it is an empty existence, like a dry reed standing in water, unable to nourish itself. The ego never brings happiness, because its playing field is external. In fact, the ego is threatened by inner development. When one begins the journey toward inner discovery, the ego will come up with plenty of arguments against it, like, 'I have more important things to do today,' or 'It's selfish of me to take time away from the family to meditate.' The ego would not like to give up its seat of power in the subconscious mind, which meditation forces it to relinquish over time. The ego likes a duel, whereas love prefers a duet.

If there is one field where the ego shouldn't take root, it is religion. Ironically, organized religion has become a breeding ground for the ego. Muslims fight with Christians, Hindus dislike Muslims, and Baptists feel contempt for Catholics. Why do religions seem to bring out the worst in us? People are unable to live harmoniously in the world because of religious differences and the root cause is ego, the belief that my faith is superior to my neighbors.

Swami Ramakrishna, who practiced each of the major religions during his life, summarized religious ego this way: "Every man assumes that his clock alone tells correct time. Christians claim to possess exclusive truth…Hindus insist that their sect, no matter how small and insignificant, expresses the ultimate position. Devout Muslims maintain that the Koran supersedes all others. The entire world is being driven insane by this single phrase: 'My religion alone is true.'" Some religionists even pray for the destruction of the world, believing that their faith will lift them into rapturous states during a global holocaust, so they can watch their non-believing brethren suffer. Vedic scriptures warn that ego poisons that which is nearest and dearest. One of the greatest assets on the spiritual path is discernment, the ability to see past the illusions created by the ego.

The sage Narada wrote, "God dislikes egotism and loves humility." It takes humility to dance in front of a half million people, especially when you're dancing alone. The saints of the world, East and West: St. Francis of Assisi, Mother Theresa, Ananda Mayi Ma, St. Bernadette, Amma, and Ramakrishna to name a few, drowned their egos in the ocean of love, and when they surfaced, they identified with the ocean, and not the individuality. It is said that Ananda Mayi Ma never even knew ego. From birth, she identified entirely with the universal Self. Humility is a trait that is honored in the East more than the West, but both sides of the globe are making progress with each other's help.

Divine Love is the best antidote for the ego because it transforms rather than confronts. How does Divine Love differ from the love one has for their family, career, or home? Divine Love recognizes that the soul of another is the same as one's own, that there is ultimately no difference between my soul and my neighbor's, no difference between a Muslim's soul and a Christian's, although many would dispute this. The essence of my child, favorite tree, or pet is the same as my own essence. We are all One. For many this truth is difficult, because it's foreign to the intellect, which differentiates. On the other hand, it's natural for the heart to understand, because it unifies. We can be confident we're moving in the direction of Divine Love when the well being of another is as important to us as our own happiness.

Windows Of The Soul

The eyes narrate the story of the soul. The dancing girl's skyward gaze and Will's feral look as he climbed out of the ocean told me that each had entered, however briefly, the unbounded realm of the Divine. I had seen the same look of wonder on the faces of pilgrims as Krishna's chariot rolled by. Before leaving Puri, we passed the parade site where a half million people had sung, cheered, and danced the previous day. The empty street was now littered with sandals. At first, I thought the pilgrims had removed their chappals out of respect for the gods, but on closer examination, I realized these were sandals that had been lost during the juggernaut that had crushed us the previous day. Our visit to the car festival by the sea had immersed us in celebration and sea, and the purifying effects of the parade of deities and procession of ocean waves had confirmed that the Self unifies one and all.

THIRTY

A Monk's Life In The Himalaya

In a hundred ages I could not tell thee of the glories of the Himalaya. As the dew is dried by the morning Sun, so are the sins of mankind by the sight of the Himalaya.

—*Skanda Purana*

An Indian Education

Our meditation program had been accepted as the leading human development program in the country. India's Fortune 100 companies had embraced it with satisfying results. We had conducted courses in every major city and state. In the process, I had lived in communities where Hindi, Tamil, Bengali, Telegu, Gujarati, and Urdu were spoken, and yet I couldn't speak any of them well. Although my failure to master the local languages was a disappointment, our managers' flawless English combined with the changing dialects on the street left me with bits of this and that, but nothing much of anything.

If there was one language I wanted to learn while in India, it was the language of the heart, which Indians communicated so well. I did my best to assimilate the gift available to all who visited the culture. The subtle nuance of gesture, both head and hand, held more meaning than any Hindi dictionary, for it conveyed feeling. It's been said that the best way to learn a language is to live in the culture where it's spoken. Having lived in India for seven years, I found that a willing heart was the only prerequisite for learning. The language relied on feeling and intuition more than words, and, although I didn't always understand what was said verbally, I often received messages as if telepathically. Perhaps the language of the heart was India's strength, and also the reason her people were childish in some ways, for Indians, like Italians, are heart people.

Ours had been an extraordinary assignment, one that began on a tourist visa, and ended up sweeping us along like the swift current of a Himalayan stream. Maharishi had predicted it from the outset. "You will be very busy," he had said. "I am sending westerners because Indians enjoy having their song sung by someone else, and because Indians admire American management." It had been a pleasure singing India's song; its melody was rich, its rhythm strong and clear.

But incessant travel and city living had exacted their toll despite the thoughtfulness we found in the Indian household. Whether the guests of an industrialist family or poor villagers, we were treated like family wherever we went. Indians have taken to heart their cultural saying 'The guest is God.'

It was a tossup whether Delhi's thoughtless government bureaucrats or its summer heat got my vote for the least agreeable aspect of Indian life, but I had learned important lessons from each. But perhaps my greatest lesson was the realization that the Indian clock kept time differently than the rest of the world. The ubiquitous 'eck minute' (one minute) really meant sometime soon, and the expression 'kal' somehow meant both yesterday and tomorrow. These vagaries gradually reshaped my concept of time until I was left with nothing but the present moment. Indians will not be hurried unless they are standing in line at the post office or stuck in traffic, in which case impatience easily overtakes them. It took commitment to adapt to 'Indian Standard Time,' but once I did, life was simpler. Although I stopped wearing a watch, I never arrived late for an appointment, and more importantly, I didn't mind when others did.

Western society and its scientific traditions train the mind to think in linear ways, to rely on verifiable analysis rather than drawing conclusions from intuition or direct cognition. Having experienced the reliability of intuition on numerous occasions, I learned to trust those inner messages, and they rarely let me down. When minor health problems needed attention, I had thorough examinations from western-trained doctors. They found nothing wrong, but when I consulted a vaidya like Dr. Triguna or Dr. Raju, I learned immediately what the problem was and received effective treatment with herbal preparations. The same was true with Vedic astrology. Useful insights were gained that no amount of analysis could match.

Linear thinking is a bit like a game of dominos. When the first block of wood is toppled over, it knocks over the second block, which in turn knocks over the third and so on, until all the pieces have fallen. Indian culture discards linear thinking as too superficial, believing the universe doesn't function that way. The Vedic tradition teaches that the mind itself creates its own universe, that each of us are co-creators, not just observers of Creation. The Vedic rishis teach that all of life is interconnected and that the distinction between living beings and non-living matter is a flawed concept; that all matter is teeming with life, be it a rock or a rock star. Having grown up with these beliefs, it's no surprise that Indians have a greater openness and receptivity to phenomena like miracles and supernormal powers.

There is much lore in Indian culture about miraculous events, so many accounts of yogis appearing in two places at once or floating in the air in a gymnasium that the unexplainable has seeped into and been accepted by the collective psyche of the culture. Stories of Ananda Mayi Ma healing a broken leg or Trailanga Swami floating on the Ganges, Ganesh drinking milk in a Hindu temple or a rock levitating at a Sufi shrine. These are accepted occurrences in India and they have helped people know that anything is indeed possible.

My own mind morphed almost daily in India. Whether in meditation or on the street, I encountered the remarkable so often that I accepted it as normal. How had my parents' names appeared on a palm leaf from south India and how did Dr. Triguna know I had been taking cold showers simply by taking my pulse? How had the stranger predicted Purari's fatal accident as well as prescribing an antidote and how did Gola Baba heal people by striking them on the back? The word normal takes on new meaning in India. Why did certain Hindu gods have eight arms or Siva's son have the head of an elephant? Daily life and spiritual life blended together in India, ultimately becoming one and the same.

The sages of ancient India explained these seemingly unfathomable events in clear terms because they understood the power of the mind, the infinite influence of consciousness. They understood that everything in the cosmos is seamlessly connected and that the power that propels Creation is at each person's finger tip. Modern science, in the process of dissecting physical reality, has cut the seamless fabric of our psyches, damaging our collective unconscious, leading us to the conclusion that we are orphans in an unfeeling world, but the rishis tell us that's not the case, that the universe is holistic and filled with benevolent beings ready to lend a helping hand. It makes all the difference in the world how you view the universe, and equally important, how the universe responds.

According to the cognitions of the rishis, the great golden egg called Hiranyagarba (Creation) is one, and not just a collection of random, disconnected parts. Not only is the great egg of Creation one, but each of us contains that great egg within us. We are the universe. The sages confirm that this truth lies hidden at the deeper levels of the mind, a unity that is not so obvious on the surface as it is at the depth. It is said that when the disciple reaches the threshold of Enlightenment, the Master bestows the final stroke of wisdom, Aham Brahmasmi, I am the Totality.

Hindus believe in a Supreme Being present in every grain of creation, and that their gods reside in the heart, that their daughters are Devi and their sons Krishna. When I asked Pateriya, who had traveled a lot in the west, what he thought the biggest difference between westerners and Indians was, he replied without hesitation, "If you ask a westerner where he lives, he points to his head, but if you ask an Indian, he points to his heart." It was the best answer I'd heard. After living in India for seven years, if I had been asked the same question, I would have also pointed to my heart. As the Kerala saint Amma once said, "The intellect cuts things, but the heart sews them together."

The Vedic concept of Deity is devoid of a God sitting in judgment on a throne far removed from his creation. For Indians, Divinity dwells everywhere, even in a car. One day a new Ambassador was parked in front of our guesthouse. As we climbed into the car, Anil was making offerings of rice and flowers on the hood of the vehicle. When I asked Anil why he was performing puja to the car, he wagged his head, and said, "Bhagavan (God) is also in car." In order to experience the depth, richness, and profundity of India's soul, I let go of old ways of thinking and embraced a rich, multifaceted reality.

The Indian post office was one of the better places to shed the western mindset. In the West, customers form orderly lines at the supermarket, bank, or post office, but not in India. Every time I went to the post office a half dozen hands shoved unstamped mail at the window to my right and left. It mattered little that it was my turn at the window. Lines don't work in India. They're too orderly.

In India I learned that the world is my family. Whenever I returned to the States to visit family, I was struck by the chasm that existed between India's poverty and America's affluence. I spent my holidays experiencing mild culture shock. Where were all the people? Parked in the driveways of every home in my parent's upper middle class neighborhood were two and sometimes three shining vehicles; the cost of each could feed an Indian village for months. But I didn't find this fact upsetting. After all, Americans are exceptionally hard working, leading the way in innovation and economic development for the entire world. I was uncomfortable with how much Americans took their affluence for granted and was uneasy about the fact that we spend more on golf vacations to Florida each year than the Gross National Product of most Southeast Asian countries.

A Spiritual Dream Comes True

On Christmas Day the wish I had made at countless altars came true. I had received instructions to have a full medical checkup without delay. The email had been sent and resent to ensure that it reached me. The message was an invitation to move to a remote part of the Himalaya. I was ready to retire from corporate boardrooms, PowerPoint presentations, power lunches, and Indian city life. The Indian adventure had exceeded all expectations, but now it was time to take a long, deep look at the Self in the seclusion of the Himalaya. I readily agreed to every point on the application, which included foregoing visits to the States.

Forty-eight hours later, wearing a gloomy expression he couldn't mask, Will put a garland around my neck as I climbed into a taxi that headed for the airport. It was a cheerless moment for both of us. We had grown close; brothers living, working, and traveling agreeably. We had been inseparable, relying on each other as much in the corporate classroom as on adventures to the border of Tibet. Will had also applied to the Himalayan ashram, but his application waited for a room to open.

It had been only a few weeks since Pundit Rao, a respected Hyderabad astrologer, had said, "You will come and go to the Himalayan ashram, but nothing permanent." His prediction had left me dissatisfied. I had been visiting the Himalaya for the past seven years and with each visit my desire to live there had grown. However, one couldn't take Punditji's predictions lightly for he had proven his genius during a talk at our management institute when he accurately predicted the exact day of the 9/11 attack that would occur two months later.

From all reports, Himalayan living was a spiritual dream come true. A hundred monks from around the world had been ensconced in their reclusive lives there for several years. Once settled into Himalayan ashram life, they didn't leave. I had seen pictures. Many of my friends had long beards, and those with hair never cut it. The smiling monks were an agreeable mix of Moses and reclusive yogi. Judging by the brightness of their eyes, the hermit's life suited them.

Pateriya Family Goodbyes

My last night in civilization was spent with the Pateriyas. It had been over two years since we'd been together, and there was much to catch up on. Pateriya relaxed with me against his cushions and talked about his cows. His favorite, Poonam, was not in her stall when I arrived. With a look of sadness, Pateriya described how Poonam had died the previous year. One of her offspring now provided the family with milk and was being sheltered in an empty room in the house.

The last time I had seen Pateriya, he had performed a homa (fire) offering that ended in the entire house being engulfed in smoke. We had been forced to evacuate the premises or suffocate. It was vintage Pateriya, and he wiggled his head playfully when I reminded him of the incident. Kusum, his oldest daughter, was now married, and her second child, a boy, was almost three months old. As we flipped through the pages of her wedding album, I marveled that the teenager we had taken to Nirula's for ice cream on Sundays was now the mother of two. Her wedding photos captured a beautiful bride ornamented in gold and wearing a scarlet sari. Pateriya still had two daughters to arrange marriages for, but when I asked about his plans for Richa, who was next in line, he seemed impervious. Pateriya was unconcerned about anything, except possibly his beloved cows.

Pateriya's head was shaved to honor the passing of his father, who had died in an accident involving one of the cows. Poonam's calf had gotten loose, and when Grandpa Pateriya caught up with her rope, the headstrong cow ran off, dragging the octogenarian on the ground for a good distance. The kindly old man never recovered. But Indian families are stoic about the arrival and departure of souls, and the family was fueled with fresh optimism by the arrival of their second grandchild. The evening was spent reminiscing five years of friendship. As I departed, the Pateriya family stood inside the gate at the edge of their property, bidding me farewell. The language of the heart conveyed everything. As my Himalayan Master had so aptly put it, "Whichever people you love the most, they are your family." The fence that separated us would soon become an impenetrable fortress of snowcapped peaks.

The road was a familiar and welcome sight. We passed Hardwar, the scene of evening aarti and countless baths in the Ganges, but somehow I didn't feel like stopping for Mataji's blessing and instructed my driver to head straight for the Himalaya. Beyond Rishikesh and the Glass House, we followed the Ganges, passing rustic villages and terraced plots as we distanced ourselves from the dusty north Indian plains. The Ganges, India's river of inspiration, flowed robustly as it twisted through the Valley of the Saints. After a three-hour journey into the mountains, we came to a landmark by the road, and I instructed my driver to stop. A nondescript trail rose over a hill and disappeared into a forest of conifers. Everyone who took that trail vanished for a very long time. I was eager to start on the path leading to my new home.

After finding a porter to carry my trunks, I headed up the trail in the direction of the ashram. Darula Ashram was an hour's hike up the mountain, a bit more for those out of shape. The ample trail was cut in the shadow of a pine forest and ascended over a succession of ridges, passing a shepherds' shelter and terraced farms along the way. It was a magical walk, a fitting end to a long journey. Twice the trail forked, but I stayed with the main route, hoping the decision was the right one. Small shrines appeared along the path, diminutive altars housing obscure gods worshipped by the hill people. Wild flowers had been placed at the base of a goddess whose features had been worn away by weather and the rubbing of hands. I puzzled at the villagers and their compulsion to create shrines when any one the magnificent firs in my midst merited an offering of wild flowers.

A talkative brook tumbled down a steep ravine. Stepping-stones aided my crossing. I stopped to splash the icy water on my face and neck, and caught a glimpse of my reflection, which would soon be changing. Gnarled moru oaks congregated in the ravines near the streams. They were the ascetic grandfathers of Himalayan forests. Further along the trail I came to an antiquated stone aqueduct that was no longer in use. It angled down the mountain from a spring higher up. I rested for a moment on the old structure before starting up a steep section of trail.

As I walked the silence magnified, and I felt the same cathedral-like atmosphere of the redwoods at Muir Woods in northern California where visitors conversed in hushed tones. I was already falling under the benevolent influence of the towering cedar and pine that blocked out all but patches of sunlight. The land itself felt holy. The gentle call of birds, wind, and rushing water carried great distances in the pristine atmosphere. In spots, a misplaced step would have sent me tumbling down the mountain. As the trail angled up a long incline, the ashram came into view above, its ochre buildings flanked by deep green forests. As I climbed the final distance to the monastery, two pack mules carrying milk canisters passed on their way down the mountain, and I leaned against the mountain to let them pass. The mules' owner gestured vaguely as he walked, smoking a bidi. Garhwali people are slightly built, which makes it easy for them to move up and down the steep trails.

At the ashram's front gate, I paused before spinning through the turnstile that kept neighboring cows and goats outside. I was about to enter a
way of life unfamiliar to humanity, a cloistered lifestyle whose dramas were
entirely internal. Within the confines of Darula Ashram, a singular lifestyle
reveled in the silence of endless meditation, a way of life sanctioned in
ancient Vedic times, but one which was on the verge of extinction in modern India. Although most of the ashram residents were old friends, I felt
uneasy as I climbed the stairs leading to a handsome rose garden in front
of the housing wing. I had hoped they would be meditating, but some
waited for my arrival. By the time I made it to my second floor room, I was
buried beneath a mound of orange garlands, buoyed by the greetings of
friends I hadn't seen in years. I felt like a soldier returning from battle.
Disguised by their long beards and hair, friends crowded around the dinner table to hear the news. Although 9/11 had reached them in letters, the
group was totally disconnected from the outside world. No television,
radio, telephone, or newspaper penetrated the ashram. An occasional aero-
gram or small care package arrived from a sister or mother, but news was
sparse, and it was that way for a reason.

View Of Ganges from Darula Ashram

I had moved rapidly since receiving word in Hyderabad in order to
arrive at the ashram by New Year. It was our tradition to spend the first
week of the year in silence. What better way to join the ranks in the sacred
Himalaya then plunging headlong into silence? Friends, already observing

it, welcomed me with hands pressed together. Baskets of fruit and enough incense to perfume Notre Dame filled my room. I had spent months in far-flung regions of the Himalaya, but Darula was the most comfortable accommodation I had seen. With balconies front and back, and private baths attached to single rooms, there was no physical privation.

The New Year began with a long meditation interrupted only by a short walk in the forest before lunch. The pristine atmosphere of the Himalaya in winter surpassed any other season. As I sat on the deck, I found my meal a distraction to the awesome panorama to the east. What eatery could boast of a wall of 20,000-foot massifs rising above the sacred Ganges as it twisted and turned through the jade green Valley of the Saints below? The view was superb and the food wasn't bad either. Surely I had arrived in heaven.

After lunch, I took a silent tour of the surrounding hills. To the east and north our mountain dropped off precipitously. A careless step on the trails and one could fall right off the mountain. On the hike, I felt almost unsteady looking down, but five hours of riveting meditation may have contributed to my giddiness. Behind the ashram, the forest rose another two hundred feet. The trail to the top offered an even broader view of the region.

From the crown I had a hawk's view of New Chirbasa, a small village nestled in a crease in the mountain. Not more than twenty yellow and white cottages were scattered among conifers and fruit trees. On the flat roofs of several homes, women knitted or operated foot-powered sewing machines. Young children bundled in woolens amused themselves, never straying far from their mothers. In the yards, a cow or two were tethered. Himalayan cows are smaller than the average, which helps them graze on the steep slopes. Not every mountainside was forested. To the north, terraced farms stepped down the mountain. The hearty Garhwali villagers lived a simple lifestyle, relying on the crops they grew and dairy from their cows to sustain themselves.

On my return to the ashram, I passed three wiry women carrying sickles for cutting fodder. The village women were reserved, but as I passed, the youngest glanced my way out of curiosity. I learned that the villagers were apprehensive about their foreign neighbors, and had requested that we not use the trails or enter the forests. This seemed like an unreasonable request, but for the most part we acquiesced. As time went by, I learned that some of the same economic dramas that plagued other parts of India also existed in our back yard, and the village folk wanted to keep those dramas private.

When not walking in the forest on sunny afternoons, I spent time gazing at the snow peaks from my balcony. Their stillness mirrored silence better than any ocean or Alpine scene I had ever seen. The swirling snow formed collars on the upper reaches of the pyramid tops. Jaonli, a 24,000 foot peak, appeared as an eagle in flight, and lesser peaks filled the skyline like the teeth of a sleeping giant. I was thrilled to have unlimited sight of a range that I had first encountered on an earlier visit to the region. Mountains are shy creatures, veiling themselves in clouds unless the mood is right.

I fell into the cadence of ashram life as easily as night descended on the valley below. I had never experienced silence like this; each breath was like the sigh of wind moving through the pines, and each heartbeat was as loud as the thumping of drums in the temple on the opposite mountain. The silence roared like the ocean at high tide, filling my meditations with a mysterious sound like the inside of a conch shell when held to the ear. Nature seemed in perpetual recitation on Darula mountain.

The Song Of Life

Melodies filled the air. Not long after sunrise, the sound of a lonely flute floated through my open window from a house on a ridge to the southeast. A wisp of silver smoke rose above the cottage, mingling for a moment with the music before moving on. Each morning I listened to the lilting song that carried from hill to hill. By midmorning, the Himalayan cuckoo took its turn. The polite bird waited until the flute recital ended before beginning its simple song. The cuckoo repeated its call twice, and then paused to listen for a response before calling again. Often a second bird, possibly a mate, replied from a distant forest, and the two conversed back and forth, one voice prominent, the other faint. Rarely did we see the shy cuckoo, although one day it posed on a limb above the trail.

When the villagers congregated at the temple on the opposite hill, the pounding of drums and chink chink of bells echoed through the hills. At the bottom of the precipice to the north, a stream stumbled over rocks, racing to merge with the Ganges. Despite the night chill, I cracked my window to listen to its muted roar. The Himalayan silence was a symphony of sound, and I cherished all of it, appreciating why those who sought solitude chose places like Darula.

In the evening, after meditation, it was the pundits' time to perform. Like a patron in a private box, I listened from my second floor balcony. Beneath lustrous stars strewn across black velvet, the chants seemed to lack a point of origin; they filled the air in all directions. After breathing the mountain air and drinking its mineral rich water, dinner seemed superfluous, a formality more than a necessity. How could prepared food compete with the nourishment of the Himalaya itself? But the fellowship of friends was also nourishment, and provided an excuse to walk in the moonlight after dinner.

I had journeyed with my friends at Darula for twenty years. We had lived together in both the Catskills and Smoky Mountains, where we progressed to more advanced yogic practitioners, but those mountains were mere hillocks compared to what surrounded us now. We had been monks in training, having never taken the formal vows required of Benedictine and Buddhist priests. Monks, I imagined, were born the way athletes and poets were gifted from birth. As I watched my friends move purposefully through the day, I decided that these guys were, in fact, the real thing. It was one thing living a monk's life with a laptop and a freezer full of Ben and Jerry's, but quite another to be cloistered five hundred miles from civilization with instructions to stay put.

Grand Larceny Over Lunch

Unprompted moments of mirth occurred from time to time. One perfect day, as we lunched on the deck and gazed at the panorama of peaks, a band of monkeys descended from the forest and launched an unexpected raid of the lunchroom. The dining room door had been left open, and the marauders seized the opportunity to pilfer fruit and baked goods before being chased out. Everyone reveled in the bold attack. As the thieves made their getaway, chased off by mock gestures of hostility, only the ashram guards waved sticks and tossed stones with intent to inflict injury on the audacious primates.

Mighty winged creatures soared above us in search of food, but there were no rodents in this ashram, thank God. Golden eagles, griffon vultures, and lammergeiers deftly rode the drafts. The raptors were gifted flyers, gliding for minutes at a time, tipping a wing occasionally to change directions. Locals claimed the enormous bearded vultures had been seen flying off with infant bharal (blue sheep). Whether true or not, the birds were massive. One day, a large bearded vulture glided over the lunch deck, casting an eerie shadow across entire tables. Seated at one table was a sprite-like fellow named Robbie. Looking up and seeing the vulture with its nine feet wingspan, Robbie shouted in mock hysterics, "Take Alejandro!" (Alejandro was a Spanish doctor about Robbie's size). Robbie's wry plea drew peals of laughter from the lunch crowd. Such was the simple entertainment we enjoyed.

My favorite flyer in the forest was the magpie, whose long tail feathers aided its navigation. The curious bird swooped through the trees with speed and grace, landing near enough to eavesdrop, yet keeping a safe distance. Its swift flight required superb sight and agility for the forests were dense, the openings irregular. I found the magpie's alert flight as skilled as the graceful maneuvers of the eagles that rode the drafts above the forests.

The days blurred together as the months flew by. The routine fell into a rhythm that revolved around going within. Except for boiling spring water or picking puja flowers, the routine varied little. Life sustained itself easily. Led by the intuition, the awareness moved from portal to gateway in the body, points of entry to worlds of light and the enormity of inner space. The days sped by with a velocity accelerated by sojourns into dimensions where hours passed in minutes and weeks slipped by like days. Bumps came now and then as the journey gathered speed, and at times I felt like a passenger on the Starship Enterprise as it approached warp speed.

A Procession Of Blossoms

Warm winter afternoons opened yellow buds on the mustard fields in the valley below, the first signs of spring. Not long after, the mountainside bloomed ruby red. Rhododendron ornamented the hills. Scarlet balls hung in trusses from stunted trees protruding at sharp angles from the slopes. Our walks during rhododendron season favored the steep slopes where the shrubs were abundant. Fallen petals covered the ground like Kashmiri rugs, their exquisite crimson rivaling the beauty of the blossoms on the branches above. The petals made a delicious jam, and one morning, like a goral, I climbed the vertical slopes and dangled over steep drops to gather a basketful of the tasseled blossoms. The jam was tasty, although it would have taken many flowers to produce more than a jarful, and I decided that the blossoms belonged on the trees and not on my toast.

As the visual spectacle of the rhododendron faded, the alluring scent of wild rose perfumed the air. Only a handful of candidates in the world rivaled our mountain's spellbinding grandeur. Kauai, the Swiss Alps, and Grand Tetons of Wyoming came to mind, but none combined the seclusion, panoramas, spiritual ambiance, and benign year-round climate that we enjoyed. When the delicate pearl roses faded, orchids opened in shadowy ravines and in the hidden hollows of trees where light barely penetrated. Fruit trees bloomed pink and white on east-facing slopes, dropping their fragrant buds after a few days. When the forests weren't blooming, the ashram gardens were. Species of rose from England and Bhutan were in bloom most of the year in such abundance that we freshened our rooms with their blossoms.

The springtime parade of color and scent captivated me, but no more than the nimble villagers in their homespun Garhwali outfits. Balanced on precipitous slopes, the sprightly women traversed the hillsides, filling their bags with undergrowth and foliage. They were a hearty crew, venturing into the forests each day to collect fodder for their animals. By spring, most of the growth had been cut or grazed, forcing the women to walk ever-greater distances with heavy bundles strapped to their backs. But one wily old woman found it convenient to slip onto the ashram property, making her raids while we meditated. She had, no doubt, cut on our hillside for decades and didn't see any reason to waste good fodder, especially since it was close to home. The 'hack hack' of her sickle could be heard almost daily, but the bushes concealed her, and she slipped in and out through a fence in need of repair. Some took offense to the intrusion, unaware that certain foliage produced sweeter, more nourishing milk. Whether she sought our bushes for their superior quality or was simply a creature of habit, she went about her business covertly.

Mischief On The Mountain

The ashram paradise was magical, disturbed only by the mischievous behavior of a few villagers. Hardship led some locals to inflict sinister wounds on the trees on our mountain. During the night, woodcutters slunk about the forests, leaving deep gashes in the trunks of mature trees. It was illegal to chop down a healthy tree, but dead trees were fair game, so unscrupulous woodsmen caused the trees to die long before their time. The pines bordering our property had deep gashes in their trunks. It was a disturbing sight, one that outraged everyone in the ashram. At the same time, we were told it would be dangerous to intervene because the tree mafia was a ruthless bunch, and they were behind the secret operation. As we surveyed a fresh cut on a healthy conifer at the edge of the property, I was reminded of my Himalayan Master's warning "Where trees are killed, people will perish."

I heard an account of a hermit who confronted the tree mafia. He lived in the Himalayan forests and noticed gashes appearing on the pines in the woods. Suspecting foul play, he stayed up one night to find out who was hurting the trees. For hours he sat unmoving, listening for a sound.

Finally he heard a chop, and then another. The sound of the axe blows echoed through the forest around him. He knew every tree on his mountain, for along with the animals, they were his friends. Fearlessly, he made his way through the dark night, drawing close to the ominous sound of splintering wood. Soon he came across five woodsmen clandestinely inflicting deep wounds on healthy trees. Without hesitating, he walked into their camp, and stood between the axe and a conifer about to be cut. "You'll have to kill me first if you intend to cut this tree," he said, challenging the tree mafia. The headman didn't believe the holy man, expecting him to step out of the way as he prepared to swing his axe. But the saintly man refused to move. Only when he realized that the hermit was prepared to sacrifice his life did the malevolent man spare him.

One day while hiking down the mountain, I startled two woodsmen who had just felled a massive long needle pine. What had been a perfectly healthy tree now blocked the footpath, so I hoisted myself over the trunk while the men operated a two-man handsaw with great precision. As I passed by, the men eyed me suspiciously, so I continued on without speaking. By the time I returned that afternoon, the lower half of the tree had been cut into planks that were neatly stacked, waiting to be carried to the road. Transporting the load, I imagined, would be done under the cover of darkness to prevent the forestry department from discovering the crime.

The tradition of felling Himalayan forests had its darkest hour when the British denuded entire mountains to build the Indian Railway. In place of indigenous species, they seeded vast areas with long needle pine, which are ineffective against soil erosion compared to deciduous types, whose decomposing leaves add richness and stability to the soil. Because of deforestation and improper reseeding, the Himalaya loses precious topsoil each monsoon, and its rivers now carry higher volumes of water onto the floodplains, which wreaks havoc during monsoon on the populations living along the Ganges.

Divinity At Play

Sunrise at the ashram was an event I rarely missed. At dawn, it was my habit to take a walk on the trail below the ashram. The path was an ideal spot to watch the sun climb over the wall of eastern peaks. Songbirds positioned themselves on overhanging limbs, ready to greet the first rays with their cheerful melodies. I took my seat at the base of a huge deodar tree, and together we waited in anticipation for the solar deity. Light increased gradually at first, becoming swifter as the great glowing orb burst forth, silhouetting the distant massif and showering the ashram with bands of gold and yellow light. I had never seen the sun ascend so rapidly as it did over the Himalaya. The image of Surya, the sun god, riding in a chariot pulled by seven white horses seemed more than a myth, and I better appreciated why the scriptures recommended that temples and houses be built facing east. Watching Surya gallop over the peaks each day, I would never view Him as anything less than a divine being again. The tradition of deifying nature was one I enjoyed.

After the daily namaskar (salutation) to the sun, I leaned against an old deodar. Cedar was one of the few trees on the mountain that was spared the woodsman's blows because it was considered sacred. The resinous scent of its congealed sap made fine incense. I drew slow, conscious breaths under the tree, practicing yogic breathing techniques to prepare for meditation. The pure mountain air filled me with a scintillating energy.

At the end of the day, about the time the group congregated for evening meditation, the same regal setting that staged daily sunrise dramas appeared in a new costume. Attired in sublime hues, the peaks now cast themselves in a feminine role. An awesome alpine glow enveloped the summits, morphing from ginger to magenta as the light faded. The effect of the celestial theater was hypnotic, and many times I found myself unable to turn away from the show to enter the meditation hall.

The moon refused a supporting role on the celestial stage. Her monthly brilliance brought us out many nights despite uncertainties on the trails after dark. In addition to the risk of falling off the mountain, a pit viper had bitten one of the cooks one night, and there were reports that a leopard prowled the precinct after dark. So we confined our full moon sojourns to the ashram's oversized helipad, which was never used. We circled round and round like the slow-moving blades of a chopper. A casual observer might have concluded that a collective lunacy pervaded the landing pad, the circling figures in their loose white outfits being asylum inmates rather than spiritual aspirants. But we were quite innocent, if not completely sane. The moon's milky iridescence kept us from stepping off the elevated launching pad and illumined the valley so we could see the silver Ganges in the night. I found the light of the moon to be equal to the soft inner light that often flooded my meditations.

Spring came early at Darula, and the woolens and silk long johns were back on the shelf by early March. Holi was upon us, a day we expected to pass as any other, except for the morning play of our staff. Consequently, we were caught off guard when a drunken villager invaded our quiet residence. He tried vainly to force entry into several rooms, making an enormous amount of racket in the process. He hollered and pounded, but soon left in frustration. His intentions were harmless enough; after all, Holi was the great equalizer, and he saw it as a chance to get acquainted with his sphinx-like neighbors. Alcohol was a sad consequence of unemployment among the villagers, but the problem persisted wherever there was lack of economic opportunity.

The spring festival honoring the village goddess arrived. The local folks gathered at sunrise at the temple at the edge of New Chirbasa, their goatskin drums echoing off the mountain. It was an important occasion for those who relied on the goddess to bless them with a good harvest. An hour later, a procession of villagers paraded past the ashram. Drums pounded as four bearers carried a palanquin with the deity seated on it. Separate groups of men and women headed down the mountain to bathe the goddess in the Ganges. Later that morning, the villagers returned in jovial spirits, their solemn mission accomplished.

I had not been inside a temple in months, and watched with interest from my balcony, using binoculars for a better view of the goddess on her simple throne. Red powder dotted her forehead, and a garland framed her face. The Hindu gods were not remote beings. They participated at every moment, and were treated with the affection of a family member. I had grown to love the Vedic deities while living in India, and for that, I was grateful.

The Greatest Show On Earth

Two distinct dispositions characterized the panorama to the east that my binoculars brought into focus. On calm days, the icy bastions were majestic and impervious to all. On blustery days, gusts and drafts sent white powder swirling about the crags and cliff belts, changing the mood and appearance of the solitary peaks from moment to moment. I studied the snowy cornices, jagged ramparts, and ice gullies that could not be seen with the naked eye, fascinated as much by their intricacy as by the winds that crafted them. A picture of Lord Siva, the great destroyer, hung on my wall. The Maha Yogi wore a tiger skin and sat in lotus posture, meditating on top of a snowcapped peak like those to the east. Siva was a yogi's yogi, a perfect role model for aspiring mendicants. As silence grew within, Siva's presence intensified, for Siva and silence are ultimately one and the same.

There were days when internal gusting sent thoughts swirling through my head like the snow that whipped about the wind-etched peaks, but distractions were few compared to the serene hours spent anchored in the citadel of the heart, a haven where errant impulses were not allowed. Once, when a storm brewed inside, I breathed long and deep until it passed, the flow of prana cooling my body like a lubricant in an overheated engine. I felt invincible on the mountain, prepared to face demons past and present. Although karma lurked on the perimeter of our cloistered life, it never penetrated this unreachable part of the world. To be sure, I appealed to Ganesh to ward off obstructions on the path, and he was always willing to help.

The sun ascended the far side of the crystalline peaks each morning like a climber conquering a snowy summit. Rising with great speed, its position changed moment by moment. Like amber molten it poured over the horizon, and I stared in awe at the first rays each day. But some mornings a telltale pull told me an exceptional meditation was on the horizon, so I retreated to my room. On those days, my mind flew to the heart's sanctuary like a bee in search of a flower. Once inside, the inner dialogue ceased for thoughts had no role in this world, nor did the mantra, except that its form was the object of my devotion. Prema ruled the inner worlds and its kingdom was shaped by devotion. When the mind ceased its futile chatter, grace filled the vessel with an ecstatic essence. Like a hot air balloon rising above the Himalaya, I was reminded of my Himalayan Master's playful promise; "I will fill you with love until you say 'Uncle.'" Although at times the inebriation left me reeling, I refused to stop, remembering that the Master had said, "Open wider and wider, for there is no limit to how much Prema can fill the heart." Where, I wondered, was my mysterious guide who had appeared so unexpectedly and then disappeared?

When intuition and softened breath merged, pranalight circulated like an intoxicant in the bloodstream, awakening powerful energies originating at the nexus between my eyebrows. With the spiritual eye as controller, calming currents bathed my body, an involuntary response that I enjoyed. Inside, I found myself in a cave. The dweller in the heart directed devotion to the inhabitant of the cave and its occupant, in turn, responded by filling the heart with prema. Time departed along with space. The Self remained.

New Worlds Within

As the incessant activity of seven years in India purged itself from my system, I plunged again and again into pristine pools of Being. The noise of the city was wiped away by the silence that washed over me. Day after day I bathed in the silence, which contained worlds more fascinating than any pilgrimage spot I had visited. Here I had been traveling all over India, and I had finally reached my destination. I understood now. The whole experience was within me, and not just when my eyes were closed. Every Siva shrine pointed to the lingam in the heart, and every Devi temple to the cool waters of the transcendent. Every holy river originated in the glacial fields of the Himalaya, the spiritual source for all of India. The Himalaya were great lighthouses, repositories of wisdom and enlightenment available to all who came. I had witnessed the cycle of life, and now sought its ultimate source. I had attended the many religious festivals, but now desired to celebrate the One. It had been a long voyage, a journey that was beginning anew.

It had always been my meditation habit to seek the transcendent, and then enter the heart's gate with intuition as my guide. The mind knew the treasures waiting to be plundered and hastened to claim its booty. Having escaped the confines of time and space, there were vast realms to explore in the worlds within, but first one paid homage to heaven's queen. She was always accessible on her altar inside the white marble temple; her darshan was indescribable. Devotion took me to her feet to bathe and anoint them with scented water and sandal paste. From her benevolent smile, I knew she enjoyed the offering and blessed my daily visit with a shower of rose petals that sent blissful currents coursing through the body. The ritual completed, I entered Her heart. Sweet absorption followed. My tiny drop merged in the ocean of Her greatness, and eternities were spent in her gentle lap. When it was time for sleep I eagerly waited for the next sublime encounter.

Para bhakti, transcendent devotion, sustained me. Without it, I was a ship without map or compass, a vessel without anchor or mast. In the seclusion of the Himalaya, there was limitless opportunity to explore the world of Devi, and I sat up in the early hours to do so. With each dive, the vessel filled beyond its capacity. Immeasurable contentment cascaded from head to foot. I reeled in the inebriating bliss and continued diving, knowing the treasures to be inexhaustible. Like a child filling its pockets with pebbles, I sought the gems of realization: love, grace, and inner light. She smiled and nodded encouragement, and one day she placed a brilliant blue sapphire in my hand, and told me that it would help my perception. Mothers take great pleasure in their child's happiness.

My heart had opened wider and wider since coming to India. There were times when it was wrenched open by the unbearable affliction of innocents, while at other times a Master had massaged it. Teaching had been my passport to India, and the teacher always receives more than the student. Beneath the chaos and congestion of a billion people struggling to survive, the gateway to Divinity was wide open, beckoning one to enter. Maharishi had described India as a dusty mirror that, when wiped clean, would reflect the timeless wisdom of Enlightenment. I gazed into that mirror and discovered the Self.

Shambala

During one particularly deep encounter with the Self, I felt a powerful pull up. As I rose above ashram, forest, and peaks, a mystic city of light hovered above the clouds. Crystalline palaces and towering temples stood magically in the ether, and beings robed in pastel light greeted me as I approached. As I crossed a bridge to enter the city, my mind asked, 'What is this magnificence?' The word 'Shambala' formed in my awareness. So the mythical city was real after all. As I entered its luminous gates, my attention was drawn to an effulgent citadel, a temple of the most exquisite beauty and light. High above, I noticed two beings of greater brilliance than any I had seen moving about the celestial city. They were dancing on the temple's bell tower, and I felt strangely attracted to them. As I grew accustomed to the radiance enveloping the pair, I recognized one of the rapturous dancers. Siva Nataraj, the divine dancer, performed his tandava dance with perfect poise, his unkempt locks flying in all directions. His serene expression was dispassionate, his rhythmic movements animated.

Siva danced with one of equal skill. For a moment I was unable to make out his partner. The other dancer moved with grace and strength, and his jet-black hair and robes flowed as one with his agile form as he moved round and round Lord Siva. The two cosmic dancers were absorbed in ecstasy as they circled one another. Then I saw the almond eyes, those great pools of compassion that I could never forget. Could it be? Yes, it was he. Devotion flowed from my heart like water from a pitcher. 'Keshava,' I whispered from my heart. 'Keshava!' As he danced, he glanced down at me and smiled, and my heart was filled with Divine Love.

The city in the sky then faded, but the light-filled experience continued. On an internal screen, images presented themselves one after another like ocean waves. People and events passed like a living movie. I saw worshippers in this sacred land, sadhus chanting Siva's name on the banks of holy rivers, and pundits performing sunrise puja. I watched pilgrims bathing and funeral pyres blazing and devotees bowing. I looked into the childlike eyes of Swami Narayana and heard Pateriya's moonlight song. I shared the plight of a thousand beggars and watched the endless procession of villagers marching to Kumbha Mela. I viewed deities benevolent and fierce, received Balaji's blessing and touched Devi Kumari's feet. I stared into the abstracted eyes of Maya Amma, and amused myself with the painted face of a Kerala dancer.

The sight of hapless lepers and homeless children playing on city streets rolled past. I gazed in awe at Mount Sivling and Nanda Devi, and saw the ruins of ancient India. Fortresses, mosques, and temples rose to the sky; others lay in ruin. I heard bellowing conches and bus horns blaring, and Krishna's magic flute. I saw kites wheeling overhead and joy on the faces of their owners. I heard the shriek of train whistles and screeching of birds, inhaled strong incense, dung smoke, and diesel, and heard the riotous chatter of monkeys. I listened to the shrill call of the peacock and admired his exotic dance. I looked into the languid eyes of cows and sought the shelter of a banyan tree. Colored saris dried on the banks of the Yamuna. I heard clanging bells, the muezzin's call to prayer, and litany of street vendors at dawn.

I was soaked to the skin by monsoons and parched to the bone by heat. I meditated by holy rivers and bathed in the Indus and Ganges, sought refuge in caves, dined with industrialists, hermits, and truck drivers, and drew diagrams in boardrooms. I had been blessed and robbed, hospitalized and humbled. Such a full dream! Was it time to awaken? Who was the 'I' experiencing all this? I felt gratitude to Mother India, my teachers, my mantra, and the presence of Divine Love and beings of light that shared the Creator's sublime essence. Surya ascended and the moon waxed. The cycles brought change against the changeless backdrop of the Self. Karma was delivered, and grace pardoned. As my beloved Himalayan Master had said, "You will see a new world and yourself as its creator. There is no end to the possibilities. Always remember, gratitude is the key, for gratitude fuels grace." I had become a bhakta in this land of gods.

The days rolled by like an endless procession of waves washing over Mother India's feet. Her surface needs cleaning, but once polished, She will shine as in ancient times. Her wisdom is needed in this Age of Kali. Her people are humble and proud, ancient and modern, and changing. They celebrate the passing of seasons with their gods, progressing at the pace of a bullock cart and the speed of a supercomputer. India is the chaos of the city and the serenity of the Himalaya. Opposites colliding at every crossing. It was time for me to join the monks, time to bridge East and West, time to create a beautiful rainbow.

The peaks donned their sunset raiment; their rosy hue blushed within me. India in her myriad forms was indeed a mirror of truth and I found that truth in my heart.

GLOSSARY

Aacha—good

Aham Brahmasmi—a Vedic sloka that means 'I am the totality'

Akara—an organized group of nagababas

Almiera—a moveable closet

Amarkatank—a forested region; source of Narmada River

Amla—a sour fruit used in Ayur Vedic preparations

Amma—a Kerala saint; means Holy Mother

Apsarasas—alluring female beings from the astral plane

Ashram—a place dedicated to spiritual life

Ayur Veda—India's indigenous system of health care

Baksheesh—a donation

Balaji—the affectionate name for Lord Venkateshwar

Bangladesh—formerly East Bengal

Bania—merchant caste

Banjara—a tribal person

Bansurai—a wood flute

Bhagawan—a name for God

Bhairav—the fearful form of lord Siva

Bhakti—devotion

Bhajan—a devotional song

Bhog—a tiger or other large cat

Bhudevi—the goddess of earth

Bhutia—large Tibetan dog used for herding and protection

Bidi—a hand rolled cigarette

Bodhi Tree—the tree under which Buddha gained nirvana

Brahma—the Creator

Brahmasthan—the central space in a building

Bugiyal—a high altitude meadow

Cankamana—the walk made by Buddha around the Bo Tree

Chai—Indian tea

Chakra—the subtle energy centers along the spine

Champak—a hibiscus flower

Chandanam—sandal paste

Chandi Walla—a silver smith

Chandra—the moon

Chappal—footwear, a pair of thongs

Charpoy—a string cot mainly used outside

Chillum—hashish and tobacco mix sometimes used by sadhus

Chorten—a small Buddhist monument

Chowkidar—a security guard

Coir—coconut husk used in mattresses

Coolie—a porter at a train station

Dabha—an open-air roadside restaurant

Dal—lentil type soup

Darshan—the sight of a saint or the auspicious sight of a deity

Deodar—a cedar tree

Deva—a benevolent celestial being; a Hindu god

Devi Bhava—assuming the mood or personality of the Divine Mother

Dharamshala—a guest accommodation for those on pilgrimage

Dhobi—a man who does laundry, usually by hand

Dhoti—a cotton waist wrap worn by village men

Digambara—to be skyclad or naked

Diksha—to receive initiation or spiritual instruction

Djinn—a Muslim spirit or ghost

Dosa—a rice flour pancake that is very thin

Durga—the principle form of Divine Mother

Ganapati—the elephant headed son of Lord Siva

Gangotri—the source of the Ganges River

Gomoukh—where the Ganges emerges from a glacier in the Himalaya

Gopi—a female devotee of Lord Krishna

Goshala—a dairy or shed where cows are kept

Gotra—one's spiritual lineage

Graha Shanti—planetary peace

Gufa—a cave where yogis dwell

Gurkhas—Nepalese military caste, excellent soldiers

Guru—a spiritual teacher

Hansa gufa—Swami Hansa's cave

Hanuman—the monkey god hero of the Ramayan

Hanuman langur—large silver-white primates with black faces

Hari Bhagawan—hail the divine

Hatha Yoga—a system of yoga emphasizing stretching postures called asanas

Hati—an elephant

Haveli—a ranch style home

Henna—a red-brown paste painted on the hands and arms of girls

Homa—a fire sacrifice to win the favor of the gods

Idli—a steamed rice patty from a fermented batter

Ikot—a sophisticated method of weaving on a handloom

Imam—Islamic leader of prayer, one close to Allah

Jaggery—raw sugar

Jain—a small religious sect with strict practices

Jal Samadhi—burial in water

Japa—a type of Hindu rosary performed by sadhus

Ji—Sir

Jiva—individual soul

Jyotish—Indian astrology

Kali—the fierce, black form of Divine Mother

Kali Yuga—the dark age humanity is now passing through

Kanchenjunga—the second highest peak in the Himalaya

Karma—the actions one performs and the resulting response

Kartik Purnima—the harvest full moon celebration

Kaya Kalp—an Ayur Ved method for reversing ageing

Kesa—saffron

Keyala—the intuition of a saint

Kheer—a type of rice pudding

Kolkata—the original name for Calcutta

Kundalini Shakti—the subtle energy in the spine that is awakened through meditation and yoga

Kurta—a traditional, loose fitting shirt worn by villagers

Kurukshetra—the battlefield of the Mahabharata War

Kutiya—a house or dwelling

Ladhus—gram flour sweets offered to the gods

Laxman—the princely brother of Lord Ram

Lhasa—the capital of Tibet, former residence of the Dalai Lama

Lila—the play of creation

Lungi—a waist wrap that is used for work or morning bath

Mahapuja—a grand ceremony of gratitude to the gods

Maharaj—great king

Maha Rudrabishek—a ceremony of offering to Lord Siva

Mahatma—a great soul, a saint

Mahout—a man who looks after an elephant

Mandala—a circle with spiritual significance

Mandap—a hall where yagyas are performed

Mandir—a temple or place of learning

Mangal—the planet Mars

Marwaris—a community of Indian businessmen

Mata Ki Jai—a salutation meaning 'Victory to the Divine Mother'

Maun—to take a vow of silence

Mauni Amavasya—day of the new moon

Meenakshi—the fish-eyed goddess in Madurai

Mehindi—the art of body painting using henna

Mela—a religious festival

Mogul—Muslim invaders from Persia

Moksha—to attain liberation

Mount Kailash—a holy mountain in Tibet where Hindus and Buddhists go for pilgrimage

Mudra—an auspicious symbol formed by the hands

Mukti Kshetra—the field of liberation

Mukti Nath—the lord of liberation, Lord Vishnu/Avilokiteshwar

Murthi—a consecrated statue of a Hindu god

Mustang—a remote region at the border of Tibet and Nepal

Nadi Palm—an ancient method of astrologer

Nadi Vigyan—the Ayur Vedic method of pulse diagnosis

Nagar—a town or community

Namaste—a greeting meaning 'I bow down to the God in you'

Nandankanan—an animal park

Narasimha—the man-lion incarnation of Lord Vishnu

Naxalite—Maoist extremists

Nirmal Hriday—place of pure heart, name of Mother Theresa's organization

Nirvana—to achieve a state of peace and liberation

Paan—a mix of lime, betel nut, and other ingredients for chewing

Paddy—a rice field

Paise—small change

Palang—a bed

Panch Agni—five fire sacrifice

Panchavati—grove of five sacred trees

Panchayat— council of elders

Pandal—a tent for large gatherings

Paneer—fresh cheese

Parikrama—to circumambulate or circle a holy spot

Parvati—Lord Siva's consort

Pindi—a sacred stone

Pitaji—revered father

Pitris—one's departed ancestors

Prana—vital breath

Prana Pratistha—consecrating ceremony in a temple

Pranayama—a yogic breathing technique

Prasada—consecrated food from a temple or ritual

Prayag—the confluence of two rivers

Prema—love

Pundit—one who chants the Vedas and performs holy ritual

Puranic—ancient

Purohit—the officiator at a Hindu ceremony

Rajma Dal—thick red bean stew

Rajput—Rajasthani warrior class

Ram—the prince avatar of Lord Vishnu

Ramayana—The epic story of Lord Ram

Rameshwarem—the south Indian pilgrimage island
where Ram worshipped Lord Siva

Ram Raj—the golden age where Lord Ram ruled for 10,000 years

Rasayana—an Ayur Vedic formula to ensure good health

Rath Yatra—the annual car festival in Orissa

Rawaal—the chief priest at Badrinath temple

Rickshaw—a three-wheel bicycle for transporting people

Sadhu—a mendicant

Sambar—a spicy south Indian soup

Sanjivani—a Himalayan herb

Sanskrit—the language of nature

Sanyasi—one who has taken vows of renunciation

Saraswati—Hindu goddess of learning and fine arts

Saree—the traditional attire of Indian women

Satsang—spiritual gathering

Shakti—power

Shankara—the great Hindu reformer from the tenth century

Shankaracharya—one of four principle leaders of the Hindu faith

Shahtoosh—a shawl made from the Tibetan antelope

Shennai—a reed instrument like an oboe

Sherpa—a Nepalese mountain guide

Shishya—a disciple

Shraddha—Eleven day ritual for departed soul; faith

Shudra—a low caste Hindu

Shushumna—the minute passage in the spine where subtle energy flows

Sidhi—supernormal power

Siva—one of the three principle deities of Hinduism; the great destroyer

Siva Linga—the oval stone worshipped as Lord Siva

Smashan—a cremation ground

Soma—the drink of immortality eulogized in Indian scriptures

Srimad Bhagavatam—the story of Lord Krishna

Subjii—vegetables

Sundarya Lahiri—a poem by Shankara

Surya—the Hindu name for the sun

Surya Namaskar—a sun salutation; a type of yogic exercise

Swami—an Indian holy man

Swastic—health

Taraka Mantra—sacred syllable given as the soul departs the world

Teech (hain)—OK

Tulsi—holy plant; sacred to Lord Krishna

Veena—a classical string instrument

Vibhuti—sacred ash from a homa

Upanishad—ancient Vedic text

Uttapam—a rice pancake

Vaidya—an Ayur Vedic physician

Vaishya—the business caste

Vasudev kutumbh katam—Vedic saying 'the world is my family'

Veda Vyasa—the rishi credited with cognizing the Vedas

Videshi—a foreigner

Vishnu—the sustainer of Creation

Yagya—Vedic ritual

Yali—a fierce being that protects temples

Yamnotri—the source of the Yamuna River

Yatra—a pilgrimage

Yatrik—a pilgrim

Yoga asana—a stretching posture

Printed in the United States
41981LVS00008B/124